Social democracy and society

Working-class radicalism in Düsseldorf,
1890–1920

Social democracy and society

Working-class radicalism in Düsseldorf, 1890–1920

MARY NOLAN

Department of History, New York University

CAMBRIDGE UNIVERSITY PRESS

Cambridge

London   New York   New Rochelle

Melbourne   Sydney

Published by the Press Syndicate of the University of Cambridge
The Pitt Building, Trumpington Street, Cambridge CB2 1RP
32 East 57th Street, New York, NY 10022, USA
296 Beaconsfield Parade, Middle Park, Melbourne 3206, Australia

First published 1981

Printed in the United States of America

Library of Congress Cataloging in Publication Data
Nolan, Mary, 1944–
Social democracy and society.
Bibliography: p.
Includes index.
1. Sozialdemokratische Partei Deutschlands –
History. 2. Labor and laboring classes – Germany,
West – Düsseldorf – Political activity – History.
3. Düsseldorf – Politics and government. I. Title.
ISBN 0 521 23473 5

To my parents,
Jane and Joe Nolan

Contents

Preface

Although the literature on German social democracy is voluminous, much of it is methodologically old-fashioned and analytically weak. Neither in the older historiography – with its emphasis on ideas and institutions – nor in the newer work – with its focus on the peculiarities of capitalist development in Germany – does the working class on whom the movement was built and whose interest it served, or failed to serve, emerge. Strongly influenced by recent British and American studies in working-class history, which have analyzed work, culture, and community so astutely, I have sought to recapture the social history of German workers in the late nineteenth and early twentieth centuries. By asking questions similar to those posed by students of the European and American working classes, a case study such as this can contribute to comparative social history.

From its inception, however, this project was concerned with political, as well as social, history. Its aim was to integrate the history of the working class with the history of the workers' movement, to use each to elucidate the other. The institutions and ideologies ignored by many contemporary social historians thus figure prominently in this study. There are several reasons for this concern. Although recent social histories of the working class have been extremely rich theoretically and methodologically, they often succumb to the same kind of monocausal explanations and compartmentalization that traditional institutional history did. To substitute work for politics, or culture for both, however, brings us no closer to understanding the totality of working-class experience. Whether such studies reflect disillusionment with social democratic reformism or belief in working-class integration, whatever the character of working-class politics, they assume that the real working class exists outside of formal political and trade-union institutions and ideologies. Class as a political category has been supplanted by class as an economic and cultural one. This study seeks to restore political organizations and ideologies to their rightful place as a crucial – but not exclusive – determinant of class formation and class relations.

For me, as for many other contemporary social historians, a concern with questions of work and culture developed in part from involvement in the New Left. The protest movements of the last fifteen years in the United States and Europe have shown the deep social roots of discontent and conflict. But they have shown as well that the effectiveness of social dissent and protest depends strongly on the political articulation and organization that they find. The experiences of these years raise important questions about the strengths and weaknesses of different organizational forms, about the relationship of ideology to social structure and culture, and about the process of politicization. These questions are as relevant to historical investigation as to contemporary analysis.

This study of social democracy and society in Düsseldorf is thus the product of both my intellectual and political biography. It is a history of the social democratic movement from below in both its political and social dimensions. It suggests some of the political implications of the social history of advanced capitalism.

Much of the research for this work was conducted at the Stadtarchiv Düsseldorf. The director and staff greatly facilitated my work by leading me to critical sources, giving me prompt service, and providing enjoyable companionship. Thanks are also due the staffs of the Universitäts Bibliotek Düsseldorf, the Staatsarchiv Düsseldorf, and the Staatsarchiv Koblenz.

Funding for the initial research was provided by a National Institute of Mental Health (NIMH) training fellowship in social history. A junior faculty leave from Harvard University gave me the necessary relief from teaching and money to complete the project.

This book was written at the Center for European Studies at Harvard. I am deeply grateful to Director Stanley Hoffman, the staff, and my colleagues there for providing an intellectually stimulating and supportive environment in which to work.

My intellectual debts are many. Fritz Stern, who advised the dissertation from which this book grew, has offered incisive criticism and constant encouragement at all stages. Arno Mayer, whose work has greatly influenced my understanding of nineteenth- and twentieth-century European history, had insightful suggestions at both early and late stages of the project. Suzanne Berger, David Crew, Victoria de

Grazia, Michael Merrill, and Charles Sabel read earlier versions of this work and offered invaluable suggestions, many of which they will recognize in the finished book. In the process of writing I benefited enormously from the comments and support of Patrice Higonnet. Both Alex Keyssar and Vernon Lidtke read late drafts with painstaking care. Their extensive comments enabled me to present my arguments with much greater force and clarity.

My final thank you is to my close friends, who have had to live with the Düsseldorf Social Democrats longer than they or I care to recall.

M.N.

New York, N.Y.
December 1980

Introduction

This book is about the formation of class consciousness, workers' culture, and social democratic organizations in late nineteenth- and early twentieth-century Germany. It explores the radical attitudes and actions of the working class in Düsseldorf, a major industrial center in the Lower Rhine, and the role of social democracy in reflecting and reshaping that radicalism. Beginning with the legalization of the Social Democratic Party in 1890 and concluding with the unsuccessful revolution of 1918–19, this study traces the interaction between workers and their organizations on the one hand and the structural and political factors that both fostered and limited radicalism on the other. It reconstructs the learning process through which workers and their movement went, by examining the categories they used to understand the world and the means by which they tried to change it. Although this is a case study, it raises broader questions about the relationship of social democracy and society, about religion and politics, and about workers and industrialization in an era of organized capitalism and political authoritarianism.

Class, as E. P. Thompson argued, "is a relationship and not a thing." It "is defined by men as they live their own history."[1] In 1890 there were workers in Düsseldorf, tens of thousands of them, ranging from skilled cabinetmakers through semiskilled metalworkers and unskilled construction helpers to female domestics. There were Catholics and Protestants, natives and migrants, permanent city dwellers and temporary peasant workers. But there was not a working class, united by shared traditions, experiences, and consciousness. In the ensuing three decades an increasingly articulate and organized working class, aware of its own interests and striving to assert them against others, emerged in Düsseldorf. How this class formed itself and was formed by the economic, social, and political relationships in which it was embedded is one of the central themes of this inquiry.

Between 1890 and 1920 Düsseldorf workers not only became a class, but also developed a powerful and singularly radical social democratic movement. The radicalism of the working class and workers' movement was manifested in their general attitudes toward the state, society, and the economy, which they felt offered no opportunities for social integration or political reform. It was evidenced in their conviction that political equality, social recognition, and decent human treatment could be achieved only through a fundamental transformation of the existing order. As a result of their general consciousness, Düsseldorf found itself on the left wing of German social democracy. Insisting on the adherence to traditional principles, Düsseldorf's social democratic workers attacked theoretical revisionism, apolitical economism, and practical reformism, with their emphasis on the possibilities of class collaboration, political alliances, and a gradual amelioration of the ills of capitalism. They criticized as well the organizational fetishism and passivity of the Social Democratic Party (SPD), proposing instead a militant strategy, centering on the mass strike and relying on rank-and-file initiative.

As the Düsseldorf working class and workers' movement developed in the prewar years, they sought to implement a more activist and confrontational strategy on the shop floor and above all in the political arena. After 1914 they vigorously protested the war and Social Democratic support of it, leaving the SPD en masse for the Independent Social Democratic Party. In 1918–19 Düsseldorf workers enthusiastically supported not only the political revolution but also the struggle for socialism. And defeat, far from undermining their radicalism, pushed them farther left into the Communist Party. The causes, character, and limits of this radicalism is the second principal theme of this inquiry.

This study is based on certain premises about the formation of the working class and the role of workers' organizations in that process. The working class is by no means created once and for all at the beginning of industrialization. Rather, it must re-create itself at each stage of industrial capitalism, as the economy and labor force are restructured, political institutions and forms of hegemony change, and old cultural forms give way to new ones. That process of class formation is as difficult in more advanced industrial capitalist societies as in less developed ones. The diversity and divisions within the working class – be they occupational, cultural, religious, or sexual – far from diminishing, recur in ever new guises.[2] Proletarianization takes many forms, some of which encourage protest, others negotiated compromise, still others quiescence and deference. Ruling elites have more experience in maintaining their position by transformations in the labor process and by astute mixtures of concessions and repression, co-option and control through the institutions of the state and civil society. As the state becomes more interventionist and the economy more organized, the power with which workers are confronted can scarcely be countered by localized protest or unstructured resistance.[3]

Under these circumstances, working-class parties and unions play an indispensable role in creating a working class as well as in shaping its consciousness.[4] Although much current social history emphasizes work, community, and culture exclusively, these cannot adequately explain class formation in more advanced capitalist societies. Political institutions and ideologies cannot be dismissed as existing outside of or after the making of the working class, for they are an integral part of that process.

As this book will argue, Düsseldorf provides a clear illustration of this phenomenon. Although the economic discrimination, political powerlessness, and social isolation to which Düsseldorf workers were subjected made them critical of the dominant institutions and ideologies, these experiences created at most an amorphous discontent, which lacked structure, strategy, and goals. They led workers to criticize the Catholic and liberal political movements, but not necessarily to abandon them. They encouraged passivity as much as protest.

It was the Social Democratic Party, the free trade unions, and the cultural and service associations that mediated between the workers and their environment and transformed this inchoate radicalism into an articulate political consciousness. For the workers in Düsseldorf, who lacked an autonomous and shared culture, social homogeneity, and a dissenting political tradition, social democracy provided a vocabulary for analyzing society and a vision toward which to struggle. It offered a vehicle for coping with urban industrial society and protesting against the inequities of capitalism and political authoritarianism. In the process of filling these functions, social democracy created a political and economic movement and a new kind of workers' culture, which brought together thousands of Düsseldorf workers previously divided by skill and occupation, by religion and geographic origin, by experiences and expectations.

If it is necessary to examine the role of the party in class formation, it is equally essential to study the party in a new way. Most historians of

German social democracy, reluctant to venture beyond the familiar terrain of political and intellectual history, have analyzed the party "from above." Explicitly or implicitly they accept the argument that the SPD was highly centralized and that the leadership determined its theory and practice while the membership remained passive and receptive. Liberals, conservatives, and communists alike focus on the accessible and clear-cut disputes of intellectuals, parliamentary leaders, and upper-echelon functionaries and ignore both the working class and the broader economic and political context.[5] Those who deemphasize differing interpretations of Marxism concentrate on social democracy's relationship with Imperial German society, arguing that social democracy became negatively integrated and in many respects the mirror image of that which it opposed.[6] And local studies generally replicate these assumptions and methodologies.[7] What is needed is a social history of politics on the one hand and a structural analysis of the society in which the working class and its organizations developed on the other.

Working-class institutions can scarcely be understood without a deep knowledge of workers' everyday lives, options, and aspirations. The occupational and skill structure of the working class, the sociology of labor markets, and transformations in the labor process provide the framework for such an understanding, but analysis cannot rest with economic factors. One must examine the communities in which the working class lived and their relationship to the larger urban environment in which they were situated. One must investigate the cultures from which different workers came and those they created, the expectations workers brought with them and the modifications these underwent as a result of workers' experiences on the job and off.[8] To understand working-class politics, in short, one must seek to capture both the diversities and uniformities of working-class life. Only by exploring the interaction among work, community, and culture can we explain the character of social democracy.

The history of a political movement is thus the history of a particular social group, but as Gramsci has argued, "this group is not isolated: it has friends, kindred groups, opponents, enemies. The history of any given party can only emerge from the complex portrayal of the totality of society and the state."[9] It is thus necessary to examine the organization and development of the economy, as well as demographic changes and social structure. Popular culture, high culture, and the role of religion must be analyzed, as must political institutions, the party system, and their class base. And this must be done nationally as well as locally if the representativeness and uniqueness of the case study are to emerge clearly.

As will be seen, there are three sets of relationships that are of central importance for understanding Wilhelmian Düsseldorf. The economy was shaped by the highly organized, technologically advanced character of industrial capitalist development in Germany and by the close but complex ties between industry and the interventionist state. Despite certain democratic forms, the political system was authoritarian in the structure of its institutions and the content of its policies. The local ruling alliance of liberals and Catholics, like its national counterpart, discriminated against workers and effectively excluded them from any power. Finally, Catholicism, which was not merely a religion but a multi-class, mass-based social and political movement, was the dominant cultural force in the Lower Rhine region and provided the principal alternative to social democracy. The complex interaction of organized capitalism, authoritarian politics, and political Catholicism, rather than any one of them alone, set the structural and political framework within which the working class and social democracy developed. It determined the reality with which they had to contend.

If we analyze the formation of the Düsseldorf working class and the history of the social democratic movement in the ways suggested, we shall arrive at a complex explanation of their radicalism. No single factor, whether it be the structure of work, the nature of politics, or the sociology of the labor market, suffices to account for why Düsseldorf workers diverged so markedly from the prevalent image of reformist Social Democrats, integrated, if only negatively, into Imperial German society and politics.

Düsseldorf's social democratic workers became radical by virtue of who they were and what they experienced, by virtue of the diverse cultures they brought with them and the way these were remolded by an urban industrial environment and by the social democratic movement. Their relationship to capitalism and Catholicism in Düsseldorf and to the national party in Berlin pushed them to the left, as did both their numerous failures and their scattered successes. Radicalism resulted from the confrontation of Düsseldorf's working class – which was young, highly skilled, migrant and new to industry – with an environ-ment that relegated workers to a second-class status economically, politically, and socially. Radicalism came as well from the mediation of that confrontation by a social democratic movement that lacked entrenched leadership, close ties to the national party, or bourgeois support. It seemed the only viable response to a situation in which there were no opportunities for class collaboration, political alliances, social integration, or piecemeal reform. Radicalism emerged from the structural and political situation in Düsseldorf, was intensified by decades of frustrating political experiences, and finally resulted in revolution, for the Düsseldorf Social Democrats had learned that they must replace the existing order if they were to attain their goals.

The very factors that promoted radicalism in Düsseldorf, however, limited its effectiveness. Organized capitalism, authoritarian government, and political Catholicism precluded reformism but made organization and mobilization difficult and militant confrontation dangerous. Rapid industrialization and migration provided the movement with ready recruits but undermined organizational stability and educational work. Düsseldorf's isolation from the national movement created a critical distance in which radical ideas could develop, but also minimized Düsseldorf's influence on Berlin, limited its contacts with leftists elsewhere, and contributed significantly to the defeat of the postwar revolution.

The social democratic workers in Düsseldorf also contributed to their own failures. However much they broadened their appeal, they were unable to reach some important groups of workers. Despite their criticism of the national movement, they bowed to its decisions until forced to leave during the war. They created a strongly organized, politically oriented radicalism but ultimately became imprisoned in prefigurative institutions and preexisting patterns of behavior. In the revolution of 1918–19 the incompleteness of working-class formation, of the movement's learning process, and of its radicalism were to be fully and tragically revealed.

This book not only studies a particular group of workers whose history was previously unwritten but also, and equally important, alters our understanding of German social democracy in this period. It disputes the assumptions about the prevalence of reformism and the extent of working-class integration held by many historians. It explains the structural and political causes and the complex character of the radicalism that other historians have acknowledged but not analyzed. It challenges the assertion that the war and postwar militancy was a sort of aberration produced by wartime conditions, and argues that it was the culmination of a long tradition of radicalism. In proposing a different approach to the study of the working class and social democracy, it suggests categories of analysis that will make it possible to compare the different consciousness that developed in various segments of the working class and the different political outcomes in the various regions of Germany.

PART I

The era of frustration:
1890–1903

When the anti-socialist laws were lifted in 1890, the miniscule social democratic movement in Düsseldorf confidently anticipated making progress on all fronts, progress that would bring substantive reforms, perhaps even fundamental transformation. What followed was a decade of frustration and failure. The Social Democrats were unable to build an effective organization, a viable press, or a successful education program. Although they could attract nearly one-third of the voters in national elections, they were unable to recruit more than a small number of young, skilled Protestant migrant workers into the party and unions. They did not present a serious challenge to the power of industrialists on the shop floor, to the dominance of the National Liberals or the Catholic Center Party in local and national politics, or to the cultural hegemony of political Catholicism. They remained isolated from the surrounding society as well as from Social Democrats elsewhere.

The economic structure of Düsseldorf and its business cycles, the social structure and the profound divisions among workers, the authoritarian political system and the isolation of the Social Democrats, all inhibited the formation of a working class and the emergence of a powerful social democratic movement. But it was above all the position and appeal of political Catholicism that thwarted social democracy. And despite numerous experiments, the fledgling movement failed to find either a program or a strategy to defeat its rival.

The experiences of the 1890s first turned the Düsseldorf Social Democrats toward radicalism. They became vociferous critics of parliamentarism, political alliances, and proposals for altering the national party's Marxist program. But the very weakness, isolation, and failure that fostered ideological radicalism also inhibited action. They encouraged a deterministic Marxism, isolation, and passivity. The resulting discrepancy between aspirations and behavior, when added to that between the expected progress and the actual failures, ultimately

9

precipitated an intense internal party struggle over leadership and organization.

Part I will analyze this era of frustration. Chapter 1 explores the inhospitable Düsseldorf terrain in which social democracy tried to put down roots. It examines the economic and social structure, the political system, and the city's workers. Chapter 2 investigates the organizational and political failures of the Düsseldorf social democratic movement in the early 1890s, seeking the explanation above all in the power of political Catholicism. Chapter 3, on the late 1890s, focuses on the difficulties of the union movement, the Social Democrats' failed foray into municipal politics, and the problems of education and political agitation. Chapter 4, covering the turn-of-the-century revisionist controversy and the local "party war," analyzes the heritage of a decade of frustration: the allegiance to orthodox Marxism, political isolation, and tactical passivity.

1

The hostile environment: Düsseldorf in the 1890s

Düsseldorf was one of the most important, prosperous, and rapidly expanding cities in Wilhelmian Germany. Situated on the Rhine, north of Cologne and south of the Ruhr mining and basic metal centers, it had been transformed from a sleepy provincial town, without economic or administrative significance, into an industrial metropolis in the last quarter of the nineteenth century. A product of German unification and industrialization, Düsseldorf was a symbol of the economic power and pride of the Empire, a sort of German Manchester. It was "the pride and joy of its citizens and a star among German cities," to quote a Wilhelmian official.[1] But just as Düsseldorf benefited from the new order, so too it was a victim of the social problems and political conflicts that were particularly acute in an authoritarian society containing powerful remnants of the preindustrial order.[2]

Wilhelmian Düsseldorf mixed the charm of its more parochial past with the grandeur and squalor of its industrial present. Approaching the city from the Rhine, one encountered the old city, which until the eighteenth century had housed the town's princely rulers. It was an enclave of imposing government buildings, cultural institutions, and elegant parks. From this old center, the National Liberal Party and the Catholic Center Party jointly governed the city, and the subprovincial administration carried on the town's bureaucratic tradition. Painting, music, and theater flourished here as well. The "city of art and parks," however, was now dwarfed by the institutions of industry and commerce.

Enclosing the old city in a sweeping half circle was the new Düsseldorf. First came the business section, which had an impressive array of banks, shops, corporate headquarters, and economic associations.[3] With a mixture of awe and hostility, the social democratic press noted that

11

the worker must not forget that some of the largest and most important entrepreneurs are here. One only needs to think about the mammoth buildings of the Stahlwerkverband in the Bastionstrasse. In this building all the threads which direct and control far and away the most important works in the Rhenish and Westphalian iron industry run together. Or a worker can walk along the Rhine to the administrative buildings of the Mannesmann firm. This ostentatious, gigantic structure, nowhere interrupted by a friendly architechtonic line, cries out as a symbol of the power over you.[4]

To the east and northeast of the business district lay the wealthy residential areas, where Düsseldorf's predominantly Protestant entrepreneurs and their counterparts from the Ruhr lived in elegant villas and large apartments.

The industrial heart of the city lay in a broad arc around the business and upper-class residential areas. Metal was king in Düsseldorf, and the numerous metalworking and machine-making plants dominated the manufacturing districts. There was also a liberal sprinkling of construction and woodworking firms, some textile mills and chemical plants, and a multitude of small-scale food and clothing producers. Weaving around the factories and workshops and edging both into the old city and out to the town's extremities were the sprawling, predominantly Catholic working-class residential districts such as Oberbilk and Flingern. The numerous middle- and lower-middle class Düsseldorfers, who were divided by occupation and income but united by Catholicism, lived both intermixed with the proletariat and in the city's more prosperous outlying areas, such as Derendorf. Even the surrounding county, though more rural and provincial than the city, was rapidly industrializing.

The small group of Düsseldorf Social Democrats, who celebrated the end of the era of illegality in 1890, confronted Wilhelmian Düsseldorf with remarkable optimism. "The anti-Socialist laws have fallen," they announced. "All the expectations placed in them have failed miserably ... The enemy stands helpless in cowardly anxiety ... Social Democracy, however, is marching forward, proud and confident of victory."[5] This statement, so accurate in its assessment of the futility of repression, was terribly naive in its predictions. The Düsseldorf Social Democrats were to struggle throughout the 1890s with a notable lack of success, for industrial capitalism and political Catholicism had left their imprint on Düsseldorf long before social democracy became a significant force. The environment created was aggressively hostile to the working class and its organizations.

The economy

"Iron and steel first made Düsseldorf into an industrial city, and they created its reputation in Germany and the world."[6] No statement better sums up the city's economic history. The economic development of Düsseldorf, like that of late nineteenth-century Germany as a whole, centered around the heavy metal industry, much of it large scale and technologically advanced.[7] By the mid-1890s Düsseldorf had 682 metal firms, which employed 14,575 workers, or 28 percent of the labor force.[8] Düsseldorf's metal sector, unlike that of such neighboring Ruhr towns as Bochum or Essen, did not concentrate on basic smelting and rolling but on the production of semifinished and finished goods. The metal-working sector, noted for its pipes and wire products, was well developed and diversified. Machines and instruments, relatively unrepresented until the mid-1890s, became the city's special domain. Indeed, by the turn of the century Düsseldorf had become "the *city* for German machine manufacturing" and was sending mining and railroad equipment, machine tools, steam engines, and scientific instruments throughout Germany and abroad.[9]

Outside entrepreneurs, including some Belgians, had established Düsseldorf's metal industry in the 1860s. Jacques Piedboeuf; Alfred, Gustav, and Rudolf Poensgen; Friedrich Giesberts; and Hermann Flender began with small, specialized iron and steel works and then expanded and diversified their operations. By the 1890s, the Piedboeufs' Düsseldorfer Röhren und Eisenwalzwerke, the Poensgens' Oberbilker Stahlwerk, and the Flender family's Düsseldorfer Eisenhüttengesellschaft were among the giants in their field.[10] Ernst Scheiss and the Haniel family, with its ties to the Guttehoffnungshütte, were among the pioneers in the machine-making industry in the 1880s. At the end of the decade Heinrich Ehrhardt, former artisan, inventor, and self-made man, established a munitions plant, which soon expanded into the mammoth Rheinische Metallwaren und Maschinenfabrik, producing machines, railroad equipment, pipes, and ammunition as well as all the iron and steel it used.[11] Throughout the Wilhelmian era, "Rheinmetall" was Krupp's major competitor in the armaments industry.[12] In the Wilhelmian era, these early leaders were joined by such successful newcomers as Mannesmann, the major producer of pipes, and Hohenzollern A.G. and Düsseldorfer Eisenbahnbedarf, which virtually monopolized the production of transportation equipment.[13] A vast array of small and

Table 1.1. *Düsseldorf's economic growth*

Region	1895 Firms	1895 Labor force	1907 Firms	1907 Labor force	% increase Firms	% increase Labor force
Düsseldorf						
1. City	11,641	53,580	14,850	95,902	27.6	79.0
2. County	3,868	13,742	5,499	31,139	42.2	126.6
3. Total	15,509	67,322	20,349	127,041	31.2	88.7

Source: Monatsschrift der Handelskammer zu Düsseldorf, October 1910, p. 260.

medium-sized metal firms sprang up in the shadow of these giants.

Aspiring entrepreneurs found Düsseldorf a most suitable locale for the metalworking and machine-making industries. The city, which had become something of a commercial center in mid-century, was the hub of a well-developed railroad and river network.[14] This provided inexpensive and convenient access to the Ruhr's coal, iron, and steel, and greatly facilitated the export of finished goods. There was abundant vacant land, suitable for factories and working-class housing. The city sponsored numerous economic exhibitions and fairs, indicating its receptivity to the emerging industrial order. Large-scale migration alleviated the city's only major initial handicap, a lack of skilled metalworkers.[15]

The phenomenal growth of the metal industry spurred expansion in other sectors, making Düsseldorf "the economic center of Germany's most populous and industrialized region."[16] Firms multiplied at nearly three times the national average, the labor force more than twice as quickly. These rates, it should be noted, were equal to or slightly less than those for the surrounding Lower Rhine and Ruhr regions. Düsseldorf's economic growth during this period is summarized in Table 1.1.

Only a small part of Düsseldorf's growth occurred in other factory industries. Textile firms, for example, were hurt by the generally bad state of the industry in Germany as well as by the necessity of paying wages comparable to those in the metal industry, and they declined through most of the period.[17] The glass industry, which was being mechanized slowly, did much better. In the Düsseldorf suburb of Gerresheim, Ferdinand Heye ran one of Germany's largest and most modern glassmaking operations.[18] Although the new, highly mechanized paper and chemical industries prospered, they accounted for only a negligible proportion of total production and employment in the city.[19]

The consumer-goods sector of the economy, where artisan labor predominated, increased substantially as Düsseldorf's industrialization attracted thousands of workers, clerks, technicians, and their dependants.[20] Trades that were not threatened by technological change did particularly well. Thus, construction, benefiting from the population explosion and accompanying building boom was the fastest-growing sector of the city's economy.[21] Woodworking enjoyed a period of stability and prosperity. Food processors – who suffered a minimum of factory competition – flourished, as did certain elements of the clothing business, such as tailors. Other artisans fared less well. Shoemakers and hat and glove makers were forced into repair work and retail trade, while tanners and coopers were all but eliminated by mechanization.[22]

As industry and artisan work expanded, so too did trade, leading Düsseldorf to "assume more and more the dual character of both an industrial and commercial center."[23] In 1895 more than 38 percent of all firms were involved in commerce and transportation, and the proportion rose substantially over the next two decades. The vitality of the commercial sector made Düsseldorf's economy resemble that of neighboring Cologne. Düsseldorf's occupational structure was much more like that of the Ruhr towns, however, for only 22 percent of the labor force was employed in the generally small commercial establishments.[24] With the exception of a large agricultural goods trade, the commercial sector catered primarily to the needs of local manufacturing, especially metal. In the 1890s the development of a vigorous transporation industry likewise derived from the demands of industry.[25]

The municipal sector of the economy, which complemented private business rather than competing with it, grew rapidly in the Imperial period. By the mid-1890s the city employed 1,400 workers and civil servants in the gas, water, and electrical works, sewage system, and slaughterhouse. In the late 1890s the city built a much-neded new harbor and purchased the privately owned streetcar system. The city, which also managed museums, libraries, financial institutions, and a municipal theater, became the largest single employer after 1900.[26]

Düsseldorf was noted not only for production and trade. It was also the administrative center for the corporations, cartels, and economic interest groups that dominated the Ruhr and Lower Rhine. Despite the persistence of small firms, German capitalism displayed a level of concentration and cartelization unmatched elsewhere in the industrial world. Of equal importance, major capitalist interests were well organized by geographic region and economic sector in an effort to stabilize economic growth, influence fiscal, commercial, and social policy, and combat working-class organizations. These monopolies, trusts, and interest associations, which had arisen as temporary responses to the Great Depression of the 1870s and 1880s, became permanent features of German economic and political life in the 1890s.[27] A review of the major institutions located in Düsseldorf suggests that city's pivotal position in the workings of German organized capitalism. All major industrial firms, whatever their subsequent expansion, retained their headquarters there. In addition, Phoenix, Stumm, and the Siemens-Schuckert-RheinElbe Union were among the major concerns that located their administrative offices in Düsseldorf rather than in the Ruhr proper. Industrial interest groups found the city congenial. In 1871 the Association for the Protection of Common Economic Interests in the Rhineland and Westphalia, aptly known as the "Long Name Association," settled in Düsseldorf. Three years later the Northwest Group of the Association of German Iron and Steel Industrialists followed. Cartels abounded as well. In 1904 the Steel Cartel, which included the major producers in Germany and Luxemburg and regulated both production and domestic and foreign sales, built its headquarters in the city. The Association of German Ironworks, the Pipe Syndicate, the Foreign Trade Bureau for the Iron Industry, and three wire-producing cartels were also located there.[28]

By the 1890s, then, industrial capitalism had transformed all aspects of Düsseldorf's economy, creating a powerful and modern factory sector, vigorous artisan trades, and thriving commerce. And that economy was palpably dominated by corporations, cartels, and economic interest groups. Industrial capitalism fundamentally altered Düsseldorf's pre-industrial and precapitalist social order as well.

Society

In the late nineteenth century Düsseldorf was transformed from a small, provincial backwater into a bustling, sprawling metropolis. The multitude of factories, workshops, and offices had an insatiable appetite for new employees. Thus thousands and thousands of migrants were drawn from near and far by the city's economic opportunities and quickly outnumbered the stable, native population. Young, single men – some aspiring capitalists, others white-collar employees, most proletarians – became the dynamic element in a city where stalwart artisans, bureaucrats, and pensioners, overwhelmingly family men, had once set the tone. The large Catholic majority, formerly secure in its control of political, cultural, and religious life, now faced a sizable Protestant minority. Urbanization, migration, and the emergence of a new class structure interacted to create a new society in Düsseldorf.

Düsseldorf was one of the fastest-growing cities in the Rhineland and Westphalia, which were the most populous, urbanized, and rapidly growing provinces in Germany. In 1871, when Germany was unified and Düsseldorf's industrialization was in its early stages, the city had nearly 70,000 inhabitants. Within two decades the population had doubled, and at the turn of the century the city had 213,711 inhabitants and the surrounding county an additional 96,559. By 1905 Düsseldorf was the fifth largest city in Prussia, the tenth largest in Germany.[29]

Native Düsseldorfers accounted for part of this population increase, because they and their children usually remained in the city for the high wages, abundant job opportunities, and strong ties to the Catholic culture.[30] It was migrants, however, who created the new Düsseldorf. Wilhelmian Germany was a nation on the move, with nearly half the population leaving its birthplace in search of economic survival or social opportunity.[31] Düsseldorf was a veritable mecca for migrants because it offered industrial and commercial opportunities, blue-collar positions as well as white-collar ones. Wages were among the highest in Germany and, unlike the Ruhr proper, cultural and educational facilities abounded. In the mid-1890s roughly 29,000 people arrived yearly but another 25,000 left, many having stayed only a few weeks, others a year or perhaps five or ten. A few settled permanently. Most of these mobile migrants were young, single men; women, relegated to domestic service or low-paying jobs, did not move readily to Düsseldorf.[32] The newcomers came primarily from towns and cities in the Rhineland and Westphalia and thus, unlike migrants to the Ruhr, were strangers neither to the region nor to urban life.[33] A significant proportion were Protestant, and as a result the population, 80 percent Catholic at mid-century, was 70 percent Catholic in 1900.[34]

This heterogeneous army of migrants who trooped into late-nineteenth-century Düsseldorf found a very diverse society. Whereas in Ruhr towns, such as Gelsenkirchen, roughly 80 percent of the population depended on industry, the figure for Düsseldorf in the mid-1890s was only 60 percent. Nineteen percent were involved in commerce, a figure comparable to the much less industrialized Munich, and 10 percent received a livelihood from government service and the free professions. Although blue-collar workers made up the largest component of the labor force, nearly one-third of those employed held middle-class positions.[35] Both newcomers and natives experienced a society very much in flux. The industrial elite and the propertied and professional bourgeoisie had established their economic position and social identity quite clearly. The working class and the new lower middle class, however, were still in the making, and the traditional *Mittelstand* was being forced to redefine itself. Occupation, income, religion, social status, and place of origin each created conflicting loyalties and initially hindered the development of cohesive groups with clear identities.

The upper bourgeoisie, whose power was built on industry and to a lesser extent commerce, was unquestionably the dominant class in Düsseldorf. Noted for its optimism, materialism, and drive, this elite acquired its position in the late nineteenth century. Whereas merchants and manufacturers had run the textile towns of Elberfeld, Barmen, and Krefeld and the commercial center of Cologne since the late eighteenth century, entrepreneurs, overwhelmingly Protestant and migrant, had not established themselves in Düsseldorf until the 1860s and gained prestige only in the ensuing decades.[36] The industrial pioneers of Düsseldorf, the Piedboeufs, Poensgens, and Flenders, Ehrhardt, Heye, and Scheiss, and their sons who took over the businesses in the Wilhelmian era, formed the core of this elite.[37] Later industrialists, leaders of commerce, and the small group of realtors who owned more than one-fifth of the housing in Düsseldorf, supplemented the original group.[38] In addition, Ruhr corporate executives often preferred to live in Düsseldorf, rather than in the towns where their operations were located, for in Düsseldorf they "did not suffocate in dust and dirt. They heard more than just the droning of machinery . . . . They lived in a different milieu than that of the working-class cities."[39] The large size of this industrial elite is suggested by scattered income statistics. In 1892, 42 Düsseldorfers had a yearly income of more than 100,000 M and 159 earned from 35,000 M to 100,000 M. By 1906 both these groups had doubled and there were 193 millionaires. This was in a city where only 2.6 percent of the population earned more than 3,000 M.[40]

The industrial bourgeoisie of Düsseldorf was extraordinarily proud of its achievements. The memoirs of Ehrhardt and the statements of the Mannesmann brothers and the Poensgens are filled with enthusiastic descriptions of new products and production processes. The addition of each new factory to their empires was celebrated as lovingly as the birth of a new child.[41] The elite eagerly participated in the Chamber of Commerce (*Handelskammer*), and in turn that body's stance on trade and tariff issues, state intervention, and social policy reflected the attitudes of the dominant metal industry.[42] But these entrepreneurs were not interested only in economic affairs. They contributed regularly to local charities. They considered themselves the defenders of *Bildung* (culture) as well as of *Besitz* (property) and supported Düsseldorf's museums, opera, and theaters.[43] They were, in short, eminently bourgeois.

For most of Düsseldorf's leading entrepreneurs, however, being bourgeois was not enough. Like their counterparts throughout Germany, these industrialists felt inferior to the politically and socially powerful landed aristocracy. In the 1860s some resented aristocratic prominence, but by the 1870s and 1880s they abandoned all resistance and emulated aristocratic culture. The feudalization of the upper bourgeoisie had begun. Capitalists also sought state recognition in the form of titles and orders, the non-noble *Kommerzienrat* being the most popular.[44] In 1894, for example the 68-year-old Rudolf Poensgen, head of the Düsseldorf Pipe and Rolling Works, former member of the Chamber of Commerce and the city council, and worth a half million marks, was given that honor for "his special interest in all affairs relating to the iron industry and workers' welfare" and for being "always a great admirer and true supporter of the ruling house."[45] The founder of Rheinmetall refused ennoblement, insisting that "I find the name Ehrhardt perfectly good." Despite this unusual gesture, he proudly noted in his memoirs that "as my business grew, I came into contact with ever higher and more influential people, finally with ministers and ruling princes. These men believed that they should honor my work, which they considered useful for the state and the public, in the usual way. In general, I received these honors with thanks."[46]

The industrialists, imitating aristocratic life-styles, built elegant urban villas, held lavish entertainments, and employed numerous servants. In Düsseldorf there were 43 domestics per 1000 inhabitants, well above the average for large cities.[47] The elite was socially very exclusive, associating with and marrying members of its own class, aristocrats, upper civil servants, and members of the free professions.[48] Düsseldorf entre-preneurs strove for contacts with nationally prominent figures but never achieved the close personal and political ties with William II or leading ministers that such men as Krupp and Stumm did.[49]

The Düsseldorf elite was part of the new agrarian and industrial ruling class that emerged in the late nineteenth century. It adopted the prevalent nationalistic attitudes, abandoned its earlier opposition to militarism, and sent its sons to be one-year reservists in the aristo-cratically dominated Prussian army.[50] Whatever divisions were to emerge within this upper class about social reform, tariff and tax questions, and political strategies, there was an underlying consensus based on the acceptance of organized capitalism, the existing social order, and the authoritarian state.

The middle and lower ranks of the bourgeoisie were neither cohesive nor powerful. Artisans, small shopkeepers, civil servants, small busi-nessmen, and white-collar workers were in an economically precarious and often dependent position. They were divided by religion, place of origin, and occupation as well as by the multitude of economic, cultural, and historical factors that separated the traditional *Mittelstand* of shop-keepers and artisans from the *Beamter*, or civil servant, and both of these from the emerging *Angestellte*, or white-collar class. These groups social-ized with one another and intermarried to only a limited degree. They were unable to form effective, large-scale associations in a society in which organized economic power carried increasing weight.[51] Small wonder that they enjoyed little social prestige and less political clout.

Despite their disunity, the middle and lower middle classes were growing rapidly. Between 1892 and 1906 the number of Düsseldorf tax payers with incomes between 3,000 M and 35,000 M rose from just over 3,000 to nearly 7,000. Those in the 900 M to 3,000 M bracket, which included some of the highest-paid skilled workers, increased from 10,000 to nearly 57,000. New groups, such as white-collar and technical personnel, were primarily responsible for this upsurge. More traditional elements benefited less. The civil service census category and the catch-all rubric that included capitalists, top management, and all self-employed artisans and shopkeepers, declined relatively but not ab-solutely.[52] Small traders clung to precarious existences, and numerous threatened artisans opened small shops. *Mittelstand* perceptions not-withstanding, this overcrowding, and not competition from department stores and cooperatives, was primarily responsible for the crisis in retail trade.[53] The artisans' experience was more mixed. Whether an artisan maintained his traditional existence, became a "modern" small businessman, converted to repair work, or went under, however, he felt economically threatened, socially marginalized, and culturally assaulted.[54]

The anxious but proud *Mittelstand* attempted to defend itself against the simultaneous challenge from organized capital and organized labor. Taking advantage of revisions in the 1897 commercial code, master artisans formed numerous compulsory and noncompulsory guilds in Düsseldorf. In addition, they formed a citywide guild committee and an Artisan Chamber, the *Mittelstand* counterpart to the industrially dominated Chamber of Commerce.[55] The *Mittelstand*'s rejection of capitalist society was sweeping, its aspirations vast. According to the Artisan Chamber, "in contemporary economic life the guilds should become what they were in their heyday: a comradely union of artisans with the explicit purpose of promoting the common interest, not only economic but social as well.... To further the social interest the guild should concentrate on raising *Standesbewusstsein* [corporate consciousness]."[56] In the words of Paul Adam, a prominent Düsseldorf bookbinder, the guild revival movement should be supported because "the factory population goes around blindly and is in the clutches of consciously misleading instigators." Apprentices and journeymen, however, were protected from such temptations.[57] Although most artisans shared these views, they were often reluctant to join the guilds, which seldom brought either immediate economic benefits or improved social status.[58] The *Mittelstand* proved unable to ward off the impact of industrialization.

When the Wilhelmian era opened in 1890, the working class was certainly as diversified and fragmented as the middle class. Neighboring Krefeld had its weavers and spinners, Solingen its cutlery makers, and the Ruhr its miners, but there was no typical Düsseldorf worker. Metal was the largest industry, but its workforce ranged from artisanal smiths through unskilled helpers and semiskilled machine operators to skilled factory turners and boilermakers. Migrant Protestant carpenters and joiners, native Düsseldorf painters, and unskilled, staunchly Catholic migrants all worked in the booming construction business. Woodworkers and printers were highly skilled, well paid, and had strong traditions, stable family lives, and firm roots in Düsseldorf; whereas textile, chemical, and paper workers were transient, semiskilled, and badly paid. And that was only the male portion of the proletariat. Women workers, poorly paid and primarily single, were employed in commercial establishments, the sweated trades, and most frequently in domestic service.[59] Although most workers were Catholic, natives and migrants did not form a cohesive community, and the Protestant contingent was on the increase. Although most workers were migrants, that fact did not overcome differences in occupation, religion, place of birth, and length of stay. Neither culture nor community nor current economic condition united Düsseldorf's proletariat.

By the mid-1890s there were more than 30,000 blue-collar workers in manufacturing and another 9,000 in transport and commerce. Eighty-five percent of them were male.[60] Nearly 30 percent of the working class, predominantly young males, had secured high-paying, relatively skilled positions in the metal sector. Although a high percentage of them worked in large factories, thousands of others were in unmechanized artisan shops and small plants. Only those with little skill and few options – older men, migrants, and women – suffered the low pay, long hours, and insecurity that characterized factory jobs in textiles, chemicals, and paper. In the artisan sector, construction was the counterpart to metal, employing more than 6,000 skilled and unskilled workers at good wages. Another 2,400 workers had positions in the equally prosperous and prestigious woodworking trades. In more precarious artisan trades, such as food and clothing, as well as in commercial establishments, shops were small and scattered, wages low, and the proportion of female workers rising.[61] In addition to those employed in the private sector, nearly 800 workers had jobs with the city. Almost all of these were men, but only half had permanent positions, and none received good wages.[62] Finally, there were more than 6,000 female domestics.

Native Düsseldorfers, migrants from the surrounding Rhineland, and arrivals from other German provinces or foreign countries each accounted for a third of the working class. Because older workers could not get jobs in metal and construction, the migrants were disproportionately young and single. Indeed, in 1895, three-fifths of the entire working class was under 30, and another one-fifth was between 30 and 40.[63]

Despite important variations among different occupations and industries, the workers in Düsseldorf were, by contemporary standards, relatively highly skilled, well paid, and integrated into industrial society. A significant number of metalworkers in both large and small firms retained a high degree of technical expertise and a fair amount of control over the production process. Skilled workers in construction and woodworking occupied an even more advantageous position in the division of labor.[64] Only those in the peripheral factory industries and the declining artisan trades had experienced significant de-skilling and a loss of autonomy by the 1890s.

Just as the dominant elements in the working class occupied a privileged position in the division of labor, so too they enjoyed advantages in the labor market. The skills demanded by Düsseldorf's rapidly expanding economy were in short supply, leading industrialists to bid up wages until they were among the highest in Germany. Even seasonal unemployment and cyclical crises affected this large skilled group less severely than the remainder of the working class. Because many of the skilled came from small and medium-sized towns, where their families had been involved in artisan and factory labor or the putting-out system, they found the transition to work and life in the industrial metropolis somewhat easier.[65] Even more than the miners and metalworkers of the neighboring Ruhr, the numerous artisans and skilled factory workers in Düsseldorf were an elite within the proletariat.[66] According to Hans Berlepsch, a Silesian aristocrat who served as president of the government district of Düsseldorf in 1889–90, the working class in that area "distinguished itself fundamentally from that in Upper Silesia. It not only surpassed the latter in number but was significantly more intelligent, determined and capable."[67]

Yet the Düsseldorf proletariat, for all its maturity and privileged status, did share one important characteristic with its counterpart in the east – the weakness of working-class associations, economic, political, and cultural.[68] As in the other industrial centers of the region, a well-paid, highly skilled, and moderately urbanized working class existed in a near organizational vacuum. This paradoxical situation contrasted sharply with that in cities such as Hamburg, Bremen, Berlin, and Leipzig, which were strongholds of both a skilled working class and the social democratic movement.[69]

When the Wilhelmian era opened, the skilled craftsmen of Düsseldorf had by no means left their imprint on the entire working class. Whether they were employed in workshops or factories, these skilled men were still bound by traditions of exclusiveness, local autonomy, and craft control.[70] Although a recognizable elite in terms of their "objective" situation, the skilled workers neither shared a common consciousness nor formed a cohesive community. Their privileged position in the production process did not enable them to form strong organizations or control the rest of the working class. Nor did it lead them inexorably in a reformist direction. Contrary to much recent historiography, consciousness and community were not created automatically by the division of labor.[71] Cultural values, forms, and goals, which were determined by social relations within the workplace and outside, were very influential in shaping workers' self-definition and relationships to one another as well as to other classes. The complex interaction of structure and culture defined social position and the possibilities for social action.[72]

Culture was no more conducive to working-class cohesion and politicization in Düsseldorf than was the division of labor. The multiplicity of occupations, the heterogeneity of the numerically predominant migrant group, and the ever-present religious split created a kind of cultural chaos. When the Wilhelmian era opened, Düsseldorf was a patchwork of small communities, each having its own occupational, economic, religious, and cultural character, its own degree of permanence, and its own relationship to the surrounding society.

To be sure, all workers shared the same basic economic insecurity and second-class social status, "a common liability to misfortune."[73] Even the best paid could affort little beyond basic necessities.[74] All faced seasonal and cyclical unemployment and received no unemployment compensation when they were laid off. Those in the most prosperous sectors as well as those in the most retrograde experienced long hours and poor working conditions. Those not rigorously supervised by patriarchal employers in small firms were subjected to the rigid disciplinary codes of large factories, which spelled out the proper behavior for industrial workers in minute and oppressive detail.[75] All found protective legislation and insurance programs grossly inadequate.

Life off the job offered few compensations for the rigors experienced 10 through 12 hours a day at work. Skilled and unskilled alike lived in overcrowded and overpriced housing.[76] They sent their children to elementary schools, which were distinctly inferior to those attended by middle-class children, and of necessity pushed them into the labor force at 13 or 14 years of age.[77] For the children as for their parents, proletarian existence was to be a life sentence. Leisure was as problematic as work and family life, because workers, to varying degrees excluded from the dominant Catholic and nationalistic cultures, were still in the process of creating their own activities and associations.

Exploitation, insecurity, and exclusion did not in and of themselves "make" the Düsseldorf working class. Many workers undoubtedly considered their wages inadequate, the authority of supervisors and owners unmerited and arbitrary, and their overall situation unjust. Certainly the desire for "decent human treatment" was widespread, as memoirs and questionnaires show.[78] But Düsseldorf's workers were unable to forge their fragmented ranks into a class, to mold a culture that incorporated yet transcended the particularistic cultures that abounded. They lacked a common vocabulary in which to articulate shared grievances and goals. The obstacles to the creation of class, culture, and consciousness came not only from structural and cultural conditions but from political ones as well.

Politics

By 1890 the contours of Imperial Germany that shaped both Düsseldorf's participation in national politics and its municipal affairs were firmly established. Bismarck's unification and the consequences of the Great Depression of the 1870s and 1880s led to the creation of an aristocratically dominated, authoritarian state. In Europe's most expansive, technologically advanced, and organized capitalist economy, political power remained firmly in the hands of an economically declining landed nobility.[79] Industrialization transformed society but not politics, and until 1918 Germany remained illiberal and antidemocratic.

Germany was a pseudoconstitutional monarchy in which the emperor and his chancellor enjoyed vast power over domestic and foreign policy. The authoritarian executive was supported by a politically conservative bureaucracy and an aristocratically dominated army.[80] The only popular element was the Reichstag, elected by universal male suffrage, but in the absence of ministerial responsibility and parliamentary control over the budget and the military, it was more a debating society than a decision-making body. The political parties, which represented particular classes or fractions thereof – the multi-class Center Party being the only exception – were increasingly subject to the influence of powerful economic interest groups, such as the Agrarian League and the Central Association of German Industrialists.[81] The political parties, striving to achieve both their narrow economic goals and their broader social vision in a situation of relative powerlessness, displayed a peculiar mixture of "principledness bordering on doctrinaire rigidity" and "adaptability verging on outright opportunism."[82]

The social basis of the Imperial German system had been laid in the late 1870s when Bismarck united East Elbian Junkers and Ruhr and Silesian industrialists behind protective tariffs and repression of the Social Democrats. The shared interests of the state, heavy industry, and agriculture were to influence domestic policy strongly thereafter.[83] By the late 1880s this ruling alliance was being broadened to include the Center Party and the rural and urban *Mittelstand*.[84]

After 1890, when Bismarck was no longer running the state in a Bonapartist fashion, serious disagreements among the Liberals, Conservatives, and Center were to arise, creating shifting government coalitions and a zigzag course in social policy. Nonetheless, industry, trade, and agriculture and their political representatives were to remain united on two fundamental issues: support of the authoritarian state and opposition to the Social Democrats. The working class was completely excluded from the Bismarckian synthesis and its subsequent re-creations, but the danger embodied in an organized and socialist working class was the cement that held the synthesis together, provided its economic and social raison d'être, and promoted its political rigidity.[85] The more the working class pressed for reforms and challenged the existing political order, the more the established forces resisted any changes. Stagnation rather than reform, a permanent state crisis, were to become the hallmarks of the Wilhelmian era not only nationally but provincially and locally as well.

In Prussia, unlike in the more liberal South German states, provincial and municipal institutions reenforced the authoritarian character and narrow class base of politics. Prussia was the largest and politically most influential state, capable of determining national policy on crucial issues. Yet the powerful Prussian Landtag, which controlled economic, social, and judicial affairs, was elected by an extremely inequitable three-class suffrage, which assured the dominance of the Conservative and National Liberal upper classes. Municipal politics were no more democratic, as the case of Düsseldorf illustrates. The city council was elected under a three-class suffrage, which placed 90 percent of the taxpayers in the lowest class. Each class elected one-third of the council in open and oral voting. Only males over 25 who paid taxes, received no poor relief, and had resided in the city for 1 year were eligible for election. At least one-half of the council had to be homeowners. Civil service candidates, locally as well as nationally, were screened for their political reliability.[86] In short, the working class in general and the Social Democrats in particular were effectively excluded.

When the Wilhelmian era opened, two major groups were competing for control of Düsseldorf's oligarchic municipal government and for the right to represent the city in the Reichstag and Landtag. Both the National Liberal Party and the Catholic Center Party had secured crucial power positions, mobilized significant support, and embedded themselves deeply in particular social milieus.[87]

Düsseldorf's elite, with a few Catholic and left liberal exceptions, solidly supported national liberalism, the industrial capitalist party par excellence. These entrepreneurs had long since abandoned the political tenets of their liberal creed and jetisoned their faith in laissez-faire capitalism and the noninterventionist state as well. They admired Bismarck and the unified, authoritarian state he had created. By 1890 they had moved from staunch, indeed strident, nationalism to enthusiastic imperialism.[88] They displayed somewhat less unanimity on domestic issues, for Düsseldorf's diversified economy contained a variety of conflicting interests and entrepreneurial styles. Machinery and textile industrialists wanted lower tariffs to facilitate exports, whereas heavy industry favored high rates, and owners of construction firms were indifferent. Large industrialists like Ehrhardt maintained a *Herr-im-Haus* standpoint, which combined authoritarian paternalism, a modicum of company welfare, and opposition to all worker organizations. The Mannesmann and Poensgen corporations moved in the direction of bureaucratic control, while medium-sized firms, more susceptible to trade-union pressure, favored a "liberal" policy of negotiation with unions and welfare legislation.[89] These entrepreneurs shared a commitment to containing the Social Democrats and defending the existing order but disagreed about whether this could best be done with or against the agrarian aristocracy, through repression or reform.[90] Nonetheless, they were able to cooperate to develop two bases of political power in Düsseldorf, municipal government on the one hand and public and private economic associations on the other.

"Although the great entrepreneurial families in Düsseldorf never assumed as commanding a position as the Krupps in Essen, they nonetheless won an influence in the city which should not be underestimated."[91] From the 1860s on, industrialists involved themselves in municipal politics because local government decided issues that had direct economic impact and because the three-class suffrage gave the upper class indisputable advantages.[92] Alfred Poensgen was the first of the new breed of capitalists to seek a seat on the city council in the mid-

1860s and was soon followed by his brother Rudolf.[93] By the end of the century Scheiss, Haniel, Bagel, Lueg, and Pfeiffer, to name only a few, had all been repeatedly elected. The industrially dominated Middle Party, a local alliance of liberal groups of which the National Liberals were the strongest, controlled both the first and second classes, leaving only the third to the Center Party.[94] Indeed, in the early Wilhelmian era the vast majority of council members were prosperous property owners, who, regardless of party, cooperated in the defence of *Bildung* and *Besitz*.

Friedrich Wilhelm Becker, Ernst Lindemann, and Wilhelm Marx, the mayors of Düsseldorf in the Bismarckian and early Wilhelmian eras, although not themselves entrepreneurs, were sympathetic to industrial interests.[95] The same was true of the government district presidents such as Berlepsch, von Rheinbaben, and von Holleuffer.[96] On the local level, just as on the national one, the increasingly organized capitalist interests looked to the municipal government and bureaucracy for aid. These institutions, in turn, intervened extensively to promote economic growth, reduce social conflict, and enhance their own legitimacy. Although the interests of business and government were by no means identical, the areas of cooperation and consensus were broad.[97]

In Düsseldorf as throughout Germany, the National Liberals failed to adapt to the age of mass politics, remaining an elite party with no bureaucratic organization or wide social appeal.[98] They operated "within a web of familial, social and business relationships uniting a relatively small group."[99] The National Liberal Party ceased to be a serious contender for Düsseldorf's Reichstag seat as early as the 1870s and thereafter used the Chamber of Commerce, the economic interest groups, and the city council as alternatives to representation in a parliament that they considered in any case ineffective, even contemptible. The Chamber of Commerce was a state-sponsored association of manufacturers and merchants that had the dual function of transmitting national policies to its constituency and representing local interests to the national government.[100] The bureaucracy and legislature alike eagerly sought its opinion on all economic and social questions, and the dominant industrial interests in Düsseldorf, well represented among the Chamber's officials, shaped the opinions delivered.[101] The local elite also used the economic interest groups, many of which had their headquarters in Düsseldorf, to influence political parties and the state.[102]

Catholic political power in Düsseldorf had a quite different institutional and social base. In the 1870s, when Bismarck waged his bitter

Kulturkampf against the Catholic Church, the large Catholic *Mittelstand*, the handful of Catholic entrepreneurs and high civil servants, and the ever-growing Catholic working class all rallied to the Center Party, which promised to defend their religious interests against the attacks of the state and their material position from the encroachments of industrial capitalism.[103] Militant political Catholicism broke the National Liberal Party's grip on the Reichstag seat and challenged their hegemony in the provincial and municipal arenas. In the early Wilhelmian era the Düsseldorf Center Party regarded the Reichstag seat as "a holy inheritance," which must be vigorously defended because the party "had held it gloriously since the founding of the Reich."[104] The Center Party completely monopolized the third class in the city council and controlled roughly a third of the second class, assuring it a strong minority voice. The three-class suffrage also gave the Center Party, with its large middle-class constituency, a substantial minority of seats in the Landtag.

The Center Party, unlike the National Liberals, had adapted to the emerging age of organized mass politics. Although the party itself remained as elitist as its liberal counterpart, it enlisted the clergy, various parish organizations, and new economic and political associations to mobilize Catholic voters.[105] In addition, political Catholicism was buttressed by a plethora of recreational and educational organizations and a well-developed press. All this made Düsseldorf one of political Catholicism's most important industrial strongholds and led the city to play a major role in the Rhineland Center Party, which believed that its adherence to "constitutionalism, responsible capitalism and social reform" made it "the intellectual center of modern German Catholicism."[106]

Although the *Kulturkampf* was ended by 1890, Catholics were not fully accepted by the predominantly Protestant state and society, and the Center Party still strove to defend the church and gain economic and political parity for its supporters. Because the party represented regions with very different social and economic structures and classes with incompatible interests, however, it was deeply divided about how to achieve these goals. The Rhineland Center Party known as the Cologne faction urged Catholics to integrate themselves into the existing order by accepting capitalism, allying with Conservatives, and cooperating with the state. The Center Party should become more secular and less sectarian.[107] It should support the *Mittelstand* without opposing industrialization and retain the allegiance of the working class through social reform and interconfessional trade unions.[108] This left wing within the Center Party reflected conditions in cities like Düsseldorf, where Catholic industrialists were few, the middle class solid, the working class numerous, and the potential Social Democratic challenge serious.

The Center's left clashed sharply with the Berlin faction, rooted in areas like the Saar and Upper Silesia, where virtually no Catholic middle class existed and paternalistic Catholic entrepreneurs faced an unorganized, impoverished, unskilled working class, new to industrial work.[109] This right wing urged Catholics to remain isolated within the Center Party fortress, insisted on the primacy of religion, and upheld the reactionary vision of a thoroughly Christian, precapitalist society of estates (*Ständestaat*). Eschewing any accommodation with other parties, Protestants, or the state, the right argued that interconfessional associations promoted secularization and that trade unions fostered unnecessary conflicts.[110] Such intransigence vis-à-vis the established order and the working class was a luxury that the Düsseldorf Center Party could ill afford.

Although "leftist" on social and strategic issues, the Center Party in Düsseldorf was neither liberal nor democratic.[111] It defended the *Rechtsstaat* but not political reform. By the early 1890s Düsseldorf Centrists, like their colleagues throughout Germany, "were conservative in sentiment," because "however authoritarian, the German Empire corresponded to and satisfied the interests of all factions."[112] To be sure, the Center Party was opposed to militarism, unenthusiastic about nationalism, and suspicious of the Protestant state, which in turn retained a lingering mistrust of the Catholics. Nonetheless, the Center's acceptance of the authoritarian regime and its opposition to social democracy were to open the way for it to become a government party, a pillar of the established order, by the turn of the century.[113]

When the anti-socialist laws were lifted in 1890, twelve years of severe repression ended. The major legal obstacle to social democracy's expansion was removed. But the Düsseldorf Social Democrats found themselves facing well-organized political movements, which had authoritarian and strongly anti-socialist traditions and were firmly entrenched in illiberal political structures. The potential political actors were already highly mobilized. The Social Democrats would have to defeat their enemies, not merely fill a vacuum by organizing the unorganized. They would have to create their own culture and traditions rather than building on existing ones. They would have to struggle to alter institutions fundamentally rather than simply seeking power within them.

The economic and social transformation that brought forth the social democratic challenge presented both National Liberals and Centrists with serious dilemmas. The National Liberals, lacking a mass base, confronted the task of maintaining in toto the existing hierarchical, authoritarian political order that guaranteed their position. If they did so, however, they would greatly intensify the contradictions between Germany's advanced economic and social structure on the one hand and its anachronistic political order on the other, thereby exacerbating social tensions and increasing the chances of radical conflict.[114] The Center Party needed to retain working-class votes to win power locally and nationally, yet could offer those voters little beyond appeals to religious solidarity and empty promises of "equalizing justice." If the Center Party were to fight for the equality of the working class in state and society, it could not hope to ally with the Conservative Party or win favor from the state. If it offered workers parity within the party as compensation for inequality in the larger society, that would disrupt the dominance of agrarian aristocrats, the *Mittelstand*, and the clergy.[115] Both National Liberals and Centrists in Düsseldorf wanted to enjoy the economic benefits of ongoing, capitalist industrialization while preventing social conflict and political change. In the long run, it was to prove a futile attempt to square the circle.

In the short run, the expansion of industrial capitalism, which presented such problems for the National Liberals and the Centrists, suggested no easy solutions for the social democratic workers in Düsseldorf. The few hundred who cheered the end of the anti-socialist laws in 1890 discovered in the ensuing decade that "the Gold International of big business and the Black International of Catholicism dominated the town."[116]

2

Social democracy and political Catholicism

In 1890 the cabinetmakers Gustav Lehmann and Ernst Erbert and the skilled metalworkers Wilhelm Tietges, Richard Heldt, Wilhelm Gotthusen, and Richard Wittkopf were among the busiest men in Düsseldorf. They ran the largest trade unions and the popular educational association–all ostensibly nonpolitical, and published the *Düsseldorfer Arbeiterzeitung*. They campaigned vigorously for the Social Democratic Reichstag candidate Hermann Grimpe, who won one-third of the votes in the 1890 electoral contest. At year's end they led the social democratic movement triumphantly out of illegality and into the new era.

The accomplishments of 1890 were superficial, however, and throughout the first half decade the successes anticipated by the Social Democrats did not materialize. Although the Social Democrats garnered more than eight thousand votes, they could not translate electoral support into active commitment or organizational strength. Less than a thousand workers were in the dozen or so weak unions, and only a few hundred in the party. Expansion beyond a small Protestant, artisan base proved impossible. The *Arbeiterzeitung* remained a small, second-rate biweekly with low circulation. Both the party and the unions lacked meeting places and funds and sponsored only a minimum number of activities. Far from being a power in Düsseldorf, the Social Democrats scarcely even had a presence. They could not contest capitalist control on the shop floor or National Liberal and Center Party power in the political arena. In comparison to its counterparts in Protestant industrial cities, the movement in Düsseldorf was immature and floundering.

The reasons for these failures are manifold. The economic and political structure of Düsseldorf stunted the movement's development, as did the economic depression that persisted until the mid-1890s. The consequences of twelve years of illegality, the organizational *Kinderkrankheiten* of the party, and the isolation of the Social Democrats from the surrounding society and from the national party in Berlin all

32

contributed to limiting the movement's appeal and weakening its institutional structure. The most important obstacle to social democratic success, however, was the organizational and ideological hegemony of political Catholicism – a hegemony that extended to the predominantly Catholic working class.

Political Catholicism was the overriding preoccupation of the Düsseldorf Social Democrats, and of necessity they defined their political priorities and appeals in terms of their more powerful rival. The frustrations they encountered in dealing with political Catholicism and the isolation engendered by their failures were to have simultaneously a radicalizing impact on their ideology and a dampening one on their practice.

The heritage of failure

The Düsseldorf worker's movement entered the era of legality with a most inauspicious history. Although local socialists such as Ferdinand Kichniawy and Gustav Lewy were present at the birth of the German workers' movement in 1863, they were unable to nourish the local branch beyond the stage of infancy. For nearly three decades they formed and reformed political clubs and trade unions, but all were plagued by internal splits, governmental repression, and Catholic competition. Düsseldorf, like neighboring Ruhr towns, but unlike Elberfeld, Barmen, and the industrial centers of Saxony and North Germany, had no heroic past that laid secure foundations for future growth.[1]

Together with many other Rhenish cities, Düsseldorf was a stronghold of Lassalle's General German Workers' Association (ADAV) in the early 1860s. At its highpoint, the ADAV attracted more than 200 members and 600 voters. Thereafter, the local party, like its national counterpart, was wracked by virulent leadership struggles. By 1871, when political Catholicism launched its simultaneous attack on Lassalleans and liberals, the Düsseldorf ADAV was "almost completely without influence." The Center Party swept the Reichstag seat, whereas the Lassalleans, too weak to run a candidate, supported the National Liberal Party. The newly established and explicitly anti-socialist Christian Social Association quickly recruited more than 500 workers, becoming the third largest such group in Germany.[2] The competition between the red and the black had begun on a most unequal footing. Two years later, the local liberals intensified the growing conflict between the proletariat and the middle classes by definitively breaking with the Lassalleans. The isolation of the socialists was complete.

Thereafter, a few young Protestant artisans without stable jobs or residences led the miniscule Social Democratic Party. The nearly 500 socialist voters came from the same milieu. The movement made no inroads into the settled, Catholic working class, the growing factory proletariat, the dominant metal trades, or the middle classes.[3] And even this meager movement disappeared when Bismarck and the Reichstag outlawed the Social Democrats in 1878.

The anti-socialist laws were applied with extreme severity in Düsseldorf and the Lower Rhine, and initially they were quite effective. By the early 1880s, however, the printers, cabinetmakers, and metalworkers had organized small unions, all of which were to suffer a checkered history of government repression and reestablishment. Simultaneously, Lehmann, Erbert, Linxweiler, Heldt, and Wittkopf, the young artisan union organizers, held clandestine political meetings.[4] In 1887 they established the short-lived electoral association, which drew its small membership from young shoemakers, metal turners, and above all carpenters. That same year, the Social Democratic vote increased from a low of 305 (2.1 percent) in 1881 to 2,933 (10.5 percent).[5] Not surprisingly, in 1888 eighteen leading Düsseldorf Social Democrats were convicted of conspiring to violate the anti-socialist laws.[6]

When they emerged from jail, Lehmann, Erbert, and the others resumed their union organizing and founded the Association for Popular Elections and Education, which according to the police included "all important local Social Democrats."[7] It recruited from the same sources as its predecessors.[8] In 1889 the Düsseldorf Social Democrats began publishing the *Arbeiterzeitung* – an action that reflected not the strength of the local movement but the success of government harassment. In the wake of the conspiracy trial, the courts prohibited the sale of the well-established Elberfeld *Freie Presse* in Düsseldorf, thereby forcing the fledgeling movement to launch its own organ.[9] Of necessity the new paper refrained from proclaiming its socialist orientation and cautiously pledged "to combat the pernicious influence of the bourgeois press through a factual discussion of existing economic and political conditions, which will fully enlighten the workers about their situation."[10]

By 1890 the Düsseldorf Social Democrats, who possessed a sizable electorate and all the organizational accoutrements of a developed movement, were certainly stronger than ever before. Their base was small but solid, the leaders young but dedicated and experienced. The unions, far from shunning politics, cooperated closely with the party.[11] The Düsseldorf Social Democrats had little contact with comrades outside the immediate region, but nonetheless valued national party unity and discipline as the key to survival. Although they were not well schooled theoretically, they had learned from bitter experience to mistrust the state, the liberal bourgeoisie, and the Catholic Center Party.[12]

Obstacles to organization

Although the Düsseldorf Social Democrats were bitter, wary, and isolated as a result of years of repression, they viewed the situation in 1890 as distinctly promising, for the legalization of the party was but one aspect of the New Course, launched by the recently crowned Emperor William II. Rejecting Bismarck's insistence that the Social Democrats could be contained only by intensified repression, William II, from a combination of ignorance, ambition, and prudence, argued that the working class could be integrated into the existing order through progressive social legislation. He replaced Bismarck by Count Caprivi, who was anxious to lower tariffs and rule more with the liberal middle classes and the Center Party than with the conservative Junkers. William appointed the reform-minded Berlepsch to the Ministry of Commerce, convened an international conference on protective legislation, and in the February proclamation held out the prospect of far-reaching reform. This loosening of the rigid Bismarckian order occurred at a time when the economy was showing tentative signs of recovery from the weak industrial growth and severe deflation that had persisted for the previous two decades. No wonder the Social Democrats, nationally and locally, viewed their prospects so rosily.[13]

Within this new context, Lehmann, Erbert, Gotthusen, and those who succeeded them focused their energies on building the embryonic movement. They repeatedly argued that "the success of the workers' movement depends on intensive agitation," and that organization and the press were "the most important weapons which workers possess" for effective agitation. Again and again leaders told members, who in turn told potential recruits, that the working class needed an organization "which functions promptly and efficiently on every occasion."[14] The

Arbeiterzeitung constantly warned workers that the Center's *Düsseldorfer Volksblatt*, the National Liberal *Düsseldorfer Zeitung*, and the left liberal *Bürgerzeitung* "competed with one another in mendacity, malice, depravity and immorality."[15] The non-party *General Anzeiger* and *Neuste Nachrichten*, which had a virtual monopoly on the proletarian reading public, were condemned on the grounds that "today, when class conflicts are irreconcilable, one is either for the workers' organization or for the capitalists. There is no third alternative."[16]

The local Social Democrats' emphasis, perhaps overemphasis, on organizational development did not stem from a desire to escape from conflict or to remain isolated. Nor were they simply acting according to the dictates of a deterministic Marxism, which prohibited action until economic conditions were ripe.[17] Isolation and ideology strengthened but did not create a concern for organization that grew out of the workers' concrete situation. Wilhelmian society, with its multiplicity of public and private associations, its mass political parties, economic interest groups, and cultural and recreational clubs of every description, was highly organized. And Düsseldorf, which added a rich Catholic culture to this, was certainly no exception.[18]

In such an environment the Social Democrats could not gain visibility and political influence if their thousands of electoral supporters re- mained outside the party and unions. Only a powerful organization could challenge the Center Party and National Liberal industrialists. Only a paper rich in factual articles and theoretical discussions could educate workers, for most Social Democrats relied on the press as "the primary, yes, almost the exclusive source of information."[19] The Social Democrats recognized that organization was the only possible weapon of the weak and the many, that, as Eric Hobsbawm noted, proletarian movements, unlike bourgeois ones, "can only operate as real armies with real generals and staffs."[20]

In the early 1890s, however, the Düsseldorf Social Democrats failed on the organizational front. To begin with, they were unable to recruit foot soldiers. "When we look at the Socialist organization in Cologne or Crefeld," lamented the party leaders in 1893, "we have to admit with shame that Düsseldorf is not a fertile ground for recruitment."[21] Al- though more than 9,000 workers protested their situation by voting for the SPD that year, the police estimated party membership at only 200. The Social Democrats, who repeatedly complained about "the lassitude of the masses," maintained a discrete silence on the subject, suggesting that this embarrassingly low figure was correct. And because most new members had joined before moving to Düsseldorf, it was they who sought out the party, not the reverse.[22]

The view from the union side was no more encouraging. Reviewing the city's dozen, largely craft, unions in 1891, the police listed the cabinetmakers, shoemakers, printers, metalworkers, tailors, masons, and carpenters as "the most politically active and potentially dangerous," but provided no membership figures.[23] Between 1890 and 1893 membership probably declined locally just as it did nationally.[24] At the meetings of the local trade union cartel, founded in 1893, only nine or ten unions regularly sent delegates.[25] The Social Democrats had held on to their small union base in artisan trades with a tradition of organization, such as woodworking, construction, and printing, but they had not expanded into new occupations or into the factories and were certainly not able to fulfill their assigned function of "wakening and strengthening the generally weak class consciousness of workers in the Rhineland."[26]

"How is this possible in a city where our candidate received almost 10,000 votes?" asked the Düsseldorf leaders plaintively.[27] How indeed! The movement throughout Germany received a severe setback from the economic crisis of 1891–5, the last acute phase of the Great Depression.[28] In Düsseldorf the tentative signs of recovery, evident in 1890, had disappeared within a year as first metal and then textiles slumped disasterously. Unemployment spread rapidly and severely in the areas of union strength, and those still employed suffered wage cuts ranging from 10 to 20 percent in most firms to nearly 50 percent in Rhein-metall.[29] Although the Social Democrats were adept at analyzing the causes of the crisis and held several large meetings of the unemployed to explain why "contemporary society is not in a position to offer the worker a secure existence" and "socialism is the only solution," they could not alleviate the impact of the depression or counteract the fear and apathy it engendered.[30] Skilled Protestant workers might vote SPD in protest, unskilled Catholic ones in despair, but most were in too precarious a position to join weak unions and a miniscule party that could not protect them. This was especially true of the growing number employed in large plants and of those relegated to small shops.[31]

Party and union leaders exacerbated their recruitment problems by directing their agitation not to the thousands of artisan and industrial migrants who flooded the city, nor to the diverse native Catholic population, but to industrial and agricultural workers in the surrounding county.[32] Sharing with their comrades elsewhere a facile optimism, derived from an overly deterministic Marxism, they assumed that workers who confronted capitalism in polarized settings like Düsseldorf would find their way into the social democratic movement unaided. Even August Bebel, the national party leader, reflected this economism in his insistence that the party give priority to rural agitation.[33] As a result, the Düsseldorf Social Democrats ignored the occupational and cultural particularism that prevented urban workers from joining. They sponsored regular Sunday agitation tours to the partially industrialized towns of Ratingen, Hilden, Benrath, and Gerresheim, and to the more agrarian villages such as Kaiserswerth. Urban workers, armed with literature and enthusiasm, would stroll into a small town, distribute flyers and newspapers and talk to anyone who would listen. On rare occasions, they were even able to hold a meeting.[34]

It was all to no avail. The Social Democrats had no program that would appeal to the threatened petty bourgeois or the marginal farmer, whose proletarianization they viewed as inevitable and progressive. Nor did mobile, urban workers have much sensitivity for the more parochial rural dweller. Personal recruitment on the job or in the neighborhood, the Social Democrats' most effective urban technique, was impossible in a rural setting.[35] Indeed, no tactic worked. Throughout the county the police arrested social democratic agitators and confiscated their literature. Employers fired party and union members, innkeepers refused to rent rooms, and priests thundered against the red menace from the pulpit.[36] In small villages prospects were even bleaker, for as one exasperated recruiter noted:

Religious illusions still hold the people in deepest ignorance. The inhabitants are black as night ... You only need to visit such a place once on a Sunday to understand the situation. The crowds flock to church in the morning, then visit various inns and bars. In the afternoon it's back to church.[37]

The Düsseldorf Social Democrats also failed to build the institutions they considered vital for growth. In 1891 the local leaders confidently transformed the Association for Popular Elections into the Social Democratic Association, established a system of *Vertrauensmänner* (special representatives who organized locally and served as a link to the national party), and founded a local trade union cartel, but the organizations did not flourish as anticipated.[38] Dismayed, the leaders tried centralization and then reversed themselves, restructured various institutions, and pleaded with the regional and national parties for help. It was all in vain.[39] The *Arbeiterzeitung*, which changed its name to *Niederrheinische Volkstribune* in 1893, fared scarcely better. To be sure, in 1894 the paper became a daily and a year later the Düsseldorf party installed Erbert and Wasser as local editors. Autonomy was incomplete, however, for the paper remained financially and substantively dependent on the *Freie Presse*, which catered to the needs of a Protestant textile town, not a Catholic heavy industry center. The paper soaked up all the party's meager funds but still teetered on the brink of bankruptcy with a mere two thousand subscribers.[40]

The Düsseldorf Social Democrats were too weak to sustain the institutions they had created in the late 1880s. Lacking reporters or a social democratic news service, for example, the local press was forced to borrow articles from the *Freie Presse* and even from bourgeois papers in Düsseldorf.[41] The Social Democrats spread personnel and funds into ever new areas instead of concentrating them in old but shaky ones.[42] Throughout the early 1890s they publicly acknowledged their organizational inferiority to the "exemplary Center" as well as to the SPD elsewhere.[43]

Local weakness was compounded by isolation from Berlin. Although Düsseldorf's ties to the regional organization were strong, those with the national party were tenuous. It had no prominent figures, influential in national party politics. It seldom even sent yearly reports or money to Berlin. Despite Düsseldorf's repeated appeals and despite Berlin's professed concern with "storming the Center fortress," the national executive offered neither guidance nor material aid to backward areas like Düsseldorf.[44] Although Berlin never explained this neglect, it probably resulted from limited resources and discouragement about the slow progress of the movement throughout the Lower Rhine.

Finally, organizational failures were created by and in turn created an ongoing leadership crisis. The cohesive leadership group of the late 1880s, whose members were equally conversant with party, union, and press affairs, disintegrated in the early 1890s.[45] Lehmann, the most able organizer and dynamic agitator, left Düsseldorf, as did a few lesser figures. Activists such as Gotthusen and Linxweiler restricted themselves to trade-union work, and men like Heldt, Treves, and Tietges appear to have withdrawn from politics completely. Some undoubtedly regarded union organizing as the necessary prerequisite for a political party, whereas others became understandably discouraged by the movement's failures, and a third group may simply have had difficulty adjusting to the less heroic atmosphere of legality. Only Erbert, who held minor party posts, worked on the paper, served in the woodworkers' union, and founded the union cartel, remained active on all fronts.[46]

No stable cadre emerged to replace those who had left. Between 1891 and 1895, for example, Voss, Reinsdorf, Barthels, and Luther served successively as head of the Association, and new and inexperienced men were likewise elected annually to the lesser posts. Although Erbert and Fannei provided a few years of continuity in the *Vertrauensmänner* slots, they were soon followed first by Gotthusen and Rieckmann and then by Huhn, Helbing, and Phillips. The leaders of individual unions, who seldom held office in the party even though they cooperated with it, turned over equally rapidly.[47]

This instability had numerous causes. Many Social Democrats were highly mobile, remaining in town for only a few years. Many others were reluctant to run for office because of apathy, a sense of inferiority, or fear of losing their jobs. Workers employed 10 to 12 hours a day were understandably cautious about taking on additional, unpaid responsibilities that brought so few results. In 1895 and 1896 the situation became so extreme that the Social Democratic Association had to postpone its elections because no candidates could be found. Erbert and a few of the old guard attempted to train future leaders by forming reading clubs, but only a handful of workers joined, and none subsequently held office.[48] Those who took office frequently failed to serve out their terms. Gotthusen and Schmitt both resigned because of "tactical disagreements." Phillips left for economic reasons, whereas Luther went to jail for embezzlement. Schrievers and Heusgen were among those involved in "family dramas" that tarnished their reputations in a movement that valued sexual propriety.[49]

These leaders, who barely mastered their basic responsibilities, could not develop a strategy for the hard-pressed local movement or build close working relationships with regional and national leaders. Neither trained by their predecessors nor able to train their successors, most spent their brief tenure in office applying makeshift solutions to complex, ill-understood problems, and quite predictably failed to solve them.

In addition to its internal problems, the Düsseldorf movement was plagued by government harassment. The Prussian organization law limited contact between the national and local parties and prohibited women and youths from joining; other statutes restricted the unions' ability to picket or bargain collectively. These repressive provisions were enforced vigorously by the municipal and Prussian governments and applauded by Düsseldorf's employers, whether Catholic or liberal.[50] In the city the Social Democrats had difficulty finding meeting places, in the county it was absolutely impossible for, as they noted, "the government, clerical, and capitalist influence on innkeepers is equally strong everywhere and prevents us from freely proclaiming our basic principles."[51] The few innkeepers who allowed meetings were often fined by the police on flimsy pretexts or blacklisted by the military, which believed that "the detrimental influence which emanates from the SPD could easily influence soldiers."[52] The party attempted to boycott, informally and occasionally formally, these recalcitrant innkeepers, but the unions did not comply and the working class was too divided and anti-socialist for such a tactic to be effective.[53] The city council, for its part, refused to rent the municipal concert hall to organizations "with notorious social democratic tendencies," and lumped everything from the party to the workers' singing clubs under this rubric. The Prussian courts, noted for their "class justice," upheld this discriminatory act.[54] And the liberal elite applauded it, announcing that "we would complain bitterly if the beautiful rooms of our lovely art institute were desecrated by the raw words of some wild revolutionary."[55]

The social democratic press, characterized by Mayor Lindemann as "an opponent of all legal order which is more responsible for the spread of socialism than all other relevant factors," was subject to comparable attacks.[56] During the 1890s the paper's eight editors and managers went to court 144 times and, despite 51 acquittals, accumulated 5,657 M in fines and more than 71 months in jail. Sometimes the government brought charges, usually of libel; at other times irate factory owners or clerics did. In 1893, for example, Gewehr was prosecuted for writing "down with capitalism." Two years later Wessel was fined 500 M for insulting Lindemann.[57] Although such harassment was perfectly legal and certainly less serious than that in the 1880s, it served as a constant and bitter reminder to the Social Democrats of their second-class status. As they noted in an editorial sarcastically entitled "Equal Rights for All," "we live in a class state in which every man who freely and openly voices his opinion, especially if he is a Social Democrat, can be silenced."[58]

By 1894 this inauspicious local environment was complemented by an equally inhospitable national one, because the New Course collapsed before producing any significant reforms. Aristocrats, capitalists, and petty bourgeoisie alike refused to grant the working class and its social democratic spokesmen social and political equality – the prerequisites for any possible integration.[59] They applauded with relief when William II ceased wooing the working class and turned to imperialism and renewed threats of repression.

Government policy and economic crisis, misguided tactics, and ineffective leadership thus all contributed to trapping the Social Democrats in a vicious circle of low recruitment, inadequate resources, organizational weakness, and powerlessness. It was political Catholicism, with its strong working-class base, however, that doomed all attempts at breaking out.

The Center fortress

The power of political Catholicism was not the result of "a clerical swindle" perpetrated on an ignorant populace.[60] There were many reasons, material and cultural, for Catholics of all classes to support the Center Party, for it effectively mobilized and organized the Catholic community, offered a comprehensive ideology that mixed religion, politics, and economics, and advocated popular social policies. An opposition party, proud of its earlier resistance to government persecution, the Center kept the Social Democrats in Düsseldorf on the defensive for most of the 1890s.

The Düsseldorf Center never abandoned its original character as an elite party (*Honorationspartei*). Although the committee, the core of the local party, included representatives of all "estates" (*Stände*), it remained under the control of its "born members" – the clergy, middle-class professionals, journalists, and entrepreneurs. Lacking a mass base and party machine, the Center initially relied on the clergy and church organizations to mobilize and integrate Catholic voters.[61] Priests used the pulpit, the confessional, parish associations, Catholic charities, special missions, and house-to-house visits to further the Center Party cause.[62] The clergy helped preserve the hierarchical character of the Center Party and strengthened clerical control over the Catholic community by extending the church's influence into politics.

By the 1880s the Center Party realized that it had to go beyond this traditional strategy and, in the words of the Rhenish leader Hitze, "organize our Christian workers before it is too late, organize them in

Christian associations before the enemy is within our wall."[63] The clergy and Center Party politicians collaborated in establishing Catholic Workers' Associations, "whose first aim was to keep Catholic workers in their Church."[64] The organization in Düsseldorf-Hamm was typical. Headed by a priest, who was appointed by the church, the association aimed at "raising the moral and social position of the worker through Christian and legal means." It stressed "the religious life" and "the duties of one's estate" (*Standepflichten*), sponsored educational and recreational activities, and offered sickness and burial benefits. It explicitly condemned not only class conflict but all strikes and militant protest. "By entering the Catholic Workers' Associations," the statutes stated emphatically, "each member acknowledges his opposition to social democratic principles and aims."[65]

By the turn of the century seventeen such parish-based associations drew more than 4,500 members, primarily from the stable, native-born element.[66] These workers, master artisans, and small shopkeepers accepted the admonition of the Center Party leader Lieber, who on a visit to Düsseldorf stated that:

The Christian Workers' Associations have no program and need no program, for they are a program ... You [Catholic workers] should not act like the others [Social Democrats] but rather according to the principle "seek first the kingdom of God and his justice, and everything else will be given."[67]

As industrialization and conflict increased, and with them the social democratic movement, more and more Catholic workers rejected the associations' call for patience and deference. The Rhenish Center Party, fearing the loss of its industrial base once the anti-socialist laws were lifted, established the multi-class People's Association for a Catholic Germany in 1890 to "combat errors and revolutionary aims in the social arena and defend the Christian social order."[68] The People's Association, led by the clergy and financed by the church, mobilized voters without giving them influence on the Center's policy.[69] It held regular meetings, published extensive educational material, sponsored training courses for agitators, and built a mass organization to rival that of the Social Democrats, and in places like Düsseldorf, to surpass it. The People's Association gradually supplemented its crude polemics against the SPD with serious arguments about social policy and simultaneously took on the more positive task of integrating Catholics into modern society, of educating them to accept industrial capitalism rather than longing for a static *Ständestaat*. The middle-class leaders of the Düsseldorf Center Party, who sought parity within the existing order, supported the People's Association wholeheartedly, dominating its leadership and moderating its social reformist thrust.[70]

As a result, the People's Association had less appeal for the working class, and by the mid-1890s the Center Party resorted to yet another expedient to hold the Catholic proletariat, the interconfessional Christian trade unions. Established first in the Ruhr and Lower Rhine, these organizations were genuine trade unions, led by elected lay workers and enthusiastically endorsed by the Rhenish Center Party, which did not include a significant number of Catholic industrialists whose interests it needed to consider.[71] In Düsseldorf the Christian wood, metal, and construction workers' unions and a scattering of smaller ones had nearly a thousand members by 1901.[72] Although these unions insisted that wage struggles were not class struggles and that "workers should consider themselves as an estate among estates and not a class against other classes," they did sanction strikes. Their goal was neither emancipation nor economic equality but integration into a hierarchical bourgeois social order.[73] The political considerations that motivated the establishment of the Christian trade-union movement were openly admitted by the Rhenish Center Party leaders and were well known to the free union organizers, who argued that "even the dumbest must realize that the Christian trade unions were called into life not for the workers' welfare but in order to curb 'social democratic' unions."[74]

Despite this, or in many cases because of it, Düsseldorf's Catholic workers joined the Christian unions and other associations en masse. At the turn of the century, these organizations had more members than the local SPD and free trade unions. They offered an outlet for socially concerned Catholic workers, who, on their own admission, would otherwise have joined the socialist movement.[75] They provided workers with services and political representation more effectively than the social democratic movement could while enabling Catholics, especially native ones, to remain within their traditional, closed, and comfortable culture.[76] Although the Center Party did not grant the working class equality, it transformed political Catholicism into a mass movement. In the process of competing with the Social Democrats, adjusting to industrial capitalism, and seeking parity in Imperial Germany, the Rhenish Center Party made significant concessions to its proletarian supporters.

Throughout most of the 1890s the Center Party effectively contained its irreconcilable social contradictions, which were ultimately to cost it its working-class base, by means of an ideology that was as appealing and all-encompassing as its organizations. Political Catholicism constantly insisted on the centrality of religion, which after all provided its raison d'être, and on the autonomy of the church, which had been at issue in the *Kulturkampf*. Even the more secular Rhenish Centrists, who sought parity within the existing order, did not abandon the primacy of religion. Nor could they, for they depended on the clergy and church funds and appealed above all to those who believed that religion united more than class divided. They could not find an alternative identity.[77] Political Catholicism viewed religion, politics, and economics as interconnected parts of an integrated social whole and maintained that Catholic political and social theory should guide political and economic practice.[78]

By the 1890s the Center Party politicians and Catholic social theorists had abandoned the reactionary and romantic concept of society prevalent in the early and mid-nineteenth century, but they still posited a divinely ordained harmony among the various estates of society.[79] (All Center Party spokesmen, whether of the Cologne or Berlin faction, assiduously avoided the term *class*.) Rich and poor, capitalist and worker, lord and peasant, artisan and professional were not merely to coexist but to cooperate within a hierarchical yet just order. And if conflicts arose, the Center Party, which insisted on the possibility of "harmonizing justice" (*ausgleichende Gerechtigkeit*), would mediate.[80] Catholics would thus be able to face the larger society united and would provide a model for others.

This corporatist vision was accompanied by a much more modern social policy, for both lay and clerical leaders gradually recognized the enormous social problems created by industrial capitalism. Moreover, in the 1880s the aristocratic wing of the Center Party dwindled, the middle- and working-class elements expanded vastly, and rural–urban conflicts escalated, making it increasingly difficult for the Center Party to reconcile differences in its ranks by reference to the traditional order. By the 1890s the Center Party, led by its Rhenish wing, had abandoned not only its hope of returning to a precapitalist system, but also its insistence that social policy should be the exclusive preserve of the church and the family. Even though it clung to a precapitalist social vocabulary, it accepted the dynamic industrial order and advocated a responsible capitalism with extensive state-sponsored social reform.[81] Center Party leaders, such as Windthorst, Hitze, and Brandts, whatever their other differences, agreed that Catholics should cooperate with the state and other conservative Christian parties to provide social insurance and protective legislation and to encourage "the organization of the workers into an estate and their integration into the whole society."[82] Thus, the Center Party supported Bismarck's sickness, accident, and old-age insurance legislation in the 1880s, hoping as did the chancellor, that the bitterness born of the anti-socialist laws could be sweetened by the most progressive insurance system in Europe.[83]

In the 1890s the Center Party continued to push for expanded insurance benefits and factory legislation, and in addition advocated both a strengthening of workers' right to organize and protection for the threatened *Mittelstand*.[84] The Center Party hoped that demands for political reform, which were so threatening to the party and the system, could be satisfied by concessions in the social sphere, which seemed easier to achieve. In election after election the Düsseldorf Center Party proudly reviewed its record for its working-class electorate, insisting that it was "a social reform party by its very nature."[85] It condemned the SPD for preferring no legislation to partial reform, noting smugly that "it is a good thing that the workers' estate has other friends than its red patrons."[86] To bolster their case, Catholic politicians argued that Bishop Ketteler, the founder of the German Catholic social movement, had developed a comprehensive social program long before Lassalle, a disputable claim. They further asserted that "in the party [SPD] there are many rich people, even millionaires, but up to now they have not given so much as a penny to people who are doing charitable work."[87]

It proved extremely advantageous for the Düsseldorf Center Party to campaign on social policy issues. It could thereby promise significant concessions to both its *Mittelstand* and proletarian constituencies, without granting them political power within the party or the state. And the costs were low, for although guild legislation was ultimately passed in a watered-down form, no further measures for the working class were. Thus the Center Party's middle-class, aristocratic, and peasant supporters were not alienated. The Center quite legitimately blamed these failures on the government and the National Liberals.[88] William II abandoned his belief that the working class could be won over with reforms, and National Liberal industrialists had never shared his illusions.[89] The metal entrepreneurs, who controlled the Düsseldorf Chamber of Commerce, spoke for the entire capitalist class when they insisted that further social insurance would make German industry uncompetitive, additional protective legislation would limit workers' earning power and freedom, and improved collective bargaining would violate employers' inalienable rights.[90] The Center Party thus reaped the fruits of championing reform without risking any adverse consequences and put their opponents on the defensive.

Political Catholicism emphasized not only the coherence of its world view and the appeal of its policies but also the inadequacies of its opponents. The Center Party criticized the state and liberals for their anticlericalism and the Progressives for their political reformism but reserved its most vituperative censure for the Social Democrats with "their principles of revolution, atheism, and communism."[91] In election after election the Düsseldorf Center Party pitted its world view against that of the Social Democrats, appealing indiscriminately to political, religious, and social anxieties in lurid tones. In 1890, for example, one campaign flyer, "directed above all to the workers who are so easily misled and seduced," warned that "those who promise heaven on earth *could not* keep their word, even if they *wanted to.*"[92] Another quoted extensively from those sections of Bebel's *Women and Socialism* that described communal child care and housework under socialism and claimed that the Social Democrats would replace marriage and the family with free love.[93] A third asked rhetorically, "Can you men give your vote to those who will introduce the *republic, confiscate* and eliminate all *private property,* and subscribe to *atheism?*" and answered:

They are filled with fanatical *hate against all religion,* and whatever is holy for us, they ridicule with godless scorn. The holy father, Christ's representative on earth, warns us about them. Our bishops speak of their evil ways and goals. *A Catholic can and may not vote Social Democratic.*[94]

Throughout the early 1890s, most Catholic workers in Düsseldorf heeded this admonition.

Social democracy on the defensive

The Social Democrats' efforts to counter the ideological and political appeal of political Catholicism in the early 1890s had only limited effect. The Center Party chose the terrain on which to fight – religion and social policy – and that terrain proved treacherous for the Social Democrats.

The Center incessantly accused its enemy of being atheistic and anticlerical. The Social Democrats had only one reply to those charges: Religion is a private affair.[95] After a flirtation with militant atheism in the 1870s, the SPD adopted this stance during its period of illegality in an attempt to moderate attacks on the movement and in response to the growing influence of Marxism.[96] The Social Democrats argued that religion and politics were separate spheres and never suggested that atheism and socialism were associated. On the one hand, they were confident that as workers understood historical materialism and built a powerful movement, they would loose all interest in religion.[97] On the other, they realized that many workers who no longer practiced their faith regularly were not necessarily anti-religious. Even those who were could not readily be induced to leave the church formally, for that procedure entailed expensive court appearances and often brought discrimination against workers and their children in its wake.[98]

The Düsseldorf Social Democrats, like their comrades elsewhere, insisted that their fight was with the Center Party as a political movement, not with religion or Catholicism per se. Instead of rejecting Christian principles, they claimed to live up to them more fully than did political Catholicism. Whereas the church and the Center hypocritically preached hope and charity while defending the interests of the right, Social Democrats showed a genuine concern for the poor and offered the prospect of improvement in this world. Whereas the Center press was full of lies, social-democratic agitation was direct and honest. Whereas the Center prohibited discussion, the Social Democrats welcomed debate.[99] All in all, argued the Düsseldorf Social Democrats in an indictment that mixed religion, politics, and economics in imitation of their enemy, the Center was "the party of treason against the people, of rising food costs, of confessional hypocrisy, the party of ignorance, lies, and baseness, the party which incites its followers against those who think differently about politics and religion."[100]

The Social Democrats were also scathingly critical of the church as an institution, especially of the clergy, who were always referred to by the derogatory anticlerical term *Pfaffen*. Instead of being neutral, priests delivered political sermons, agitated for the People's Association, and pressured individual Catholics, especially women, to support the Center Party.[101] Backed by the lay Center leaders, the clergy tried "to prolong confessional strife for all eternity ... to mislead the people into wasting their power in religious disputes, to poison and simplify all knowledge with religious trimmings ... to drive out intelligence and replace it with the narrow-minded faith of the middle ages."[102] Nor did the Social Democrats refrain from *ad hominem* attacks on priests who failed to lead exemplary lives. Rumors of alcoholism were spread as gleefully as tales of uncharitable priests who made impoverished widows pay for their husbands' funerals.[103]

Only in rural areas in the county, where the population was deeply religous and the church correspondingly powerful, did the Social Democrats curb their anticlericalism. On their Sunday agitation tours, the city comrades, who at other times complained so bitterly about the power of religion, refrained from criticizing the Center Party's misuse of Catholicism. They distributed the *Rheinische Volksfreund*, a calendar that contained stories of rural poverty and oppression as well as articles on the community of interests between the city and the country. It listed saints' days and parish fairs in a concession to the realities of the recipients' lives, but otherwise avoided all mention of the Center Party or Catholicism.[104]

Despite these efforts the Düsseldorf Social Democrats had little success in neutralizing the explosive religious issue. Indifference was a weak position from which to fight, yet they could neither pretend to be more positive nor dare to be more critical. For those Catholic workers deeply immersed in the culture, religion did permeate politics and economics, and the Social Democrats' attempt to relegate it to a small, private sphere was seen as destructive of both Catholicism and an entire way of life. Many working-class Catholics believed that the divinely ordained social order was indeed hierarchical, authoritarian, and conservative, just as the Center Party maintained.[105] The Social Democrats could only win these workers on economic and political grounds, not general ideological ones. Yet in the 1890s they had great difficulty doing that, for they could not compete with the Catholic economic and social organizations. Nor could they prove that the Center Party's social policy was detrimental to working-class interests.

The Düsseldorf Social Democrats repeatedly argued that political Catholicism's social theory and policy were *arbeiterfeindlich*, or hostile to the working class. The Center Party preached a class harmony that merely confused and subjugated Catholic workers. It praised an insurance system that paid meager benefits, had excessively complicated regulations, and left rural and home workers uncovered. Protective legislation was likewise limited and factory inspection underfunded. Less than half of Düsseldorf's factories were inspected in the 1890s, for example, and accident rates rose steadily.[106] As a result, the Düsseldorf Social Democrats, like their comrades elsewhere, refused to compromise their principles for piecemeal reforms that were politically motivated. They recognized that no adequate social legislation would be passed unless the working class had political equality within a genuinely parliamentary system. In short, they saw that the social question could have only a political answer.[107]

Understandable as the Social Democrats' position was, it proved singularly ineffective as a means of attracting supporters, for what was perfectly suitable to Protestant regions was terribly problematic in Catholic ones. The Social Democrats offered the workers only negative criticism, whereas the Center Party could point to positive if insufficient reform. By insisting on the primacy of political change, the Social Democrats alienated Catholic workers, who questioned the desirability of democratization.[108] Of equal importance, many workers simply took no interest in social policy, for national legislation did not have the direct impact on their lives that provincial and municipal measures did.[109] Workers' memoirs, for example, fail to mention the insurance system, and the Düsseldorf police reported that the local population viewed the introduction of old-age insurance "apathetically."[110]

Frustrated by being forced to fight on the Center Party's chosen terrain, the Düsseldorf Social Democrats sought aid from the national executive, but the 1893 party congress rejected the request for special agitational materials. Subsequent efforts by the Düsseldorf leaders to establish a separate association for social policy issues failed "due to the lack of interest on the part of workers."[111] Imperial Germany's social policy did not overcome the workers' sense of injustice nor integrate them into state and society, but it was not the issue that the Social Democrats could use to woo loyal Catholics from the Center Party or arouse the indifferent to political protest.

In the early and mid-1890s, however, the Düsseldorf Social Democrats were forced to rest their case against the Center Party almost exclusively on that issue, because the Center was not a member of the ruling coalition of National Liberals and Conservatives. As an opposition party it could take credit for measures likely to be popular with the working class and *Mittelstand* and still avoid responsibility for failed reforms or renewed repression. However much the Social Democrats suspected that the Center was at heart conservative and opportunistic, they lacked the necessary proof. After all the Center Party staunchly opposed the

Table 2.1 *Reichstag elections in Düsseldorf in the 1890s*

Year	Total vote	Percent of total vote	City	Percent of vote	County	Percent of vote
		Social Democrats				
1890	7,573	28.2	5,701	31.6	1,872	21.1
1890	8,228	33.2	6,251	38.4	1,977	28.2
1893	9,396	28.2	7,342	31.8	2,025	19.9
1893	9,123	34.9				
		Center				
1890	12,476	46.5	7,453	41.4	5,023	56.7
1890	16,511	66.6	9,987	61.3	6,524	76.6
1893	15,214	45.8	9,560	41.4	6,559	55.6
1893	17,017	65.1				

Source: Stadtarchiv Düsseldorf, III 10104, 1890; 10105, 1893.

1893 Army bill. A year later, after some hesitation, it helped bring down William II's proposed Revolution bill, a renewed anti-socialist law.[112] Political Catholicism was thus a more formidable opponent than national liberalism or conservatism, and the Social Democrats were to pay heavily at the polls, just as they did in party and union membership, for their inability to breach the walls of the Center fortress.

In the Reichstag elections of 1890 and 1893 the Düsseldorf Social Democrats, who ran the popular and articulate Hermann Grimpe, the working-class editor of the Elberfeld *Freie Presse*, won between a quarter and a third of the vote. The Center Party, whose candidate was the wealthy bourgeois lawyer and judge, Kirsch, who had played a leading role in the 1888 socialist conspiracy trial, however, won two-fifths in the first elections and more than three-fifths in the run-offs.[113] As Table 2.1 shows, the SPD vote increased encouragingly in the city, but the Center Party made commensurate progress, and the county remained "black as night." The Center not only controlled 70 to 75 percent of the Catholic vote but also received massive support from liberals of all shades in the run-offs.[114] The Social Democrats drew their support from those elements excluded from the dominant Catholic culture and the smaller liberal parties. Roughly two-thirds of the socialist voters were Protestant workers, the remainder Catholic ones, probably migrants who were at best poorly integrated into Düsseldorf's parishes and Catholic association life.[115] Düsseldorf was one of the few cities where the Social Democrats did not draw on bourgeois votes to supplement their proletarian ones, for the Catholic middle class stood behind the Center Party, and the Protestants voted National Liberal or Progressive.[116] The Center fortress was not visibly tottering even though its proletarian foundations were being slowly eroded by industrialization, migration, and secularization.[117] As the government noted with pleasure in 1893, the Center Party was "continuing the fight against the Social Democrats and expresses its opposition to this party very energetically and successfully."[118]

Inchoate radicalism

The manifold failures of the Düsseldorf Social Democrats in the early 1890s both reflected and reinforced their isolation from the dominant Catholic culture, other political parties, the local working class, and the national movement. This isolation, in turn, created the space within which the Düsseldorf Social Democrats could interpret their situation and disappointing experiences in a manner that emphasized the primacy of class, the exploitative character of capitalism, and the impossibility of reformism in an authoritarian state.[119] Frustration, weakness, and isolation thus encouraged a radical consciousness. But the Social Democrats' deterministic Marxism and their particular situation in Düsseldorf simultaneously fostered tactical passivity.

Given the character of Düsseldorf and the situation of the workers' movement there, it is hardly surprising that the Social Democrats enthusiastically adopted Marxism, albeit in a vulgarized form.[120] They found Marxist class analysis, with its predictions of growing polarization and exploitation, highly relevant to an area where rapid industrialization and an authoritarian state had enabled organized capitalism and entrepreneurial power to develop in particularly stark forms. The Düsseldorf Social Democrats did not espouse Marxism, with its historical materialism and end goal of socialism, in order to distinguish themselves from bourgeois politicians, for their short-run program of democratic and social reforms sufficed for that.[121]

Rather, the Social Democrats used Marxism as a means of explaining the existing situation of the working class. They filled their paper, brochures, and speeches with concrete examples of local factory firings and accidents, of long hours and low wages, of large profits and high-handed capitalist behavior. And they invariably argued that "the source of all misery which afflicts the working class . . . is the fact that the only property which the worker has is his labor power, and he can only use that by selling it to the owners of the means of production. So long as this situation persists, the working class will . . . live in a more or less severe state of distress."[122] Capitalism and class conflict, they insisted, had created a society whose moral foundation was "the freedom of men to exploit other men," and whose legal system "made such a mockery of equality before the law that it offends and almost destroys the sense of justice of whole classes."[123] They illustrated these abstract indictments with telling local incidents, published in a regular newspaper column entitled "When Two Do the Same, It's Not Necessarily the Same." The political system reflected class power no less than the legal and economic ones did. The Social Democrats accused the Prussian Landtag of bringing "hunger and defeat for the people. Gifts and the surrender of popular rights for the factory owners and Junkers." They detailed "the damages done to the material and spiritual health of the people" by the national government and "the vanity, avarice, and hypocrisy of the ruling classes."[124] Marxism, in short, provided an analysis of the Social Democrats' current situation and past experience.

Marxism also offered them hope in the face of their failures. They found the labor theory of value appealing because it affirmed the worth of the workers' production that the dominant society denied. Of greater importance, Marxism held out the promise of social transformation in the face of existing weakness and oppression.[125] As the editors of the *Arbeiterzeitung* confidently stated in 1890:

The Social Democrats have the comforting certainty that, no matter how furiously capitalist society develops, no matter how energetically it protests, everything that it subjects to its boundless profit frenzy and scheming contributes to undermining its own foundations. To the same degree that capitalism is undermined, social democracy is strengthened . . . Due to this fact one can calculate with almost mathematical certainty the victory of socialism.[126]

The same factors that encouraged the Düsseldorf Social Democrats to adopt Marxism made them shy away from an interpretation of it that stressed the potential of parliamentary activity and the possibility of class alliances and political coalitions. Although they pledged allegiance to the SPD's Erfurt program of 1891, whose first part contained a deterministic Marxist analysis of capitalism's development and socialism's advent and whose second part outlined an agenda of short-range reformist goals, they were consistently pessimistic about the possibility of winning concessions from the existing system. "It is certain, " wrote the *Volkstribune* editors in 1893, "that in areas of highly developed capitalism like the Rhineland and Westphalia, the trade unions will *never* grow in relationship to the power of capital such that they can win their demands for the improvement of the condition of the workers if the entire power of capital proclaims its 'no.' "[127] To be sure, the Social Democrats insisted that the unions and the party should struggle for improvements, as this would raise class consciousness, but they were convinced that "only a radical transformation of society, only a complete new ordering of production will help."[128]

Given their fundamental mistrust of reformism and their weakness vis-à-vis political Catholicism, the Düsseldorf Social Democrats were even more ambivalent about parliamentarism than the SPD as a whole. And parliamentarism was the crucial issue dividing the movement in the early 1890s. During the era of illegality Social Democrats had been allowed to run candidates for the Reichstag and the parliamentary delegation had become the effective movement leadership. Thus both the local and national party became increasingly involved with parliamentary activity. But at the same time, the adoption of Marxism, which gave primacy to economic development, and the recognition of the weakness of the Reichstag, led Social Democrats to deny that parliament could be the instrument of fundamental social change.[129] After 1890, in the euphoria engendered by the post-legalization expansion and in the absence of ready alternatives, many Social Democrats moderated their critique of parliamentarism. Confident of socialism in their own lifetime, they ceased to ask whether or what kind of parliamentary activity would hasten its advent.

Not so the Düsseldorf Social Democrats. "The importance of parliamentarism should not be overestimated," insisted Albert and Helbing during the 1893 election campaign. "The speeches of our deputies in the Reichstag should be directed to the public and should be of a more principled nature."[130] Since the Reichstag was not an instrument of popular sovereignty, it should not be a major arena of social democratic activity.[131] The views of the Düsseldorf movement were most succinctly stated in the resolutions that they submitted to the 1892 and 1893 national party congress:

Considering that parliament can be and should be only a means of agitation, be it resolved that from now on – except for important votes – only a few deputies attend the sessions of the Reichstag in order to clarify our standpoint. All other representatives have the duty to hold public meetings in the various provinces of the Reich in order to make clear to the real people the correctness and feasibility of our ideas.[132]

Although the national executive refused to discuss the proposals, the Düsseldorf Social Democrats maintained that "our party can never and must never seek its main task in parliamentary participation."[133]

The Düsseldorf Social Democrats exended their criticism to other policies and practices of the national leadership as well. Sensing a growing laxity in the movement, Albert and Erbert urged the national executive to denounce militarism unequivocally and to condemn Georg Vollmar when he first aired his reformist views. In heated party meetings held in preparation for the 1892 national party congress, Kimmel and Helbing accused the executive of becoming dictatorial, and Held urged the party to institute participatory democracy.[134] Fearing that a cult of personality was developing, the local party requested that "the national executive forbid the manufacture of all objects with pictures of noted personalities, since such objects never contribute to the enlightenment and conversion of the working population."[135] Finally, the Düsseldorf Social Democrats, who were isolated from the national movement, urged biannual congresses, arguing that the enormous expense of yearly meetings was not justified by their limited value.[136]

The Düsseldorf Social Democrats' rejection of parliamentarism and deep suspicion of centralized leadership resembled the views of the Jüngen, the left opposition that surfaced nationally in 1890–1.[137] Like-wise, both groups had difficulty developing positive, radical alternatives to the tactics they criticized. Yet there appears to be no direct connection between the Jüngen, who were predominantly intellectuals based in Dresden, Berlin, and Magdeburg, and the Düsseldorf leftists, who were working class and had few contacts with their comrades elsewhere. Although their critiques were similar, they arrived at them from different starting points. The Jüngen began with a theoretical analysis that stressed voluntarism and opposed any social reforms, whereas the Düsseldorf Social Democrats were responding to local conditions and their isolation from Berlin. As representatives of a weak movement, they could not advocate voluntarism as a realistic course; as spokesmen for other workers, they could not afford the luxury of condemning all social welfare measures.[138]

Under scathing attacks from Bebel, the Jüngen withdrew from the SPD to form the Organization of Independent Socialists in 1891, whereas the Düsseldorf Social Democrats, who were most vocal from 1892 on, never considered leaving the national movement. Although one Düsseldorf police report from 1892 mentions a branch of the Independent Socialists, no other did, suggesting that it was most ephemeral and insignificant.[139] Düsseldorf radicalism was nurtured by the local situation and articulated by local spokesmen in isolation from dissidents elsewhere.

As a result of their experiences the Düsseldorf Social Democrats thus became radicals rather than reformists, even though their radicalism was not well developed theoretically. The leaders strove to give workers a class outlook, "a new vocabulary and a new set of concepts which permitted a different translation of the meaning of inequality."[140] But the very conditions that fostered a radical class consciousness prevented it from being translated into practice. Political authoritarianism, economic oppression, isolation, and weakness were not the prerequisites for militant confrontation. Such tactical caution harmonized badly with their understanding of German society and the goals of social democracy. Until the movement and the environment in which it operated changed, however, the Social Democrats could not develop an alternative strategy.

3

A false start

The fortunes of the Düsseldorf Social Democrats seemed to pick up in the late 1890s. After twenty years of depression, the economy entered a sustained upswing. After nearly thirty years of opposition, political Catholicism became a supporter of the policies of the conservative Junker–industrial alliance. In this more auspicious environment, the social democratic unions were finally able to recruit members and mount strikes. The movement made its first tentative forays into municipal politics. Finally, the party concentrated on developing an effective program of education and agitation.

Appearances were deceptive, however, and social democratic expectations were disappointed. The late 1890s saw a replication in the economic sphere of earlier problems in the political. Despite a certain level of mobilization, unions remained organizationally weak and tactically ineffective. Nonetheless, the simple attempt at unionization encouraged employers to organize against the Social Democrats as effectively as the Catholics had. In the municipal arena, the Social Democrats gained footholds only in marginal institutions, and even those were bitterly contested by the Center and Christian unions. The party's educational programs failed both to train the organized and attract the unorganized. As a result, the frustrations and failures of the early 1890s were to continue in the latter half of the decade.

Unionization

The free trade unions began to expand rapidly in 1895, the true founding date for the union movement not only locally but nationally as well.[1] Expansion reached its limits, however, with the skilled, male workers in a few selected sectors. The fledgling union movement was increasingly able to strike yet seldom able to win due to internal weakness, legal

57

restrictions, state intervention and, above all, employer intransigence and organization.

After 1895, in the wake of economic prosperity and industrial expansion, hundreds of workers flocked to the unions each year. Secure in their jobs or confident of finding other ones, they were more willing to assume the risks that union membership entailed. And as more joined, the benefits increased, even if the dangers did not disappear. In 1896 the 1,312 free trade unionists comprised only 3 percent of the Düsseldorf working class. Thereafter the Social Democrats complained repeatedly that "the aggressive terrorism of big business in league with the vicious work of the clergy threatens to nip all working-class activity in the bud." The national movement dismissed Düsseldorf as a place "where not much could be done."[2] By 1900, nonetheless, 4,672 men (for there were few women union members) or 9 percent of the working class were organized. Even though 900 belonged to the Gerresheim glassworkers union, which was soon to be decimated by the failure of the glass-workers' general strike, the increase was impressive.[3] Not all workers, however, were able to translate their grievances into organization and protest.

Skilled artisans in the woodworking and construction trades, which were largely unmechanized and small scale, reaped the fruits of the organizational seeds laid in the late 1880s. Twenty percent of the workers in each sector joined, and these men dominated not only the local union movement but the party as well. The construction unions of the masons, carpenters, plasterers, and painters prospered as industrial and residential building was undertaken on an unprecedented scale. Those of the more peripheral trades, however, were so small as to be unviable. And the strongly Catholic, easily replaceable, migrant construction helpers remained "unconcerned and apathetic" despite the formation of an unskilled construction workers' union.[4] The cabinet-makers, wheelwrights, and brushmakers who had united to form the woodworkers' union in 1893 were strong not only in medium-sized establishments but also in the small shops whose owners were in the compulsory guild. The free trade unionists had won control of the mandatory journeymen's committee, thus bringing class conflict into the heart of an institution whose anxious supporters wanted to transcend or surpress it.[5] The Düsseldorf woodworkers were both militant unionists, who urged their national organization to demand the eight-hour day and oppose union unemployment benefits, and enthusiastic Social Democrats, who supplied the party with many of its leaders.[6]

The industrially organized German Metalworkers Union (DMV) did not fare nearly as well. As the Rhenish congress of the DMV noted in 1896, "in the government district of Düsseldorf (at best with the exception of the city of Düsseldorf) the metalworkers' organization has as good as no importance, and certainly does not have 'a power position.' "[7] By 1900 nearly a thousand joiners, turners, mechanics, pipefitters, and file makers had joined the DMV, but this was only 7 percent of Düsseldorf's metalworkers and most of these were skilled migrants, working in medium-sized plants or small, guild shops. Spiegel, Walbrecht, and other local DMV leaders organized impressive educational programs that drew between 150 and 250, but such activities were a substitute for action.[8] The DMV was crippled by its failure to gain a foothold in the large factories of Poensgen, Scheiss, Mannesmann, and Ehrhardt. The union likened these factories to prisons and lamented that "nowhere do the employers act more brutally than in the Rhineland," but it remained powerless against them.[9] The inability to organize the sprawling and vital metal sector seriously weakened the Düsseldorf workers' movement and contributed to making the Lower Rhine the least organized industrial region in Germany.[10]

Although the Social Democrats had established unions in all branches of manufacturing except paper and chemicals, the smaller organizations were more symbolic presences than viable associations. There were only forty unionists in Düsseldorf's large but depressed textile industry, which was notorious for wage cuts, fines, and firings.[11] In the garment trades and food processing, where small shops or home industry predominated, unions scarcely existed. Shoemakers were more highly organized but still unable to ward off the devastating impact of factory competition.[12] Even the printers union, so impressive elsewhere, recruited less than a third of the workers, for as the trade-union activist Lohse remarked critically, "an inveterate Düsseldorf printer can absolutely not be moved to join a union."[13] The Social Democrats met with no success among transport workers and did not even think about organizing those in the commercial sector.

It was thus above all skilled, male workers, many of them artisans, most with a tradition of organization, who formed the backbone of the Düsseldorf union movement. They worked in medium-sized factories and workshops and increasingly in smaller guild establishments but almost never in the numerous large plants. Both Protestants and Catholics were overwhelmingly migrants. Although many had had previous experience with urban living and artisan if not industrial work, they found no ready place in Düsseldorf with its native Catholic control of social and political life and its liberal, capitalist domination of the economy and municipal affairs. For those unintegrated workers, the unions offered not merely a means of economic self-defense but also an alternative community that provided solidarity as well as psychological and social support in dealing with the anonymity and often hostility of a new environment.[14] Indeed, in the 1890s they fulfilled the latter function more successfully than the former.

In the early 1890s legal harassment and employer intransigence, reinforced by economic crisis and union weakness, led to a diminution of strikes nationally and their virtual cessation locally.[15] In the second half of the decade, however, strike activity picked up. Although the size and frequency of strikes were still low in comparison to other industrialized regions[16] and many economic sectors remained unaffected, the transformation was significant enough to boost workers' morale, worry the local authorities, and frighten both industrialists and guild masters into organizing against the unions.

Strike activity, like union strength, was concentrated in the wood, construction, and metal industries. Although two of the three sectors had industrial unions, strikes usually involved only one craft. Wood and construction workers began by striking individual firms but soon escalated to citywide actions. Thus in 1897, 200 carpenters struck thirty construction firms, winning an increased minimum wage and better hours despite loud outcries from guild masters.[17] One year later the cabinetmakers, the backbone of the powerful woodworkers' union, began a rolling strike, walking out on a few firms at a time to demand a nine-hour day and a 15 percent wage increase. After two months, during which first small and then large firms were tackled, the demands had been won for more than 900 workers in 49 shops. Simultaneously, the carpenters staged a general strike, albeit an unsuccessful one.[18] The weaker metalworkers engaged in smaller, shorter strikes, which usually involved only a few dozen workers in a firm and ended in defeat.[19] In several instances the DMV, too weak to strike, proclaimed a boycott, but that tactic also failed, for it required a strong movement rather than being a substitute for one.[20] Overall, Düsseldorf workers won considerably fewer contests than their comrades elsewhere, and their successes came only where workers were highly organized and employers small and divided. Large firms could not be forced to recognize unions or bargain collectively.

Workers walked out most often over wages and hours. The predominance of economic strikes, hardly surprising in view of the previous quiescence and the onset of inflation, was not an indication of moderation or integration. Wage demands, which the national leadership encouraged, often "crystallized more diffuse, less articulate political ambitions."[21] They were part and parcel of the larger struggle over the power to decide how society's wealth would be distributed and by whom.[22] Far from being antithetical to radical change, such demands were steps on the path leading toward it.[23]

Nearly a third of the strikes were called to protest hiring and firing practices, supervisors' behavior, and forms of pay. In 1896, for example, molders struck the Senyff and Heye foundry, demanding the rehiring of a dismissed Social Democrat and the firing of the foreman Schmits, "a person who rose up to his present status from the position of helper and now treats the workers as though they were beneath contempt."[24] Two years later the DMV boycotted all foundries because they resorted to blacklists, arbitrary discipline, and frequent Sunday work.[25] These disputes about control questions were not, as some have argued, an expression of small-group solidarity. Rather they manifested broader class consciousness and a determination to gain legal and real equality, for workers' rights to engage in union and party activity were almost always at issue.[26] Because the stakes were high, these strikes always ended in defeat.

As workers became increasingly organized and active, employers used many expedients to wage the class struggle from above. And that struggle was waged with a high degree of success. When unions were weak and strikes small, employers simply forbad unions, blacklisted "troublemakers," and made workers sign pledges never to join a union. Ehrhardt went so far as to fire all DMV members summarily in retaliation against a *Metallarbeiterzeitung* article critical of Rheinmetall.[27] Employers refused to negotiate with strikers and in instance after instance hired scabs, often from outside Düsseldorf. Both factory owners and workshop masters frequently appealed to the police to curb pickets and attempted to influence public opinion through indignant, often lurid, strike reports in the bourgeois press.[28] Employers used existing cartels, interest associations, and the guilds to combat strikes. By the late 1890s, however, employers in wood and construction, who faced growing militancy, a divided public opinion, and what they considered to be inadequate state intervention, added a new weapon to their arsenal – the employers' association.

In the wake of the 1898 cabinetmakers' strike, more than eighty employers in the woodworking sector, imitating their colleagues elsewhere, formed an association "to counter all unjustified demands in an effective, united manner."[29] Noting SPD support for the strike, they concluded that "instigation from outside" and not real dissatisfaction had caused it. They optimistically predicted that unrest would cease if "loyal, contented workers" were but protected from agitators.[30] The construction firms employing carpenters responded similarly to the 1898 general strike. In both cases, the new organizations not only devoted themselves exclusively to combating unions and strikes but also united smaller guild employers with larger, nonguild ones.[31] The employers' associations showed that employers, like workers, were becoming new men, who had learned new forms of behavior that showed few remnants of previous paternalism or individualism.[32]

The provincial and municipal administrations exacerbated the escalating conflict between capital and labor by adopting a legalistic stance, which severely constrained workers but failed to satisfy industrialists and guild masters.[33] The anti-labor bias of the law was clear. Although paragraph 152 of the commercial code removed all prohibitions on the formation of unions, for example, the very next clause prescribed three-month jail sentences for anyone "who through physical force, threats, insults or oaths determines, or tries to determine, that someone will participate in such an agreement [union or strike] or prevents someone from withdrawing from such an agreement."[34] Trade unionists repeatedly complained of both general police harassment and excessively severe enforcement of paragraph 153 against pickets.

The police maintained that unions were political organizations, whose activities the police were legally entitled to oversee.[35] In the early 1890s the unions had usually complied with police requests for membership lists, but when Commissioner Hentze demanded the names of all members in 1897, Lohse, the head of the cartel, flatly refused, announcing that "it is not out of the question that employers would be allowed to see these 'blacklists' in order to dismiss those on them."[36] The following year three local union executive committees were each fined

15 M for withholding their records.[37] Strikers were frequently hauled into court, and although the charges were seldom serious, the proceedings both intimidated workers and wasted their scarce time and money. In 1898, for example, the Social Democrat Bösch was sentenced to one week in jail and expelled from Gerresheim for being "a nuisance." Later that year the Springorum Company submitted the names of all strikers to the police, who then brought charges against those who had failed to register their residence.[38]

Local authorities were explicit about their support of capitalist interests. As early as 1896 the government warned that "these [union] organizations are a factor which will have to be reckoned with sooner or later and which can only be energetically checked by the counter-organization of the entrepreneurs."[39] During strikes the police assured anxious employers that they were protecting those willing to work to the fullest extent possible under the law. But employers were far from satisfied with either the police or the law that they were enforcing. The police received a steady stream of letters from individual firms, guilds, and employers' associations, complaining that pickets were "swearing at, insulting, and at times even threatening those willing to work."[40] Wilhelm Hupp and Paul Lindt, who headed the Employers' Asociation for the Wood Industry, summed up the conservative sentiment of local capitalists when they urged the government to prohibit all union boycotts of firms and lamented that "we stand powerless against each and every demand of the workers as long as they can engage unhindered in picketing and everyone willing to work is subject to proscriptions which we are unfortunately not in a position to counter."[41]

Because neither the employers nor the Social Democrats felt that they could rely on the state as ally or mediator, each clung intransigently to hardened positions and organized their forces ever more massively to defend them. Both large capitalists and guildsmen preferred pressuring the state for more repressive legislation to negotiating with the unions. They did successfully check the union challenge. This was hardly behavior that would convince trade unionists that Wilhelmian society had a place for the working class and that political neutrality was possible. Quite the contrary. Throughout the 1890s the unions and the party cooperated closely with one another, sharing the same theory and considering themselves part of a common workers' movement.[42] Frustration on the economic front, like its counterpart on the political one, encouraged workers to turn a deaf ear to those who advocated collaboration with other classes and the abandonment of long-range goals while predicting a gradual amelioration of the workers' plight. Reformism required a minimum of reformist success to be convincing, and the Düsseldorf Social Democrats did not experience that in their union activity. Nor were they to find it in their efforts to win influence in municipal institutions.

The morass of municipal politics

The Düsseldorf Social Democrats were painfully aware of Catholic and liberal hegemony on the local level but were unable to challenge it.[43] They neither ran candidates for the city council nor drew up a municipal program. Like their comrades in Berlin, they believed that national politics were both more important and a more promising arena of activity.[44] Discriminatory suffrage regulations on the one hand and the movement's unstable migrant base on the other further discouraged involvement in municipal government. Thus the Social Democrats dismissed Düsseldorf's ruling Center–liberal coalition as "a reactionary mass, which misses no opportunity to rob the Social Democrats of their rights," and left municipal government uncontested in its hands.[45]

They could not ignore social policy institutions such as the worker–employer mediation courts (*Gewerbegerichten*) and the health insurance boards (*Krankenkassen*) so readily, however, for these touched workers' lives directly and were partially managed by elected worker representatives. Despite their criticism of state social policy, the Social Democrats were forced to try to influence its implementation.[46] In 1893 the trade-union cartel established an information bureau, run by the retired umbrella maker Lohse, which dispensed free advice on the insurance system, the commercial code, and civil law. By 1900 more than 1,700 workers a year sought Lohse's help, but the bureau offered only individual and legal solutions to problems that were collective and political.[47]

Of necessity, the Social Democrats also ran candidates for the mediation court, which handled wage and social policy disputes between individual workers and their employers, and the health insurance boards, which managed the day-to-day operations of the system.[48] This involvement was both part of the trade unions' drive to protect workers' material interests and build an alternative community and part of the party's effort to occupy existing political space and acquire public visibility. Social democratic participation contested Catholic and National Liberal power on the local level, where it was most visible, and marked the beginning of the politicization of all aspects of municipal life – a politicization that intensified class conflict rather than integrating the proletariat.

In the early 1890s, 700 to 800 workers a year brought cases before the mediation court, and nearly half won full or partial redress. Yet the Düsseldorf Social Democrats regarded the court as a limited, reformist institution, which merely alleviated the crassest forms of exploitation. Young workers, recent migrants, and women were all disenfranchised, and municipal employees were excluded from the court's jurisdiction. The court prohibited social democratic functionaries from representing workers, pressured plaintiffs to accept unfair compromises, and often failed to enforce settlements.[49] The *Volkstribune* summarized the SPD's indictment when it wrote that:

The mediation courts were established by a class state. They document by their structure – workers on the one side, employers on the other – the sharply antagonistic class conflicts in society. The class divisions within the court prove how foolish the conciliatory policies of the Center are. If the Center were right, the state would not have had to establish mediation courts.[50]

Nonetheless, the Social Democrats used the courts and participated in elections in order to seek minor improvements and clarify the limits of reformism.

In the 1892 election the SPD, by dint of quiet but persistent agitation won 950 votes as against 160 for the Catholic Workers' Associations and 118 of the Hirsch-Duncker slate.[51] Party and union members jubilantly claimed that "the working class in Düsseldorf sees social democracy as the only genuine representative of the working people."[52] Two years later they were again victorious, but this time the municipal government refused to convene regular court sessions and disqualified two SPD deputies.[53] These actions, which understandably embittered the Social Democrats, were followed by a counterattack from the Center and Christian unions, which suddenly realized the dangerous consequences of their previous indifference.

Abandoning their passivity in 1896, the Catholics transformed the once insignificant and nonpartisan mediation court elections into "a question of party and religion." Using their full arsenal of ideological and organizational weapons, they made the mediation court contest a mini Reichstag election. The Social Democrats, thrown on the defensive politically and organizationally, were defeated by a vote of 2,350 to 1,800.[54] Two years later they were trounced even more soundly. Father Schmitz, addressing a victory rally of Christian trade unionists, optimistically predicted that "the older, more reasonable workers are beginning to draw back from the Social Democrats."[55] In 1899 the Center Party triumphed yet again, and the Social Democrats ruefully noted that "we Düsseldorfers live in a Catholic stronghold of the Center and must still work enormously hard."[56]

The local Social Democrats had somewhat more success with the local health insurance boards, which Bismarck intended as an alternative to social democratic influence, not a means of enhancing it. Both the SPD and the Center Party left elections to their respective unions. This benefitted the larger free trade unions, which by 1897 controlled the metalworkers' and factory workers' boards, covering 9,000 employees. The Christian unions, however, dominated the 17,000 workers in the artisan, clerical, and general workers' boards. Moreover, another 21,000 workers were in insurance programs managed by individual firms, and 2,000 were in guild-run plans. All in all, the Social Democrats remained too weak to influence the administration of programs or implement reforms in costs and coverage.[57]

Two other areas of local social policy – or lack thereof – attracted the attention of Social Democrats in the 1890s: unemployment and housing. Although the Düsseldorf city fathers prided themselves on their progressive social attitudes, they proved unreceptive to social democratic programs and proposals for cooperation.

The Social Democrats met the first rejection of their reformist overtures in the early 1890s, when unemployment rose precipitously. The local party petitioned the city council to open a municipal labor exchange but received no hearing. In 1893 and 1894 social democratic leaders and unemployed workers even went directly to Mayor Lindemann, who first claimed that the city had no money and then urged workers to apply for jobs individually. Those who tried were given a "character test" and if discovered to be Social Democrats were told to turn to "their instigators and ranters" for help.[58]

The housing crisis reinforced the Social Democrats' sense of powerlessness. By the late 1890s Düsseldorf faced an accute housing shortage and skyrocketing rents because of rapid population growth, land speculation, and builders' reluctance to construct working-class apartments, which were difficult to finance, paid low returns, and had an unstable tenancy.[59] Numerous families shared the fate of a worker who wrote the *Volkstribune* that:

My family and I have already been homeless for fourteen days. Four children are staying with friends, and my wife, three children, and I are with the Pütz family. Despite great effort I cannot find an apartment anywhere, even though the mayor has given me a voucher, indicating that he will pay our rent. Moreover, the poor house is full.[60]

The Social Democrats appealed to the more progressive Mayor Wilhelm Marx, who proved willing to subsidize rents temporarily, house sixty to seventy homeless people a day, and provide aid for low-cost housing. He flatly refused to construct public housing, however, and deliberately excluded the Social Democrats from the newly formed housing commission, appointing only Christian and Hirsch–Duncker unionists.[61] The city thus failed to develop a long-term housing program and gave the Social Democrats no opportunity to cooperate in policy making.

The Social Democrats' efforts to collaborate with bourgeois groups in establishing a tenants' association proved even less fruitful. Although several party members served on the association's planning committee, believing that "a tenants' association five to six thousand members strong or stronger, would be a power with which landlords would have to reckon," they quickly resigned in protest. Only two thousand people joined, and the thoroughly bourgeois leadership limited itself to passing paper resolutions for piecemeal reforms.[62]

In areas such as Bavaria and Baden or cities such as Bremen and Hamburg, where the SPD and unions were strong, the middle classes' liberal, and municipal government more democratic than in Prussia, social democratic participation in city politics, the mediation courts, and housing programs undoubtedly did produce results and enhance working-class power. It promoted reformism and "the integration of the workers into the life of bourgeois society."[63] Exactly the reverse was true in Düsseldorf, where such activity exacerbated economic and political conflicts, intensified the Social Democrats' isolation, and confirmed their sense of impotence. Their venture into the municipal arena in the 1890s convinced them that they had not missed any opportunities to play reformist politics. There were none to miss.

Agitation and education

The Social Democrats were no more successful in their agitation and education than they were in their economic and social policy battles.

Although the leaders insisted that "the first and foremost duty of a Social Democrat is to know what socialism is and what it wants," they were unsure how to facilitate such understanding.[64] The rank and file shared the belief that "knowledge is power." Indeed, many workers were attracted to social democracy precisely because it offered them so much more than their formal schooling with its emphasis on religion, nationalism, and monarchism.[65] But they were as uncertain about what they wanted to learn as the leadership was about what it should teach. And neither group had a program for attracting the unorganized.

Local leaders faced nearly insoluble dilemmas in trying to develop educational programs that would be politically effective as well as popular. A national focus was needed to give workers an understanding of German society and to counterbalance the movement's local weakness, but a local one was required to make general, theoretical arguments concrete and to promote activism. Given the low level of organization and politicization, it was necessary not only to train the committed but also to recruit the indifferent and hostile. Given the impoverished schooling of workers, it was necessary to teach them about economic development, contemporary politics, and social theory as well as history, science, and culture, while avoiding a superficial general education. In the 1890s neither the press nor party meetings, the two main vehicles for recruitment and education, were able to fulfill the diverse demands made on them.

Volkstribune editors Wessel and Erbert, reflecting local sentiment, wanted the press to serve the political needs of the party, provide general education, and appeal to the unorganized. Unfortunately, they lacked the necessary financial and educational resources. The editors promised "to devote detailed attention to political and social developments at home and abroad," for example, but like their movement counterparts elsewhere scarcely mentioned foreign affairs, thereby severely limiting workers' knowledge about international capitalism and foreign workers' movements.[66] The *Volkstribune* covered national politics at greater length by borrowing analytical articles from such SPD papers as *Vorwärts* and the *Leipziger Volkszeitung* and reports on Reichstag proceedings from the local bourgeois press. All too often, it was the availability of material and not political considerations that determined what was printed. As the decade wore on, coverage of the national party and unions improved somewhat, but in general the paper reflected Düsseldorf's isolation rather than overcoming it.[67] The editors discussed theory by drawing lessons from concrete situations rather than presenting Marxism as an abstract dogma, and they were scarcely more well versed in Marxism than their readers.

The *Volkstribune*'s local news coverage was very rich, for nearly every day workers sent in reports on union meetings, strikes, factory conditions, and neighborhood incidents, which were printed verbatim. Although these articles lacked analysis, they did provide a rich chronicle of the injustices of working-class life and the activities of the Social Democrats. They promoted solidarity among the diverse factions of the Düsseldorf working class by providing information about common conditions and complaints. Reliance on amateur journalists created headaches for Erbert and Wessel, who continually urged workers to "send only incontrovertible facts. Name names and give witnesses . . . Be triply cautious with your communications, for social democratic editors have better things to do than sit in jail."[68] But such rank-and-file participation greatly increased interest in the paper.

For all its inadequacies, the *Volkstribune* was the most effective vehicle for strengthening workers' identification with social democracy. By 1898 it had as many subscribers as there were trade unionists and was read by at least one in four social democratic voters.[69] It was not, however, a suitable instrument for recruiting the unorganized, who found its coverage too narrow and serious and its political rhetoric either objectionable or incomprehensible. The *Volkstribune* was certainly not "a very considerable power" that the movement's opponents were "forced to notice" as its editors boasted.[70] The Centrist *Volksblatt* had five times as many readers, and the *General Anzeiger* and *Neuste Nachrichten*, with a combined circulation of 58,000, found their way into most proletarian homes.[71]

The Düsseldorf Social Democrats, united about the functions of the press, were divided about those of meetings. Men such as Erbert, Schmitt, and Cretschmar, who led the Social Democratic Association, strove to educate the organized and involve them intensely in the local movement. Helbing, Jammer, Windhoff, and the other *Vertrauensmänner* wanted to recruit new workers and increase interest in regional and national party affairs. Collaboration between the two groups left much to be desired. In early October of 1897, for example, Schmitt scheduled the association's elections and Jammer and Windhoff sponsored a discussion of the upcoming national party congress. The following week Erbert addressed a mediation court election rally, sponsored jointly by the party and cartel. In addition the association held a lecture on contemporary poets, and the *Vertrauensmänner* arranged a talk by Clara Zetkin on the position of women. In early November the association discussed the gold standard and capitalist society, while the *Vertrauensmänner* turned their attention to the British metalworkers' struggle for the eight-hour day.[72]

This mixture of activism and eclecticism, which made enormous demands on workers' limited time without focusing their energies, characterized programs throughout the decade. It reflected the inexperience of the leadership, which changed hands yearly. Each new officer implemented a different program in an effort to boost the perennially low attendance, but few succeeded.[73] Lacking local talent, leaders had to rely on whichever outside speakers were available. They did not know what would be politically useful and popular, and received little advice from the rank and file. Nor was guidance forthcoming from the national leaders, even though they regarded education as vital for promoting both unity and the belief that socialism was "the logical result of historical development."[74] Imbued with a strong economic determinism, the national leaders were supremely confident that the movement would flourish and socialism arrive whatever specific programs were offered. The Düsseldorf Social Democrats quickly lost the naive optimism of their comrades in Berlin.

In the early 1890s the Social Democrats concentrated on training the urban, organized worker rather than soliciting new recruits. Association leaders Voss, Reinsdorf, and Barthels were torn between offering a general education, to compensate workers for their previous deprivation, and a more narrowly political one, to train competent agitators and organizers. Each year, they offered several well-attended lectures on such theoretical topics as the party program, nationalism, and religion and socialism.[75] Discussions of the class character of German education and law were less well received, for workers preferred the *Vertrauensmänner*'s lectures on current affairs or the unions' analyses of economic questions.[76] Whenever possible, the association held talks on art and poetry, in which relatively few workers were interested, or on science, which fascinated them.[77] Workers' preferences were shaped both by the relevance of the subject and the skill of the available speakers.

In 1895 Erbert and Luther, worried by the association's stagnation, opted for the political alternative. They selected speakers who shared their anti-reformist views to discuss domestic politics and Marxist theory. Workers responded enthusiastically to Welsch's analysis of the German political situation, Binde's discussion of bourgeois intellectual thought, and Lehmann's critique of the Center. More theoretical lectures by Lütengau on the party program, by Gewehr on the agrarian question, and by Binde on cooperatives "were happily very well attended."[78] The following year 130 workers went to a talk on the theory of value, and double that number to one on Marxism.[79] Even if the police were correct in their claim that "many present did not understand the talks," the attendance attests to a lively interest in learning about Marxism – an interest denied by many students of the SPD.[80] Except for occasional readings of Hauptmann's *The Weavers*, the association abandoned cultural topics and general education.

The 100 to 150 workers who participated regularly in the association received a solid political education. But most Social Democrats were mobile migrants who remained too short a time to do more than vote SPD or perhaps join a union. Because most lived in the outlying working-class neighborhoods, they found the trip to the one party pub in the central Altstadt too long, especially for week-night meetings.[81] Most significantly, the vast majority of workers shunned the movement completely.

Aware of this, the *Vertrauensmänner* shifted the locus of party life from the association to public lectures and rallies, aimed at attracting the unorganized or hostile. This strategy certainly brought the party in contact with more workers, for 200 to 300 came regularly to talks on contemporary politics, 400 to 600 attended the lectures by prominent speakers, such as Hermann Molkenbuhr and Clara Zetkin, and 1,300 turned out for the charismatic Karl Liebknecht.[82] Workers found such knowledgeable and polished speakers a vast improvement on the association's lecturers, who were frequently criticized "for not really knowing their subject," "confusing everything," and even for "not being modern Social Democrats, for they did not have a materialist analysis."[83] Yet workers who attended such public lectures neither received systematic political training nor learned socialist theory well. At best, the new strategy taught the theoretical value of solidarity without offering workers the practical experience of it. It convinced workers to vote Social Democratic without winning them for the party. By 1898 only 350 of Düsseldorf's more than 33,000 male workers had joined, and for the next three years membership stagnated.[84] As the metalworker Max Sendler remarked with disgust, "the Düsseldorf workers come to party meetings when there is something new. They applaud and shout 'Bravo' but nothing else happens. When they leave, everything remains the same."[85]

The association did not fill the resulting educational lacuna, for its dispirited leaders retreated once again into eclecticism. Only in 1899 did they offer a serious and coherent program. Woltmann from Barmen delivered several lectures on anatomy, physiology, and Darwinism to nearly a hundred workers. Evolutionary natural science, which harmonized so well with the party's deterministic Marxism, was more popular than the second series on the fundamentals of economic thought, which attracted only sixty.[86]

Although the Social Democrats understood the dilemmas of education and agitation by the late 1890s, they continued to be thwarted by them. The working class seemed as intractable as the economic and political environment, and the frustrations of agitation and education fed directly into the continued failure of the movement politically.

The transformation of political Catholicism

In the late 1890s the Düsseldorf Center Party warded off the social democratic challenge just as effectively in national politics as it did in the local arena. The People's Association built an elaborate mass organization with district and block leaders, held regular educational meetings, with specially trained speakers, and distributed popular literature on all issues of dispute between Catholicism and socialism.[87] The clergy and Center Party leaders urged Catholic workers to engage in "person-to-person agitation in workshops, streets, and bars."[88] Worried by the sudden growth of the free unions after 1895, they strongly promoted the Christian trade unions. If the Catholics consciously imitated their opponents, they did so from a position of strength. Even Grimpe grudgingly acknowledged that "as a result of its conflicts with the government, this party [the Center] is politically astute, tightly knit, and has an unusually effective apparatus for agitation . . . and the party possesses such financial strength that its power cannot be broken from one day to the next."[89]

The results of the 1898 election confirmed the Center's dominance. With more than 70 percent of all Catholics voting along religious lines, the Center Party won 49 percent of the vote in the first election and 64 percent in the run-off, whereas the Social Democrats, with 29 percent and 35 percent, respectively, barely improved on their 1893 showing.

Indeed, they suffered heavy losses in several inner-city proletarian neighborhoods and overall attracted only 8,400 of the more than 13,000 working-class voters.[90] The Center Party proudly announced that "social democracy has been brought to a halt in the Rhineland," by a party that "unites religious conviction, true monarchical sentiment, and honest enthusiasm for social reform."[91] Reviewing their losses a few years later, the Social Democrats blamed them on Catholic workers who "have been content to be the trainbearers and electoral beasts of the Center lawyers, the Center rentiers, the Center doctors, the Center counts, and the Center millionaires ... and to celebrate feast days with Father Neumann, Father Schmitz, and Father Schmidt."[92]

Neither the Center's optimism nor the SPD's despair was entirely justified, however, for in fact Catholic working-class voters formed roughly half of the SPD electorate but only 43 percent of the Center's.[93] Catholic leaders were experiencing increasing difficulty in recruiting soldiers to defend their seemingly invulnerable fortress. Older, native-born working-class supporters did not defect, but newer, younger migrants refused to enlist. With the exception of the relatively weak Christian trade unions, Catholic associations were closely tied to parishes and seem to have recruited primarily from those long involved with the local church. Because they were too religious, hierarchical, and conservative, they were unable to attract more mobile workers who had broken out of traditional social relationships and authority patterns. Many migrants found that the rapidly growing free trade unions offered better economic protection and a more hospitable community.[94] Many others were repelled by the new policies that the Center Party adopted.

In the late 1890s the Center completed its transition from pariah to pivotal party in Wilhelmian Germany's pseudoparliamentary system. The integration of the Center Party into the ruling coalition began in earnest under Chancellor Hohenlohe, Caprivi's successor, who solicited Catholic support for the Civil Code of 1896 and participation in the alliance of agriculture and heavy industry that his minister Miquel reconstructed in the late 1890s. Leading Centrists, anxious to promote the party's religious interests and political power, abandoned their opposition to militarism and imperialism as well as their qualms about allying with Protestant Conservatives. In 1898 the Center Party threw its decisive votes behind the first Naval bill, not in order to promote the economic interests of its constituents, for the expense of the vast armaments project bore heavily on the Catholic lower middle classes, peasants, and proletarians, but in order to secure its parliamentary power and end its isolation.[95] The Center affirmed its new role as a government party by endorsing the second Naval bill two years later.

Just as the Center's ties to the government and the Conservatives pushed it to the right, so too did pressure from Catholic agrarians and artisans, who "were in a nastier mood than many Catholic workers and were better organized."[96] Once in the ruling coalition, the Center Party deemphasized social welfare for the working class, advocating instead "social policies" for the *Mittelstand* and landlords, that is, guilds and tariffs.[97] The former were passed in 1897, the latter after the turn of the century.

The liberal Rhenish Centrists supported this new orientation, because it furthered not only the religious interests and political power of the party but also the social integration of middle-class Catholics. It significantly limited political Catholicism's flexibility vis-à-vis the working class, however, for in order to maintain its pivotal position the Center Party had to support numerous measures, such as the Naval bills, guilds, and ultimately tariffs, which negated its self-proclaimed reputation as "a friend of the working class." The transformation of the Center Party was part of a broader restructuring of economic and political relationships at the turn of the century, which revived the Bismarckian stalemate and reunited the Junkers and heavy industrialists by means of imperialism and tariffs.[98] By tying its political fortunes to this alliance, the Center Party became of necessity an opponent of political and social reforms, which would disrupt the delicate balance.

The Social Democrats rejoiced at the metamorphosis of the Center Party, believing that it vindicated their critique and improved their political prospects. In the long run it was to do so, but the Düsseldorf workers could not launch an immediate and effective attack on the Center fortress. To be sure, in the 1898 Reichstag campaign, they lambasted the Center for committing "treason against the working class" by supporting the Naval bill, failing to secure tax reform, denying rural workers the right to organize, and offering only weak opposition to the Penitentiary bill, which proposed to outlaw picketing.[99] Erbert, Grimpe, Sendler, and a host of lesser leaders ringingly denounced the Center as "a fawning government party" whose pro-capitalist and pro-agrarian biases were clear for all to see.[100]

Though accurate, this indictment did not prove persuasive to indifferent or hostile workers. After some hesitation, the Center Party opposed repressive legislation, and the Reichstag thus failed to pass it. The plight of rural workers was not of great concern to an urban proletariat with problems aplenty of its own. The local party and union leaders, trapped in a self-defeating economism, tended to argue all issues in terms of their impact on the workers' pocketbook, but the workers did not feel the cost of naval building until after the turn of the century, when tariffs were raised to unprecedented heights. Only then did they become fully aware of the Center's transformation, and only then could Social Democrats relate workers' everyday experiences with inflation and discrimination to questions of military spending and Catholic policies. In the late 1890s their arguments seemed remote from the insecurities and injustices of proletarian life.

Much of the time the Social Democrats were forced to fight on the Center's chosen ground of religion and social policy. Because they were pessimistic about the possibility of reform, they made no predictions about the fruits of a leftist electoral victory. Although they did not hide their desire for socialism, they never discussed it extensively. In short, they offered a critique of political Catholicism, organized capitalism, and Wilhelmian society but no concrete improvements in the short run or vivid and inspiring alternatives in the long run. It was a peculiarly negative stance for a movement so optimistic about radically transforming humanity and society.

By the turn of the century it was clear that the optimistic developments of the late 1890s marked a false start rather than the first stages of sustained growth. The Social Democrats had failed to contest capitalist power on the shop floor or Catholic dominance in local and national politics. The Social Democrats ended the decade as they had begun it – the representatives of a minority of young skilled male workers, predominantly Protestant, overwhelmingly migrant. This decade of frustration was to solidify the Düsseldorf movement's commitment to orthodox Marxism and isolation, but it was also to precipitate an acute organizational crisis, a veritable party war.

4

Ideological unity and organizational disarray

A decade of failure and frustration profoundly shaped the theory and strategy of the Düsseldorf Social Democrats. Isolation and defeat, intensified by the turn-of-the-century economic crisis, confirmed their skepticism about parliamentarism and reformism and their opposition to proposed alterations in the party's program and practice, which emanated from the right. Their experiences made them receptive to a conception of revolution that emphasized economic development and not working-class activism as the crucial component of a socialist transformation. Their advocacy of orthodox Marxism, isolation, and tactical passivity both reflected and reinforced the weakness of the local movement and the stalemate of national politics.

Their experiences and the lessons they drew from them conditioned their negative and dismissive response to the revisionist controversy that shook the national movement at the turn of the century. They condemned Bernstein's proposals for revising Marx's economic analysis and reorienting the SPD's political strategy, and lashed out bitterly at bourgeois intellectuals who stirred up futile controversies. But they rejected revisionism without articulating an activist and radical alternative. They thus found themselves closer to the party's mainstream than they had previously been – or ever were to be again. Like their comrades elsewhere, they found that deterministic, orthodox Marxism offered hope in the face of failure and legitimated isolation and passivity. It did not, however, provide a way out of the dilemmas and disappointments of the 1890s.

The same failures that unified the party ideologically divided it organizationally. In response to renewed economic recession, continued Center Party success, and government harassment, the Social Democrats fought bitterly over questions of party structure, the press, and leadership. They groped desperately for organizational solutions to problems that were social, political, and tactical, and they virtually crippled the movement from 1899 to 1903. The "party war," as it was called by the combatants, diverted attention from the struggle with the Center Party and the revisionist controversy on the one hand, and yet dealt with serious organizational issues on the other. Its resolution through the restructuring of the party and press and the recruitment of stable, effective leaders did not solve the political and strategic problems the Social Democrats faced, but it did prepare them to exploit changes in the economy, the composition of the working class, and the politics of the Center.

Orthodoxy and inactivity

After the early 1890s the inchoate radicalism of the Düsseldorf Social Democrats developed into a more sophisticated but less radical espousal of orthodox Marxism. This transformation took place in three stages – or more accurately, in the debates around three issues: reformism, the nature of revolution, and revisionism. The Social Democrats confirmed their allegiance to Marxism but defined it in an increasingly determin-istic manner. They rejected proposals to alter the party's program, electoral practice, and alliance policy but offered only organization, isolation, and patience as alternative tactics. The gap between theory and practice widened, and the radical edge to their earlier critique was lost. Their attack on reformism and revisionism was particularly vehement, but their strategy was hardly radical. For a brief moment they stood in the movement's mainstream rather than on its left.

By the mid-1890s the Düsseldorf Social Democrats had stopped debating the merits of parliamentarism, even though they doubted its effectiveness. Isolated local protests were doomed by the national party's strong commitment to electoral politics on the one hand and the lack of a ready alternative to them on the other. Reformism had many faces, however, and the Düsseldorf Social Democrats, like their comrades elsewhere, shifted the grounds of struggle to the party's agrarian pro-gram and Prussian electoral policy. The ensuing controversies forced them not only to decide crucial tactical questions but also to reassess the validity of Marxism.[1]

In the late 1860s the social democratic movement adopted what it con-sidered to be a principled and radical stance on the agrarian question, one that prophesized the extinction of the small peasant and the emergence of large-scale collective farms.[2] For the next two decades, while the Social

Democrats ignored the issue theoretically and practically, Junkers and peasants, severely hurt by the Great Depression, built an alliance on a platform of grain tariffs, anti-Semitism, anti-urbanism, and political conservatism.[3] Workers and peasants, the SPD, and the Junker–peasant alliance inhabited different worlds, economically and ideologically, except in Bavaria. In the early 1890s the South German wing of the SPD, operating in a more democratic and less industrialized region where the Center Party was relatively weak, moderated its agrarian program, cooperated with other parties, and won support from small farmers. In 1894 Georg Vollmar, the Bavarian party leader, urged the national movement to follow suit, and an agrarian commission was formed to study his suggestion. In 1895 it advocated support for small farmers and state socialist measures but, following an acrimonious debate, the Breslau party congress resoundingly rejected the controversial reform proposal.[4]

The Düsseldorf Social Democrats initially ignored the dispute, for they had just abandoned rural agitation as hopeless. By 1895, however, they recognized the larger issues at stake and began a concerted campaign against Vollmar. Erbert and Wessel assiduously solicited articles for the *Volkstribune* from Bebel, Kautsky, and Adler, who shared their views, while refusing space to the South Germans. Local leaders ridiculed the slogan, "go to the country and make the peasants Social Democrats," arguing that urban Catholic workers must be recruited first.[5] They condemned positions "which denied and obliterated the proletarian, revolutionary character of the party" in order to win peasant or bourgeois support. Several hundred workers turned out to discuss the agrarian committee's report and voted overwhelmingly against each and every part.[6] After Breslau, the *Volkstribune* summed up the local mood by noting with satisfaction that "rural agitation will not cease. On the contrary, it will be directed into the proper channels. We will do our best to win those who can be won: the rural proletariat."[7]

In fact, the rural proletarian could not be won any more easily than the small farmer, and the Düsseldorf Social Democrats hardly tried to recruit him. Throughout the Rhineland, the conservative Agrarian League and the Catholic Peasant League had long since articulated agrarian discontent and organized the countryside. There was no group to whom the Social Democrats could have appealed with a more reformist program. Thus even though their decision was based as much on an abstract defense of traditional principles as on a concrete analysis of the peasantry's social position and political outlook, it was correct.

The same mixture of isolation, failure, and principle led the Düsseldorf Social Democrats to oppose participation in the Prussian Landtag elections. In the 1890s successive national party congresses first recommended participation, then prohibited it, then reversed that decision, and finally, in 1898, left the matter up to the local party. But Düsseldorf never vacillated. As Ludwig Schmidt argued, participation was futile under the three-class suffrage. "We should remain revolutionaries."[8] Abstention was the only policy that could be reconciled with both orthodox Marxism and the impotence of the Düsseldorf movement. Thus in 1900 several hundred party members resolved that although others had the right to participate, "under the prevailing conditions, the Düsseldorf party comrades refuse to do so ... All our political opponents in Düsseldorf are so unworthy that the class-conscious proletariat cannot extend a hand to them or form an alliance with them."[9]

This pessimistic analysis was certainly not exaggerated. In the absence of agitation for suffrage reform, however, nonparticipation was a purely negative policy. By developing a principled defense of it, the Social Democrats made a virtue out of necessity. As with parliamentarism and the peasantry, they drew no positive tactical deductions from their doctrinal positions, adopting instead a passivity akin to that of the party's mainstream.

Theoretical certainty and utter tactical confusion were nowhere more evident than in the speech that Erbert delivered to more than six hundred workers on May Day 1897. He opened with the ringing declaration that:

We are born equal to the propertied classes, and we believe we are entitled to participate in all the discoveries of mankind. Because we believe this, we demand – we do not ask – that you treat us as men, that you guarantee us the rights that we insist on as the producers of all value.

But how was this to be achieved? Erbert despaired of parliament, where working-class representatives "are not in the position to achieve anything positive." Social policy simply showed that "the possessing classes have nothing for us." Technological progress brought workers only lower wages and greater exploitation. He admonished workers "to look to self-help," "to unite and work against capitalism," and "to win public opinion for us," but did not suggest any more specific tactics.[10] Finally, Erbert, like his comrades, urged workers to wait patiently for the social revolution that economic conditions would inevitably bring.

Throughout the first, frustrating decade of legality the Düsseldorf Social Democrats consoled themselves with a deterministic conception of revolution. They advocated a total transformation of society, but argued that "the most important of all social revolutions are economic."[11] Like their comrades elsewhere, they considered such an economic revolution not only desirable but also inevitable, even if the timing was not predictable.[12] As Erbert and Wessel reminded their readers repeatedly, "the most strenuous efforts of the proletariat would not alone suffice to liberate society from its present, unjust conditions if capitalism itself did not carry the seeds of its own destruction."[13]

The task of the working class was to synchronize its actions with that economic process. At the movement's annual commemoration of the 1848 revolution, Grimpe, Lehmann, Erbert, and Sendler always praised the heroism of the artisans and workers who had fought on the barricades, but insisted that the revolution had been doomed from the start because "the economic preconditions for proletarian rule were not developed."[14] They drew only negative lessons from such economic analyses. Don't act! Don't become impatient! "According to scientific socialism," the *Volkstribune* admonished, "it would not be a revolutionary act if individual men, groups, or parties attempted to bring about the social revolution. *The times themselves must be ripe.*"[15]

Locally as well as nationally, warnings against revolutionary adventurism were used to condemn violence, thereby further encouraging passivity in practice as well as determinism in thought. Grimpe and Erbert stated emphatically that "we neither *want* a violent revolution nor *could* we make such a revolution."[16] Moreover, "the goals and spirit of those who struggle is the main thing and not fighting on the barricades."[17] Adopting a note of practicality, Sendler reminded his readers that "building barricades is in any case impossible since the governments of large cities have paved the streets."[18] Lehmann stated that "historical development has gone so far that it will no longer come to an open struggle. We at least do not want it." Having absorbed the teachings of Bebel and Kautsky, he insisted that society, and not social democracy, would bear the onus of resorting to violence.[19] Finally, Grimpe, summing up the outlook of the late 1890s, argued:

The means of struggle are not fists and guns but healthy human understanding (*gesunder Menschenverstand*). The times change and with them the means of struggle. Whereas earlier the working people did not know how else to express their discontent except through brute force, now they quite correctly go forward in an organized class struggle. This comon intellectual struggle is the most dangerous for our enemy. [20]

No one envisioned an alternative between the extremes of armed uprising and quiet organization.

Düsseldorf Social Democrats specified neither how the organized intellectual class struggle should be waged nor how it related to the desired revolution. They urged workers to promote proletarian solidarity by building the party and unions, but always advocated this in the Kautskyan sense of organizing for the revolution rather than organizing the revolution.[21] They discouraged the workers from seizing power but denied that they could gain it electorally. Not a single speech on the history of 1848, the nature of capitalist development, or the prospect of socialist revolution foresaw a parliamentary road to socialism. At most the Social Democrats implied that they would inherit power when capitalism collapsed.[22] Thus, much as men like Grimpe and Erbert insisted that "the political struggle with the weapons of organization and the vote has also its heroism,"[23] they could not explain wherein that heroism lay – especially in areas such as Düsseldorf, where those struggles had led only to humiliating defeats.

The relation of education and revolution was equally unclear. Spiegel stated emphatically that social democracy must "educate the workers so that they know where they have to go and where their interests are best represented."[24] According to Grimpe, "no amount of heroism, no amount of martyrdom can substitute for the clear insight of the proletariat into the course of historical development, into the essential preconditions of its liberation."[25] Neither man suggested that such education would enable workers to shape the historical process. Like so many other Social Democrats, they concentrated more on teaching workers that Marxism was a science with which to understand the world than on persuading them that socialism was a practical task that would be achieved by changing it.[26] Only Ludwig Schmidt, speaking on the fifty-first anniversary of 1848, offered a somewhat more activist analysis. "We must transform men's minds so that they know what they want. We must go so far that no one needs a leader and everyone know what he wants. Everyone must do his part."[27] His prescription, which was, to be sure, distressingly vague, fell on deaf ears.

The Düsseldorf Social Democrats viewed the "future state," as they called a socialist society, with the same passivity and determinism as they did the revolution. It was something that would happen as a result of historical forces, not something they would actively create and whose character they should thus debate. Indeed, local leaders, like their national counterparts, criticized discussions of life under socialism as a kind of revolutionary escapism, which diverted attention from the hard and necessary tasks of the present.[28] May Day and March 18, the commemoration of 1848, were almost the only occasions when the Düsseldorf leaders speculated in however cursory a manner about the future state. In 1902, for example, Windhoff promised a May Day crowd of several hundred that the working class would one day succeed in "eliminating oppression and throwing off the chains of servitude." Wessel, speaking to more than 400 workers gathered in another locale, painted an unusually detailed picture, "of the fundamentals of the social democratic future state." "Better protective legislation" and "world peace" would be essential elements in the new order. "The many millions which are sunk into the sea and blown into the air will be used to promote culture and the well-being of the working class." Finally, "the workers will not be excluded from culture, because there is more, or at least as much intelligence in proletarian heads as in those of other classes."[29]

If these remarks were hardly illuminating about economic and political arrangements, they nonetheless accurately conveyed the working class's desire for equality and respect, for humane treatment, and the opportunity to lead a fulfilling life. Simple, nonrevolutionary goals, some have said.[30] Perhaps, but the Düsseldorf Social Democrats, despairing of the current order, believed that they could be realized only in a socialist society.

These discussions of revolution, past and future, however unsatisfactory to speakers and audiences alike, served several important functions – or so the leaders hoped. The Social Democrats sought to give the working class "an historical consciousness and thus knowledge of its past in order to accomplish its mission."[31] This was no easy task in a country without strong traditions of dissent and successful revolution. They hoped to reclaim "the history of the defeated," which, in Grimpe's words, "had been covered with lies by the victors."[32] In the schools, the army, and the press, the working class was exposed to a nationalistic and conservative interpretation of history in which, noted the *Volkszeitung* angrily, "the March heroes [of 1848] have been betrayed and forgotten by the cowardly bourgeoisie."[33]

The Social Democrats did not succeed in creating from the despair and distant memories of 1848 a viable revolutionary tradition that could both mobilize the working class and legitimize the workers' movement.[34] Defeat did not breed optimism, even though it was blamed on "unripe economic conditions." Heroism was not inspiring, for there was no hope of emulation. The leaders analyzed past revolutions in order to teach patience and caution. Their followers may well have learned only passivity and pessimism.

Belief in the inevitability of socialist revolution probably had a similar unintended impact on the rank and file. Certainly it offered the assurance of victory, despite powerlessness and oppression in the present.[35] It was a response to and a positive confirmation of the isolation of the movement and the working class as a whole, yet it promised an end to that marginality and subordination. It helped the Social Democrats deal with their contradictory position in German society and provided them with an analysis of that society, which appropriately reflected "the ambivalence of an historical situation which one could call the end of the era of European revolutions."[36]

Yet the theory of revolution drew only general and abstract connections between their profound pessimism about the short run and their total optimism about the long, between the cautious tactics that were sanctioned and the revolution that was desired. Although some Social Democrats undoubtedly found hope and consolation in this theory, many others were surely confused and frustrated by its lack of theoretical specificity and meaningful tactical prescriptions. In North German, Protestant, industrial regions and in South German, Catholic, and less developed ones, where the movement had a long history of success with organization, education, and elections, it was easier for Social Democrats to believe that such practices were linked to radical social change, or at least that they were worthwhile until the economic revolution swept all before it. This sense of efficacy and validity was much less prevalent in areas like Düsseldorf.

The Social Democrats also discussed revolution in order to arouse workers' interest in its end result, socialism. Yet they failed to make socialism a vivid and meaningful alternative to the present.[37] Although the movement clearly articulated workers' desire for equality, decency, prosperity, and culture, it did not portray adequately how these would be realized in a socialist society. Leaders and theoreticians justified their silence now on the grounds of ignorance or pragmatism, now on those of science combating utopianism. But workers were eager for such knowledge, as evidenced by the fact that party members and trade unionists alike read Bebel's *Women and Socialism*, with its detailed vision of the future state, far more widely than any other theoretical work.[38] And large numbers turned out for those rare meetings devoted to discussions of life under socialism.[39] Local Social Democrats, such as Lehmann, Erbert, and Grimpe, following national figures, such as Bebel and Kautsky, failed to heed workers' legitimate request to know where they were going, and in so doing, dampened their eagerness to get there.

At most, the conception of revolution that the Düsseldorf Social Democrats developed in the late 1890s reenforced workers' rejection of reformism without offering them tactical guidance or a clear sense of the end goal. Thus, when a new challenge from the right arose at the turn of the century, leaders and followers alike were to reject it more as a result of their experience with and analysis of contemporary society than in anticipation of the realization of an alternative one.

The revisionist controversy erupted in the late 1890s when Eduard Bernstein, a prominent movement theorist since the 1880s, proposed substantial revisions in Marx's economic analysis and in the SPD's political practice. Rejecting the Marxist dialectic, Bernstein proposed an evolutionary approach to history. After studying capitalist development and political conflicts in Germany and above all in England, where he had lived for several years, Bernstein concluded that the contradictions of capitalism were not driving it inexorably toward a final crisis and socialism. Rather, polarization, immiseration, and class struggle were diminishing, thereby making it both possible and necessary for the working class to join with liberal middle-class elements in an alliance that would seek democratic and social reforms by peaceful, parliamentary means. Revolution was no longer inevitable, and socialism was only the ethically desirable and not the historically necessary result of such a reformist, evolutionary process. Or, in Bernstein's famous phrase, which so shocked orthodox and radical Social Democrats, "the movement is everything, the end goal nothing."[40] Given Bernstein's stature and the support that he received from both the reformist South German Social Democrats and trade-union leaders, his attempt to reconcile revolutionary theory and reformist practice by fundamentally altering the former was indeed a serious threat to the status quo.

The Düsseldorf Social Democrats greeted Bernstein's proposals with the same negativism and unequivocal orthodoxy as they had Vollmar's on the agrarian question. They took their stand on revisionism, or "the

Bernstein problem" as they preferred to call it, as soon as his *Evolutionary Socialism* was published in 1899. Raising all the themes to which they would return in the next three years, men like Erbert, Wessel, and Windhoff insisted that Bernstein's economic analysis was faulty, his political prognosis utopian, and his tactical suggestions simply impossible.[41] His proposals threatened the identity of the movement and the morale of the working class. In the first of many ringing affirmations of the party's current course, the *Volkstribune* announced:

Our party is not a philosophical discussion club, which can loose itself in endless debates. Rather, it is a fighting party. A fighting party like the SPD, which is the principled enemy of all other parties, needs *firm* principles, and it needs a *firm* end goal. A political party which abandons its end goal abandons itself. We assert this not only in order to maintain the spirit of those who struggle, but also because it is an objective fact. The end goal of the SPD is the transformation of the economy, the socialization of the means of production.[42]

From 1899 until 1903, when the SPD officially but ineffectually condemned Bernstein, the Düsseldorf Social Democrats seldom discussed revisionism, in part because they underestimated the seriousness of the challenge and the breadth of its support and in part because they were involved in organizational problems and power struggles closer to home. They remained thoroughly hostile to Bernstein, however. In 1902, for example, Wessel and Erbert argued in the *Volkszeitung* that social reforms should not be confused with social revolution, for piecemeal concessions could not eliminate the necessity of overthrowing capitalism. Although valuable and desirable, democracy was not the end goal. Nor could it be fully realized except under socialism. At a 1903 discussion of the Erfurt program, to which more than 200 workers came, August Schulte argued that conflict and exploitation were increasing, making the interests of capital and labor more irreconcilable than ever.[43]

The fact that the revisionist controversy was played out against the background of the 1900–3 economic crisis made such arguments persuasive. In the Düsseldorf metal industry, for example, three to four thousand workers lost their jobs between 1900 and late 1902, and Rheinmetall alone fired more than one-third of its work force. Many firms shortened the work time, thereby reducing wages by 25 to 30 percent. At the labor exchange there were two applicants for every job.[44] Strike activity virtually ceased. The only major confrontations, the strike by the 700 workers of the Gerresheim "glass kingdom" over the right to organize and that by 1,500 masons and construction helpers, ended in bitter and total defeat.[45] Thus, although the Düsseldorf Social Democrats lacked the expertise to refute Bernstein's economic arguments point by point, they rejected them from their limited knowledge of Marxist theory and, more important, from their own experience with recession, unemployment, inflation, and strikes.

They were equally critical of the tactics that Bernstein advocated and of the underlying assumption that politics should take precedence over economics. They acknowledged that no one could predict "whether socialism would be reached in one leap, step by step, or through a slow and steady process of development," and conceded that alliances would be permissable if the SPD did not thereby compromise its principles.[46] But they found no progressive middle class in the Rhineland with whom to cooperate. Neither the National Liberals, who were once again working with the Conservatives, nor the Center Party, which joined the ruling block just when Bernstein published his magnum opus, were the potential allies that revisionism presupposed. The Social Democrats' experience in the Reichstag and mediation court elections had convinced them of their isolation and led them to question the value of formal political institutions. As Woltmann, a Barmen Social Democrat who frequently spoke in Düsseldorf, argued, "universal suffrage is only an illusionary right which exists on paper. The only genuine rights are those behind which economic power stands. It is thus the task of the working class to gain economic power."[47]

The weak Düsseldorf movement had no union or party functionaries, no city councilmen, and only a handful of deputies on the health insurance boards and mediation courts. In short, there were hardly any of "the practical men" of working-class origin, who had broken out of their isolation by means of successful reformist work and who were the main supporters of revisionism elsewhere.[48] Unlike Social Democrats in such cities as Bremen, who opposed revisionism because it endangered reformism, those in Düsseldorf attacked it precisely because it advocated reformism in its most extreme form.[49]

The Düsseldorf Social Democrats, who defined themselves in terms of their principles and aims more than in terms of their meager concrete achievements, were convinced that if the party altered its theory, it would lose its identity. They saw revisionism, quite correctly, as an explicit rejection of the traditions that had "nourished collective memory and class consciousness."[50] As Erbert argued in the *Volkstribune*, abandoning socialism "would represent a complete break ... We would no longer be Social Democrats but merely Democrats."[51] The end goal must be everything or the movement would be nothing. For the Düsseldorf Social Democrats, Marxist theory offered hope in the face of repeated failure and served as a substitute for the tradition that they lacked. Abandoning it would create confusion and dissention in the ranks. As one member argued passionately before the 210 workers who came to discuss the 1901 Lübeck party congress, if the SPD failed to condemn Bernstein, "no one can know today how our organization will look in later years. It could come to pass that old and good party members will be expelled from the organization precisely because they hold firm to the old principles."[52]

All these dangers were stirred up by a controversy that the Düsseldorf Social Democrats considered tedious and unproductive. Grimpe and Windhoff, the delegates to the 1901 national party congress, complained that "the Bernstein problem" had been blown up all out of proportion. A year later 100 members endorsed a resolution regretting that the Munich party congress "lost so much time due to the fight among the academics."[53] The *Volkszeitung* suggested, with a mixture of sarcasm and seriousness, that "Bernstein should try fighting on the outside, that is, against our enemies, and not devote himself exclusively to brooding over problems."[54] The Düsseldorf Social Democrats did not underestimate the importance of theory or seek to emancipate themselves from it, as did those reformists such as Auer, who espoused *Praktizismus*, a desire to avoid theoretical questions entirely and pursue reformist work.[55] They did object to what they considered incorrect theory and to "the hair-splitting arguments of our highly learned theoreticians."[56]

The longer the revisionist controversy dragged on, the angrier the overwhelmingly working-class Düsseldorf Social Democrats grew at Bernstein and his fellow "washed-up academics," who, in the words of Zilles, "have no proletarian experience or sensibility."[57] To the Düsseldorf movement, the academic was an unknown entity, a priori suspect because of his birth, superior education, and propensity to look down on workers. When several bourgeois intellectuals became vociferous proponents of revisionism, the Düsseldorf Social Democrats attacked them as part of their defense of the revolutionary, proletarian character of the SPD. According to Grimpe, many bourgeois intellectuals "dedicated themselves to socialism only when they failed in their careers. Once they established a firm foothold and became functionaries, they were lax in fulfilling their duties."[58] The local party wholeheartedly endorsed the

Dresden party congress' condemnation of intellectuals who wrote for the bourgeois press.[59] "If a Social Democrat cannot earn money by writing, he should learn another trade," remarked the metalworker Milow indignantly. "The party does not exist to give individuals a helping hand financially." When Schildbach and Walther disagreed, the audience drowned them out with shouts of disapproval.[60] The local Social Democrats opposed expelling bourgeois intellectuals, but urged the national leadership to watch them carefully. All agreed that intellectuals were needed to elaborate the party's doctrine.[61] As the *Volkszeitung* noted, however, all too often

They disturb social theory, which has developed during the two decades of the modern workers' movement, by their eternal doubts, and in their practical activity they do not represent the interests of the entire movement. Rather they use their formal education to limit the mental horizons of the workers.[62]

In Düsseldorf, as in so many other areas, the Social Democrats defended Marxism without embracing militant tactics. Orthodox theory, isolation, and reformist work all coexisted without undue tension, because the latent contradictions were analyzed only by the reformists and revisionists.[63] As a result, the Düsseldorf Social Democrats did not recognize the seriousness of the doctrinal and tactical differences within the movement. The very fact that they reduced revisionism to "the Bernstein problem" is indicative of their terrible shortsightedness. Lacking knowledge of the movement elsewhere, they blithely assumed that all other groups shared their conception of revolution and of German capitalism and politics. Thus, they regarded Bernstein as no more of a threat to party unity than Vollmar had been, for neither was considered representative of substantial sectors of the movement.[64] The bourgeois parties and the government might gloat over growing reformism and predict impending splits, noted the *Volkstribune*, but "such idle talk is so silly that it does not deserve serious refutation."[65] Already after the 1901 Lübeck party congress, the Düsseldorf Social Democrats announced enthusiastically that "social democracy is unified. We disagree over details... We are divided over the 'how' of our struggle... We all want to struggle. We want to fight as part of the class struggle and for a great goal... the end goal of the expropriation of the expropriators!"[66] When the 1903 Dresden party congress overwhelmingly rejected revisionism, the Düsseldorf Social Democrats were pleased and relieved, but hardly surprised that "the revisionists suffered defeat upon defeat."[67]

During these years the Düsseldorf Social Democrats were closer to the emerging party center, led by Bebel and Kautsky, than they had been in the early 1890s or were to be after 1905. Like the national party leadership, they retained both their reactive, defensive tactics and their isolation from state and society. Like them they rejected Luxemburg's call for an active, offensive strategy, centered around the militant fight for social reform, which would raise political consciousness, intensify the class struggle, and maximize the interaction between social democracy and society.[68] Düsseldorf, like Berlin, found the Kautskyan synthesis of revolutionary theory, reformist tactics and isolation appealing not because it served as an "integrating ideology" that unified the party, but rather because it offered an analysis of and means to deal with the ambiguous, stalemated society that was Imperial Germany.[69]

The national and local movements came to Kautskyanism by different historical paths, however, and applied its particular mix of revolutionary theory and reformist practice to quite different situations. The national party, operating from a position of relative strength, used Kautskyan centrism as a means to protect its organizations while maintaining its identity and aspirations. The Düsseldorf movement, stuck in a position of embarassing weakness, adopted Kautskyanism in order to defend principles and explain away the lack of practical accomplishments or radical action. The strong and the weak came together briefly behind a common strategy. Yet once the Düsseldorf Social Democrats overcame their powerlessness, they were to abandon Kautskyan passivity in favor of more militant confrontations with state and society. And the ground-work for that shift to the left was laid during the revisionist controversy, when the Düsseldorf Social Democrats, so unified in their condemnation of Bernstein, fought so bitterly to reform the party's organization, press, and leadership.

The party war

On the national level, the turn-of-the-century movement crisis was primarily theoretical and tactical, but on the local level it was above all organizational. Stagnation in the economy brought stagnation in the movement. By 1902 fewer than 4,000 workers were in the trade unions and only 530 had joined the party.[70] According to Erbert, "no sooner is a worker won for the trade unions or the political organization than he quits. They don't benefit him. They don't protect him from wage cuts and unemployment. He thinks he should save the money he once paid out for dues."[71] The party lacked visibility and structural coherence; the press was plagued by financial and editorial problems; and no stable, effective leadership emerged. Although the Social Democrats finally won the mediation court elections in 1901 and again in 1902, the government instituted proportional representation in order to preserve the influence of the Catholics.[72] In the national arena, the alliance of Conservative Junkers and National Liberal industrialists reconsolidated itself around agrarian tariffs and naval building, and the Center Party approved both in order to enhance its parliamentary power and promote its religious interests, albeit at the material expense of most of its constituents.[73] As a result of this unfavorable economic and political conjuncture, the Social Democrats made little headway against the Center, big business, or the government.

Unable to alter the hostile environment within which they operated, the Social Democrats increasingly looked inward, seeking organizational solutions to problems that were social and political. Frustrated on so many fronts, they convinced themselves that if they could only find the proper organization for the party and press, success in all other areas would follow. In these years, they indeed made a fetish of organization, not because they were unwilling to act, but rather because they were unable to. For nearly five years, the Düsseldorf Social Democrats devoted themselves to experimenting with different forms of organization, establishing a fully independent press, and settling the interminable power struggles that resulted from these efforts. The issues were serious, but the battles of unprecedented intensity and bitterness absorbed all the movement's energies and temporarily paralyzed it. When the virtual civil war was over, however, the movement was stronger and the Social Democrats more united and self-confident then ever before.

The movement's organizational problems stemmed in part from the dual party structure, dictated by the Prussian organization law, which prohibited national political associations. Although the separation of the city-based, centralized Social Democratic Association and the county-oriented, loosely organized *Vertrauensmänner* system was irrational and counterproductive, the Social Democrats could legally reform only the individual parts.

In 1898 they centralized the *Vetrauensmänner* system by appointing one man to supervise the rest.[74] Simultaneous efforts to decentralize the floundering Social Democratic Association proved more controversial. The county *Vertrauensmann*, Windhoff, argued that "up to now all our efforts to increase membership have been futile ... The association absolutely must be given a helping hand and this can only be done by establishing district organizations."[75] Erbert, Spiegel, Lohse, and Kunisch insisted that decentralization would destroy the association, which they led and regarded as "the highest abode of *Bildung*." The members, after some hesitation, endorsed the reform, but it neither attracted new recruits nor bolstered sagging attendance nor compensated for the missing sense of direction. When the association leaders demanded that all those affiliated with the *Vertrauensmänner* join the association as well, nonmembers protested furiously that they were being treated as "second-class Social Democrats" and that membership entailed too many risks and too few benefits.[76] After months of angry debate, the demand was dropped.

Although this decision temporarily quieted the controversy, it did not prevent the consolidation of two factions, which split first over conceptions of party organization, then disagreed about how to run the paper, and finally fought bitterly for exclusive leadership of the local movement. The larger and ultimately victorious group drew its supporters from the city and its leaders from the association. Veterans of the movement, such as Erbert and Huhn, played a major role, but the most prominent figures were relative newcomers to Düsseldorf, such as the cabinetmakers Wilhelm Schmitt and Peter Berten, the metalworkers Max Milow and Rudolf Walbrecht, and the storeclerk Emil Westkampf. They were overwhelmingly Protestant, migrant, and remarkably young. Erbert, at 36, was the old man in the group.[77] The opposing camp was based in the county and led by the *Vertrauensmänner*, who were also young, Protestant, and migrant. Windhoff, a factory worker, whom the police described as "a very intelligent and articulate man" and "an extremely energetic agitator," was the undisputed leader. He received invaluable support from Wessel, the editor of the *Volkstribune*.[78]

The conflict resumed in 1900, when the Prussian government dropped the legal barriers to a unified structure. Berten, Erbert, Schmitt, and Huhn, believing that the loose party around the *Vertrauensmänner* produced "very questionable consequences," required all urban Social Democrats to join the association, retaining the *Vertrauensmänner* system only in the county where "it is not yet possible to establish formal organizations." Windhoff and his allies claimed that such discriminatory measures would curb free speech, expose workers to police and employer harassment, and discourage activism in the county. Both factions argued their cases at a series of stormy meetings, which drew crowds of 150 to 300 workers.[79] The rank and file, previously indifferent to local party affairs, realized that questions central to the development of the movement and their relationship to it were being debated.

Windhoff persuaded most Social Democrats that centralization would be ineffective, dangerous, and undemocratic, and in November 1900 more than 500 voted to restore the old dual structure. "The hatchet is buried," noted the *Volkstribune* editor Wessel with satisfaction. "Three weeks ago we appeared to be hostile brothers. Now we are brothers and comrades." And the unresolved differences? They were papered over with the vague formula that "the association should be the backbone of the party, and the *Vertrauensmänner* should be coordinated with it."[80]

Centralization had not been a panacea, but decentralization worked no better than in the past. Moreover, short-lived experiments with radically different structures created confusion and accelerated the deterioration brought on by the economic crisis. By late 1901 the demoralized leaders of the association even debated dissolving the organization.[81] Finally, unable to resolve the controversy, both factions tabled it and turned to the equally urgent problems of the press.

Party and union leaders, Social Democratic workers, and even the paper's editors had become bitterly critical of the *Volkstribune*, for its circulation was low, its finances precarious, and its coverage thoroughly inadequate. Relations between Düsseldorf and Elberfeld grew ever more acrimonious, and when the *Freie Presse* unilaterally decided to expand itself and the *Volkstribune*, thereby making the latter prohibitively expensive, the angry Düsseldorf Social Democrats established their own, fully independent paper.[82] The first editorial captured the party's enthusiasm about the *Düsseldorfer Volkszeitung*. "What the Düsseldorf working class had hoped for for more than a decade, what still appeared to be utopian a few months ago, has now become a happy reality: Düsseldorf has an independent daily organ of the Social Democratic party." The editors promised to produce "a fighting paper for workers

and artisans, for the little people... for the exploited and the en-
slaved."[83]

This initial euphoria quickly evaporated, for the Social Democrats had
to devote all of their energies and much of their money to keep the
venture afloat. Even though, as the Lower Rhine Agitation Committee
proudly noted, "the Düsseldorf comrades worked extremely diligently
for their paper," doubling the number of subscribers, it remained nearly
bankrupt, and its first two managers had to be fired for incompetence
and financial corruption.[84] Wessel argued that "the party executive
should intervene for once and support the *Volkszeitung*. We need it
desperately, more desperately than many districts with so-called 'big
men' as leaders."[85] National and provincial spokesmen, however, not
only refused aid but also chastised Düsseldorf for insubordination.[86] The
Social Democrats, feeling more isolated and mistreated than ever,
renewed their determination to build a viable press, but whereas the
Schmitt faction advocated a complete reorganization and new personnel, the Windhoff group recommended only minor changes in the
status quo.

The *Volkszeitung* thus became "a source of annoyance" for one and all.
At the numerous party discussions about the press, which were
punctuated by occasional fistfights, each faction flung exaggerated
charges of financial and sexual misdeeds at the other and called their
opponents "Lumpen"— the most insulting label one class-conscious
worker could pin on another. The warring factions did bury their
differences temporarily when they agreed almost to a man that the strike
of the women who delivered the paper was "treasonous."[87] Antifeminism could not create lasting bonds, however, and the struggle
resumed with its former intensity. The Social Democrats took out their
frustration, accumulated during a decade of failure, on one another. As
Berten pointed out, Düsseldorf seemed to be "the district where the
most can be accomplished... Therefore the unsatisfied ambitions of
individuals never rest."[88]

Although "many workers became aware of the socialist movement as a
result of the controversy,"[89] initially involving themselves in the debates
and agitating for the new paper, by 1902 they avoided the endless
meetings, where repetitive discussion led to no agreement. They
cancelled their subscriptions to the *Volkszeitung*, whose contents deteriorated as its debts mounted.[90]

The crisis came to a head in July 1902, when the printer Greven refused any further credit and the paper stood on the verge of collapse. The Schmitt faction, seizing the initiative, won widespread approval for having the party take over formal ownership of the paper, whose editors were now required to present periodic public reports. The association leaders, Schmitt, Berten, Born, Böttcher, Kremser, Milow, Huhn, and Jantzen, won election to the press commission, thereby securing control over the *Volkszeitung*.[91] The Social Democrats seemed on the way to restoring unity and establishing efficiency. However, the paper's publisher, Wasser, would neither cooperate nor resign, and Windhoff and his supporters cancelled their subscriptions. Undeterred, the Schmitt faction fired Wasser and published the paper under the slightly altered title, *Volkszeitung, Organ für das werktätige Volk am Niederrhein*. After promising that "nothing about the entire unbearable row would appear in the *Volkszeitung*," Düsseldorf finally received aid from the national party.[92]

Encouraged by their victory, Schmitt, Berten, and their allies persuaded a majority of Social Democrats that "the entire leadership of the party must be given to the association and the *Vertrauensmänner* system must be dissolved." All urban party members were required to join the association, unless this would endanger their jobs, and the urban Social Democrats took steps to establish branches of the association in the county.[93] After years of failure with decentralization and dual leadership, the Social Democrats were firmly convinced that only centralization would promote efficiency, combine recruitment and education, co-ordinate national and local concerns, and restore peace between the city and the county.

The Windhoff faction, defeated, dislodged from power, and deserted by the vast majority of workers, angrily refused to accept unity on these terms and launched a doomed campaign to reverse the recent reforms. The county party declared its independence from the city association, and Windhoff, Wasser, and Büchter repeatedly disrupted meetings of the association. They even sponsored their own gatherings, where they not only impugned the integrity of the association leaders but also urged their followers to cancel their *Volkszeitung* subscriptions – and with some success. Finally, Windhoff pressed libel and embezzlement charges against Erbert, Böttcher, and Peters in the courts – the courts so detested by the Social Democrats.[94] Grimpe wondered in despair "how these men can still call themselves party comrades."[95]

By the fall of 1903 the majority of Social Democrats, repelled by the opposition's actions as well as by their growing syndicalist tendencies, expelled Wasser, Windhoff, and Büchter.[96] The opposition immediately appealed the decision to a party mediation court, which enthusiastically endorsed the reforms but reprimanded Schmitt, Huhn, and Walbrecht for maligning their opponents. It found Wasser, Windhoff, and Büchter guilty of putting up "unjustified and stubborn" resistance and agitating against the *Volkszeitung*, but refused to expel them on the grounds that their irrational behavior was produced by the prolonged "party war."[97] Both sides, unhappy about this inconclusive judgment, appealed to the national party control commission, which upheld the lower decision but went on to expel Windhoff, who was judged "conscious of the injustice of his actions at the time he was engaging in them."[98] Although he, as well as Wessel and Büchter, who had resigned from the party in protest, continued to agitate, their support dwindled to virtually nothing.[99] Many Social Democrats had been willing to dissent within the party, but few were ready to attack it from without. The experience of illegality had taught them to value unity above all else.

With the opposition defeated, Schmitt, Berten, and their allies completed their reform of the *Volkszeitung*, firing Wessel, who had aroused much opposition by his incompetence, sympathy for Windhoff, and dismissal of socialist literature as "trash." On the recommendation of the national party, they hired Heinrich Laufenberg, an experienced journalist and former Center Party intellectual.[100] The choice was to prove a happy one. They then created a uniform and centralized organization, adding four rural districts to their eight urban ones. Each elected its own leaders, who were responsible for collecting dues, conducting agitation, and holding meetings "on interesting and educational themes."[101] In late 1904 Gewehr, the chairman of the Lower Rhine Agitation Committee, noted with satisfaction that "the activity of the comrades in Düsseldorf deserves special mention. Since they introduced their new organization, the situation there has developed well."[102]

The Schmitt faction not only reformed the organization and the press but also provided the movement with the stable and effective leadership that it so sorely lacked in the 1890s. Berten, Schmitt, Milow, Walbrecht, and Westkampf, who gained wide experience in the protracted party war, were to guide the Social Democrats in the coming period of expansion and militant confrontation with expertise and confidence.

The benefits they brought the movement outweighed the loss of Windhoff and his supporters, a loss that severely weakened the already shaky county party.

By late 1903 the Social Democrats had resolved their most acute internal difficulties. Although they still faced serious external obstacles, they were able to deal with them more effectively, for they no longer sought organizational solutions to problems that were social and political. Equipped with a centralized structure, a viable press, and talented leaders, the Social Democrats were able to take advantage of the growing conservatism of the Center Party, the continued influx of migrants, and the return of economic prosperity. They were to enter a period of unprecedented expansion in which they learned the emptiness of reformism and the limits of radicalism. The years of frustration had finally ended.

PART II

Ambiguous success and radicalization:
1903–1912

After the failures and frustrations of the 1890s and the turmoil of the turn of the century, the Düsseldorf Social Democrats entered a decade of unprecedented expansion and accomplishment. Possessed of a new confidence and sense of direction, they reversed previous defeats, became active in ever more political and cultural areas, and gained a high degree of autonomy from their comrades elsewhere and their opponents at home. The working class, once divided between staunch supporters of the Center and the politically indifferent, was mobilized and educated by the Social Democrats. As thousands of workers flocked to the movement, the party and unions gained a public visibility and organizational stability undreamed of in the 1890s. The Social Democrats significantly limited the Center Party's power in national and municipal politics and steadily eroded the social and ideological power of political Catholicism. Even the unions, despite setbacks, flourished as never before.

Structural changes in the economy and the working class, the growing conservatism of political Catholicism, and the successful resolution of the "party war" laid the groundwork for this impressive progress. But it was the Social Democrats' ability to take advantage of these changes that transformed possibilities into actualities. They developed party, union, and cultural organizations that served workers' educational and recreational needs, defended their material interests, and offered them an alternative community. They solved the agitational and educational dilemmas that had crippled them in the 1890s.

These accomplishments, however, despite the claims of many historians, did not lead the Düsseldorf Social Democrats to become more integrated into the state and society or more reformist theoretically and tactically. Quite the contrary. They moved from the national party's center to its left wing in the years from 1903 to 1912, becoming severe critics of parliamentarism, reformism, and bureaucratization and enthusiastic proponents of the mass strike. They advocated tactical innovation and confrontation rather than passivity. As they discovered, progress was uneven and circumscribed. Numerical growth and organizational strength could not be translated into effective political and economic power. Expansion did not end the Social Democrats' isolation from the institutions and values of the dominant society. Both success and failure, the character of the Düsseldorf movement and the nature of its environment, the limits of reformism and the allure of radicalism pushed the Social Democrats steadily to the left and yet prevented them from acting fully on their convictions.

Part II will analyze the ambiguous success and radicalization of the Düsseldorf movement between 1903 and 1912. Chapter 5 will present a sociological portrait of those who joined the movement, who shaped its institutions and ideology and were shaped by them. Chapter 6 will analyze the construction of an effective party organization and a workers' culture, both of which were central to the creation of a unified working class in Düsseldorf. Chapter 7 will investigate the continued struggle between the Center Party and the SPD as well as that between unions and employers in the period from 1903 to 1906, the years of greatest optimism. Chapter 8 will trace the Social Democrats' subsequent move to the left in the struggles around Prussian suffrage, nationalism, militarism, and budget voting. Chapter 9 will explore the movement's frustrating return to a more reformist practice in national and municipal politics after 1910.

5

Skilled migrants, peasant workers, and native Catholics

Between 1903 and 1912 an ever-expanding number of Düsseldorf workers moved from sporadic protest to sustained political activity. Some were attracted by social democracy's militant defense of working-class economic interests, others by its principled struggle for political reform, and a third group by its rich associational life. And neither political setbacks nor economic recessions turned workers away from the movement as they had in the past. Party membership rose from 950 in 1903 to 2,560 in 1907 and topped 7,000 by 1912. Trade-union growth was even more spectacular, expanding from 5,403 in 1903 to 13,030 in 1907 and on to 24,920 in 1912.[1]

Far from recruiting a representative sample of the Düsseldorf working class, however, both the unions and the party drew disproportionately from select groups of skilled, migrant, and relatively young workers. An examination of who these workers were, what situations they found themselves in, and why they joined the movement will not only provide a profile of the membership, missing from most studies, but will also help explain the radicalism of the Düsseldorf Social Democrats. It will illustrate how social democracy was able to benefit from continued industrialization and migration and serve the interests of those drawn into Düsseldorf's work force while the Center Party proved unable to meet the needs of new proletarian groups. Because detailed information on party and union membership and on the structure of the labor force is available only for the 1896–1908 period, the analysis will focus on those years.[2]

A workers' propensity to join a union or socialist party cannot be deduced from any single factor, economic, political, or cultural. Models which assume that the working class behaves homogeneously and in response to the state of the economy and the standard of living are clearly untenable. Reductionist theories, which assert that a worker's attitudes and actions are structurally determined by his or her position in

99

the production process are likewise problematic, for although they acknowledge diversity within the working class, they simplify its origins and deny self-activity to the workers. Nor are noneconomic monocausal explanations more credible. Although political forces are integral to the creation of workers' consciousness and behavior, full citizenship, like prosperity, does not necessarily integrate workers. Nor does authoritarianism automatically provoke rebellion any more than does economic crisis. Culture is one force that shapes a worker's life-style and perceptions, but it is neither all-powerful nor immutable.[3] Workers make their own history, albeit under circumstances given rather than self-chosen, and diverse groups of workers make it in quite different ways. The given circumstances, structural, political, and cultural, go far toward explaining the distinct patterns that emerge.

It is necessary to analyze the economic structures that workers encountered, above all the organization of work, for the objective situation in which they found themselves varied enormously and could lead workers with similar backgrounds to act in markedly dissimilar ways. But it is equally important to determine the world views that workers brought to their work situation. Differing attitudes toward industrial work, skill, authority, independence, and urban life, as well as expectations about life experiences, led diverse groups of workers to react in varied ways to the same situation. A worker's world view, in turn, was determined by a complex of factors – birthplace and social background, migratory patterns, religion, education, and job training. Very often, the expectations engendered by the world view and the opportunities available were radically at odds, forcing workers to redefine the former, alter the latter, or both.[4]

The following chapter will delineate the opportunities available in Düsseldorf, the expectations of its workers, and the strategies employed to cope with discrepancies between them. Using records on the 4,259 adult males who joined the Düsseldorf SPD between 1896 and 1908, it will examine the importance of occupation, religion, birthplace, and age.[5] It will explain why certain groups of workers turned to social democracy as a means of interpreting and coping with their political, social, and work situations and how, in turn, social democracy was able to shape that response.[6]

The socialism of skilled workers

Although Düsseldorf had a mixed economy and diversified social structure, the social democratic movement was overwhelmingly prole-

Table 5.1. *New party members from 1896 to 1908 by skill level and class*

	1896 (36 of 37)[a]		1897 (28 of 210)		1898 (23 of 41)		1899 (129 of 186)		1900 (33 of 149)		1901 (116 of 167)		1902 (52 of 223)	
	No.	%	No.	%	No.	%	No.	%	No.	%	No.	%	No.	%
Skilled, semiskilled	34	94.4	23	82.1	19	82.6	95	73.6	27	81.8	102	87.9	44	84.6
Unskilled	1	2.8	5	17.9	4	17.4	33	25.6	6	18.2	13	11.2	8	15.4
Independent	1	2.8	0	0.0	0	0.0	1	0.8	0	0.0	1	0.9	0	0.0

	1903 (0 of 305)		1904 (23 of 104)		1905 (365 of 525)		1906 (859 of 1116)		1907 (907 of 941)		1908 (228 of 235)	
	No.	%	No.	%	No.	%	No.	%	No.	%	No.	%
Skilled, semiskilled	0	0	15	65.2	307	84.1	658	67.6	632	69.7	159	69.7
Unskilled	0	0	6	26.1	49	13.4	191	22.2	269	29.7	65	28.5
Independent	0	0	2	8.7	9	2.5	10	1.2	6	0.6	3	1.3

[a]Number with occupational data out of total number of new members.

Source: Stadtarchiv Düsseldorf, III 6923–33, 1896–1908.

tarian, as Table 5.1 shows. Although blue-collar workers comprised only 55 percent of the labor force in 1907, they accounted for 99 percent of the more than 900 new party members. Between 1896 and 1908, records list only 33 small tradesmen, store clerks, office workers, administrators, innkeepers, and the like. These figures underrepresent the actual number of petty bourgeois and bourgeois members, for 49 fell into this category by 1908, but they do accurately indicate their relative insignificance.[7] Academics and intellectuals, who figured prominently in the party in Bremen, Berlin, Munich, and Leipzig, were likewise all but absent in Düsseldorf. Laufenberg was simply the rare exception who proved the rule. Berten admitted that he "forgot to register now one or another, when it involved well-known businessmen or civil servants," but it is highly unlikely that the Catholic and liberal business communities or the strongly nationalistic and conservative bureaucracy harbored many secret Social Democrats.[8] As a result, 98 percent of the total membership in Düsseldorf in 1906 was working class as opposed to 92 and 77 percent, respectively, in Leipzig and Munich, which had comparable economic and social structures, and 85 percent in more industrial Dortmund.[9]

The overwhelmingly proletarian character of the party reflected the rigid class divisions in Düsseldorf. The traditional lower middle class looked to the guild movement and political Catholicism for guidance and protection, whereas the new white-collar class, among whom no unions existed, turned either to the Center Party or to liberal groups of one political shading or another. They found adequate channels for political representation outside the social democratic movement. Intellectuals occupied a marginal position in a city with a powerful Catholic hierarchy, a cultural life supported by the business elite, and no university. Most remained either hostile or indifferent to the SPD, and, as we saw earlier, the SPD reciprocated.[10] The composition of the party, which paralleled that of the unions and electorate, also increased class antagonisms. The more proletarian the party became, the less attractive it was to disaffected bourgeois groups and, conversely, the longer such groups remained outside the party, the less interested it became in trying to recruit them. The Social Democrats saw no reason to modify their goals, theory, or tactics in the hope of attracting bourgeois elements, which might well prefer a conciliatory course. The movement catered exclusively to working-class interests, for the working class unequivocally dominated the movement.

In Düsseldorf, as throughout Germany, skilled and to a lesser extent semiskilled workers joined most readily, accounting for 76 percent of all new recruits over the twelve-year period. The unskilled, which included all those described as workers, factory workers, unskilled metal and construction workers, and day laborers, began joining in numbers only after 1905, but accounted for 30 percent of the new recruits and 14 percent of the party's total membership by 1908. The predominance of the skilled resulted not only from their economic and cultural position but also from their numerical preponderance in the working class as a whole. In 1907, 60 percent of all workers in Germany were skilled or semiskilled, and in Düsseldorf, where the machine-making and construction industries dominated, the percentage was probably even higher. The vast majority of new members were employed in the industrial sector even though only three-quarters of all blue-collar workers were. In 1907, for example, 75 percent of the recruits fell under this rubric, and the 20 percent who held unclassifiable unskilled jobs probably worked where the majority of politically active and strongly unionized skilled workers did.[11]

The SPD, like the unions, recruited most unevenly from workers in the industrial sector, as Figure 5.1 shows.[12] Although metal was undisputably king in Düsseldorf, employing one-third of the blue-collar labor force by 1907, metalworkers did not join the union or the party as readily as their less numerous comrades in construction or woodworking. Metalworkers were 98 percent male, relatively highly skilled, and well paid, receiving 4 M to 6.50 M per day by 1906. Throughout much of the period, however, they were proportionately underrepresented in the party, accounting for only 22 percent of the total membership as late as 1906. Only in 1908 did they reach the 33 percent mark. The industrial DMV was the largest union in the Düsseldorf cartel, but in 1907 it had recruited only 4,035 of the city's 20,443 metalworkers, and only one-eighth of these were also party members. Within the union, and presumably within the party also, the most skilled craftsmen, namely, the fitters, turners, and molders, predominated.[13] This disappointing record can be explained only by looking at the organization of production, the recruitment of different occupations, the policies of employers, and the response of workers.

The metal sector consisted on the one hand of machine building, instruments, and other metalworking, employing more than 16,000 workers, and on the other of basic iron and steel, employing roughly

Figure 5.1. Percentage of the working class and of party recruits in different sectors of the Düsseldorf economy. The statistics for the entire working class cover all skill levels; those for the party include only skilled and semiskilled, because information on the unskilled is inadequate to assign them to a sector. Note that the occupational statistics for the working class are for 1895; the party statistics are for 1896. *Sources:* See Tables 5.2 and 5.4.

4,000. In the machine and metalworking sectors, the labor process had not been rationalized to any significant degree, and skilled workers were able to exercise the full range of their technical expertise and enjoy relative autonomy on the shop floor. Despite changes in technology and the organization of production in the decade before World War I, which weakened the position of some skilled workers, such as the turners, these sectors remained a bastion of the skilled working class from which most of the union and party members were recruited.[14]

Not so heavy iron and steel, where mechanization, intensification, and dequalification had proceeded much farther and where the union barely had a foothold. As a 1910 DMV investigation of the iron, steel, pipe, and wire industries in Germany stated with awe, "the simply unmeasurable accomplishments of modern technology are most successful and most thorough in the iron industry."[15] It went on to admit with dismay that this technological change, far from benefiting the worker or shortening the work day, had intensified work, without even a compensatory pay hike. At the Mannesmann pipe factory, for example, workers doubled productivity in three years under the pressure of increased supervision. In the rolling mill workers had to do setup during their lunch break and for no extra pay. At Rheinmetall technological changes decreased employment in some divisions while zealous foremen increased productivity in others.[16]

As we saw, metalworkers had no collective bargaining. Wage rates varied enormously, not only among plants but within them as well. In both machine building and iron and steel there were well-developed and managerially controlled piece-rate scales, and attempts were made to imitate American premium bonus and incentive systems.[17] Different skill levels and occupations were ordered into finely graded hierarchies, which had little technical justification but which aroused resentment and increased competition among workers. In the Düsseldorf Pipe and Iron rolling mill, for example, Martin furnace workers earned from 3.90 M to 6.35 M depending on their job, whereas the three classes of puddlers received from 6 or 6.50 to 8 or 8.50 M. In the Oberbilker tin rolling mill, helpers made 4.50 M a shift on piece rates, cutters 4 M, walzers 5.72 M, and oven workers 9.40 M.[18] Unionized members in metalworking and machine making generally worked ten hours a day, but employees in basic iron and steel had twelve-hour shifts, which allowed virtually no time for political or union activity. The propensity to organize, as the Social Democrats were well aware, moved inversely with the length of the working day.[19] Although the DMV tried to unite workers with different trades, skill levels, wages, and work days, more often than not it failed to recruit precisely because of them.

The fragmentation and compartmentalization caused by the division of labor was intensified by the diverse origins of different groups of workers. Skilled metalworkers were recruited primarily from artisanally trained craftsmen, who had broken their ties with the land, were committed to industrial work and urban life, and wanted an autonomous and challenging job.[20] Their craft and the culture and community built around it gave these workers a clear sense of their identity as workers and of the rights and recognition that were their due. Both their world view and their current position as either skilled or dequalified semiskilled workers provided a basis from which they could organize and protest.[21] The unskilled and many of the semiskilled came from agricultural backgrounds and either still lived on the land or returned there periodically. They identified primarily with their rural roots and regarded industrial work as a temporary expedient to raise the income necessary to remain on the land. What limited skills they possessed had been learned in the factory and were often specific to it. They showed little interest in their work, and from a mixture of fear, deference, and instrumentalism, followed orders and settled for low wages. The two groups came from different geographic regions as well as social backgrounds, and this further increased the likelihood that skilled and unskilled would compete rather than cooperate if they interacted at all.[22]

The size and structure of the metal industry was geared to isolating workers. In metalworking only 21 to 30 percent of the workers were in plants with fewer than 50 employees, in machine making only 16 to 24 percent, and in heavy iron and steel a scant 4 percent. More than 25 percent of all machine makers, however, and 49 percent of iron and steel workers were in factories employing 500 or more.[23] The work situation in these large firms undermined what little solidarity might have survived skill hierarchies, wage differentials, and cultural differences. In heavy industry many were forbidden to leave their machines, and noise, a fast work pace, and prying supervisors further reduced contact among workers.[24] Large machine-making firms like Rheinmetall were organized into a series of relatively autonomous small and medium-sized workshops. Such compartmentalization both isolated the skilled from the semiskilled and unskilled and increased the latter's dependence on foremen. It virtually precluded that informal on-the-job contact that was so vital both to trade-union recruitment and politicization.[25]

These large firms also practiced a mixture of authoritarianism and welfare paternalism that effectively curbed organization.[26] The Düsseldorf Social Democrats repeatedly complained that large plants like Springorum, Haniel and Lueg, Oberbilkerstahlwerk, and Hohenzollern Lokomotiv were more like prisons than factories. They fired activists, blacklisted "troublemakers," and sometimes required workers to pledge that they were not and never would become trade-union members.[27] Men like Ehrhardt, whose biographer described him as "an outspoken master who forced his will on others," were proud of their *Herr-im-Haus* stance.[28] Factory ordinances, such as that from the Ernst Scheiss machine tool firm, listed in painstaking detail the workers' obligations and the steep fines for failure to fulfill them but made no mention of wages, hours, or workers' rights.[29] More than 60 percent of the Rhenish and Westphalian iron and steel workers surveyed by the DMV complained that they were treated unsatisfactorily or badly. Those in Düsseldorf were no exception. At Rheinmetall workers objected to being called "Lumpen" and told to "shut up" if they complained. At the Düsseldorf iron and steel works, workers claimed that foremen not only swore at them but also hit and kicked adolescent employees.[30] In 1900 the large firms formed the Union of Employers in the Metal Industry in Düsseldorf to curb unionization and cooperate in case of strikes.

But they did not restrict themselves to repressive measures. In 1903, for example, 72 city and 36 county firms had management-run insurance programs. By 1910, 25 provided housing for some employees. Others offered libraries, lectures, singing clubs, and athletic facilities.[31] Such welfare institutions, established from a mixture of anti-socialism, paternalism, and economic rationality, both bound workers to the company and greatly increased the costs of unionization and political activity.

Although workers throughout the metal industry disliked conditions in the large firms, protest took the form of quitting more often than organizing. This was especially true among the unskilled and in basic iron and steel.[32] And high turnover rates made unionization still more difficult. Not surprisingly, the Düsseldorf Social Democrats recruited primarily in the small and medium-sized metalworking and machine-making firms, which were a peculiarity of Düsseldorf and employed fewer than half of its metalworkers. Those who were organized "enjoyed a reputation for being solidly behind the class struggle,"[33] but that radicalism was largely a product of their weak and beleaguered position in the face of organized capital and technological change.

Workers in the numerous artisan trades of the construction and woodworking industries were the most highly unionized and politicized groups in Düsseldorf as they were elsewhere.[34] As Figure 5.1 indicates, construction workers were consistently and quite dramatically over-represented in the party. In the late 1890s carpenters and joiners participated most readily, whereas thereafter painters, roofers, and above all the rapidly growing masons became active. By 1907, 3,654 of Düsseldorf's 8,070 construction workers were in one of the five skilled and one unskilled building unions, and one-sixth of these had joined the party as well. The 302 masons, 96 carpenters, 63 plasterers, 35 painters, 17 roofers, and 91 unskilled helpers represented a quarter of the total membership. Social democracy was even more popular in the much smaller woodworking trades. In 1907 nearly one-third of Düsseldorf's more than 3,000 woodworkers were union members and 307 were in the party. Although woodworkers comprised only 5.4 percent of the working class, they were the third largest block within the party.[35]

The highly skilled and overwhelmingly male workers recruited into both sectors had generally received an artisan training even though they had never been nor could they ever hope to be independent masters. They had learned not only the skills and secrets of their trade but also its ethos of craft control, autonomy, pride in workmanship, and egalitarianism within the artisan community. Carpenters, masons, wheelwrights, and cabinetmakers worked in trades that had a long tradition of organization. Until the third quarter of the nineteenth century, the journeymen's organizations within the guild system created solidarity, taught collective forms of action, and provided a vehicle, however weak, for asserting social and economic interests against the masters.[36] Such associations fostered the development of craft unions, which established firm roots in the 1870s and weathered the repression of the 1880s better than most.[37]

Many skilled construction workers and woodworkers probably came to social democracy by a route similar to that of the cabinetmaker and movement leader Berten. Berten grew up in a small Rhenish village where his father eked out a precarious existence doing carpentry work for local farmers and making weaving stools for the regional putting-out system. He helped his father as a child and after finishing elementary school learned cabinetmaking from him. In 1891, at the age of 18, he became an itinerant journeyman, for job prospects in the countryside were meager indeed. Moving from city to city in the Lower Rhine, he rounded out his training, learned the realities of urban, proletarian life, and became a Social Democrat. While employed in Dortmund, he encountered the woodworkers union and signed up without hesitation. A few years later, after participating in lively political discussions at union meetings, he joined the party as well.[38] Far from being an impediment to unionization and politicization, the craft tradition in Germany, like its counterpart in Britain and France, encouraged them by giving workers both a commitment to urban life and industrial work and a sense of the rights that were due those with skills.

Construction and woodworkers, like skilled workers in small and medium-sized machine-building firms, enjoyed an advantageous position in the division of labor and on the labor market. In the wake of rapid urbanization and industrialization, construction was the fastest-growing industry in Düsseldorf, woodworking prospered, and the demand for labor was high except during recessions.[39] Of equal importance, neither mechanization nor rationalization was extensive. Carpenters and masons lost some of their autonomy and planning initiative to architects and new building firms, and both large businesses and small guildmasters tried to cut costs by intensifying the pace of work. Woodworkers were forced to specialize somewhat.[40] By and large, however, construction and woodworkers did not suffer displacement or deskilling.

The structure of both industries further aided organization. Although construction was becoming increasingly concentrated, in 1907 between one-third and one-half of the employees still worked in firms with fewer than 50 employees.[41] Workers moved from one employer to another, depending on the availability of work, and from one building site to the next. Carpenters, masons, roofers, painters, and plasterers thus had extensive contact with other members of their own trade and with other trades as well. Far from being segregated into their own tasks, the unskilled worked intimately with the skilled, especially the masons. This led in 1910 to the merger of the masons and their helpers into the industrial Construction Workers' Union. Cooperative work and informal camaraderie did much to overcome the differences between the skilled artisans and the unskilled, who like their counterparts in metal, were frequently from the land and still tied to it.[42]

The situation was different but no less favorable in woodworking. Workers were less mobile, but the various woodworking trades had extensive contact with one another in the numerous small and generally unmechanized firms of that sector. They also exploited the guild revival to their advantage. Nearly 50 percent of all woodworkers were in shops with fewer than 20 employees, and by 1904 more than 38 percent of those shops had joined the cabinetmakers' guild, partly in order to prevent unionization and restore patriarchal relationships. Social Democratic woodworkers, however, used the journeymen's committee, which the guild was legally required to establish, as a means of strengthening the influence of the union and party. The process was repeated among carpenters. By 1907 the guild chamber lamented that "the Social Democratic party leadership absolutely controls the journeymen."[43]

Wood and construction workers benefited from the handicaps that accrued to employers as a result of the small scale and labor-intensive character of the industries and their dependence on local markets and seasonal work.[44] Both small guildmasters and larger building and wood-working firms knew that the intransigence of the metal entrepreneurs was a luxury they could ill afford. Neither the guilds nor the employers' associations, which encompassed guild and nonguild firms alike, were powerful enough to prevent unionization or curb strikes. Company work rules contained few of the draconian provisions so frequent in metal. Employers had wanted the state to pass restrictive picketing laws in the late 1890s, but when the Penitentiary bill failed in the Reichstag in 1899, they accepted defeat, recognized the unions, and bargained collectively with them on the local and regional levels. To be sure, employers fought all concessions strenuously, even resorting to a massive lock-out in woodworking in 1906.[45] Yet they knew that they were engaged in a prolonged war with a powerful opponent and could at best hope for periodic negotiated cease-fires.

As a result of all these advantages, both construction and wood-workers were able to form strong unions, which won local and regional collective contracts. Wages, once described as "too much to die and too little to live for," rose by 1906 to 4.50 M a day for helpers, 5 M to 6.50 M for masons and 5.50 M to 6.50 M for carpenters. This at least partially compensated for the seasonal unemployment, which ranged from six to twelve weeks, and for the decline in the secondary employment among construction workers. Although many unskilled, both German and foreign, worked part of each year in agriculture, most of the skilled were entirely dependent on their primary earnings.[46] Wood and construction workers, who often de facto enforced a closed shop,[47] were able to maintain the egalitarianism of the craft community and prevent the divisive wage hierarchies so prevalent in metal. They also secured a ten-hour day, thereby assuring enough free time for both family life and movement work. By winning these benefits, the trade unionists paved the way for yet more extensive organization. And this in turn fed still more workers into the party, for the skilled in both sectors were well aware that they maintained their position only through constant vigilence, struggle, and organization – political as well as economic. Rather than falling into a narrow craft exclusiveness, these workers sought political power commensurate with their economic position and provided political leadership for the rest of the working class.

No such solidarity was evident among the remaining highly skilled group, the printers. Although nearly half of the city's 1,200 printers were unionized by 1907, only 51 had joined the party. To the dismay of other workers, Düsseldorf's printers, like their colleagues throughout Germany, were elitist and convinced that the indispensability of their skills made purely economic struggles efficacious.[48]

Workers in Düsseldorf's remaining factory industries, chemicals, paper, and fats and oils, formed less than 4 percent of the proletariat and provided only a handful of party recruits. These industries were technologically advanced, highly rationalized, and recruited their unskilled and semiskilled labor force from among marginal workers with no previous training. By 1903 a third of all chemical workers and a quarter of those in paper were women. These vulnerable workers made only 3 M to 3.50 M for a ten- or twelve-hour day if male and 1.50 M to 2 M if female. Roughly half worked in plants with 50 to 500 workers. None of these industries had a tradition of organization, and none developed unions. Although a few workers joined the unskilled factory workers' union, most, to quote the *Volkszeitung*, "were so economically oppressed and intellectually deadened" that they tolerated deplorable work conditions and wages "in silent resignation."[49] The situation was hardly more promising in the Gerresheim glassworks. Mechanization was being slowly introduced in the wake of capital's victory in the 1901 strike, and "Russians were being lured there en masse, only to be threatened immediately with expulsion if it were even suspected that they belonged to an organization."[50]

Workers in food, clothing, and shoemaking, who formed more than 12 percent of the working class, belonged to the disadvantaged artisan sector that could be neither unionized nor politicized readily. Mechanization threatened the skilled in all three areas, forcing many into specialization, repair work, or the factory, and creating new unskilled and semiskilled strata. Employers, large and small, intensified the pace of work, hired an increasing number of women, and where possible, used subcontracting and putting-out. Between 1895 and 1907, for example, the proportion of women in food rose from 10 to 20 percent and in clothing from 51 to 63 percent. Although there were large breweries and bakeries and a few sizable tailoring establishments, 40 percent of those in food, 60 percent of those in clothing, and more than 70 percent in shoemaking worked in shops with fewer than six employees.[51] And most small firms were in the tailors', bakers', and shoemakers' guilds, which were much more effective at maintaining a patriarchal relationship in their shops than at warding off factory competition.

Workers in these sectors lacked a tradition of organization, and the structure of the industry perpetuated that. To be sure, 14 percent of the skilled male tailors and a comparable proportion of the skilled shoemakers were unionized, and the brewery workers formed a fairly powerful organization. Despite strikes and even boycotts called by the union cartel and party, however, these men were unable to win decent wages and reasonable hours for themselves.[52] They could do nothing about the extreme exploitation of women and male apprentices. If construction and woodworkers showed that some artisans could hold their own while industry and capitalism expanded, food, shoe, and clothing workers proved that many more fell victim to those forces.

Longshoremen were the only group in the commercial sector at all receptive to social democracy. By 1907 nearly 900 had joined the newly formed union and had won a ten-hour day and wages ranging from 4 M to 6 M. Hotel and restaurant employees, as well as blue-collar workers in trade, remained unorganized. Forty percent worked in firms with less than six employees; many actually lived with their employers, and a growing proportion were female. Some were trapped in deference, whereas others had "a certain social arrogance" that led them to shun working-class politics. They had no tradition of organization and received little attention from a movement hard-pressed to organize workers in central industries such as metal.[53]

The Düsseldorf Social Democrats, in summary, were primarily skilled construction, wood, and metal workers, who had an advantageous position in the labor market and division of labor. They had received artisan training and absorbed the culture of the skilled trades. They regarded themselves and were regarded as full-fledged and permanent members of the urban, industrial working class. They had, as well, particular patterns of migration that make them, unlike many other workers, migrant or native, receptive to social democracy.

Permanent migrants and peasant workers

Düsseldorf, with its expanding and diversified economy and relatively high wage scale, was a mecca for migrants from all social classes. It attracted both those forced out of their preindustrial background by poverty and those who came voluntarily in search of opportunity. Some stayed permanently, but most remained a few months or years before moving on to another town or returning to their rural roots. By 1907 migrants made up two-thirds of the working class and more than four-fifths of the domestics.[54] As Table 5.2 shows, the Social Democrats recruited almost exclusively from this migrant element. Since native Düsseldorfers were remarkably sedentary, whereas those who had moved once usually did so again, the proportion of migrants in the total party membership was probably somewhat smaller than these figures suggest. Nonetheless, the Düsseldorf SPD was clearly a party of the "outsiders."

Political Catholicism had claimed the allegiance of the native-born working class before social democracy became a significant force. And native workers were particularly receptive to the Center Party's over-tures. Although the native working class does not appear to have had a markedly different occupational structure than its migrant counterpart, a larger proportion of it was Catholic. Native workers were born and raised in a strongly Catholic environment, where family and neigh-borhood ties reinforced religious ones and social life revolved around the parish and Catholic associations. Far from being unmobilized and therefore potentially receptive to new political ideologies, they were fully integrated into the Catholic milieu, albeit as junior partners. If these workers were to reject political Catholicism, they would have to break not only with their past but also with their present, to leave not only a political party but a way of life. Not surprisingly, few did, leading Social Democrats such as Künisch to complain about "the human material with which we have to work."[55] Between 1896 and 1902 only 53 natives joined. In 1903 alone more than 40 followed suit, but that was simply a temporary protest against the Center Party's support of grain tariffs. Not until 1907 did Berten note "a remarkable change for the better," and a year later the *Volkszeitung* stated proudly that an ever larger percentage of members were native Catholic workers.[56] The growing conservatism of the Center was beginning to alienate even some of its most loyal supporters.

Table 5.2. *Birthplace of new party members*

		Düsseldorf		Major cities[a]			
Year	New members	City (%)	County (%)	Ruhr/Rhine (%)	Other (%)	Other (%)	Foreign (%)
1897	156	4.5	1.3	7.1	9.6	76.3	1.3
1900	84	8.3	3.6	2.4	9.5	73.8	2.4
1903	301	13.3	2.3	4.7	7.0	72.4	0.03
1906	639	11.1	1.6	5.6	8.9	72.0	0.8
1908	148	18.2	2.0	6.8	6.8	65.5	0.7

[a]Cities with more than 100,000 inhabitants in 1905.
Source: Stadtarchiv Düsseldorf, III 6923–33, 1896–1908.

The migrant population in Düsseldorf, which numbered more than 141,000 in 1905, was extremely heterogeneous. Fifty-two percent of all migrants were from the Rhineland, and the majority of these, in turn, came from the economically well-developed areas within a 50-kilometer radius of Düsseldorf. Neighboring Westphalia, which had a similar economic structure, provided nearly 15 percent of the newcomers. Migrants from more distant provinces, who had come in relatively small numbers in the late nineteenth century, accounted for 28 percent of the new arrivals by 1905. The remaining 5 percent were foreigners, primarily from Holland, Belgium, Austria, and Italy. Some of these migrants came from areas that were economically underdeveloped in comparison to Düsseldorf, others from towns with a similar industrial structure but a lower wage scale. A slim majority of migrants came from small and medium-sized towns, whereas only a third had been born in rural areas and a surprisingly high 15 percent in cities of more than 100,000. An additional 11 percent had lived in a major city before arriving in Düsseldorf. Nearly 60 percent were men and most, whether male or female, were between 20 and 40 years of age. A large proportion but not a majority were Protestant. Finally, although some had left their homes permanently to settle in Düsseldorf or another town, many others regarded urban, industrial work as a temporary expedient that would enable them to return to the land.[57] It was the permanent migrants from more urban backgrounds, Catholic as well as Protestant, who joined the social democratic movement, whereas the temporary and very transient remained outside the party and unions.

Many of those who moved to Düsseldorf neither intended to remain nor did so. Throughout the period, outmigration was nearly as high as inmigration, and many of those who left had only recently arrived. At the end of 1905, for example, one-third of those who had come since January and two-thirds of those who had arrived in 1904 had departed.[58] Adolescent artisans and factory workers, who were permanent members of the industrial work force but had not settled down to one job or one town, composed part of this unstable, floating population. Although some became involved in the social democratic movement, and many others would in their 20s, most teen-agers were either too transient or preferred amusements to politics. Foreign workers, whether skilled or not, were also temporary migrants, who were more interested in returning home than striking roots and struggling in Germany. The social democratic movement lacked the resources to try to persuade them otherwise, even though it realized that unorganized foreign workers undercut the economic and political position of German ones.[59] Finally, the small Polish-speaking contingent from the east was, according to Berten, "unreceptive due to the language barrier and religious fanaticism."[60]

The majority of temporary migrants were neither youths nor foreigners, but peasant workers who, whether they had left the farm on a one-shot basis or regularly sought industrial work, were concerned above all with earning enough to maintain themselves and their families on the land. Some, such as the unskilled construction workers from the Eifel, came seasonally. Others, like the unskilled in iron and steel, stayed for more irregular and often longer periods. None, no matter how precarious the rural situation, intended to stay for good. They had an instrumental attitude toward their dead-end, unskilled jobs. They were even more detached from urban life, with which they had little social or political contact and which they viewed with indifference or hostility.[61] Many came from economically backward and strongly Catholic areas such as the Eifel, Kempen, Cleve, and Geldern. Often they were directed to their destination by their parish priest, stayed in Catholic hostels, and kept the faith.[62] Nothing in the background from which they came or the work situation they encountered in Düsseldorf encouraged union involvement or political activism. These peasant workers did not want to find meaningful industrial work or adjust to urban life, but rather aspired to escape both. Only if that escape route were cut could they be mobilized.[63]

Migrant artisans, skilled factory workers, and some of the semiskilled were much more receptive to social democracy – and not merely as a result of the interaction between their training and expectations on the one hand and the work they found on the other. These men moved with different intentions than those of the peasant workers, and migration had a very different impact on their political behavior. They, or their families before them, had broken their ties with the rural world and preindustrial forms of production. They generally came from small and medium-sized towns where they had learned an artisan trade or done factory work. They were committed to industrial work, and whether they moved from necessity or by choice, sought skilled, high-paying work that offered autonomy and, if possible, craft solidarity. These workers were also socially and psychologically committed to urban life. Ten to twenty percent of the new recruits each year had been born in cities of more than 100,000, and others had spent time in them. All knew that they would remain in Düsseldorf or a comparable town and therefore needed the means to cope with a hostile environment.[64]

Although few of these migrants had joined the movement before coming to Düsseldorf, they were more open to new political attitudes and organizations by virtue of either having broken with their past or coming from a past conducive to activism. They looked to the party, the unions, and the associations of the social democratic culture to help them better their work situation, win political concessions, and adjust to urban life. The movement thus offered both a community for workers inextricably enmeshed in an industrial capitalist economy and urban society and a vehicle for improving, if not fundamentally altering them. And the Catholic permanent migrant joined almost as readily as his Protestant counterpart.

The skilled Protestant migrant was undoubtedly the best potential recruit, for by definition he was excluded from the dominant Catholic milieu as well as from the upper-class and quite conservative liberal culture. The interconfessional Christian unions were in practice overwhelmingly Catholic appendages of the Center Party. The liberal Hirsch-Duncker trade-union movement, after prospering briefly at the turn of the century, had entered a period of strife and decline that reduced its membership to 800 by 1907. The Protestant Workers' Associations, which according to the police "provided the nationalistically inclined Protestant worker with a firm bulwark against the destructive effects of socialist agitation," attracted scarcely more followers.[65] In a society where all spheres of activity were politicized,

Protestant migrants could look only to the social democratic movement to represent their interests and offer equality and solidarity in its institutions. Without social democracy they would have been as isolated and adrift as the peasant workers – indeed, more so because they had no alternative world to which to return.

The ever-growing number of skilled Catholic migrants also found their way into the movement. Nearly all Catholics in the leadership came from this group, and the Catholic majority in the SPD electorate did as well. As worker autobiographies show, migration weakened traditional relationships and attitudes and increased the likelihood of coming into direct contact with social democracy. Catholic workers generally left home, lost the faith, or loosened their ties with the church, and only then became Social Democrats.[66] According to the *Volkszeitung*, the migrant "was liberated from the tyranny of tradition and from his literal belief in every word uttered by the clergy."[67] Thus, many who arrived in Düsseldorf were already seeking an alternative to political Catholicism, and like the Protestants, discovered that there was nowhere else to turn but to the social democratic movement. Others who were still religious may have tried to assimilate into Düsseldorf's Catholic milieu but found it either closed or too conservative. Catholic culture, which held the native working class so strongly, could not adapt to the needs of migrants, who demanded more politically and socially at a time when the class conflicts within political Catholicism enabled it to give ever less. As we shall see, the political fortunes of the Düsseldorf Center Party were ultimately to be decided by these Catholic migrants.

Social democracy thus continued to be a movement of the mobile and marginal rather than the stable native born, but capitalist development made migrants the predominant element in Düsseldorf. And these migrants were receptive not only to social democracy but also to radicalism. They had broken with traditional authority patterns and social relationships as well as preindustrial modes of existence. Yet within Düsseldorf they occupied a distinctly marginal social and political position, which was particularly galling in view of their economic centrality. They were either excluded from the dominant culture or had explicitly rejected its very moderate postulates. Unable to leave their situation or find allies with whom to reform it piecemeal, they sought radical solutions.

Although migration brought many workers into the movement, it was not an unmixed blessing. Even skilled workers, permanently committed to urban, industrial life, moved when opportunity beckoned or, as was more common, unemployment struck. In addition, during major strikes and lock-outs single workers had to leave town in order not to deplete union funds. As Table 5.3. shows, working-class mobility bordered on instability and led to an incredibly rapid turnover in party and union membership in Düsseldorf as in other cities. In 1906 and 1907, for example, the party gained nearly 2,000 new members but lost almost 1,000. Seventy-one percent of those who left did so because they moved from Düsseldorf, whereas only 16 percent were expelled for non-payment of dues and 12 percent simply quit. Thereafter the percentage migrating out was even higher.[68] In order to organize, educate, and integrate these highly mobile workers, it was, as we shall see, absolutely essential for the party and unions to have a stable core of functionaries.[69] A certain irreducible level of bureaucratization was dictated by the unalterable facts of working-class life.

Politics and age

The skilled Catholic and Protestant migrants in the primary labor market who formed the bulk of the union and party members were quite young. Indeed, the receptivity to social democracy correlated very closely with age. In the years between 1896 and 1908, 50 to 65 percent of the party's recruits were in their 20s, 10 to 15 percent in their early 30s, and another 10 percent in their late 30s. The mean age of those joining hovered between 27 and 29. The party had almost no success in attracting workers in their late teens or those over 40. Although Düsseldorf's industries attracted a young labor force, younger workers were nonetheless recruited out of proportion to their representation in it. The Catholic Workers' Associations, by contrast, drew primarily from those between 30 and 45 and had a sizable contingent of those over 45.[70]

The age at which workers joined reflected not the particular histories of different generations but rather the common experiences and expectations of those who became permanent members of the industrial working class in late nineteenth- and early twentieth-century Germany. The 27- or 28-year-old who joined in 1896 had known prolonged recession, frequent high unemployment, and political repression, whereas a worker of the same age who joined in 1908 had enjoyed prosperity and legality for the movement. What they shared was a similar life pattern.[71]

Table 5.3. *Party membership fluctuations*

	1905–6		1906–7		1907–8		1908–9		1910–11	
	No.	%	No.	%	No.	%	No.	%	No.	%
Total new members	1,888		1,968		1,183		1,307		3,911	
First time joining	1,818	96.3	1,694	86.1	966	81.7	1,074	82.2	3,242	82.9
Joined elsewhere	70	3.7	274	13.9	217	18.3	233	17.8	669	17.1
Total leaving	354		987		915		1,372		2,006	
Emigrated	290	81.9	700	70.9	693	75.5	1,052	76.7	1,647	82.1
Unknown	25	7.1	0	0.0	0	0.0	0	0.0	0	0.0
Quit	23	6.5	118	12.0	81	8.9	132	9.6	102	5.1
Stricken[a]	11	3.1	160	16.2	136	14.9	178	13.0	237	11.8
Dead	5	1.4	9	0.9	5	0.5	10	0.7	20	1.0

	1911–12		1912–13		1913–14		1914–15	
	No.	%	No.	%	No.	%	No.	%
Total new members	4,654		2,527		3,148		955	
First time joining	4,015	86.3	2,087	82.6	2,778	88.2	764	80.0
Joined elsewhere	639	13.7	440	17.4	370	11.8	191	20.0
Total leaving	3,022		2,255		2,743		4,167	
Emigrated	2,599	86.0	1,915	84.0	2,223	81.0	1,331	31.9
Unknown	0	0.0	0	0.0	0	0.0	0	0.0
Quit	124	4.1	85	3.8	181	6.6	249	6.0
Stricken[a]	268	8.9	226	10.0	308	11.2	335	8.0
Dead	31	1.0	7	0.3	31	1.1	91	2.2
Drafted							2,161	51.9

There is no information available for 1909–10.

[a] For nonpayment of dues in most cases.

Sources: "Jahresberichten der Sozialdemokratischen Partei Düsseldorf," *Volkszeitung,* July 13, 1906; July 23, 1907; July 23, 1908; July 28, 1909; July 21, 1911; July 26, 1912; April 25, 1913; April 22, 1914; April 23, 1915.

The vast majority of working-class children received only an elementary school education, and many worked part time before joining the labor force permanently at age 14. Most adolescent boys chose their initial jobs rather haphazardly, taking any available opportunity or seeking high pay rather than choosing a trade in which they were interested or following family tradition. Whether they seved an apprenticeship or took a semiskilled factory job, they were likely to change jobs and often locale repeatedly for the next five to eight years. They had neither secure jobs nor families to tie them down, and all faced the possibility of military service. Although they lacked the options of the peasant workers, many "had the feeling that they did not have to remain permanently in their occupation, that they could still perhaps change their fate."[72]

Their experiences and expectations militated against union and party activity, and the state and the movement reinforced this tendency. The government prohibited minors from joining political parties, and systematically harassed the ostensibly nonpolitical youth association that the Social Democrats formed after 1909. The Social Democrats, for their part, were slow to concern themselves with the problems of young workers. Nationally the unions neglected young workers while the party sought to subordinate the independent and quite radical youth movement that sprang up in various cities after 1904.

Locally, the Social Democrats, quite young themselves, did not worry about whether the next generation would carry on their work. They did not even begin to discuss the youth question until the national party prompted them and Catholic, Protestant, and nationalist associations began to organize adolescents. In 1909 they finally established a youth commission. Within a year more than 200 teen-age boys and girls were participating regularly in its activities, and by 1912, 800 subscribed to the paper *Arbeiter Jugend*.[73] Although neither the party nor the police described these young workers, it is probable that they came from the same background as those who joined at a later age.

Workers in their 20s and early 30s had more job security and geographic stability than their younger colleagues. They had generally settled into an occupation and were enjoying their peak earning years. Yet they also had more responsibilities and expenses, for many were married and had children. Unlike adolescents or peasant workers, they could not view inadequate wages, periodic unemployment, poor education, bad housing, and lack of upward mobility as transitory phenomena. A 24-year-old with 10 years' work experience, a man in his early 30s with 16 to 20 years on the job, could hardly sustain such an illusion. From necessity and realism they became involved in the movement.

Older workers seldom joined the party or union. If a worker had not become active after 40 years of proletarian life and 25 or more of work, he was unlikely to change his mind in middle age, when his earning power was declining and his economic position becoming more precarious. The small number of new members in their 40s and 50s had probably joined the party elsewhere and then migrated to Düsseldorf.[74]

The Düsseldorf SPD not only recruited young workers but overall had a younger membership than many other locals. On the one hand, the party's belated growth meant that there were few veterans of the years of illegality or even the 1890s. On the other hand, the high turnover assured a steady influx of men in their 20s.[75] There was not the generation gap between members and leaders in Düsseldorf that there was elsewhere. The average age of the two dozen top leaders in 1908 was only 38, whereas the average age of the 29 lower-echelon leaders was 36 and those who were to join the leadership between 1909 and 1914 were 31 in 1908.[76] The young members, like the young leaders, were new to politics and venerated neither the established party and union organizations nor the grand old men of the movement. They were unencumbered by the vested interests and anxious conservatism that characterized older Social Democrats, and as a result were much more receptive to radicalism.

Women

Women have been strikingly absent from our analysis of the social democratic movement because they were not included in the membership statistics collected before 1909 and, even more important, because they were marginal to both the work force and social democracy in Düsseldorf. The experiences and expectations of proletarian women made activism improbable, often impossible.

As a result of industrialization, women lost their previous economic position and found work only with difficulty, for Düsseldorf was dominated by metal, wood, and construction rather than textiles, food, and clothing, where most women were employed.[77] Düsseldorf women had low-paying, insecure jobs in the secondary labor market if they had jobs at all. In 1895 there were nearly 34,000 male workers in manufacturing and commerce and only 5,546 female ones. Another 2,040 women were casual laborers, and 6,078 were domestic servants. By 1907 the number of domestics had increased by half again, whereas the number of wage workers had doubled even though women remained concentrated in the relatively unimportant, unprosperous, and unorganized sectors of the economy. Nearly 3,000 women worked in clothing and cleaning, where they formed well over 50 percent of the labor force in the numerous small, unmechanized firms of that sector. Another 3,000 were in trade, and more than 1,200 were waitresses, chambermaids, and dishwashers. Nearly 800 women worked in textile factories and almost 700 in the food business. Only 267 of the 20,710 metalworkers were women, whereas a mere 71 were employed in wood and exactly 6 in construction. As late as 1904, more than 70 percent of the 3,000 women registered with the insurance fund earned only 1 M to 2 M a day. By contrast, only 6 percent of the male workers were paid so abysmally.[78]

Women workers were even younger and more transitory than their male counterparts. In 1902, 57 percent were under 21 and only 15 percent were married. Few remained in Düsseldorf's shops and factories, for little in the work was appealing or liberating. Not only were wages extremely low in the nonunionized sectors where women were concentrated, but hours were also longer, and women were often forced to take home additional work in order to survive. Factory inspection, inadequate in any case, focused on large firms in which few women were employed. Not surprisingly, most women withdrew from industry and domestic service once they were married and had children. They took work into their homes or did more casual jobs in the neighborhood, going back to the factory only when their husbands earned too little, were sick, or died.[79] In their lack of commitment to industrial work, these women were similar to peasant workers. But they had no alternative world to which to retreat. Rather, they moved in and out of the labor force in order to assure the survival of a working-class family in an urban, industrial society.

The large group of domestic servants was even more removed from both the native born and the skilled migrant working class. Like the peasant workers, whose daughters they often were, they came directly from farms or small villages in the area around Düsseldorf or in neighboring Westphalia and remained closely bound to their past. Their personal relationships were with the families for whom they worked or with their own families in the countryside, not with the Düsseldorf working class.[80]

Many Catholic women were much more religious than men. Although few male workers had formally left the church, most male Catholic workers who migrated to Düsseldorf did not participate in Catholic associations or heed the authority of the clergy in political matters. Among women, however, there was not this strong correlation between mobility and declining religiosity, for both migrants and natives were closely tied to the church. They participated actively in the Catholic associational life, read the Catholic press, and were subject to moral pressure from the clergy. According to the Social Democrats, for example, priests visited women at home and urged them to pressure their husbands to quit the movement.[81]

This economic and social situation led to weak unionization and political indifference among women and to hostility toward them among men. Women were objectively difficult to organize due to the structure of the industries in which they worked, the feminization of the labor force in them, and their lack of a trade-union tradition. Because women were temporary workers in marginal sectors, men made little effort to unionize them, despite social democracy's theoretical commitment to women's work and politicization. Indeed, neglect often verged on a kind of proletarian antifeminism, for women, lacking options, accepted miserably low pay and thereby depressed the wage level. Such behavior by the unions and party in turn generated apathy or antipathy in women workers.[82]

Efforts to break out of this vicious circle in the early 1890s were short-lived and unsuccessful. At the suggestion of the national party, the Düsseldorf Social Democrats formed an Educational Association for Women and Girls in 1892 and a Women's Agitation Commission a year later. At first only ten or twelve women, all of whom were married to leading Social Democrats, participated, but after a year their number had risen to forty or fifty. Because women were prohibited from joining political parties, the women's organizations were separate and ostensibly nonpolitical. Neither the police nor the courts regarded such formal autonomy as real, however, and by 1894 both the Educational Association and the Agitation Commission had been fined and dissolved.[83] Repression killed the little activism that had developed in Düsseldorf's inauspicious economic and cultural climate.

For the rest of the decade the male Social Democrats hardly even discussed the woman question, let alone acted on it. The *Volkstribune*, summing up the prevailing opinion, asked "is there any purpose in wanting to 'make' a women's movement?" It quickly answered in the negative, arguing:

Women, already backward as a result of their schooling, are scarcely involved in public life. They spend all day doing housework and hardly have a spare hour for reading and party activities. Thus it is hardly surprising that women remain backward, especially since numerous comrades scarcely concern themselves with the progress of women in a political sense.

The political attitudes of women were thus explained and excused by their social situation, but at the same time women were criticized and dismissed because they were not only backward but were seemingly condemned to remain so forever. The Social Democrats saw women not as a promising or even neutral element but as an explicitly negative one. Yet their only strategy for dealing with them was to chastize "the numerous comrades, married for years ... who have not managed to convince their wives of the truth of our theories."[84]

When the women's movement revived after 1902, it owed little to the male Social Democrats. Rather, Gotthusen, Weiss, Wiertz, and Kählen, all of whom were nonworking women married to local Social Democrats, took the initiative. After three years of failure, during which the restrictions on women's political involvement were eased but not removed, they succeeded in establishing both a Support Organization for Women and Girls with 25 members and a loosely structured Women's Organization with 160. A year later the *Volkszeitung* enthusiastically claimed that "there are several hundred members in the women's movement," but failed to specify who they were.[85] Nor are other sources available. Presumably most were older women, employed in factories and shops, for such women joined in other cities. Although some nonworking wives of Social Democrats were active as well, few unmarried women or domestics were likely to have participated. Female Social Democrats remained a rarity until after 1908, when the government lifted all prohibitions against party membership. Then, as we shall see, women joined en masse, becoming a strong and militant element in the movement.

These workers whom we have examined – largely young, male migrants, relatively highly skilled and religiously mixed, were the raw material from which the successful social democratic movement in Düsseldorf emerged. They were simultaneously committed to industrial work and urban life and unintegrated into the dominant social and political order. Privileged in some respects and powerless in others, they were unable to fulfill their hopes and expectations in the hostile environment of Düsseldorf. As they turned increasingly to social democracy, they built a rich associational life, which both met their particular needs and laid the institutional basis for challenging political Catholicism and industrial capitalist power.

6

Party building and popular culture

After the resolution of the party war, the Düsseldorf Social Democrats turned from quarreling about how the party should be built to building it. They concentrated on breathing life into the new structure by making the party a viable presence in every working-class neighborhood in the city and county. They sought to improve the *Volkszeitung* and expand political education programs as well as to enlarge the leadership cadre. At last they established an effective mass movement that offered workers responsibilities and opportunities and challenged the organizational superiority of the Center Party.

Not content to remain a political party narrowly conceived, the Social Democrats strove to create a rich associational life that would teach workers alternative values, fulfill their needs for education and recreation, provide social services, and offer the experience of camaraderie and equality. They created a politically oriented workers' culture as part of their efforts to occupy the existing political space and compete with political Catholicism, to unify Düsseldorf's disparate workers and offer concrete aid to those opposing the dominant system.

These new and refurbished political and cultural organizations played a central role in attracting workers to the movement and integrating them permanently into it. They brought social democracy into working-class neighborhoods, into daily contact with workers' lives, and this compensated for social democracy's relatively weak base in Düsseldorf's factories. These organizations enhanced social democracy's ability to compete with political Catholicism and combat employers and the state. Finally, they helped unify the heterogeneous workers of Düsseldorf into a cohesive class – or at any rate, they unified those young, migrant, relatively skilled workers who flocked to the movement and whose interests it reflected and served. Success on the organizational front, however, did not translate automatically into power in the larger society, and the workers' culture that was created had an ambiguous relationship to both the dominant society and the political work of the party.

Overcoming organizational inferiority

The core of the social democratic movement was the party, and the Düsseldorf Social Democrats first directed their energies to strengthening that previously frail institution. In the years after 1903 they secured meeting places throughout the city and established a well-functioning district structure. They were able to convert electoral support into party membership and in turn to educate those new Social Democrats thoroughly. They overcame their previous institutional inferiority vis-à-vis the Center Party. And all this was accomplished under the guidance of a local leadership that was stable and effective without becoming oligarchic or bureaucratic.

In 1903 the SPD in Düsseldorf had nearly 24,000 supporters at the polls, but only one in four of these was a union member and only one in twenty-five had joined the party. Thereafter the Social Democrats were able to translate votes into membership both because they had improved their organization and because it was operating in a more favorable environment. By the 1907 Reichstag election, half of the 25,000 SPD voters were in a union and one-tenth were in the party. Twenty percent of the working class (and 24 percent of male workers) were unionized, and the ratio of union to party members had dropped from a high of nearly 13 to 1 in 1901 to just over 5 to 1, a figure that compared favorably to that in other major cities such as Frankfurt am Main, Munich, and Leipzig.[1]

Although encouraged by developments on the trade-union front, party leaders such as Grimpe, Berten, and Schmidt lamented that far too many workers remained "just trade unionists" and that the party reached only the committed or nearly converted and not the indifferent.[2] True as these criticisms were, the party had made significant progress in establishing roots among new groups of city and county workers and creating a richer, more intense relationship between the movement and its members.

The Social Democrats had least success penetrating the county, which, despite industrialization and urbanization, remained a stronghold of political Catholicism. In Ratingen the glasscutter Mager, the metalworker Markgraf, and Ferdinand Herweg were very active after the turn of the century, but they attracted only a few dozen workers to their educational association.[3] According to one discouraged movement agitator:

If you go to the Ratingen pubs on Sunday and listen to the workers talk, you think they are really determined to improve their existence. Naturally only around the bar. Ask one or another to join a trade union or political organization and suddenly they say their condition is quite satisfactory.[4]

The party managed to establish footholds in the towns of Hilden, Rath, Benrath, and Erkrath, but found that "in the industrial centers around Düsseldorf there is a whole series of comrades who are not able to be active politically . . . Currently the fear among comrades in the county is very great."[5]

In more rural areas the situation was nearly hopeless. One party worker complained that "when we go into houses with *Morgenroth* [a special publication for rural agitation], we are thrown out. They hate the magazine."[6] A Social Democrat distributing election flyers in Gustorf reported that "the entire day the Gustorfers warned me that I would not come out of the village alive." And when the bicycle club Solidarity rode into the hamlet of Stürzberg, they were chased away with pitchforks and dogs.[7]

Progress in the city was much more substantial. After 1904 the Social Democrats created thriving district organizations, whose engaged leaders conducted agitation, recruited members, and sponsored a wide variety of educational and social activities. In 1906 they tried to supplement this structure with a system of block captains.[8] As Berten noted, "the lack of sedentary party comrades was a major difficulty in implementing the block captain system, just as in general the fact that workers frequently change their dwellings impedes our organizing efforts.[9] Gradually, however, the party prevailed upon "older, resident party members to dedicate themselves to this detail work."[10]

Lacking meeting places in most proletarian neighborhoods, the Social Democrats begged and cajoled innkeepers to rent rooms. From 1903 to 1906 their efforts were in vain. Bitterness mounted over such "second-class" treatment, for as the Social Democrats argued, "the influence of our movement is constantly growing, and the innkeepers are ever more dependent on us." In 1906 the party abandoned persuasion for more forcible methods and proclaimed a boycott against all innkeepers who refused to allow political meetings. The *Volkszeitung* published daily lists of recalcitrant owners, and the boycott commission criticized unions and individual workers who failed to comply, insisting that "people who openly trample on our decisions do not belong in our ranks."[11] Over the next few years the Social Democrats coerced innkeepers throughout the city to open their doors to the movement.[12]

The Social Democrats were finally able to reach the worker in his neighborhood, and a worker needed to go no further than his local pub to participate in party activities. The movement, lacking firm roots in the factory, had at last established them in the community. The greater visibility of the movement and greater frequency of meetings and agitation facilitated both recruitment and education, for speeches and discussions were more effective than the written word with poorly educated and overworked proletarians.[13]

After 1903 members were much more involved in party life than they had been in the 1890s, both because the movement was more active and visible and because the party war had encouraged participation and illustrated the need for better organization and education. Workers not only conducted ongoing agitation but also attended meetings regularly. Gradually, "the *Zahlabend*, when members . . . gathered in the pub to pay contributions and talk things over, became not only the most important social institution of Social Democracy at the grass roots but also the focus of political opinion."[14] And political opinion was focused in very particular ways by the educational efforts of the leaders as well as by the interests of the rank and file.

The Social Democrats explicitly rejected the eclecticism that had characterized, and often crippled, their earlier educational programs in favor of a rigorously theoretical and political orientation. According to Spiegel, "it is necessary for the working class to learn the fundamentals of socialist theory."[15] Berten insisted that "meetings should discuss the party program and similar subjects which will promote the theoretical development of the comrades."[16] *Volkszeitung* editor Laufenberg argued that "the more the proletariat delves into theory and develops its tactics in line with it, the more quickly and certainly it will master threatening difficulties and the more confidently it will fight its battles.[17]

Workers responded enthusiastically to this emphasis on theory, history, and strategy. In 1905 and 1906, for example, more than 1,100 workers came to hear Spiegel and Kremser discuss the implications of the Ruhr miners' strike. Schulte's lecture on cultural development and historical materialism drew 250, whereas 200 heard Laufenberg's analysis of British municipal socialism and 160 his exposition of Engels' thought. More than 400 came to Molkenbuhr's talk on militarism, navalism, and colonialism. The district meetings, unlike citywide ones, relied on less experienced and less educated local speakers and shied away from theory in favor of history and radical critiques of existing institutions. In February 1905, for example, Jäcker presented an indictment of the mediation courts, Kremser spoke on the relationship between the party and the union movement, and other districts discussed the Prussian constitution and the International.[18] The party no longer offered workers general or remedial education, which had been appealing to the least politicized; rather, it offered a focused and coherent political training, which created a competent and confident rank and file.

Following the highly structured format adopted in the 1890s, all meetings opened with a report on the previous meeting, continued with a formal lecture, and concluded with a discussion period. Citywide meetings and public rallies intimidated members and encouraged passivity, for workers had to leave their familiar neighborhoods, mingle with hundreds of strangers, and listen to polished outside agitators. Having little education or speaking experience, they were understandably reluctant to question and criticize.[19] District meetings retained the old structure but proved more conducive to participation. They attracted from twenty to ninety of the most active Social Democrats, who knew one another well, and were held in neighborhood pubs that were more intimate and informal than downtown halls. Known local speakers were less polished than outsiders, and the rank and file, who often resented their lack of expertise, felt free to criticize them. Sometimes speeches were followed by silence or only a brief remark from the district leader, but quite often a lively discussion ensued.[20] For the core of the movement's membership, the district meetings partially fulfilled their assigned task of "training the comrades, giving them encouragement and stimulation and educating them to become discussion speakers."[21]

The education that workers received at party meetings was supplemented by the *Volkszeitung*, which was no longer aimed at the indifferent or hesitant but rather at those who, in Berten's words, "are advanced and enlightened in terms of principles and politics."[22] By 1906 the paper's 6,000 subscribers included all party members and two-thirds of the trade unionists but only one-quarter of the voters. Under the editorship of Laufenberg, who was an experienced journalist and an expert on political Catholicism and Marxism, the *Volkszeitung* intensified its attack on the Center Party, expanded its analysis of political and economic developments, and even improved its coverage of foreign news.[23] Special sections on science and culture, serialized novels, and supplements for women and youth were added in an effort to make the *Volkszeitung* more competitive with the Catholic *Volksblatt*, the *General Anzeiger*, and the *Neuste Nachrichten*. Laufenberg, Berten, and Erbert also devoted much more attention to the history, current practice, and internal debates of the movement. Finally, the editors used every possible opportunity to show the relationship between everyday experience and socialist doctrine, for as Laufenberg noted, "it is false to underestimate the theoretical education which the press not only can give the party comrades *but which under the given circumstances, it must give them*."[24]

These changes in organization, education, and the press were carefully planned and nurtured by the cadre of talented leaders who emerged during the crisis and were to guide the party until World War I. Peter Berten, a skilled woodworker with exceptional abilities as an organizer and agitator, was the dominant figure after 1904, serving frequently as head of the Social Democratic Association, paid party secretary and, after 1908, editor of the *Volkszeitung*. The movement's only bourgeois intellectual, Heinrich Laufenberg, who according to the police was "as intelligent as he was radical," exerted an enormous influence over both the press and the party from 1904 until his departure for Hamburg in 1908. The turner Emil Westkampf was almost as prominent as Berten and Laufenberg, holding numerous party offices before taking over the position of secretary from Berten. The metalworkers Heinrich Jäcker, Max Milow, Karl Spiegel, and Rudolf Walbrecht, all of whom were active in the DMV, played a vital role as district leaders and public speakers. The printer Heinrich Pfeiffer, who arrived in Düsseldorf in 1904, managed the education commission, and the fitter Hugo Schotte the *Volkszeitung*, while Heinrich Fischer from Weimar headed the newly established workers' secretariat. Ernst Erbert, the one vetran of the 1890s, and Wilhelm Schmitt, the key figure in the crisis years, devoted themselves principally to the trade-union cartel.[25]

These leaders, unlike their predecessors, were paid functionaries for the *Volkszeitung*, the party, individual unions, the cartel, or the secretariat.[26] As such they were able to acquire and transmit political knowledge, organizational expertise, and oratorical skills. They could coordinate the activities of the various institutions in which they worked.

Of perhaps greatest importance, they provided an element of stability and continuity for a membership that was as mobile as the working class from which it came.[27] These functionaries received a somewhat higher salary than most workers, had a great deal more job security, and enjoyed a degree of respect, power, and responsibility denied most of their fellow proletarians. Despite these advantages, they did not develop a petty bourgeois life-style, status, or self-perception. Nor did they become a closed elite, advocating cautious reformist policies.[28] However right Michels may have been about the oligarchic and bureaucratic character of the national leadership, he was certainly wrong about this, and probably many other local cases.

The Düsseldorf leaders were similar to those whose interests they represented and from whom they had been recruited. They were skilled workers from wood, metal, and to a lesser extent construction and printing. Nearly all were migrants, and several had lived in other Ruhr Catholic industrial centers before settling in Düsseldorf. More than two-thirds were Protestants, and only two of the two dozen top leaders were native Catholics. In contrast to their counterparts in areas where the movement had been established early, they were remarkably young, the average age in 1906 being 36. The Düsseldorf leaders saw themselves as an integral part of the working class and were seen as such by the dominant society. For reasons of class, politics, and religion, they were excluded from the established order, and the status they enjoyed within the working class was denied them outside it. Indeed, as the most visible symbols of the social democratic movement, they were actively harassed by the clergy, the Center, the police, and the courts. Half the leaders had criminal records, most from convictions for libel or violation of paragraph 153.[29] Certainly neither the traditional *Mittelstand* nor the emerging white-collar class considered these leaders petty bourgeois.

The Düsseldorf leaders were too new to their positions to have developed a closed caste mentality. Those from inside had risen to prominence in an open contest with the rival faction, whereas those from outside Düsseldorf, such as Fischer of the Workers' Secretariat, had been selected by a written competition.[30] They lacked national stature and close ties with national movement leaders, many of whom were indeed cautious, reformist, and in certain respects petty bourgeois. Far from being subservient to Berlin, the Düsseldorf leaders were frequently critical of it.[31] In short, the new leaders provided stability and efficiency without bureaucratic oligarchy. Rather than being reformist, they were to become the champions of radicalism after 1906.

As a result of their electoral and organizational progress, the Düsseldorf Social Democrats no longer felt inferior to their comrades elsewhere. Indeed, they assumed a leading role in the Lower Rhine region, speaking authoritatively rather than apologetically at regional party congresses, giving aid to less developed areas, such as neighboring Neuss, and providing a Reichstag candidate for their comrades in the nearby textile town of Mönchen-Gladbach. In 1906 they began publishing a monthly, *Korrespondenz Blatt*, which provided agitational materials for the region.[32] Düsseldorf did not usurp regional leadership from Elberfeld and Barmen, but it gained autonomy and responsibilities undreamed of in the 1890s.

The organizational balance of power between social democracy and political Catholicism also changed. As the Social Democrats recruited ever more workers and the Christian trade unions began to criticize the Center Party, political Catholicism looked to social democracy for organizational innovations.[33] The Center established a workers' secretariat, modeled on the social democratic one and staffed by workers. It encouraged the unions to form a cartel in imitation of their opponents. In municipal elections, although not in provincial ones, the Center Party slate included token working-class candidates.[34]

The Center's concessions to its proletarian base were more cosmetic than substantive. The Center Party did not commit itself to fight for working-class equality within the larger society or within the party. It could not, for after the turn of the century the powerful Berlin faction launched a massive attack on the Christian trade unions, insisting that only clerically led, anti-strike Catholic Workers' Associations were compatible with political Catholicism.[35] This controversy precluded reforms that might threaten clerical control or bourgeois and aristocratic privilege.[36] Thus the Center continued to be "the party which profited most from the agitational activity of its mass organizations and was least shaped or altered by them."[37] But the rate of profit was falling. Although the concessions satisfied workers who were already involved in the Catholic milieu, they were judged inadequate by many younger, migrant workers. The Düsseldorf Center Party gradually lost the organizational advantage it had long enjoyed over the SPD.

As the Social Democrats developed a more visible and active movement, they created a more knowledgeable, cohesive, and committed working class. The party became not only the defender of working-class material interests but also an alternative community, which offered workers opportunities denied them in the dominant society. The organizational expansion both consolidated previous gains and provided the structure and confidence that was to enable the party to become more active and radical in subsequent years. And party building, defined in relatively traditional terms, was accompanied by the creation of a rich social democratic culture.

The organization of popular culture

Once the frustrations and failures of the 1890s were behind them, the Düsseldorf Social Democrats seized the initiative culturally, just as they did organizationally. They sought to create a politically oriented working-class culture that would embody alternative norms and values and offer workers the experience of practical solidarity through a variety of associations and celebrations. This culture (a term that better connotes both the Social Democrats' aspirations for autonomy and the autonomy actually achieved than does the term "subculture"[38]) defined itself in opposition to both the dominant society and the proletarian cultures that developed more spontaneously around work and community. The Social Democrats wanted to avoid the exclusiveness, religiosity, and emulation of the bourgeoisie typical of many skilled workers and simultaneously to escape the defensiveness, conservatism, and self-containment of the unskilled. Their culture neither glorified the preindustrial past nor provided escapist diversions from the present but rather sought to work actively toward a socialist future.[39] It did so by emancipating workers from many aspects of the dominant culture, redefining some bourgeois ideas and institutions, and appropriating a few cultural forms in toto.

Although the Social Democrats accorded primacy to economic and political struggles, they recognized that man does not live by bread or politics alone. They valued not only politically relevant knowledge but also literature, art, and music, both classical and popular, and tried to give workers the opportunity to develop all aspects of their lives. The creation of a social democratic culture was a means of meeting working-class needs for education, recreation, and service and thereby assuring that they would enjoy at least some of "the fruits of civilization" from which the dominant society excluded them.

Yet the Social Democrats also viewed culture instrumentally. They developed a rich associational life as part of their effort to occupy existing political space and define new areas as relevant to the conflict between social democracy and German society. The culture both served as a substitute for the dissenting tradition that Germany lacked and provided structural support for those opposing the system.[40] Cultural activities were to strengthen commitment and raise consciousness, but not supplant politics. As the movement leaders constantly reminded their followers:

A good comrade is not someone who joins the workers' singing, athletic, swimming, stenographic, health, and other organizations or regularly attends the activities of the educational commission but only someone who is an active member of the party and trade union.[41]

Finally, and perhaps most important, a class-conscious culture was a vehicle for overcoming the cultural barriers that divided skilled and unskilled, migrant and native, Catholic and Protestant in Düsseldorf's fragmented working class. As an examination of associational life, educational programs, and festivals shows, the social democratic achievements on the cultural front were impressive, but their political impact was much more ambiguous.

An extremely diverse set of recreational, service, and educational organizations, some of which dated from the late 1890s, others of which were founded after 1903, formed the institutional framework of the social democratic culture. By 1907, 350 Düsseldorf workers had joined the athletic associations; nearly 200 participated in the singing groups that had sprung up in nearly all proletarian neighborhoods. Eighty acted with the theater club, Sunrise; whereas another 70 were in the bicycle club, Solidarity. Thirty-five were members of the workers' stenographic association. And that was only in the city. In Düsseldorf county another 350 Social Democrats participated in a comparable range of activities.[42] These organizations, which were quite clearly modeled on their bourgeois and petty bourgeois counterparts, provided recreational opportunities and sociability to their members and aided the larger movement at elections and celebrations.

Service organizations concentrated on easing the economic and social burdens of proletarian life. In 1904 the popular but inefficient information bureau was replaced by a workers' secretariat, manned by the full-time functionary and experienced legal advisor, Heinrich Fischer. The *Volkszeitung* proudly announced that "a new period in the history of the Düsseldorf workers' movement has begun . . . a long-desired goal of all comrades has been fulfilled."[43] By 1907 more than 8,000 workers a year, 68 percent of whom were organized, came with problems about insurance benefits, work contracts, and civil law.[44] In 1897, when the party's opposition to cooperatives had subsided into neutrality, 76 Düsseldorf comrades established one. For several years, as President Jammer correctly complained, the party and unions remained "very passive" and "only a miniscule portion of workers recognized the advantages of consumer cooperatives." By 1905, however, more than 2,000 workers had joined the cooperative, which was on its way to establishing outlets throughout the city, and the People's Bread co-operative bakery had been formed in the wake of a bakers' strike and boycott of commercial firms.[45] The money for all these ventures was raised locally.

Many of these activities, as well as those sponsored by the party and unions directly, were held first at the trade-union house and then at the new headquarters opened in 1909. The Volkshaus, built by the move-ment from the contributions of its members, was the pride of the Social Democrats. It was an impressive symbol of their visible presence and growing power in Düsseldorf. Of equal importance, it was, in the words of *Volkszeitung* editor Berten, "a home . . . a fatherland . . . a home where workers are master and not dependent on the goodwill of speculating parasites . . . a home in which they can raise themselves above the misery of daily life, if only for a few hours."[46]

In 1904 Düsseldorf party and cartel leaders, urged on by Laufenberg and Berten rather than by the national party, initiated an educational program. The project, which reflected their faith in the efficacy of "intellectual weapons" and their concern about the perennial shortage of trained speakers and functionaries, sought to provide political education to the committed rather than to bring basic literacy or general knowl-edge to the unorganized.[47] According to Giebel, "we must expand people's knowledge as fighters in the class struggle and train them to be good agitators. Grammar and spelling are less important. It's the ability to think which must be developed."[48] In 1904 and 1905 Laufenberg, Giebel, and Schotte offered eight- to ten-week courses on the ideology of the Center and on basic socialist theory. All together more than 100 Social Democrats participated enthusiastically, and in late 1906, the party and cartel, encouraged by their initial success, established a formal education commission. It continued "to educate the comrades in the fundamentals of our outlook," through courses on economic history, social theory, and Marxism, thereby reinforcing the educational orienta-tion of the association and the *Volkszeitung*.[49]

The Düsseldorf Social Democrats, unlike their comrades elsewhere, did not fall prey to what Haberland described as the temptation "to become involved in all possible areas of knowledge and aesthetic fields."[50] They did, however, hold occasional evenings of music and poetry, and after 1905 regularly sponsored visits to the municipal theater and opera from a conviction that "making classical literature available to the working class meets a real need."[51] Although some party leaders viewed these cultural activities as nonessential, and a few even opposed them as dangerous diversions from politics, the workers flocked to them, and most leaders insisted that "the struggle for socialism is simultaneously the ascent of the masses to culture."[52]

The Social Democrats made commemorative occasions, like associations, an integral part of their culture and a valuable adjunct to their political activities. May Day, the trade-union festival, social events, and funerals offered workers alternatives to religious feasts, nationalist celebrations, and commercial entertainment. These "invented traditions" simultaneously isolated the Social Democrats from the dominant culture and unified disparate elements within the working class.[53] The Social Democrats used such opportunities to demonstrate their strength and solidarity to themselves as well as hostile onlookers and to proclaim their general goals and values. Although such festivals were not, as the Social Democrats took pains to point out, "convenient opportunities for drinking bouts, where hard-won, paltry wages are squandered," they did enable members and their families to relax and escape the monotony of proletarian life.[54]

May Day was the social democratic holiday par excellence, the most carefully planned, the most political, and the most controversial event on the movement's calendar. On that day the Social Democrats protested the entire character of capitalism, proclaimed their internationalism, and celebrated the "people's springtime."[55] The Düsseldorf Social Democrats, like their comrades elsewhere, accorded a very special, if not entirely clear, meaning to May Day, but the prosaic reality of the event never matched the almost millenarian ideal.

In the 1890s the Social Democrats had been too weak to stage a militant and massive protest on May 1. They consistently endorsed the idea of a one-day strike, encouraged "spontaneous" walks – because the police forbade demonstrations – and held protest meetings to demand the eight-hour day and pledge "to do everything possible to improve the condition of the working class and eliminate capitalism."[56] Participation ranged from a few hundred in the early 1890s to nearly a thousand by decade's end. Thereafter attendance picked up, but the festive element began to outweigh the political one.[57] Party leaders such as Grimpe, Schmitt, and Erbert, convinced that May Day should be "a massive protest of workers against exploitation by capital . . . against war in every form," fought successfully against that trend.[58] In 1903 more than 4,000 workers turned out, marching and singing throught the streets of Düsseldorf and listening to political speeches by Nostrop, Sendler, and Windhoff. As the *Volkszeitung* proudly noted, "many a bourgeois made a bewildered face as he saw the lively Reds parade by like a brigade of soldiers."[59]

The Social Democrats could not sustain the momentum, however, and in 1904 the event resembled a spring festival more than a political demonstration. Even though 5,000 to 6,000 attended the Sunday events, the *Volkszeitung* lamented that the bourgeoisie was justified in laughing at May Day rather than fearing it. Party leaders once again strove to revive the "idealism and revolutionary-demonstrative character of May Day."[60] In 1905 the Social Democrats urged their supporters to "demonstate for the eight-hour day and for world peace," and reminded them that "these major demands are inextricably bound up with all the other hopes and wishes for the future which derive from our revolutionary world view."[61] Six hundred workers appeared for the morning political meetings, and three thousand for the afternoon "walk." When the national trade-union congress suggested abandoning the one-day strike entirely, Berten, Laufenberg, and other leaders insisted that the workers had no interest in quiet evening celebrations and condemned "petty" union leaders for calculating whether the sacrifice was worthwhile.[62] The rank and file was equally unwilling to abandon the ideal, even if many were fearful of implementing it.

The following year the *Volkszeitung* asserted that "the idea of May Day is breaking ever more ground in the unions," but this optimism proved unfounded, for union resistance and government refusal to issue a parade permit or rent the municipal auditorium discouraged many workers from celebrating.[63] As so often in the past, workers were reluctant to run the risk of striking when the local movement was weak and the national one ambivalent about such militancy. Police harassment, employer threats, and social democratic timidity thus limited confrontation to "spontaneous" walks and verbal bitterness on all sides. Despite the movement's expansion and confidence in other areas, the Social Democrats were still not able to make May Day the inspiring radical celebration they wanted and needed.

In addition to May Day, which had been established by the Second International as a purely proletarian holiday, the Düsseldorf Social Democrats developed their own summer festival to compete with the numerous Catholic parish fairs on the one hand and the nationalist celebration of Sedan, Germany's 1870 victory over France, on the other. After trying unsuccessfully throughout the 1890s to make the Lassalle memorial into such a popular event, they initiated a trade-union celebration, modestly billed as "a common outing" in 1901.[64] Within a few years the cartel was proudly describing the festival as

a demonstration of workers, who with justified self-confidence have stepped out into the streets from the factories and workshops in order to hold a parade of the army of class-conscious fighters . . . Although the form is merry, it is a serious warning to the ruling class that the organization of workers is expanding further and further, that the army of wage slaves is ever more strongly united.[65]

The march, replete with band and flags, with which the festival opened had strongly political overtones, but the remainder of the day was a vast carnival, offering something for everyone. There were games, sports, dancing, children's activities, booths, and performances by the social democratic singing societies and sports clubs. By 1906, six thousand trade unionists, or nearly half the movement, marched, and more than twelve thousand people celebrated.[66]

Although the Social Democrats concentrated on creating their own celebrations, they did not ignore traditional holidays, such as Christmas, Easter, and Pentacost. They held their own festivities not only to divert workers from religious ones and to expose the hypocrisy of the Catholic church, but also to redefine these holidays in a socialist light rather than rejecting them completely. A typical Easter editorial from the *Volkzeitung* illustrates how this was accomplished. "The class-conscious proletariat also celebrates Easter," insisted the paper, "but in its own way. Fasting and praying never satisfied anyone. The hungry proletariat knows that all too well." It then went on first to secularize and then to socialize the event. "Easter is the festival of resurrection, of the awakening of nature . . . For the proletariat this spring is a symbol of the people's spring for which we long so passionately, of that sunny time of socialism for which we stuggle, for which we are prepared to suffer."[67]

The Social Democrats also sponsored innumerable purely social events. There were hikes and picnics in the summer, dances and family parties in the winter, and regular social evenings at the neighborhood party pub, which according to the police were "very popular."[68] These events, like the associations and clubs, enabled workers and their families to socialize regularly with other comrades.[69]

The Social Democrats tried to develop special commemorations not only for all occasions in a worker's life but for his death as well. Like workers throughout Europe, they were most anxious to give a dignified burial to their comrades, who had suffered so many indignities in life. They escorted them to the grave with all the solemnity and defiance that the movement could muster – and that the police would allow. Several hundred workers attended social democratic funerals in the 1890s, and 2,000 to 3,000 thereafter, for funerals were more than personal testaments to the individuals involved. They were political demonstrations of a special kind, at which Social Democrats could pay tribute to the personal characteristics they found most valuable politically. In eulogy after eulogy workers were commended for activism, commitment, discipline, a sense of responsibility, and high standards of personal and political morality, regardless of whether they had in fact been such exemplary comrades. Their death, whether it resulted from accident, illness, or suicide, was cited as another example of how economic hardship and political repression ground down and snuffed out proletarian lives. The city government, upset by the political character and public visibility of such funerals, sometimes prohibited speeches, at other times songs and occasionally even wreaths with red ribbons. A sizable police contingent accompanied every Social Democrat to the grave.[70] In death as in life, the Social Democrats were denied equality and peace.

As the first decade of the twentieth century drew to a close, it was thus possible for a Düsseldorf Social Democrat to spend his (or more rarely her) nonwork life entirely within the ambit of the movement. In addition to attending party functions and doing union work, he could spend his leisure singing, cycling, or studying with his comrades. His family could purchase food from the cooperative, secure legal advice from the workers' secretariat, information from the *Volkszeitung*, and books from the union cartel library. His wife could join the women's movement, his children the youth association, and all could celebrate proletarian holidays and other festivals. Many of these activities would occur within the familiar environment of the neighborhood party pub or the downtown Volkshaus. Even a worker's relationship to the institutions of high culture could be mediated through the movement. Not all workers participated fully in this craddle-to-grave network of associations and activities. But for many, the movement was the central institution in their lives, unifying work and community, politics and personal life.

The Social Democrats devoted themselves to building this rich culture not out of an aversion to action, love of isolation, or organizational fetishism, but rather because the sphere of popular culture in Imperial Germany was thoroughly politicized. Like the workers' movement, the state and the institutions of civil society viewed culture instrumentally and organized actively, now imitating the Social Democrats, now seizing the initiative. The government, the schools, and the military, fearing that workers would reject the existing order, and political Catholicism, worrying that they would defect from the Center, competed directly with social democracy by providing associations for many proletarian needs. And as the Center became more conservative and integrated into the authoritarian state, it supported the dominant culture's efforts to imbue the working class with an ideology of monarchism, nationalism, imperialism, religiosity, and deference.[71]

The Catholics established not only Workers' Associations and trade unions but also educational programs, recreational clubs, consumer cooperatives, and legal-aid bureaus.[72] Large factories such as Rhein-metall and Oberbilkerstahlwerk sponsored singing groups, and the nationalist German Athletic League recruited working-class sup-porters.[73] The Social Democrats maintained that these associations, far from being neutral, were "hypocritical, patriotic associations" and "the tools of political reaction."[74] The state, long concerned about "the danger of their [the Social Democrats'] energetic work in precisely these kinds of organizations," encouraged and eventually funded nationalist and religious recreational and cultural associations as well as youth groups.[75] Summing up their experience in the first decades of legality, the Social Democrats noted that:

In confirmation preparation and communion instruction the clergy calls attention to the Christian youth associations. The school teacher does the same. He praises the patriotic athletic organizations, the youth militia, and the youth division of veterans organizations. The pupils receive some patriotic advertise-ments from which they can read about the alleged greatness and glory of Germany. Nor do these men forget to warn of the dangers of the evil Social Democrats.[76]

The national government also ran continuing education schools, and, after 1911, its Prussian counterpart launched an extensive, expensive, and explicitly anti-socialist adolescent-welfare program.[77]

Given the activism of the state and political Catholicism, it was politically necessary for the Social Democrats to create their own culture, because if they did not fulfill workers' nonpolitical needs, other groups, with anti-socialist politics, would.[78] Their cradle-to-grave network of associations did not simply offer workers the chance to enjoy middle-class culture without middle-class control or to experience an equality and solidarity denied them in bourgeois and religious organizations.[79] The culture did not represent an escape from action but was part of the Social Democrats' active confrontation with the organizations and ideologies of the state and their Catholic opponents.[80] Progress on the cultural front was important not only in its own right but was also a prerequisite for the creation of a politically conscious and unified working class and workers' movement. Indeed, the Social Democrats always stressed these political considerations, rather than the status ones, when urging workers to join their cultural associations.[81] If the Social Democrats forced their opponents to play mass politics, it was the state and political Catholicism that pushed the Social Democrats to organize popular culture. And once the competition began, both the Social Democrats and the dominant society escalated it, until everything from singing to food shopping had become an intensely political affair.

Although government officials and Catholic leaders believed that such cultural associations and celebrations were effective adjuncts to the party and unions, the Social Democrats, who constructed a popular culture as much from competition with their opponents as from conviction, were more ambivalent. They accepted the necessity of acting in this sphere but repeatedly insisted that "the duty to agitate for the party takes precedence over clubs and amusements."[82] They recognized that cultural activities not only made enormous demands on workers' limited free time but also, and more important, that their form and content had ambiguous political consequences. The Social Democrats were damned if they organized culturally and damned if they didn't.

The Social Democrats both borrowed from the dominant culture and strove to maximize their autonomy from it. Their independent organizations, which frequently imitated bourgeois forms, might encourage hierarchy, passivity, and the emulation of dominant norms. More frequently, however, they helped workers develop skills and "learn to express themselves and assume responsibility,"[83] for without middle-class control, middle-class culture and the workers' relationship to it was transformed. Social democratic cultural activities transmitted a rudimentary Marxism and advocated new values, such as solidarity, collectivism, indifference to religion, and internationalism. They also introduced workers to the high culture of the dominant society and stressed such bourgeois values as respectability, self-improvement, sexual morality, sobriety, and discipline, albeit as prerequisites for effective political work and not for individual mobility.[84] Overall, the social democratic culture was suffused with both a mixture of Marxism, influenced and attenuated by the dominant culture, and a negotiated or mediated version of dominant values.[85] The culture embodied a clear sense of class identity and opposition to the dominant society without offering a complete alternative to that society in the present or a clear sense of what that alternative would be in the future.[86]

In important ways the social democratic associations, educational programs, and holidays aided the party politically and organizationally, reinforcing political principles by developing them in a variety of settings. The social democratic singing clubs, for example, held frequent concerts, and according to the party press, "their songs often have a deeper, more effective and more permanent agitational effect on the spirit and soul of the workers than the most intelligent two-hour speech."[87] Political songs, as Vernon Lidtke noted, "helped to provide a sense of identity for people within the labor movement" and "symbolized the differentiation of labor-movement members from others in German society."[88] Although the sports clubs never discussed politics explicitly or agitated publicly, they constantly reminded their members to serve their party, union, and class.[89] All these organizations also "provided a ready-made communications network...for political action."[90]

The social democratic culture strengthened members' identity with their class by emphasizing the centrality of class to all aspects of workers' lives and enabling them to define all their activities consciously in terms of their class position. The social democratic associations and celebrations did not "play the integrative role...but on the contrary tended to preserve rather than to break down social differentiation."[91] By meeting a variety of working-class needs, the Social Democrats lessened workers' dependence on the institutions of the dominant society. By providing the physical and social space in which an alternative community could develop, they both attracted migrant workers, seeking a place in a new urban, industrial environment, and lessened the risks of being a dissident in a city dominated by political Catholicism and organized capitalism.[92] By offering workers the experience of practical solidarity, they helped unify the culturally fragmented Düsseldorf working class.

The Social Democrats also used cultural activities to mediate between the party and more indifferent male workers, women, and youth. Many were drawn first to concerts, festivals, or social nights at the pub, where they learned the rudiments of social democracy and overcame their hesitations about more explicit political commitment.[93] Through much of the Wilhelmian era, the law prevented women and minors from participating in any but such ostensibly nonpolitical gatherings. Of the several thousand unorganized workers who received free advice from the workers' secretariat each year, some may well have joined a union or the party as a result of their experience, and many probably voted SPD as a token of thanks. Although the consumer cooperative does not appear to have attracted the unorganized, it undoubtedly made the unpolitical wives of many Social Democrats more receptive to the movement. In short, the culture provided the Social Democrats with valuable help in politicizing a young, transient, politically inexperienced and Catholic working class.

Facets of the culture, however, had a more problematic relationship to the political work of the SPD, for the culture's forms and content were eclectic and its impact ambiguous. The education courses, for example, offered a Marxist analysis of capitalism and political authoritarianism in Germany, whereas the cultural events exposed workers to the art and literature of the dominant society with no critical discussion whatsoever. It was not so much the heritage being transmitted as the means by which it was conveyed and the spirit in which it was received that divorced high culture and politics and led the Social Democrats unwittingly partially to nullify in their cultural programs what they sought to accomplish in their educational ones. The social democratic culture encouraged workers to strive for intellectual self-improvement, which could either be regarded as an end in itself or used as a basis for claiming equality with the bourgeoisie and demanding reform of education and culture.[94]

Cultural institutions competed with the party for the limited time and energy of workers – and often won. Party leaders constantly urged workers "to avoid such activities and attend meetings where you can be enlightened about the condition of the working class," and noted sarcastically that "it would be desirable if party meetings were as well attended as social events."[95] Yet they could not resolve the dilemma. For the party to be strong, it needed the social democratic culture, but the culture diverted workers from the party.

The culture offered workers a security, status, and sociability denied them in religious and bourgeois institutions and isolated them from the surrounding society. They enjoyed self-respect and satisfactions that no doubt sometimes blunted their activism and militancy. Neither equality nor solidarity nor isolation, however, automatically demobilized and depoliticized the Düsseldorf working class. For all it offered workers, the culture could not suspend the operation of class relationships. Nor could it protect workers from domination, discrimination, and exploitation. The dominant society constantly impinged on the social democratic milieu. Workers could use the self-esteem and skills they gained within the culture to attack the dominant society as readily as they could use them to prevent confrontation and build a subordinate culture of consolation. The Social Democrats isolated workers not in order to avoid action but as part of their active conflict with the dominant institutions and ideologies. And as subsequent chapters will show, the organization of popular culture was perfectly compatible with the radicalization of social democracy in Düsseldorf.

7

Expansion and optimism

For the Düsseldorf Social Democrats the years immediately following the revisionist controversy and local party crisis were among the least tumultuous but most constructive and optimistic of the entire Wilhelmian era. The movement's expansion coincided with an economic boom, and the Social Democrats were as active on the shop floor as in the political and cultural arenas. Established unions flourished, new ones cropped up, and strike rates rose markedly. Workers were frequently disappointed with the results, however, for their efforts were thwarted by industrialists and guildsmen on the one hand and the Christian trade unions on the other.

Although national politics were stalemated in this period and Prussian and municipal ones closed to the Düsseldorf Social Democrats, they made significant progress in their campaign against political Catholicism. The Center Party's support for increased grain tariffs and its pivotal position in the conservative ruling alliance at last provided the Social Democrats with concrete proof of the Center's hostility to the working class and enabled them to choose the terrain on which it was most advantageous to fight. The tremendous gains that they made in the 1903 Reichstag election and the split in the Christian workers' camp convinced the Social Democrats that the Center fortress would soon topple if they but organized and agitated as before.

Social democracy and the shop floor

After 1903 the trade unions, like the political and cultural wings of the movement, emerged from the doldrums. Economic prosperity, party consolidation, and electoral success were aided by union expansion and activism and encouraged them. Thousands of workers joined established unions, and hundreds set up new ones in formerly unorganized sectors. Strike rates, which picked up in 1904, reached unprecedented heights in

1905 and involved different groups of workers but did not diminish dramatically in 1906. In addition, workers in different unions both cooperated more frequently and experimented with new tactics. As in the past, however, worker organization generated employer counter-organization, and militancy brought repression in its wake. Although more and more workers looked to the free trade unions, rather than the cautious Christian ones, to defend their interests, they were increasingly frustrated by the results of their efforts. Union activity, like so much else in Düsseldorf, was to promote radicalism and isolation rather than reformism and integration.

Although the first tentative signs of economic recovery appeared in 1903, textiles and machine making continued to do poorly, and not until late 1905 did both government and business move from cautious optimism to enthusiasm about a boom in all sectors, especially metal.[1] The upswing in the economy brought expansion in the labor force from only 51,000 workers registered with the health insurance system in 1903 to more than 70,000 in 1906. Trade-union membership likewise rose from 6,622 in 1904 to 13,807 in 1906, but remained concentrated in the traditionally well-organized areas of construction, wood, and to a lesser extent metal. The DMV, for example, had 1,555 members in 1904, the carpenters union 294, and the printers 325. Unionism picked up in the previously weak food and clothing sectors, and cement workers and longshoremen, unskilled and formerly unorganized, established unions with 200 and 110 members, respectively.[2]

The expansion and diversification of the union movement meant that many more workers came into contact with social democracy on the job. As unions were neither officially recognized by employers nor established on the shop floor, all members were urged to agitate informally among their co-workers, old and new. For many workers such conversations provided an introduction to social democracy and marked the first step in their politicization.[3] Growth meant that the free trade unions far outstripped their Christian competitors, whose claim to offer a viable union alternative was less and less persuasive. The Center's position was thus being undermined on the shop floor as well as in other arenas. Finally, expansion and diversification meant that industrial militancy was once again on the agenda, and this time was not restricted to the traditionally active groups.

The well-organized carpenters opened 1904 with a major strike, a strike that illustrated the prevalent pattern of union activism, employer intransigence, police intervention, and Christian trade-union caution. After more than 100 unionized carpenters had extracted an hourly wage increase, the abolition of all piecework, the regulation of hours, and bonuses for work in the county, 166 of their fellow workers struck ten large construction firms and eleven small guildmasters. The carpenters were optimistic that the demands, which had first been recognized in 1901 but not implemented as a result of the economic crisis, would be readily granted because construction was booming and carpenters were in short supply. Although one or two employers did give in after a few days, most construction firms held out at least three weeks, and the guildmasters remained intransigent for three months.[4] The guild was better organized and more frightened about the future of artisan work than earlier, and large construction firms were prosperous enough to avoid making concessions for the sake of expediting work. The Social Democrats had not reckoned with such strenuous opposition. Nor had they anticipated vigorous police harassment and the erratic, indeed disloyal, behavior of the Christian trade unions.

As in past conflicts, the police did not attempt to break the strike, but they did enforce the decidedly anti-working-class picketing and libel laws with unprecedented vigor. Instead of merely picketing construction sites, the carpenters patrolled the railroad station as well in order to turn away out-of-town scabs through persuasion or intimidation. The police, who complained that such pickets were "especially zealous" and "endangered convenience, safety, peace, and quiet," regularly broke up crowds of workers, escorted scabs to their new employers, and in the process arrested 27 trade unionists for libel, disorderly conduct, and violation of paragraph 153. Although half were subsequently acquitted, the remainder received sentences ranging from one to sixteen weeks.[5] Police harassment upped the costs of an already expensive strike and frightened workers anxious about future job possibilities, but it failed to satisfy employers, who demanded yet more decisive intervention on behalf of "the right to work." The miniscule Christian carpenters union not only refused to support the strike, just as the Christian bricklayers had a year earlier, but also negotiated a separate agreement for a smaller wage increase and longer hours. It even recruited scabs from outside Düsseldorf. The guildmasters, eager to diminish the power of social democracy, readily collaborated with the Christian unionists, and the incensed Social Democrats labeled them traitors and strikebreakers.[6]

In the late summer a confrontation between 600 plasterers and stucco workers and their employers followed the same basic scenario. Although workers preferred the advantageous tactic of striking only one or two firms at a time, they were forced by the employers' organization to act on a citywide basis.[7] Although the Christian unionists walked out with their social democratic co-workers, they soon reached a separate agreement with the guilds and construction firms and promised to provide 200 strikebreakers. After six weeks, which were marred by surprisingly little police harassment or worker violence, the employers capitulated to the Social Democrats, thereby nullifying the agreement of the Christian union, which lost power and credibility.[8]

In the 1890s the Social Democrats had oscillated between accusing the Christian unions of being "encircled by the black spirit" and dividing the working class, and admitting that Christian unions were better than no organization at all. They argued that if a Christian union engaged in strikes and job actions, which was often the case in the 1890s, it would be treated by employers just as the free unions were, which indeed happened.[9]

As the attack on the Christian unions from the Center's Berlin faction, the Catholic Workers' Associations, the Fuldauer Bishops' Conference of 1900, and the papacy escalated, however, the Christian unions moderated their policies. Fearing for their existence yet unwilling to abandon the union field to the Social Democrats, they strove both to use strikes and to promote a community of interest between capital and labor. They spoke of humanizing industrial relations and, like the Center, looked more favorably on the state and its national ambitions. They recognized, albeit with a certain resignation, that political Catholicism would not and could not grant them parity within the movement or society. They tried to carve out a middle position between the free unions and the Catholic Workers' Associations, which would enable them to defend workers' interests with dignity and autonomy but not offend the most influential religious and secular powers in the Catholic milieu.[10] Although such a middle position could be articulated theoretically, it could not be translated into practice, and time after time the Christian unions opted for anti-socialism over union militancy, just as they did in 1904.

Throughout 1904 metal remained calm, even though the police reported that the DMV "was agitating strongly," and the pipefitters guild complained that relations between masters and journeymen were "bad primarily due to the influence of the union."[11] The only important, well-publicized strike involved a controversial control question. Ten helpers in the Töller pipefitting firm refused to pay an additional 5 M to the 50 M security deposit, already put down for tools, and further demanded the firing of their particularly hard-driving foreman. Töller, backed initially by his fellow guildmasters, denounced this challenge to employer power, insisting that "it's my business if I withhold more. It does not concern anyone else. If someone doesn't like it, he can quit."[12] After three weeks of futilely searching for strikebreakers, however, Töller submitted the conflict to the guild mediation office, which rejected his claim. Both the workers and the DMV, which had gained eighty new members by agitating around the Töller controversy, were pleasantly surprised.[13] Many masters, however, were embittered that their mediation office had sided with the journeymen. They could reconcile themselves to raising wages for several hundred workers more readily than to relinquishing power to ten. As the regional guild paper, the *Westdeutsche Gewerbezeitung*, noted with indignation, "the journeymen claimed to want to interfere in the personal rights of masters." It warned that "if we want to remain masters in our house, in our workshop, we must close our ranks tightly. Therefore, be watchful and united, united, united!"[14]

The bakers' strike, like that of the Töller metal workers, was small in scope but far-reaching in its implications, for it showed social democracy's new ability to use the boycott. In late July the formerly quiescent bakers pressured four bread factories to grant wage increases, overtime pay, and a twelve-hour day and then struck the four other firms that refused. The party and cartel, recognizing that the thirty-two strikers would be easily defeated without support, proclaimed a boycott. They held hugh rallies and distributed thousands of flyers. Workers pressured local stores to carry only unboycotted bread, and the *Volkszeitung* published daily lists of those who complied. In late August the cooperative bakery "People's Bread" opened, and by early September was supplying more than 100 shops. The very fact that the Social Democrats could plan and execute such a boycott proved that they had made great strides in overcoming the sectional divisions within the working class and creating not only a sense of solidarity but also assertiveness. They had become a force to be reckoned with in the everyday life of the community. But they were still not able to defeat their opponents. Because the struck firms refused to settle and the Christian unions denounced the campaign, the Social Democrats lifted the boycott after five months and the disheartened bakers returned to work under the old terms.[15]

Both nationally and locally the renewed activism of 1904 paled in comparison to that of 1905. That year, which opened with the large and bitter Ruhr miners' conflict, saw a half million German workers strike. If the return of prosperity made activism possible, the rising cost of living and aggressive employer efforts to cut wages, intensify the pace of work, and curb unions made it necessary. And politics fueled the strike wave as well as economics. Within Germany workers were angered and frustrated that the post-1903 wave of reaction, far from ending, gained momentum. Liberals and Conservatives restricted suffrage on the provincial and municipal levels and threatened to do the same nationally. Abroad, the Russian Revolution offered both inspiration and seeming confirmation of the efficacy of militancy.[16] Düsseldorf was no exception to the general trend. Government statistics list nineteen strikes involving 220 firms, 105 of which were shut down completely. The largest number of workers striking simultaneously was 3,235 as compared to 538 in 1904, and nearly 8,000 were employed in the struck firms as against 1,150 the previous year.[17]

Throughout the turmoil of 1905 the Düsseldorf DMV remained the quietest of the major unions – a testament to the intransigence of employers, the weakness of the union, and the caution of its leaders. Employees in some large and medium-sized factories won modest wage increases without striking, for orders were abundant and employers were anxious not to lose men with skill. There were virtually no strikes for wages or union recognition against either the well-organized large-scale capitalists or the smaller ones that were protected by them. At most the rank and file, often against the wishes or without the knowledge of union leaders, would call a small strike to protest the arbitrary firing of a worker, who was usually a union activist, or the behavior of a foreman, who was an ex-worker but "acted like a noncommissioned officer." Such control disputes indicated the intense anger over severe employer discipline but generally ended in failure, thereby increasing employers' hostility without enhancing union strength. For all its growth, the DMV was still no match for Ehrhardt, Mannesmann, and their ilk.[18]

Developments in clothing were more encouraging and indicated the spread of militancy to new groups. In late March, Düsseldorf's 400 journeymen tailors struck seventy-five small firms. After two weeks employers, guild and nonguild alike, recognized the union and granted a small wage increase, which, according to the *Volkszeitung*, "set a limit to the confused conditions and shameless exploitation in the payment of workers."[19]

No sooner had the tailors' strike ended than the brewery workers became involved in a major conflict, whose regional character heralded a new level of confrontation. The dispute began in neighboring Cologne and spread to Düsseldorf when the Cologne brewers persuaded the recently formed Ring Brewers Association to call for a lockout. Düsseldorf's 387 unionized brewery workers responded with a pre-emptive strike, and the cartel and party announced a boycott of Ring beer. Workers in other cities in the Rhineland and Westphalia followed suit, and an eight-week battle ensued.[20] At issue were not wages or hours but the control of hiring, firing, and discipline. As the Employers' Association announced indignantly:

If the leaders of the brewery workers demand that they have a say in the filling of individual posts in the different breweries and if they sow discontent at every dismissal of a union member by claiming that it is a question of disciplinary punishment . . . then that far surpasses what is permissable.[21]

It accused the striking free and Hirsch-Duncker unions of "terrorism" and appealed to "fair-minded workers" to recognize employers' rights and subvert the boycott.[22] The Social Democrats claimed that the owners wanted to crush the union so as to "remain master in the house" and called meeting after meeting to convince workers that "breaking the boycott is reprehensible behavior."[23] Both sides pressured pub owners, mobilized their press resources, and distributed thousands of flyers to workers and bourgeoisie alike. The Christian unionists once again supported capital.[24]

By June both sides negotiated a settlement, for the breweries through-out the region were beginning to suffer from the boycott, but the Social Democrats were having difficulty enforcing it widely because of Center Party opposition and some free trade-union disobedience. Although the Social Democrats called off the boycott in return for union recognition, it proved a pyhrric victory for the workers. The breweries reneged on their promise to rehire all the strikers, and by year's end union member-ship had dropped to eighty.[25]

Construction workers continued to be very active. More than 1,100 bricklayers, who had been severely defeated in their general strike of 1902, engaged in several major confrontations with the city's largest construction firms, such as Boswau and Knauer and the Allgemeine Hochbaugesellschaft. By uniting skilled and unskilled to attack firms individually, they won significant improvements in wages and hours.[26]

The largest, most demoralizing conflict occurred in woodworking, where 101 employers and 1,168 workers from the free, Christian, and Hirsch-Duncker unions fought one another for three months. This massive confrontation shattered the peace that had reigned in the industry since 1901, when a mediation office, with representatives from the unions, the guild, and the employers' association, was established to settle disputes and facilitate collective bargaining. Early in 1905, however, the mediation office failed to arbitrate a firing controversy and was subsequently unable to persuade workers and employers to renew their contract. When wage negotiations broke down, the employers unilaterally imposed terms and threatened to dismiss anyone who refused to submit to them. All woodworkers walked off the job, claiming they were locked out, whereas employers insisted they were striking.[27]

Each side settled in for a war of attrition. The employers displayed a remarkable degree of unity, and within the first two weeks only one large firm accepted the unions' terms. By the end of the first month only 359 woodworkers in forty-four firms had won contracts. Another 481 workers had left Düsseldorf in search of jobs, and the three unions had spent more than 52,000 M on the struggle. Both the unions and the employers' association–guild alliance maintained a united front and actively sought to rally public support through the press, flyers, and meetings.[28]

As the struggle dragged on for weeks and then months, tempers frayed, and the conflicts among strikers, scabs, employers, and the police escalated. The workers not only posted pickets at all shops and watched the railroad station, but also cajoled and frequently coerced scabs and held demonstrations of 100 or more workers and their families in front of the shops of particularly hated employers.[29] The employers' association, the guild, and individual firms sent indignant letters to the police, complaining that employers could not come and go "without being subjected to the most serious insults and assaults" and that "the terrorism against those willing to work is unbelievable."[30] They urged the police to escort strikebreakers from the railroad station, send reinforcements to shops, and make more arrests. When the authorities failed to comply, the employers' association argued that "the Düsseldorf police are apparently not up to the situation."[31]

The police, whose professional pride was wounded by such insults, insisted that they were giving every possible protection to those willing to work and reminded employers that picketing per se was not illegal. They refused to send reinforcements to working-class neighborhoods on the grounds that "experience has shown that through such police measures strikers are only embittered, and the lumpen elements, who are always looking for trouble, are attracted.[32] Despite such statements, the police did crack down. They arrested several schoolboys who yelled "strikebreaker." Most were so young that they had to sign their statements with X's. At the request of the police, School Superintendent Kessler asked all teachers to forbid their students to participate in unlawful assemblies or to insult scabs. And in the course of the strike thirty-six workers, most of them cabinetmakers, were arrested for violating paragraph 153. Twenty-five received fines or jail sentences.[33] The Social Democrats were as little impressed by the legalism and ostensible neutality of the police as the employers were.

After three months the woodworkers resumed work on the employers' terms. According to the union, "it is temporarily counterproductive to continue fighting. The colleagues would damage themselves too much economically."[34] The employers' association, created in the wake of the woodworkers' successful strike of 1898, had now defeated them, and the painful progress of a decade had been nullified. Union strength and militancy could not be translated into material improvements or expanded rights.

In 1906 the overall level of industrial conflict remained high in Düsseldorf, but its character changed. There were no major strikes, lockouts, or boycotts, and the traditionally most active workers were quiet, either because they had not recovered from recent defeats, like the woodworkers, or because they were still enjoying the benefits of past victories, like the carpenters. Nor were workers in food and clothing able to maintain their momentum. Metalworkers, masons, longshoremen, and laborers in cement and stone picked up the slack. Although fewer firms and employees were involved, more workers in large firms, formerly free of labor disputes, came into contact with union militancy.[35] Seven hundred molders walked out of Düsseldorf's six largest foundries, for example, and held out for four months until they were forced to return under the old conditions. More than 200 of Düsseldorf's unskilled and recently unionized longshoremen staged a series of successful strikes for increased wages, overtime pay, and a clear specification of job content. The cement and concrete workers, another unskilled and newly organized group, pressured several large firms to grant a wage increase, and then 324 struck those that refused. In addition, unionists in county towns such as Benrath and Hilden struck more frequently.[36]

The union drives and strike activity of these years produced ambiguous results. Workers definitely improved their economic situation in certain respects, as a 1906 trade-union cartel survey of one-fifth of Düsseldorf's organized, predominantly male workers revealed. Although factory workers, cigar makers, municipal employees, longshoremen, and one-half of all masons earned 3.50 M a day or less, most metalworkers made 4 M to 5.50 M if paid by the hour and 4.50 M to 6.50 M on piece rates. Woodworkers averaged between 4.50 M and 5.50 M, whereas in construction wages ranged from 4.50 M for the unskilled to 5 M to 6.50 M for some masons and nearly all carpenters. These rates, for the ten-hour day that most workers had won, were substantially higher than the 2 M common in textiles and restaurants and the 3 M to 3.50 M typical in paper and chemicals. They made Düsseldorf workers among the highest paid in Germany.[37]

Wage rates alone, however, do not tell the whole story. Workers not only had more than 8 percent of their wages deducted for insurance payments but were also frequently fined for lateness and alleged poor workmanship.[38] In addition to cyclical crises and seasonal unemployment, which hit sectors such as construction particularly hard, the workers surveyed lost an average of nearly three weeks work due to sickness and temporary layoffs.[39] As hours decreased, the pace of work intensified and accident rates rose commensurately. By 1905, 74 of every 1,000 workers suffered an injury on the job.[40] Finally, the steady increase in the cost of living was bringing the previous rise in real wages to a virtual standstill.[41] The working-class gains were thus meager and tenuous and were to be rapidly eroded by continued inflation and renewed recession after 1906.

Worker militancy gave the unions and the social democratic movement as a whole a power and visibility they had previously lacked, both in organized sectors and among new groups of workers. The free trade unions became the only serious defender of working-class material interests and played a vital role in mobilizing disaffection on a more permanent basis and in politicizing economic protest. The union movement became an integral part of the community that the Social

Democrats established as an alternative to both the Catholic milieu and the institutions of bourgeois, nationalist Germany. Without the expansion of the union movement, the social democratic occupation of political space would have been far from complete, just as without social democratic progress on the political, organizational, and cultural fronts, union activism would have been less militant and perceived as less threatening by employers, Catholic workers, and the state.

The expansion of the unions was paralleled by that of guilds and employers' associations, however, and working-class militancy generated employer intransigence. In Düsseldorf, as throughout Germany, both employers' associations and guilds proliferated, and their members cooperated much more effectively than in the 1890s. As workers escalated their demands, employers sought to resist allegedly exorbitant wage claims, disruptive social democratic agitation, and detrimental collective bargaining. They often succeeded by using blacklists, firings, lockouts, and other repressive measures.[42] On the basis of bitter experience, Düsseldorf's union leaders complained that "in our heavily industrialized region factory absolutism proliferates most arrogantly and draws strength from the artificially created divisions in the workers' movement."[43] In electoral politics, as in economic struggles, the Social Democrats were to move from optimism through disappointment to anger in these years.

Center conservatism and social democratic attack

In the 1890s political Catholicism had accepted first industrial capitalism and then Wilhelmian politics. It had abandoned its critique of militarism and nationalism, allied itself with conservatism and national liberalism, and advocated a social policy for the *Mittelstand* rather than the working class. Yet it held on to much of its proletarian support, convincing workers that religion was more important than class. After the turn of the century, however, the Center Party became an enthusiastic proponent of agrarian tariffs, which had extremely detrimental economic and political consequences for the working class, and its claim of "harmonizing justice" rang hollow. On an unprecedented scale, Catholic workers inside and outside the Center criticized the party. Many turned to the social democratic movement, which was at last able to seize the political offensive and relate its critique of capitalist economics and Catholic politics directly to workers' everyday experience. The long siege of the Center fortress entered a new stage.

Tariffs were hardly a new issue in Germany. They, and the controversies surrounding them, had become an integral part of economic and political life during the Great Depression of the 1870s, when Bismarck introduced both agrarian and industrial protection. He thereby cemented the alliance between heavy industry and Junker agriculture on which the Empire was built and secured for the national government a remarkable degree of financial independence from the individual states and the Reichstag. In the early 1890s, however, the New Course challenged both the economic and political principles of Bismarckian protectionism. In order to satisfy industrialists, pacify workers, and conciliate foreign powers, Chancellor Caprivi reduced rates from their 1887 high but kept them well above the 1879 level. Although the prosperous industrial sector was pleased, Germany's permanently depressed, high-cost agriculture was not. Recognizing the threat to their economic and political power, the Junkers utilized their government connections and mobilized the peasants in the Agrarian League in order to combat Caprivi's reforms. By the late 1890s, the Conservatives, with the aid of William II and the National Liberals, had already dismantled much of the New Course. In 1900, when Bernhard von Bülow became chancellor, the Caprivi tariffs were up for renewal, and the campaign for revision began in earnest.[44]

Bülow, who had grown up in cosmopolitan Berlin, was neither an aristocrat nor a landowner, but he shared their outlook, having been educated in an anti-industrial and anti-capitalist tradition.[45] Convinced that Germany could be governed only with the Junkers and that a strong agrarian sector was necessary for economic, social, and national reasons, Bülow proposed to raise grain duties 45 to 100 percent, meat and dairy products even more, and to alter the rates on hundreds of raw materials, semifinished goods, and finished industrial products. The proposed tariffs, which far exceeded the high 1887 rates, aroused nearly universal indignation. The Conservatives intransigently insisted on still greater concessions, whereas the National Liberals and Progressives complained bitterly about those already made, and the Center moved from ambivalence to endorsement. Only the Social Democrats launched a massive national campaign against the tariffs, soliciting 3½ million signatures on a petition and engaging in extensive parliamentary obstruction. In addition, Bebel and Auer, who were convinced that the

tariff issue would split the Center and permanently alienate its proletarian base, urged their comrades in Catholic regions to campaign
vigorously and exclusively against "bread profiteering."[46]

The Düsseldorf Social Democrats enthusiastically embraced the tariff
issue as a means of attacking their enemy and uniting their own torn
ranks. "We must lead the struggle with all possible energy," urged the
Volkstribune in mid-1900, "and begin now to develop our agitation on a
grand scale."[47] For the next three years the Social Democrats hammered
home on this issue in the press, in brochures, such as *Down with Bread
Profiteers*, and at numerous meetings that drew from 100 to 500
workers.[48] Grimpe angrily labeled the proposed tariff "an assault on the
nation" and "a crime against humanity."[49] Its passage, argued Kremser,
would mark "the triumph of might over right."[50] According to Berten,
the "hunger tariff" was the work of "robber barons and speculators" who
were securing benefits for large landlords at the expense of small farmers
and above all workers.[51] In minute detail, social democratic agitators
spelled out the appalling cost of the tariff. Since the average working-
class family spent 60 percent of its income on food and the poorest even
more, the planned tariff increase would put more than 8 million
German families or 38 million people below subsistence and increase
child mortality and disease.[52] The widely read pamphlet, *Black or Red?*,
emphasized that most workers already paid 10 to 20 percent of their
incomes in indirect taxes, whereas higher-income groups paid only one-
twentieth as much.[53] If the Bülow tariff passed, it would cost every
worker three weeks' wages![54] As Erdmann passionately argued at a rally
attended by more than 100 workers, the tariff was "a cruel governmental
injustice . . . a form of brutal class rule and base agrarian selfishness."[55]

No wonder the Social Democrats were incensed at Bülow's proposals.
No wonder they attacked the Center Party so mercilessly for supporting
them. The Center's behavior was not an aberration, insisted Kremser in
an argument repeated by most of his comrades. Rather, it was the logical
culmination of that party's increasingly conservative, indeed treasonous
behavior on economic, social, and military questions. By supporting
Bülow and doing the agrarians' "parliamentary dirty work" for them, the
Center showed just how one should judge its claim to be "a party of
truth, freedom, and justice."[56] The brochure *Black or Red?* neatly
summed up the Social Democrats' indictment by noting that "the
Center's tax and tariff policies provide the clearest proof of that party's
hostility to the working class."[57]

The Center Party, upset but unpersuaded by the barrage of criticism from its enemies and its faithful alike, mounted an aggressive defense of its position. Reichstag deputy Kirsch and Landtag representative Schmitz spoke out publicly in favor of the "moderate" tariff, which both the state and the agrarian sector needed. They admitted that food prices would rise, but insisted that workers could well afford the increase.[58]

The People's Association, which took an unequivocally pro-tariff stance, launched an intensive campaign to persuade dissident Catholic workers that tariffs were not only essential for the society but also beneficial to the proletariat. No longer relying on general ideological arguments about "harmonizing justice," the Center and its allies argued their case in hard economic terms. In addition to aiding agriculture, the People's Association pamphlets claimed, tariffs were necessary to ward off foreign competition, secure improved trade treaties, expand domestic markets, and end rural migration, which lowered urban wages. "If the social democratic proposals for free trade were passed," insisted one Center author, "our entire industry would be destroyed and the workers would be thrown into the street."[59] The Center and People's Association quoted – usually out of context – statements by Social Democrats such as Schweitzer, Bracke, Schippel, Hasenklever, and Kautsky that were favorable to protection. In addition, they accused the Social Democrats of obstructing parliament and stirring up "revolutionary feelings" with "big words" while blocking all practical reforms. On occasion the Center stooped to calling social democratic leaders millionaires, who had no understanding of proletarian life, or Jews, who "are not suitable representatives of the workers' estate."[60]

The Center supplemented its defense of tariffs with discussions of its social policies, praising past accomplishments in glowing detail. Kirsch argued that the Center had repeatedly shown its "practical friendliness to the working class."[61] The People's Association published numerous pamphlets with titles like *What Has Been Done to Protect Workers in the Most Recent Social Legislation?* and *Progress in the Area of Social Insurance.* Social policy was a much more comfortable terrain for the Catholics, but they did not merely rest on their record. The Rhenish wing, fearing for its urban, proletarian base, pushed the national party to insist that any excess tariff revenues would be used to establish an insurance fund for orphans and widows.[62] Tariffs and social policy were thus effectively linked in the Center's tariff agitation, and it was years before it became clear that the legislation passed was a dead letter. The People's Association, for its part, promised that the Center Party would push not only shorter hours, better insurance benefits, and housing reform, but also improvements in the right to organize. "The workers' estate has the right to strive for equality . . . to participate in the progress of culture," insisted the People's Association, but quickly added, "as long as the workers pursue these goals on the basis of the current social order."[63]

The Center Party won the parliamentary round of the tariff battle. After prolonged, acrimonious debate, the Conservatives, the Free Conservatives, the Center, and some National Liberals composed their differences. The Junkers realized that the "Agrarian Chancellor," as Bülow called himself, could not and would not support their exorbitant demands. Industrialists, owing the agrarians a quid pro quo for their support of the Navy bills and wanting to diminish foreign competition in order to cut the costs of social insurance, dropped their opposition. The Center, which had lost its adamantly low-tariff leader, Lieber, succumbed to pressure from the People's Association and its own rural locals.[64] In December 1902 the four parties altered parliamentary procedure to circumvent SPD filibustering and pushed through the Bülow rates.

Passage of the 1902 tariff eliminated the last remnants of the anti-Bismarckian New Course and completed the turn-of-the-century restructuring of economic and political relationships. The cartel of anxiety between Junkers and heavy industrialists was restored, but as befit the age of mass politics, the old and new *Mittelstand* and the Center were now incorporated into it.[65] This revived and refurbished *Sammlungspolitik* gave, in Eckert Kehr's succinct description, "the fleet, *Weltpolitik* and expansion to industry, tariffs and the maintenance of the social prominence of the Conservatives to the agrarians and, as a result of this social and economic compromise, political hegemony to the Center."[66] To the Social Democrats it gave nothing.

The *Sammlungspolitik*, which restored the Bismarckian stalemate, was a tour de force by the Junkers that secured their position, furthered the extensive feudalization of the bourgeoisie, and pushed the Center decisively to the right. It was directed against the Social Democrats and effectively precluded any political integration of the working class. After 1902 substantial political and social reform was all but impossible, for any change would disrupt the delicate balance and threaten Junkers, industrialists, and the Center alike. The permanent crisis of the Wilhelmian state was intensified. There were to be no more turning points where German history failed to turn for accidental or mysterious reasons.[67]

Before the long-run implications of the tariff became clear to its opponents, the short-run consequences became evident to its supporters. The Center Party had persuaded its parliamentary allies of the benefits of the Bülow tariff more effectively than its proletarian base. Although the Rhenish Center Party defended the Christian trade unions, it had not given them a voice in the tariff decision. Although the national party expressed concern for social policy, going so far as to call a Workers' Congress for all non-social democratic organizations in 1903, it failed to act in this area legislatively. At a time of severe recession, it had placed new financial burdens on a working class already hard-pressed by indirect taxes. And when Reichstag elections loomed on the horizon in 1903, the Center Party pleaded with workers to consider "the common good" and quietly accept the tariff legislation. Giesberts, head of the West German Catholic Workers' Associations, forbade his followers to cooperate with Social Democrats on issues like the tariff "for religious and patriotic reasons."[68] As one Catholic author put the official position so unequivocally, "the representation of religious interests is even more important for the Catholic workers than the political representation of economic demands."[69]

Unfortunately for the Center Party, many Christian trade unionists throughout the Rhineland simply refused to accept these arguments. From 1901 on they began to speak out against the tariff, often attending social democratic rallies on the issue. Although union leaders declared the tariff to be a political question that was outside the competence of their organizations, protest continued, and Düsseldorf became its main center.[70] In 1902 the *Volkszeitung* reported with pleasure that "the class consciousness of these proletarians who have been miserably led around by the 'glorious' Center is beginning to awaken ... Recently the newly aroused Christian workers have courageously held open meetings in order to sit in sharp judgment over the bread profiteering of the Center."[71]

The Center's response was swift and harsh. In the words of one dissident Christian union spokesman, "the top party leaders and the secretaries of the People's Association led their columns into these meetings, which were called by Center voters, in order to shout down the opposition of the little man to the reactionary Junker policy of the

Center."[72] Although these workers still claimed to be loyal adherents of political Catholicism and certainly did not join the SPD, they did run a splinter, anti-tariff candidate in the 1903 Reichstag contest.

The Social Democrats made spectacular gains in that election, which was a rude shock for the overconfident Center Party. In the first round of balloting, the Düsseldorf SPD polled 20,375 votes, an astonishing 90 percent increase over their 1898 showing. This far surpassed the 40 percent increase in the Düsseldorf electorate as well as the party's 42 percent increase nationwide and 74 percent increase in the Lower Rhine region. The splinter Christian trade-union candidate ran very poorly, but the Center Party could hardly take heart at this, for it attracted only 21,628 supporters, a mere 21 percent increase.[73] The run-off was, to be sure, not as close, for most liberals and many dissident working-class Catholics threw their weight behind the Center, which polled 27,084 votes as against 23,762 for the Social Democrats. The margin of victory, however, was much narrower than in previous years. Overall in the government district of Düsseldorf the percentage of voting Catholics who backed the Center fell from 72 percent in 1898 to only 67.5 percent.[74] More significantly, in both rounds the Social Democrats in the city of Düsseldorf won more votes than the Catholics. The Center fortress was visibly weakened and was prevented from falling only by the loyal Catholic troops from the more rural county. Even they were less reliable than before, and the Center Party won only 51 percent of the county vote in the first round.[75]

The Social Democrats were clearly making major inroads into the Catholic proletariat, especially its migrant elements. Political Catholicism had been able to attract and hold Catholic workers when it was critical of industrial capitalism, political authoritarianism, strident nationalism, and costly militarism. As long as the Center was an opposition party, it could reconcile the conflicting interests of its multi-class constituency, and offer workers a vehicle for protest. As long as it was supported by a rich associational network that was more powerful and extensive than that of the Social Democrats, political Catholicism defended workers' interests and provided a supportive and integrated milieu. By 1903, however, the Center Party had become a vital pillar of the existing order. Its electoral machine and its cultural, educational, and recreational organizations were barely as strong as those of the Social Democrats, and its unions were not.

Many Catholic workers nonetheless remained within the Center fold from political conviction, religious faith, social ties, or simply habit. Many others, however, were alienated by the Center's anti-working-class policies. In a time of economic crisis and high unemployment, they were no longer impressed by the proud claim of Christian trade-union leader Schiffer that "we do not confuse our demand for the recognition of the equality of rights for the working class with complete equality." They were not convinced by People's Association spokesman Peiper that their goal should be simply "recognition for the workers' estate within economic, social, and political life."[76] Their vote for the SPD expressed a rejection of "harmonious justice" and an ill-defined "common good" that brought them so little. It expressed dissatisfaction not only with the transformation of the Center but also with economic crisis, political discrimination, and social exclusion.

The Center Party refused to acknowledge the deep ideological and political causes of its setback. The *Düsseldorfer Volksblatt* maintained that many social democratic voters were not political dissidents but rather personal failures, for "he who has misfortune seeks a scapegoat in order not to take responsibility for his own failings, and he follows those who cry the loudest that things must change"[77] But if anyone was guilty of scapegoating, it was the Center. During the electoral postmortem it shrilly accused the Social Democrats of "lies and distortions" and generally underhanded campaign practices. The Catholic press complained about the passivity of the party, whereas the party blamed the dissident trade unionists. Leaders criticized the ineffectiveness of subsidiary organizations, especially between elections. And everyone chastized the allegedly apathetic Catholics "who still do not understand how deadly serious the situation is."[78]

The Center never reevaluated its policies preferring to minimize the tariff issue by arguing that if discontent had really been pervasive, the SPD would have done better still. Perhaps the Center had no choice. By 1903 it was firmly committed to a strategy of defending Catholic interests by occupying the pivotal position in parliament, and to retain that position, it had to support the government, Conservatives, and National Liberals on crucial issues such as the tariff and military spending. The Center knew that its policy was costly, but refused to discuss its working-class losses publicly. Only the National Liberals, long since excluded from contention in the Reichstag contest, had the courage to ask the question on all bourgeois and Catholic minds. "Given the enormous increase in the social democratic vote ... what will happen five years from now?"[79]

After 1903 the Social Democrats redoubled their efforts to win Catholic workers and assure even greater success in the next election. They continued to attack the Bülow tariff, which was scheduled to go into effect in 1906, labeling it "a harsh application of the Malthusian principle," and claiming that it would exacerbate the inflation that had begun in 1903.[80] On the basis of recent experience, Berten confidently predicted that "the time of mass hunger and mass misery is the golden time for the propagation of our ideas. In it the worker learns the principles of socialism as clear as day. He learns that the means of production must become his if things are to be different for him."[81]

As the Social Democrats realized, economic conditions did not automatically generate the desired responses, and the learning process could not be furthered by the tariff issue alone. After 1903 tariff agitation had a defensive and somewhat futile quality, for the parliamentary battle had been definitively lost on the one hand and the economic impact had not yet become evident on the other. The Social Democrats needed another issue that, like the tariff, would expose the Center Party's policies and undermine its credibility. They needed a means of relating socialism to the workers' everyday life in order to provide "an interpretation of experience, a language for conceptualizing class relations that helped to sharpen and broaden the sense of class consciousness."[82] Because no suitable economic or political issues emerged in the national or local arenas, the Social Democrats turned to religion. It was not to be a happy choice.

Prior to 1904 the Social Democrats had wisely recognized that religion was the Center's trump card and sought to eliminate it from political discussion. Thereafter they attempted to prove that Catholic theology and historical materialism were perfectly compatible and that any true Christian could, indeed, should be a Social Democrat. Laufenberg, who had been a Center intellectual and journalist before joining the SPD, championed this orientation. He argued that Christianity was originally "a purely proletarian class ideology, an explicitly pauper philosophy" that was "based on a primitive communism of consumption." Gradually the church developed a hierarchy, separated itself from the community, and abandoned its early collectivism. As a result, "alongside the ideology of proletarian free will and the right to existence, there developed an ideology of authority and right of property, which suited the hierarchy and the possessing classes in general." The church preached each to the appropriate audience.[83]

Laufenberg insisted that "the proletarian side of the Christian ideology should be played off against its clerical counterpart, against the Christianity of the ruling classes," for Christianity could promote revolution as well as acquiesence.[84] In a series of impassioned but highly intellectual pamphlets, Laufenberg sought to do just that. *Falsehood and Deceit or Christian Reaction and Christian Business* repeated the standard social democratic critique of Catholic social policy and analyzed the contradictory implications of Catholic social theory. *Can a Catholic Be a Social Democrat?* argued that "in the present it is precisely the Social Democrats who most strongly emphasize the genuinely ethical side of Christianity," and therefore sincere Catholics should join the SPD. *The Legend of the Worker-Pope* mercilessly criticized Leo XIII and the encyclical *Rerum Novarum* to which the Catholic Workers' Associations and Christian unions constantly appealed.[85]

Laufenberg's arguments, which leading local and regional Social Democrats repeated,[86] proved less than persuasive. They were too sophisticated and abstruse for many working-class Catholics, who had little if any knowledge of Christian theology, church history, or Catholic social theory and who did not regard religion as something to be analyzed and intellectualized. Whether workers accepted the vision of a hierarchical order of estates or rejected it, they believed that Catholicism unequivocally advocated such a society.[87] Discussions of primitive Christian communism could not convince them otherwise, for there was no popular left-wing Catholic tradition to which the Social Democrats could appeal. The attempt to redefine the relationship between religion and politics did not speak to a felt working-class need or offer an interpretation of a significant experience, as the tariff agitation had. Thus, it fell on deaf ears. The Center did not even bother to refute the new attack, preferring simply to repeat its claim that social democracy was anticlerical and atheistic.[88]

After 1903 the National Liberals and Conservatives, like the Center, bolstered their defenses against the SPD. They called for decisive action against "the inner enemy" and discussed with renewed interest altering the suffrage by means of a coup. They vehemently opposed any extension of social reform or improvement in the right to organize. Finally, they established the Imperial League against Social Democracy, which was to rally popular support against the left.[89]

The growing intransigence of the right and Center fostered a fearful and defensive mentality among Social Democrats in many areas of Germany. In Düsseldorf it increased their pessimism about reforming existing political institutions.[90] The *Volkszeitung* complained about the joint dictatorship of "the golden international of big business and the black international of Catholicism."[91] Kremser ridiculed a political system that "always protects the strong."[92] In 1905 Grimpe argued that the Dresden party congress's rejection of revisionism was vindicated by the subsequent behavior of the government and the bourgeois parties.[93] But until the Prussian suffrage campaign of 1906–10, no one could find an issue that would mobilize workers against the threat of reaction.

8

Move to the left

Between 1903 and 1905 the Düsseldorf Social Democrats had displayed an optimism born of pride in their accomplishments on the one hand and confidence in the correctness of the party's theory and tactics on the other. Thereafter, they questioned traditional strategy and developed an angry militancy that was directed not only at the state, the Center Party, and capitalist interests, but also at their more conservative comrades within the movement. This transformation was initiated by the labor protest, suffrage agitation, and mass strike debate of 1905–6, intensified by the 1907 election, fought on the explosive issue of nationalism, and subsequently fueled by renewed economic crisis, inflation, growing tax inequities, and military spending. In 1910 the second and unsuccessful Prussian suffrage campaign confirmed their adherence to the emerging left wing of the SPD, which advocated a more militant, confrontational strategy and dismissed the possibility of class alliances and substantial social or political reform.

During these years the Düsseldorf Social Democrats went through a learning process in which they debated and experimented with a variety of centrist and left positions, rejecting most of the former and embracing the latter. Although they continued to combat political Catholicism as vigorously as ever, they turned ever more attention to the state on the one hand and their more reformist comrades within the movement on the other, for both, it was felt, hindered the development of social democracy. Despite their growing numbers and visibility, the Düsseldorf Social Democrats experienced not a negative integration into society, which engendered reformism, but they experienced rather an isolation, which encouraged radicalism. Yet the very structures and social forces that promoted radicalism made it difficult to translate left policies and tactics into practice.

Prussian suffrage and the mass strike, round one

In late 1905 the Düsseldorf Social Democrats, in conjunction with their comrades throughout Germany, launched a campaign to reform the inequitable suffrage systems in northern Germany, above all Prussia. The suffrage campaign, which waxed and waned until 1914, was the most sustained, bitter, and militant battle fought by the Social Democrats. Their demand for universal male suffrage in Prussia challenged the Imperial German political and social order and placed political Catholicism in an ever more uncomfortable position vis-à-vis its working-class supporters. Yet precisely because universal male suffrage in Prussia had such revolutionary implications, neither the government nor the Center Party would support it, preferring to cling to the precarious stalemate that excluded the working class. During the prolonged campaign a social democratic left, offering a strategic alternative to the reformism of the right and the passivity of the center, emerged, and the Düsseldorf Social Democrats were to join it.

The enormous power of the Prussian Landtag, the governing body of Germany's largest and strongest state, explains the intensity of the struggle. Next to the Reichstag, the Landtag was the most important political institution in Germany, and in certain areas it alone had competence. The Landtag controlled the Prussian police, judicial, and prison systems; managed education, welfare, and factory inspection; and passed legislation regulating political organizations. Its lower house, the Diet, was elected by a suffrage system that divided the electorate into three income classes in such a way that roughly 8 million third-class voters elected one-third of the deputies while 750,000 second-class and 220,000 first-class ones chose the remaining two-thirds.[1] Introduced during the era of reaction following the 1848 revolution, this system also provided for indirect election and open voting. It enabled the Conservatives and National Liberals to dominate the Landtag and use it to influence national government policy and assured adequate representation to the Center, while excluding the Social Democrats completely. Unless the Prussian Landtag was reformed, Junkers, industrialists, and their Catholic allies would continue to prevent genuine parliamentary government with ministerial responsibility and control of military and foreign policy on the national level. Until the three-class suffrage was abolished in Prussia, it would persist in other states and cities. As the Social Democrats noted bitterly, "in most civilized countries of the world the class struggle is fought within a democracy. In Prussia, however, it is fought over the issue of democracy."[2]

That fight did not erupt in the 1890s, when Social Democrats throughout Prussia ignored the Landtag and its suffrage. After the turn of the century, however, the national party endorsed electoral participation, and the Düsseldorf Social Democrats, succumbing to outside pressure, reluctantly ran a slate. The results of the 1903 election were even worse than the pessimists had expected. In Düsseldorf only 44 of the 1,200 electors chosen were Social Democrats, and Prussia-wide the SPD failed to win a single mandate despite its more than 315,000 votes.[3] After the 1903 Reichstag election in which the SPD won 3 million votes, Liberals and Conservatives attacked the already restrictive suffrage systems in Saxony, Hessen, Lübeck, and Hamburg. Although massive and militant suffrage agitation occurred in Belgium, Sweden, and Holland, the SPD did little against the wave of reaction. In late 1905, however, the Russian Revolution, Austrian suffrage protest, and the German strike movement sparked an almost spontaneous campaign.[4] Social Democrats throughout Germany, alternating between optimism about the abolition of existing inequities and fear about the future of universal male suffrage nationally, launched a partly offensive, partly defensive struggle. The Düsseldorf Social Democrats, who had long maintained that electoral participation without such a struggle was unprincipled and self-defeating, eagerly joined in.

The Düsseldorf Social Democrats began with a massive educational effort. Laufenberg, Grimpe, Berten, Erbert, and Schmitt denounced the three-class system, which, they argued, was supported by a timid bourgeoisie that had once labeled it "a disgrace and a scandal." Income requirements and open voting were maintained solely to intimidate workers and curb the SPD. Every speaker detailed the power of the Landtag and documented its most blatant anti-proletarian actions.[5] The Social Democrats, incorporating suffrage into their ongoing critique of political Catholicism, argued that "the Prussian three-class system finds one of its most energetic supporters in the Center."[6] Abandoning the resignation that had characterized much of their previous rhetoric, the Social Democrats urged workers "to arise courageously in a powerful mass and announce your will loudly," warning them that "you deserve the deprivation of rights which has occurred if you continue to tolerate this system patiently."[7]

The National Liberals provided the most strident opposition to suffrage reform, for they had failed to build a mass party capable of winning Reichstag representation and owed their political prominence on the municipal and provincial levels to the three-class system. The liberal *Düsseldorfer Zeitung* argued adamantly that universal suffrage would be as detrimental in Prussia as it was nationally, for it would give the balance of power to the Center and benefit the lower classes. It was thoroughly unacceptable "to German men who have been raised with patriotic feeling and believe in the future of the fatherland."[8]

The Center Party, which stood to gain Diet seats from reform, nonetheless remained neutral, hoping that the entire conflict would disappear quickly. Its leaders supported neither universal suffrage nor genuine parliamentary government because these reforms would alienate the Center's National Liberal and Conservative Party allies and undermine its pivotal position in the Reichstag. The Center could not champion workers' rights in society at large when it denied them equality within its own ranks. And parity in either sphere would disrupt the delicate social equilibrium on which the future of political Catholicism depended. Yet the Center could not defend the existing suffrage against the express wishes of the Christian trade unions, for it could not risk a major confrontation with its unhappy working-class base so soon after the tariff controversy.[9] The contradictions within the Center could no longer be papered over with appeals to "harmonizing justice." Uneasy silence was the strategy of last resort.

While Catholics, Liberals, and government officials refused to discuss suffrage reform, the Social Democrats moved quickly from education to protest. The national party, anxious to channel rank-and-file militancy, planned massive meetings throughout Germany for January 21, 1906. Red Sunday was to commemorate the first anniversary of Bloody Sunday in Russia and simultaneously demonstrate the extensive working-class support for universal suffrage.[10] The Düsseldorf Social Democrats, previously marginal to national party activities, now cooperated with their comrades elsewhere in denouncing institutionalized political discrimination. The self-confidence they had recently gained led them to expand their critique of German society, not moderate it.

Yet they did not consider it either feasible or desirable to endorse new means to reach new goals. On the one hand, they lacked experience with such tactics as street demonstrations and political strikes and were reluctant to experiment without encouragement from Berlin. Moreover, local leaders conceived of the mass strike as a purely defensive weapon, "not to win rights but to defend them and if necessary to restore lost ones."[11] On the other hand, the euphoria engendered during the 1905 strikes persuaded them that massive but peaceful protests could be extremely powerful. Thus, rather than setting the rules of struggle, they argued, to quote Schmitt, that "if the government acts in a western way, so will we. If it uses eastern tactics, however, then we refuse all responsibility for the results."[12]

Although government officials did not imitate their Russian counterparts, they abandoned what the Social Democrats described as "a correct but certainly not benevolent attitude" toward the workers' movement.[13] Prussian officials forbade all outdoor meetings and street demonstrations, and the Düsseldorf police, believing that "there is a desire to demonstrate among Düsseldorf's radical element," raided the trade-union house, the *Volkszeitung* offices, and the homes of Laufenberg, Berten, Walbrecht, Erbert, and a dozen other leaders.[14] Although "they searched with painstaking thoroughness... not only going through laundry and cupboards but even lifting sleeping children from their beds," they found only a few hundred flyers.[15] The party tried to minimize the intimidating impact of "these glorious deeds of our police" by sarcasm and ridicule, and insisted that they "have accomplished what we ourselves previously failed to do... They have shaken the workers from their political sleep."[16] The National Liberals, who shared this assessment, urged the Prussian officials to display "somewhat more composure," and argued that if left to run its course, "the entire action, which has been set in motion with so much noise, will peter out without effect."[17]

Precisely that happened on January 21. At least 2,000 workers attended the four rallies, where Laufenberg, Fischer, Schmitt, and Jäcker denounced the Landtag as "a caricature of popular representation." Several thousand more were turned away for lack of space.[18] As the *Volkszeitung* proudly noted, "Düsseldorf has never seen such a demonstration." The police were heavily armed and soldiers were stationed throughout the city, showing, according to Laufenberg, "how our ruling Junkers plan to use the army against the internal enemy."[19] The Social Democrats gave them no excuse to intervene, however, for every speaker warned workers to avoid provocative statements and watch out for police infiltrators. Berten assigned local union leaders to see that the meetings dispersed quietly.[20] The display of state power had not been so ineffectual after all.

After Red Sunday, the tide of radicalism began to ebb. The massive display of working-class strength failed to impress the government or convert the Center, but it did frighten the national party executive and the general commission of trade unions, both of which worked to curb rank-and-file suffrage protest. At the same time the domestic strike wave subsided and the Russian revolutionaries suffered a definitive defeat.[21] The Social Democrats could neither continue the campaign using traditional means nor agree on alternatives.

The national debate that followed ʼthe first round of the suffrage campaign centered on the mass strike and brought to the surface the irreconcilable divisions not only between the party and the union movement but also between the right and the emerging left within the SPD. When the mass strike was first discussed in the wake of the 1905 Russian Revolution, most Düsseldorf leaders endorsed it "not as a means of attack but of defense." They acknowledged that "a growing aversion to and agitation against universal suffrage goes hand in hand with the concentration of capital," but asserted that "as long as the proletariat is allowed the possibility of bringing its influence to bear legally by means of equal, direct, and universal suffrage, there is hardly any cause to think about political strikes."[22]

Nonetheless, all but a few trade-union functionaries, such as Ahrens, condemned the decision of the 1905 Cologne trade-union congress to suppress completely discussion of the subject, arguing that the workers must prepare for all contingencies with every possible weapon. "If the masses are not ripe for a mass strike," argued Giebel, "we must educate them for it."[23] When the Jena party congress sanctioned discussion of the mass strike as both an offensive and a defensive weapon, Berten, Laufenberg, Schmitt and their allies were jubilant. Even if much of the rank and file remained indifferent to the problem, the principle had been established and educational work could begin.[24]

The following year their optimism was deflated but not destroyed. In a series of secret meetings with the national party executive, the trade-union general commission announced its refusal to discuss or support a mass strike. The previously subordinate unions were demanding veto power over the party and sabotaging a strategy that required a suspension of the rigid division between economic and political struggles, short- and long-run goals.[25] When the protocols of this conference were published in mid-1906, a bitter debate erupted in Düsseldorf. Although Jantzen and a few other union functionaries defended the general commission's stance on the grounds that unions should concentrate exclusively on improving the workers' material position, most Düsseldorf leaders were critical. Milow spoke disparagingly about the unions' reprehensible lack of interest in theory. Berten attacked them for refusing to discuss the mass strike, which was impossible at the moment but might be necessary in the future. Fischer blamed the entire controversy on the unions' failure to remember that the movement's end goal was socialism, not simply piecemeal reform.[26] Pfeiffer struck a popular theme when he argued that "it's not a question of whether or not we want a mass strike but of whether or not we quietly submit when reaction throws us to the ground."[27] Düsseldorf did not seek to put the mass strike on the immediate agenda or make it part of the party's practical work but rather to have it recognized in principle and discussed in practice.

Despite their anger, the Düsseldorf Social Democrats minimized the seriousness of the conflict between the party and the unions. Clinging to the illusion of unity that had sustained them so long, they, like radicals elsewhere, entirely misinterpreted the meaning of the 1906 Mannheim party congress. Instead of recognizing that giving the unions parity with the party on major decisions was a stunning victory for the forces of reformism, they believed that "not only the party but also the powerful German trade unions have unanimously agreed to the mass strike as a possible weapon."[28]

Although the priorities of the leaders were clear, the position of the members was not. Relatively few came to discussions of national party affairs, for they were still trapped in the isolation, parochialism, and political passivity from which the leaders were emerging.[29] Subsequent events were to make them more aware of the necessity of abandoning centrism and participating in national party controversies, for the Prussian suffrage campaign opened a period of growing conflict both between social democracy and society in Düsseldorf and between the national party's emerging left and the right and center. These struggles were to isolate and radicalize the Düsseldorf working class.

Throughout 1906 relations between Social Democrats and the state in Düsseldorf deteriorated. Far from being an isolated incident, the intensive police harassment prior to Red Sunday marked the beginning of a "new course," dictated by the regional and Prussian governments. The police continued to search homes and confiscate literature; the judiciary barred *Volkszeitung* editor Eskuchen from sessions of the provincial court; and local officials and private citizens filed more than thirty-five charges of libel and slander against the paper. Schotte, who served as the sacrificial responsible editor through much of this period, spent more than five months in jail for libeling a variety of stalwart citizens, including the mayor of Erkrath, a drunken policeman, and a Düsseldorf factory owner. He was even punished for "ridiculing Prussian state institutions" when he called the Landtag "a world unto itself, existing outside the people, outside Europe and outside all intelligence."[30] The *Volkszeitung* amassed 1,800 M in fines. Schotte remarked bitterly that "the current situation in Düsseldorf promises to be even worse than it once was under the anti-socialist laws. It is clear that a social democratic movement cannot exist without being persecuted."[31]

Although the prediction was exaggerated, the Social Democrats were justifiably upset. All their energies were absorbed with protest meetings and endless court appearances by Schotte, Erbert, Laufenberg, Höch, and Müller. They barely rallied their forces for the late fall municipal elections and then failed to win a single seat. By year's end they were exhausted and demoralized. Despite union growth, the strike wave had brought few concrete gains. Red Sunday had been exhilarating, but the campaign it was to herald had quickly fizzled out. The new course had shown how easily the government could disrupt the movement and throw it on the defensive. Much of the optimism of 1904–5 had vanished. The remainder was to be destroyed in early 1907 when the Social Democrats were forced into an unexpected and unwanted Reichstag election.

Nationalism and politics

In mid-December 1906, Chancellor Bülow, the architect of the 1902 tariff and the National Liberal–Conservative–Center alliance that had governed since, dissolved the Reichstag. For months his government had been under attack for wasting millions on Germany's small and scattered colonies, which brought neither profits nor prestige nor military advantage. The colonial office tolerated administrative abuses, even atrocities, and the military was waging a war of extermination against the Hereros in South West Africa. Scathing criticism came not only from the SPD, which Bülow regularly ignored, but also from the Center. Rather than investigating the charges, Bülow took his case to the people.

The resulting Hottentot election was a plebiscite in part about *Weltpolitik*, that popular slogan which Germany had such difficulty translating into concrete power, and in part about the chancellor's right to manage foreign and military affairs without parliamentary supervision. It was an attempt, in the tradition of Bismarck, to divert attention from domestic affairs and to use nationalism to rally liberals and conservatives of all shadings against the Social Democrats. As befit the age of mass politics, however, Bülow sought to mobilize wide support for his position, recruiting the aid of such organizations as the Navy League, the Pan German League, and the Imperial Association against Social Democracy.[32] And this strategy did convince most Germans to support expansion abroad at the expense of parliamentary government at home. It brought to an abrupt halt two decades of social democratic electoral progress and forced the movement to reassess its practice – with highly divisive results.

Bülow's maneuver caught the Social Democrats by surprise, for both the national and local parties had been preoccupied with the Prussian suffrage campaign and its aftermath. Of greater importance, it forced them to fight about nationalism, an issue they had scrupulously avoided because any position they might take would be controversial and costly. Ostensibly the Social Democrats were internationalists, to employ their positive term, or "men without a fatherland," to use the derogatory label of the dominant society. Yet national party leaders, such as Bebel, insisted that they were loyal to the German nation if not its existing political institutions, and preached international brotherhood only on May Day. They adopted a policy of "not a man and not a penny" to the existing military, but the executive refused to sanction any sustained anti-militarist agitation. The Social Democrats opposed all military appropriations and criticized Germany's strident and expansionist foreign policy – significant actions in a society with no bourgeois opposition – but they promised support for a defensive war. The party program advocated a militia, but the party never pushed for that alternative to the Prussian army.[33]

The SPD's muddled stance on colonialism and militarism had its roots in the program and practice of the party, the strength of nationalist sentiment among the middle and upper classes, and the ambiguous attitude of the working class toward the German state. Marx and Engels had no theory of imperialism that would enable workers to situate it in the overall development of capitalism, and Hilferding, Luxemburg,

Kautsky, and Lenin had not yet produced their works, which would set the terms for subsequent debates.[34] The SPD had no strategy for curbing militarism and, if necessary, preventing war. Revisionists and reformists urged the party to develop a beneficial nationalism, and even a socialist colonialism, in order to win wider support in the bourgeoisie as well as the proletariat. Kautskyan centrists and trade-union leaders were lukewarm about internationalism and feared reprisals against anti-militarism. The left saw war as inevitable but was only beginning to advocate using the mass strike against it. All were acutely aware that the German middle classes had long since abandoned liberalism for nationalism and regarded power abroad as compensation for impotence at home. The deadlock among the Social Democrats, which was replicated in the Second International, eliminated any pretext for state intervention, but alienated the middle classes and confused the working class.

The divisions within social democracy reflected and reinforced working-class ambivalence toward state and society. On the one hand, workers received a strongly nationalistic socialization in the schools, churches, and military, as well as in the popular press and mass culture. Some looked forward to military service as one of the few respites from the drudgery of proletarian life. Others admired the Emperor along with Bebel or in place of him. On the other hand, many other workers resented their political subordination and economic oppression, disliked the discipline and indoctrination of the army, and opposed a state that preferred imperial glory to social welfare and political justice.[35]

Rather than trying to clarify these contradictory attitudes, the Social Democrats preferred to ignore them, and Düsseldorf, despite its left leanings, was no exception. Speakers mentioned militarism and nationalism only when an imperialist crisis, such as the Spanish–American War or the Boer War, erupted. In 1906 a mere two, rather poorly attended, district meetings raised the recently exposed colonial scandals. When attacking military expenditures, which occurred frequently, the Social Democrats couched their critique in terms of cost, not nationalistic motivation or expansionist implications, and their pledges of allegiance to internationalism each May Day seldom went beyond the general and rhetorical. Walbrecht and Gewehr both argued that war was inevitable under capitalism, for example, but the former advocated pacifism whereas the latter endorsed defensive struggles against Russia, the enemy of the working class everywhere.[36] Manasse, addressing a May

Day rally, claimed that "the internationalism of the proletariat expresses itself in the common support for freedom, human rights, and world peace, for a social order in which...a worker's life is not spent like a winter day without heat and sun."[37] No one offered a strategy for attaining these goals, however, or insisted that they should be an integral part of the party's practical work. In short, both locally and nationally the Social Democrats were ill prepared to fight an election about *Weltpolitik*.

In 1907 they were forced into such a contest under the worst of circumstances. The National Liberals and Conservatives predictably rallied behind Bülow, and the various imperialist associations organized public opinion most effectively. The Progressives, led by a younger, more nationalistic generation that was anxious to share in power, also joined the colonial camp.[38] Only the Center Party, long a loyal supporter of the chancellor, became an unrelenting critic of colonial mismanagement and was, in turn, the target of vitriolic attacks, unmatched since the *Kulturkampf*. As the Catholic *Düsseldorfer Tageblatt* noted with glee:

The Social Democrats presently find themselves in a desperate situation. The Center Party stands in opposition to the government as the defender of the constitutional rights of the people and the ruthless critic of our colonial abuses. Therefore, the Social Democrats cannot throw around the slogan about the "government party."[39]

The Düsseldorf Social Democrats found this situation, so reminiscent of the 1890s, not at all to their liking. Their initial response to the impending election was to concentrate on purely organizational preparations.[40] Technical expertise, adequate funds, and enthusiastic party workers, however, were no substitute for effective arguments against the torrent of nationalistic propaganda. Precisely these were lacking in 1907.

Some Social Democratic agitators, such as Laufenberg and Spiegel, focused on the exorbitant price of dubious colonial ventures. Attacking the policies of the state rather than the economics of capitalism, they cried out passionately that:

Untold millions disappear into the pockets of swindlers who are decorated with state medals. The cultivators of murder weapons, the army and navy, greedily strangle the vigor and power of the nation, drive the debts of the Empire to insane heights. In order to protect and secure the goods, the foul pleasure seeking of a small minority, the people are driven into the abyss.[41]

Others, ranging from prominent outsiders such as Singer and Molkenbuhr to local leaders such as Fischer and Jäcker, blamed the

Center Party entirely for Germany's foolish and corrupt colonial policy. Although the Center objected to certain abuses, it nonetheless endorsed the principles of *Weltpolitik* and had approved all previous appropriations. As Grimpe claimed, in an oft-repeated charge, the Center's current oppositional posture was simply self-serving wheeling and dealing.[42]

Both arguments fell flat. The working class did not feel the economic costs of colonialism as immediately as those of the tariff. The party could neither readily illustrate those connections nor convincingly place all responsibility for colonialism on the shoulders of its arch enemy. The Center was, after all, attacking the government, and its previous support for militarism and nationalism had always been opportunistic and equivocal. The Center's hostility to the working class was much less evident in foreign policy than in domestic. Finally, by reducing colonialism to a question of taxes and Catholic machinations, the Social Democrats blinded themselves to the ideological appeal and political uses of nationalism.

The Center Party, enjoying the electoral advantages of its oppositional position, argued its case with an assertiveness not seen since the mid-1890s. It adroitly attacked colonial monopolies, administrative mismanagement, and abuses against the indigenous population without rejecting colonialism per se. This position appealed to bourgeois Catholics, long critical of the Prussian state, and to the increasingly nationalistic Christian trade unionists, both of whom wanted a humanitarian, religious colonial policy.[43] The Center proudly reviewed its social policy record, and even defended its stance on tariffs, ridiculing the Social Democrats for "once again beating the drum about this issue."[44] Finally, it adroitly exploited fears that government and liberal attacks heralded another *Kulturkampf*.

Despite their unpreparedness, the Social Democrats had approached the election with a naive optimism. That was quickly dispelled by the first round of voting, when they won only 25,389 votes as against 29,259 for the Center and a remarkable 14,664 for the previously insignificant National Liberals. As the *Volkszeitung* noted with dismay, there was "an elemental outburst of bourgeois class instinct against the working class." The Social Democrats controlled a smaller percentage of the electorate than they had in 1903, and their ranks were increasing more slowly than those of the Catholics and Liberals. The early February run-off was even more of a debacle, for many discouraged workers stayed away from the polls, while Catholic nonvoters and National Liberals appeared in record numbers. As a result the Center Party swept the election by a vote of 33,317 to 25,233. In urban Düsseldorf, which the Social Democrats had captured in 1903, the Center triumphed by nearly 3,000 votes.[45] Political Catholicism, given a new lease on life by the nationalism of the Protestant middle classes, had reversed its previous humiliation.[46]

The Düsseldorf Social Democrats took scant consolation from the fact that they did much better than their comrades in other Catholic districts.[47] They hardly noticed that for the first time the Center Party won less than 50 percent of the vote in the rapidly industrializing county. If they realized that the Center's working-class base was continuing to defect, they were too demoralized to comment on it. Yet defecting it was. Because both the Protestant and Catholic middle classes united in opposition to the SPD, the left relied almost exclusively on proletarian votes. If all of the nearly 7,000 Protestant working-class voters supported the SPD, they would have accounted for only 37 percent of the total, as against 44 percent in 1898. More than 11,000 Catholic workers now voted SPD, whereas only 7,000 backed the Center, two-thirds of whose electorate came from the middle and lower middle classes. And these workers were not turning to the social democratic movement simply out of frustration at election time. One in every two was in a union and one in ten in the party.[48] Such unspectacular progress hardly fulfilled the enormous expectations raised by the 1903 election and the subsequent progress on all fronts. The Social Democrats' former patience, born of failure, was exhausted, and they wanted tangible power.

National results intensified the bitterness engendered by the local setback. The party won scarcely more votes than in 1903, and it lost 38 of its 81 parliamentary seats, including two in the Lower Rhine. Bülow remained securely in power, backed by the classic Bismarckian alliance of National Liberals and Conservatives, and the Center moderated its criticism of an obviously popular colonial policy. The Social Democrats were more isolated than ever. In the ensuing electoral postmortem, reformists and radicals were to give very different diagnoses of the party's ills.

1907 had a radicalizing impact on the Düsseldorf Social Democrats not because they were defeated, an experience with which they were all too familiar, but because the gap between their expectations and the results was so enormous. 1907 reflected and reinforced the isolation and exclusively proletarian composition of the movement. It denied the party the minimal success that would have been necessary to make reformism seem feasible. It proved beyond all doubt that political Catholicism and nationalism had an extremely tenacious hold over the middle classes and sections of the working class as well. In the wake of their defeat, the Düsseldorf Social Democrats intensified their critique of both reformism and the gradualist parliamentary strategy practiced for so long.

Neither reformists nor radicals could deny that the bourgeoisie had deserted the SPD en masse in 1907. Whereas Bernstein, Calwer, and others urged the national party to moderate its rhetoric and policies so as to win back the middle classes, the left in Düsseldorf and elsewhere condemned compromise positions and electoral alliances.[49] At the 1907 Essen party congress, the Düsseldorf Social Democrats proposed that the party forbid all support for bourgeois candidates, whether left liberal or Catholic. Düsseldorf favored, to quote Laufenberg, "an unrelenting, stubborn, and energetic struggle against bourgeois society."[50] Although the congress rejected the resolution and Bebel reprimanded Laufenberg for his intransigence, the Düsseldorf Social Democrats remained convinced that all their progress was due to uncompromising opposition to the Center, whose "allegedly democratic past" was deceptive.[51] At the regional party congress, Düsseldorf stated its position unequivocally. "It is an illusion to assume that we would have greater success if we gave more consideration to the strata which lie between the employers and the working class. This is completely impossible here in the lower Rhine. Here everything is black and white."[52]

Because the social and political situation in the Ruhr was antithetical to reformism, the Düsseldorf Social Democrats rejected the right's pleas for more "practical work" and less "sterile dogma."[53] "Our agitation must express the standpoint of the proletarian class struggle clearly and unambiguously," insisted the *Volkszeitung*.[54] Far from being too radical, the party had not been radical enough in 1907. Too much energy was devoted to negative criticism of social legislation and tax policies.[55] "That is all necessary," argued Berten, "but we should not forgo pointing out the end goal of our movement. If we had done that our electoral agitation would have been greatly strengthened. The masses realize that . . . things will only get better when the ax is laid to the root of the problem."[56]

Düsseldorf also defended a principled position on colonialism and militarism. After the Hottentot election, both Bebel and the reformists denied that the SPD was anti-nationalist. They advocated a reformed and efficient army and a beneficial, social colonialism that would replace the current destructive, capitalist variety, which exploited foreign peoples in the interests of a small bourgeois minority. Led by Laufenberg, the Düsseldorf Social Democrats accused the SPD of "lacking the necessary revolutionary energy."[57] At the Lower Rhine party congress, they and their regional comrades voted overwhelmingly for Düsseldorf's strongly anti-colonialist resolution, which stated that "the party congress rejects any socialist colonial policy which would base a right of 'guardianship' on the differences in cultural levels among various people. Such a policy compromises the principled position of the party and is irreconcilable with the proletarian class struggle."[58] The Düsseldorf Social Democrats were equally critical of militarism, insisting that the movement undertake more vigorous agitation on this issue. Some leaders, such as Laufenberg and Werner, favored using the mass strike to prevent war, whereas Jäcker and other trade-union functionaries declared it futile. Both sides were too insecure to push a vote when the Düsseldorf party discussed the 1907 congress of the International, at which this issue had been raised.[59]

The Düsseldorf Social Democrats thus emerged from the 1907 election more convinced than ever that the workers had no allies, that reformism was impossible, and that compromises would cost the movement its identity without winning it new adherents. Their intransigent position separated them not only from the surrounding society but also from the right and center elements within the SPD. Their isolation provided them with the critical distance necessary to develop a radical alternative to the analysis offered by Berlin. It forced them to assess their own experience and rely on their own resources.

Economic crisis and trade-union stagnation

After the Hottentot election the economy took a precipitous downturn, and as in the past, economic crisis intensified class antagonism but undermined the workers' ability to defend their interests. Moreover, the depression of 1907–9 marked more than a temporary worsening of the terms of struggle for the Social Democrats. It initiated a period in which the working class was thrown decisively on the defensive by German industry's efforts to organize capitalist interests, reorganize production, restructure relations between capital and the state, and employ new tactics against the labor movement. Both the immediate crisis and the more general transformation led to a deterioration in the condition of the German working class in the years before World War I. In Düsseldorf, recession and rationalization were to make sustained radicalism seem desirable, indeed necessary.

The economic crisis of 1907–9 was even more serious than the turn-of-the-century depression. As production dropped and prices fell, unemployment rose, wage cuts multiplied, and profits dwindled. "It was a time of pronounced economic depression," according to the city government, and "the labor market has almost never been this bad." During 1908 health insurance membership in Düsseldorf declined by more than 3,000. In metal alone more than 1,800 jobs were lost, and firms such as Hohenzollern Lokomotiv, which retained their workers, cut wages. The municipal labor exchange, which had 71 jobs per 100 applicants in 1907, had only 45 per 100 in 1908 and actually found work for only 38 percent. The situation scarcely improved in 1909.[60]

As the economy worsened, industrialists redoubled their efforts to increase productivity through technological change, work reorganization, and new payment systems. In basic iron and steel, chemicals, and paper, mechanization was extensive; whereas in metalworking and machinery, in woodworking, and on the docks, it was being introduced piecemeal, a power lathe here, a power saw or crane there. Although industrialists did not attempt to introduce a full-fledged version of Taylorism with its minute control of the laborer through time and motion studies, both factory and artisan firms did intensify the pace of work by altering piece rates and experimenting with bonus systems. In addition, management took charge of setting piece rates, which had once been negotiated by workers and foremen, and introduced time clocks.[61]

The reorganization of the shop floor was accompanied by increased collaboration among the already highly organized capitalist interests. Employers' associations, established locally and regionally in the late 1890s and nationally in 1904, became increasingly cohesive and militant. Workers' demands were countered with threats of reprisals, and even small strikes were frequently met with massive regional and national lockouts. Employers' associations not only sought to make economic conflict prohibitively expensive, but also tried to rescind collective bargaining where it existed and lobbied energetically but unsuccessfully for a prohibition of picketing, aimed at "protecting those willing to work."[62]

These cyclical and structural changes weakened the Düsseldorf union movement, which lost 21 percent of its membership in 1907–8 and did not recover those losses until 1910. Between mid-1907 and mid-1909 there were only fifteen strikes involving 717 workers, and ten of these ended in complete failure for the unions.[63] Most were defensive struggles against the corrosive impact of recession, rationalization, tariffs, and inequitable taxes. This proved to be a labor Sisyphus, for in the years after 1906 the growth of real wages slowed in some sectors and stagnated or actually declined in others.[64]

In the few union struggles that occurred during the depression, the tendency of powerful employers' associations to turn local conflicts into regional and even national battles became more pronounced. When Düsseldorf's journeymen gardeners staged their first strike to improve notoriously low wages, for example, the masters immediately locked out the entire work force. Guild and nonguild tailoring establishments did the same nationally in order to impose a most disadvantageous contract. Construction firms locked out stone cutters locally to achieve a similar end. In 1908 plasterers and paving stone workers withstood regional lockouts, called to impose contracts that decreased wages and increased hours, but longshoremen failed to resist a similar attack.[65] As Tobler, the head of the painters union, noted, "the employers love to play with the idea of bleeding the unions to death."[66]

Initially the unions responded to these lockouts by admonishing their members to discipline, organization, and caution. In addition, they sought to counter the anti-socialist sentiment of the middle classes and government, which had intensified markedly since 1903, by rallying public opinion to their side. The gardeners, for example, circulated a most deferential flyer, describing their miserable conditions, listing their modest demands, and noting the poor quality of scab labor. The tailors appealed to the humanitarian sentiments of Düsseldorf's citizens, arguing both on their own behalf and on that of the singularly exploited home workers. They urged the public to pressure firms to settle before artisan shops succumbed needlessly to factory competion. (The tailor's guild, it should be noted, used this same argument against the workers.)[67]

In the bitter 1910 conflict in construction, workers responded more aggressively. The powerful employers' association called a nationwide lockout in order to impose a uniform national contract that would introduce piece rates and establish labor exchanges, both managed exclusively by the employers. What the unions had long feared came to pass. More than 175,000 construction workers were locked out, and the six-week contest of wills cost the union nearly 9 million M. Yet the union survived – indeed, it even gained new members – and because its strength so nearly matched that of the employers, the state finally arbitrated an agreement that introduced the ten-hour day, increased wages modestly, and dropped all plans for a uniform national contract and an employer-controlled labor exchange.[68] Masons in several large cities, including Düsseldorf, refused to accept the settlement, however, arguing that their real wages would actually decline over the life of the contract because of inflation. Despite opposition from the leadership, 600 masons and helpers struck twenty Düsseldorf firms in late June. According to the police, "the employees are acting independently, without the understanding of the leaders, for the leaders have lost all authority here since the national union accepted the decision of the mediation court."[69] Without national support, however, the Düsseldorf rebels were fighting a doomed battle. After a few weeks they unhappily resumed work under the objectionable contract terms.[70]

Those employers who did not use the lockout were equally determined to limit concessions and stop the spread of collective bargaining. Increasingly they defeated workers – even those who stayed out for weeks and months. The tailors and painters were able to defend the idea of collective bargaining and secure minor wage increases because the free and Christian unions remained more united than the numerous small employers in the construction and garment industries. Carpenters, however, were unable to win a wage hike, and lost one-sixth of their membership after the defeat. A three-month strike of marble workers failed completely, and although nearly 300 pipefitters forced the recalcitrant guild to accept a contract, the terms were only slightly better than before.[71]

During the dockers' strike, the Wicking'sche construction materials supply firm sent the police a most revealing justification for employer intransigence. Workers' wages had risen excessively because of the disorganization of the employers, and the resulting high wages aroused envy and protest among those less well off. Wage cuts would curb such disaffection and were moreover justified because the introduction of cranes had lightened work loads. The letter also advocated the abolition of seniority so as to limit insubordination among secure workers. Although most companies did not state their aims so explicitly, they shared similar attitudes and pursued similar policies. In the crisis-ridden metal sector, for example, industrialists used the recession as an excuse for wage cutting, but when prosperity returned in 1910 they pointed to competition or, as at Mannesmann, to "improved machinery... which forces us to reduce the old piece rates in relationship to the increased productivity."[72]

Employers were even more intransigent about control issues than wage ones. When more than 100 Catholic and socialist masons walked out to protest the firing of a Christian trade-union leader, the firm immediately hired replacements. The eighty turners who struck the Woest machine factory to demand a public posting of piece rates returned to work after six weeks, having extracted no concessions. When forty masons struck the Düsseldorf Pipe and Tin Rolling Mill to demand higher wages in place of a yearly bonus, the firm labeled the action "a power play of the union against the firm," and insisted that "nothing can be granted since a question of principle is involved."[73]

Both wage and control disputes were waged with increasing violence. In the plasterers' lockout and the longshoremen's strike, for example, there were shooting incidents between pickets and scabs. The police escorted those willing or foolish enough to work, limited picketing, and made numerous arrests.[74]

Even those workers, such as carpenters and woodworkers, who fared much better than their comrades in metal by 1910, were barely able to recoup their recent losses and maintain the status quo. Rank-and-file resentment of the meager results gained by traditional tactics grew to unprecedented proportions. The carpenters were least dissatisfied, for they finally forced the guild to sign a contract that raised wages to the level promised but not paid in 1907 and slated still further increases for 1912. Masons, as we saw, protested their settlement strongly. The woodworkers were the dubious beneficiaries of one of the first national collective bargaining agreements in Germany. The national union signed a contract that was bitterly criticized by the 1,600 Düsseldorf woodworkers who attended the ratification meeting. Angry union members complained that the national leaders had failed to exploit the return of prosperity and insisted that they were entitled to both higher wages and shorter hours. After acrimonious debate the contract was finally accepted "against a strong minority."[75]

Düsseldorf workers, so hard hit by the recession, thus did not benefit from the return of prosperity. Like their counterparts elsewhere in Germany, their position relative to other classes worsened. Employers, such as the engineering firm Franz Schülter, might bitterly lament that "it is no longer possible to conduct business peacefully in Düsseldorf against the wishes of the trade unions," but both labor and capital knew that capital was still dominant.[76]

The working class was excluded from Imperial Germany economically and socially as well as politically, and there seemed no way to break out of this second-class status. Social democratic successes on all fronts after 1903 had aroused the ire of industrialists and government officials alike and led to increased police and judicial harassment of trade unionists. Such "class justice" did not curb the workers' movement, but it did "destroy the credibility of the judiciary and promote the alienation of the organized working class from a state which was perceived as an instrument of class rule."[77] Union organization and militancy had precipitated employer organization and rationalization that weakened the workers' position structurally and politically. This dismal situation encouraged a cautious reformism among national trade-union leaders that found an echo among some local functionaries, but it promoted dissension and militancy among the rank and file.[78] Economics, like politics, pushed the Düsseldorf Social Democrats steadily to the left.

Radicalization

In the wake of the 1907 social democratic electoral defeat, the classic Imperial German alliance of agrarian Conservatives and industrial National Liberals was recreated. Although the left liberals replaced the Center Party as the junior partner, the Bülow bloc was no more reform-minded than its predecessor. Quite the contrary. The ruling classes continued "their ceaseless attempt to ban the danger of domestic change once and for all."[79] Between 1907 and 1910 they blocked all tax reform despite skyrocketing military expenditures, defended the three-class suffrage despite massive protests, and thwarted any significant improvements in the right to organize. Neither the Bülow bloc nor the blue–black coalition of Conservatives and Centrists with which Chancellor Bethmann-Hollweg ruled after 1909, was able to repress the social democratic movement. But they were able to perpetuate structures that prevented reform.

The social democratic response to this stalemate in national politics was deeply divided. The South German party practiced reformism on the regional level, whereas center leaders preached patience, isolation, and passivity. Only the emerging left, of which Düsseldorf was a part, advocated a radical extraparliamentary strategy, centering on the mass strike.

Taxes and budgets first stirred up controversy by confronting the SPD with the possibility of cooperating with bourgeois groups. These fiscal issues forced the party to choose between long- and short-range goals, principle or expediency, economics or politics. In short, the revisionist controversy was rekindled but this time as a question of practice rather than theory.[80]

The Social Democrats had been divided about whether to vote for provincial budgets since the 1890s. The South Germans, who enjoyed more democratic conditions and greater political representation, insisted that the issue was purely tactical and that approval was permissible if the budget contained provisions beneficial to workers and peasants. North Germans, on the contrary, staunchly defended the principle "to this system not a man and not a penny" and passed repeated resolutions to that effect at party congresses. In 1908, however, the Social Democrats in both the Bavarian and Baden parliaments voted for their budgets, and the controversy erupted anew.[81]

The Düsseldorf Social Democrats, who had passed a nearly unanimous resolution against budget approval as recently as 1907, eagerly supported the effort of radicals and centrists to condemn the breach of discipline. The *Volkszeitung* launched a vituperative attack on "the South German tactic," labeling it a distortion of "positive cooperation" and arguing that conditions in Bavaria and Baden were not so different from those in Prussia.[82] At a large and lively party meeting, which reflected the membership's growing interest in theoretical and strategic disputes, Berten roundly denounced those who sought to transform the SPD into "a bourgeois radical reform party." He argued that "we have no cause to give up our principles and our tactics. The capitalist system with its injuries cannot be eliminated by concessions to the ruling class and its government." When the DMV functionaries Walbrecht and Spiegel dissented, they were shouted down by the vast majority, who regarded the budget issue as a matter of principle and party discipline. The rank and file, led by the radical local party functionaries, endorsed the 1908 Nürnberg party congress's condemnation of the South Germans and resolved that "we expect that the party leadership will introduce the necessary steps against every violation of the resolution in order to preserve the self-respect and unity of the party."[83] If agreement on principles did not exist, then it had to be enforced by discipline where possible and expulsion where necessary.

Although the budget issue receded in 1909, the questions it had raised were posed anew by the government's proposed financial reform. The national government supported itself completely through tariff revenues, indirect taxes, and contributions from the federal states, all of which benefited agrarians and industrialists at the expense of the lower classes. These had kept the government solvent in the 1880s and 1890s. Between 1896 and 1908, however, military expenditures, which accounted for 90 percent of the budget, doubled. Even though indirect taxes had risen from 7.15 M per capita in 1884 to 26.52 M in 1909, the state went heavily into debt. By 1909 the situation had become so serious that Bülow proposed supplementing the usual indirect taxes with a token direct one. His reform plan would raise 400 million M by increasing a variety of indirect levies and 100 million M by introducing an inheritance tax. He hoped to win Conservative support for the first bill and SPD backing for the second. His calculations proved false, for although National Liberals and Progressives were willing to accept some change, the Conservatives refused to give up any of their fiscal privileges and the Social Democrats were bitterly divided. The reformists urged support for the inheritance tax, because the Erfurt program endorsed direct levies and the indirect burdens would be passed in any case. The radicals advocated rejection because the new revenues were to be used solely for armaments and would not lighten the workers' burden.[84]

Düsseldorf championed the radical cause without hesitation, opposing any support, intentional or otherwise, for militarism and criticizing those who sought "to make parliamentary activity the alpha and omega of the party's work."[85] They hammered home the cost of "this monstrosity of the Hottentot election," as they called the finance-reform plan. They attempted to reach the indifferent through an appeal to their pocketbook and to mobilize the committed by politicizing an economic issue that affected all workers, regardless of occupation, religion, or culture. As with the tariff, the popular response was encouraging. According to the *Volkszeitung*, "the new tax burdens drove the proletariat into lively political activity."[86]

It was not only social democratic workers who were demonstrably unhappy. The police reported that Christian trade unionists were "rather irritated" by the Center's support for indirect taxes but not for the death duty. Clerical and lay leaders had "their hands full trying to justify the position of the Center to the workers."[87] The *Westdeutsche Arbeiter-zeitung*, sent to all members of the Christian trade unions and the Catholic Workers' Associations, defended the Center Party vigorously. Matthias Schiffer, the head of the Central Association of Christian Trade Unions and a Reichstag deputy, visited Düsseldorf to argue that the new revenues were vital to national security and that workers could easily bear the additional tax burden.[88]

Despite the popularity of the Social Democrats' arguments, the Conservatives and the Center, against the wishes of not only the SPD but the National Liberals and Progressives as well, passed the indirect taxes and defeated the death duty. The Conservative Junkers had proven themselves the strongest power within the Empire, and the Center joined with them in order to regain its pivotal political position. Christian trade unionists did not defect en masse, as the Social Democrats had predicted, but the finance-reform plan did further erode the Center's credibility with Catholic workers, especially migrant ones.

In the wake of the budget and finance-reform controversies, the Düsseldorf Social Democrats became increasingly critical of the national party's indecisive stance. "The party must be clear about the way to its goals," argued the *Volkszeitung*, "if it wants to retain the allegiance of the masses who are necessary for its victory."[89] And the way to its goals, Düsseldorf believed, was not through reformism. Berten summed up the mood in the entire Lower Rhine by asserting that:

Our party has a radical tradition in the industrial west, and we consider it impossible for revisionism to win a foothold here. This is because the economic and political pressures that bear down on the workers in our region are so strong. Through them the masses are forged together and learn class consciousness and revolutionary thinking.[90]

The next round of the Prussian suffrage campaign, which opened in 1910, confirmed this analysis, for it showed that the constitutional issue could be "solved only by revolution."[91]

Far from letting the suffrage campaign die after 1906, the Düsseldorf Social Democrats, together with their comrades in the Lower Rhine, had made a strenuous effort to revive it. When the Prussian Landtag opened in late 1907, they held several large but peaceful meetings to condemn "the parliament of class and privilege." At one such rally Jantzen exposed the duplicity of the Center, which "acts as if it wants the Reichstag suffrage for the Landtag but has done nothing to introduce this suffrage." At another Laufenberg urged his comrades "to awaken the mistrust of the Christian workers, so that they are not cheated once again ... We must demand that the leaders of the Christian workers cooperate with us. We must force them either to act or drop their mask."[92]

In early 1908, when Bülow submitted a meek and meaningless reform proposal to the Landtag, 2,000 workers attended a meeting to protest "being treated like political helots in Prussia."[93] A few days later, several thousand staged their first street demonstration, "spontaneously and without leadership," or so it was claimed. Four and five abreast they marched chanting and singing through the business district and down the Königsalle, Düsseldorf's "most elegant promenade street," to the city hall and provincial government offices. In the words of the local party leaders, it was "a day of honor for the working class ... a day of political protest such as the current generation of iron and steel millionaires has never experienced."[94] Henceforth, they argued, street demonstrations should be used "to strengthen the committed ... to inspire outsiders ... to show the ruling class that the issue in question has taken deep roots in the masses."[95]

Düsseldorf had no immediate opportunity to use their new weapon, for the Bülow proposal was defeated and, except for the celebration of March 18, the suffrage agitation died. The Social Democrats, who had revived the commemoration of the 1848 revolution in 1906, viewed that event exclusively in terms of the suffrage issue. Instead of depicting revolutionary struggle and defeat, as they had in the 1890s, they described constitutional change and bourgeois treason. Instead of talking abstractly about revolution in a situation where they considered it impossible, they spoke only about limited current struggles. And they had no prescription for action. Except for a vague reference to strikes, Fischer was silent on the question of tactics, whereas Spiegel advocated only agitation, enlightenment, and organization. Although more than 1,900 had attended the March 18 celebration in 1906, by 1908 only 800 turned out, and many found the message disappointing.[96] By altering March 18 the Social Democrats had abandoned their efforts to create a revolutionary tradition, if one will, a revolutionary mythology, without advancing the suffrage campaign.

Their efforts to channel worker protest into the upcoming Landtag elections proved equally futile. The rank and file, convinced of the injustice of the system, saw little sense in voting until it was reformed. Even if they met the property and residence requirements for the third class, they were reluctant to risk their jobs under a system of open voting when it was evident that the SPD could not win a single seat. They considered protest meetings and street demonstrations more effective than the ballot. As a result, the Social Democrats won only 7,139 votes as against 19,737 for the Center.[97] After this defeat the suffrage issue subsided for the next year and a half.

During that period the Social Democrats continued the political education in which they had been engaged since 1905. Using party meetings and education commission courses, local leaders, such as Berten, Arzberger, and Laufenberg, sought to expose the membership to history, economics, and Marxism in greater depth. Abandoning the eclecticism and parochialism of earlier years, they discussed the national movement's theoretical and tactical controversies extensively. In 1908, for example, the general meetings that discussed economic crises, the mass strike, and religion and socialism were all well attended, proving, the *Volkszeitung* argued, "that the discussion of the points of our party program arouses the interest of party comrades."[98] In 1909 the most popular topics at district meetings were the goals of social democracy, the fundamentals of Marxism, and the theory and tactics of political Catholicism.[99]

The education commission reinforced this political orientation. In 1908 Berten gave a course on social theory, Müller covered economic history, Arzberger taught Marxist economics, and Quitzau lectured on the Erfurt program. As one enthusiastic participant wrote to the *Volkszeitung*, "Comrade Quitzau understood how to explain the development of socialist theory in an easily comprehensible way. The number of participants at the end was almost as great as at the beginning, a clear proof that the students were pleased with the theme and presentation."[100] In 1909 and 1910 nearly 300 Social Democrats attended the lecture series on economic theory and economic development, given by Otto Rühle of Berlin.[101] As the police noted with dismay, the attention given to education "had contributed significantly to making trade unionists interested in the party and deepening the comrades' understanding of the party's purpose and goals."[102] It also made the Social Democrats more critical of the party's right and center, more cognizant of tactical options, and more receptive to radicalism, as the 1910 round of the Prussian suffrage campaign showed.

The Düsseldorf Social Democrats, who had been optimistic in 1906 and uncertain in 1908, were pessimistic, impatient, and radical in 1910.

Four years of economic crisis and inflation, increased taxes, and intransigent coalition governments had heightened the workers' sense of injustice, exploitation, and isolation. And the Social Democrats were able to articulate these discontents, to give this inchoate radicalism a concrete political direction in the suffrage campaign.

Round two opened in January 1910 when the Prussian party leaders, inspired by their comrades elsewhere and pressured by their own rank and file, convened a congress to discuss the suffrage question. The reformists such as Bernstein urged their comrades to adopt a moderate posture and cooperate with National Liberals, Progressives, and even Centrists. The vast majority of Prussian Social Democrats, however, opted emphatically for extraparliamentary tactics and demanded that the party launch a "suffrage storm." Düsseldorf endorsed the idea enthusiastically. On January 22, the anniversary of Bloody Sunday and Red Sunday, the campaign opened with large rallies throughout Prussia. In Düsseldorf alone more than 3,000 workers attended seven protest meetings. Although the announcements for the event had stressed that "the class-conscious proletarian must leave no means untried in order to help his justified cause to victory," none of the speakers discussed tactics concretely and the workers dispersed quietly.[103]

A few weeks later the government announced its "reform" proposal, and the calm was shattered. Chancellor Bethmann-Hollweg, anxious to placate the National Liberals, promised to institute direct election and allow certain educated persons to vote in the second rather than the third class. That was the entire substance of the measure! The enraged Social Democrats labeled the bill "an insult, a scandal," and promised to teach the government that it could not dupe the people with such "fake reforms."[104]

On February 13 several thousand angry workers packed the four protest meetings, where Berten, Arzberger, Haberland, and Jäcker adopted an aggressive tone and, according to the police, "intimated, in contrast to earlier gatherings, that the people must now announce their will publicly."[105] After the meeting 3,000 to 4,000 workers marched and sang through the streets of Düsseldorf, drawing several thousand new supporters along the way. As in 1908, they taunted their bourgeois and Catholic opponents who filled the sidewalks and cafes in Düsseldorf's fashionable downtown district and, in addition, visited the homes of Mayor Marx and Reichstag deputy Kirsch.[106] Although the police were convinced that "there was a will to demonstrate in every participant," they did not intervene on the grounds that "such movements lose support more quickly ... when the police adopt a wait-and-see attitude."[107] This sensible policy, which drew criticism from the provincial government, prevented confrontations but did not dampen the growing militancy.

While the Landtag debated the government's outrageous reform bill for the remainder of February, the Düsseldorf Social Democrats continued their agitation. They singled out political Catholicism for particular criticism, arguing that "the Center Party has the power to realize suffrage reform in Prussia. The Center leaders merely need to add their troops to the army of Social Democratic suffrage fighters and the opposition of the Prussian rulers to a democratization of the Prussian constitution would disappear like the chaff before the storm."[108] The Center offered no such cooperation, however, for it would lose its privileged political position in a more democratic order. The *Westdeutsche Arbeiterzeitung* openly opposed universal suffrage, and the Christian trade unions, despite pressure from their rank and file, refused to endorse the reform campaign on the grounds that it was a "political question."[109]

The Düsseldorf Social Democrats were forced to fight alone and with more militant tactics. Under Berten's editorship, the *Volkszeitung* vigorously defended street demonstrations, arguing that "even wide circles of the bourgeoisie recognize them as an effective means of winning a democratic suffrage."[110] On March 6 the Social Democrats practiced what they preached. Six thousand workers packed the Apollo theater to hear Karl Liebknecht condemn the three-class suffrage, denounce the Center Party, and proclaim that the problem would be solved in the streets, not in parliament. Afterwards 15,000 to 20,000 workers marched through the city without police interference.[111] Shortly thereafter Arzberger threatened that "if the people are not given universal suffrage ... the previous demonstrations will have been mere skirmishes before the real battle."[112]

In the light of recent events, Berten, Arzberger, Haberland, and other local leaders became convinced that "the struggle of the proletariat today is something very different from all earlier mass movements."[113] Their reassessment of the role of organization and leadership and their challenge to the SPD's prevalent economic determinism marked the culmination of a long development. Berten, for example, had begun this process in 1906, when he took courses with Luxemburg at the Berlin party school. She taught him, he later acknowledged, that "one cannot talk of an automatic development from a capitalist economy to a socialist one. Capitalism lays the basis for a socialist society but the working class must bring it about."[114] Others, such as Haberland, Milow, Pfeiffer, and Fischer, gradually learned from experience that a more activist strategy and even the offensive mass strike were necessary. Far from being a reformist brake on the rank and file, these leaders were a radical impetus to it.

Throughout the spring of 1910 they argued that all too many Social Democrats labored under the misconception that "offensive struggles against the state power" could be as carefully planned and executed as the day-to-day work of the party and unions. The *Volkszeitung*, summarizing local opinion, maintained that in the Prussian suffrage campaign:

There is no evidence of a rationally drawn up plan . . . No, the passion, the spontaneous outrage of the masses determined the momentary action . . . There was little or no central direction . . . The leading organs of the workers' movement have left the initiative to the masses themselves to employ new methods of struggle.

The success of such a struggle depended not on the form of organization but on the spirit of the workers. "The lesson to be learned from the suffrage movement," insisted Berten, was this:

Everything depends on the masses. And the working masses themselves must be filled with the consciousness that they not only have *to carry out* decisions but have *to make them* as well . . . Only where they take the initiative themselves, lead their own organizations on new paths, and push the national leadership forward is it possible for our struggle to move forward powerfully.[115]

These views were repeatedly articulated even though the national executive had explicitly prohibited all discussion of the mass strike in February 1910. Moreover, they found a strong echo among party members who not only turned out en masse for rallies and demonstrations but discussed tactics as well. In March, for example, the 11th district had "a lively discussion about the previous street demonstrations." Several districts read Luxemburg's pro–mass strike pamphlet, *What Next?*[116] In the 4th district:

Most speakers were of the opinion that the working class must employ ever new forms of struggle in order to defy capitalism at a given moment. It was regretted that in the suffrage struggle further means had not already been used. It was further emphasized that the political mass strike could be a most effective weapon for the proletariat.[117]

Buoyed by this wave of popular militancy, the Düsseldorf Social Democrats wanted to continue the fight. "The land of the schnaps Junkers" had never seen such popular demonstrations, argued the *Volkszeitung*, adding overoptimistically that recent events proved popular protest could have a significant impact on state and society.[118] The Social Democrats gleefully claimed that the Center had been thrown on the defensive and the police confirmed this assessment, noting that "the opposition to the suffrage proposal of the government ... had gripped not only those workers who are under social democratic influence, but also makes itself visible within the Christian workers' movement and in the democratic and liberal bourgeoisie."[119] No wonder the Düsseldorf Social Democrats had as little sympathy with the passivity and isolation of the party's center faction as they did with its right wing.

But they and their fellow radicals in the Lower Rhine won no support from the national executive and the trade-union general commission for either sustaining or escalating the struggle. While the Lower Rhine Social Democrats talked of a mass strike, the national leaders did everything in their power to end the suffrage campaign completely. Although the Düsseldorf Social Democrats bitterly resented this, they did not continue on a radical path alone.

The failure to act did not mean that there was no genuine radicalism, that talk of a mass strike represented only the traditional working out of pent-up frustration by means of verbal aggressiveness.[120] In the spring of 1910 the rank-and-file mood in Düsseldorf and throughout the region was militant and volatile. Actions the Social Democrats had deemed impossible a few months earlier now seemed feasible and desirable. As the Lower Rhine leader Dittman argued in late 1910:

Here we have a mass movement such as we have never known. The most encouraging thing is that this movement has grown out of the masses. It is the masses who decided to storm the Junker fortress. It is perfectly understandable that the masses, as a result of the unheard of pressure from all sides, finally believe that mass action and the mass strike are necessary.[121]

A mass strike was by no means certain, but it was by no means impossible – if support were forthcoming from the national party executive and union leadership.

The Düsseldorf Social Democrats, like radicals elsewhere in Germany, would not and could not act alone and against orders from Berlin. To be effective, the mass strike had to be implemented nationwide. Although Düsseldorf had contact with other radical locals in the region, it lacked knowledge of, let alone regular communication with, radicals elsewhere. The very isolation from Berlin that fostered independence and a critical spirit promoted isolation from sympathetic comrades as well. And radical leaders of national stature, such as Luxemburg and Liebknecht, had done little to overcome this situation.[122] Finally, the Social Democrats, whatever their political persuasion, placed a high value on party unity and discipline, for these had saved the fledgling movement during the years of illegality. Dissension was acceptable. Undiscipline and departure were not.

Embittered and frustrated, the Düsseldorf Social Democrats staged one final outdoor rally in mid-April. Fifteen to twenty thousand workers, including "many thousands who had formerly not been active in our movement or had been indifferent to it," attended. Enthusiasm still ran high among the rank and file, but the leaders knew that the campaign was over. Street demonstrations had not brought the desired reform one step closer. The party had either to risk the mass strike or drop the campaign entirely. Otherwise it would lose credibility with the workers. Thus, although Haberland and Berten promised the cheering crowd that if peaceful means failed the mass srike would be used, they urged no immediate action. Indeed, they specifically requested that the workers disperse quietly, and the order was obeyed.[123] The limits of radicalism had been temporarily reached.

If the Prussian suffrage campaign of 1910 convinced the Düsseldorf Social Democrats of the necessity of going beyond parliamentarism, it was the behavior of their South German comrades that showed them the dangers inherent in it. Since 1908 the revisionists and reformists had begun to violate party resolutions instead of merely criticizing them. The Düsseldorf Social Democrats reacted sharply, from both principled disagreement and fear for party unity. They urged the national party congress to condemn the seven Swabian Social Democrats who had broken precedent by paying their respects to the court. When Bernstein published an article in the bourgeois *Berliner Tageblatt*, an action forbidden by the 1903 Dresden party congress, the *Volkszeitung* angrily concluded that "one would assume that someone who cannot recognize the correctness of our party's principles and program would have the courage to draw the appropriate conclusions."[124]

Sarcasm gave way to rage in mid-1910 when the Baden Social Democrats again voted for the budget. This gross breach of discipline, coming immediately after the collapse of the suffrage movement, upset not only radicals but also many centrists. In Düsseldorf the *Volkszeitung* began a derisive polemic against "the intelligent, diplomatic policies" of those Social Democrats "who lay so much weight on positive cooperation with bourgeois governments."[125] At the yearly district conference, usually devoted to mundane business, the Social Democrats talked of little else but the Baden revolt. According to Berten:

Such an approval of the budget means a recognition of the existing order, but such a recognition of the existing order leads logically to compromise and bloc politics, to the diplomatic weighing and balancing of conflicts of interests within bourgeois parties, to a politics of the moment, determined by the mood of the moment.

Such politics, he concluded "do not give the masses a principled education or awaken class consciousness." The well-attended conference unanimously endorsed a resolution that "condemns the budget approval of the Baden Social Democrats most decisively – not merely because of the brusk disregard of the decision of the party congress but also because of the views of the Baden comrades on parliamentarism in general."[126]

There was strong sentiment in Düsseldorf for expelling the Baden deputies, who considered "propaganda for the end goal of socialism a danger for the party" and were thus lost to the cause. Nonetheless, Düsseldorf realized that the rank and file in Baden was influenced by the leadership and would probably leave as well. Thus the Düsseldorf Social Democrats endorsed the resolution of the Magdeburg party congress that condemned the action but threatened automatic expulsion only for the next offense. Haberland, the new SPD Reichstag candidate for Düsseldorf, joined the group of leftists whom Dittmann had brought together to counter the growing strength of the right.[127] And the local party leadership, adopting an ever sharper tone, attacked "all opportunistic, revisionist attempts to collaborate with our opponents and the capitalist state as well as all attempts to loosen the unity, determination, and discipline of the party."[128]

Between 1906 and 1910 the Düsseldorf Social Democrats thus moved from the party's orthodox but passive center into its activist left wing. Led by such radical local functionaries as Berten, Arzberger, and Milow, the Social Democrats were able to mobilize and politicize a growing number of workers. They articulated the grievances of those who, regardless of background, occupation, or religion, were hurt by inflation, recession, and technological change, discriminated against by taxes, tariffs, and suffrage regulations, and excluded by political Catholicism and liberalism alike. The movement not only championed their immediate interests and offered them refuge from a hostile environment, it also provided an analysis of industrial capitalism and political authoritarianism, a prescription for action, and a promise of social transformation. More specifically, in these years the Düsseldorf Social Democrats insisted that the contradictions of capitalism and the conflicts within Imperial Germany were irreconcilable. Although they did not oppose either trade unionism or parliamentary activity, they argued that neither would fundamentally change the existing order and that neither should be the exclusive preoccupation of the movement.[129]

While many of their comrades turned to revisionism or an atheoretical reformism, they defended orthodox Marxism, insisted on the primacy of long-range goals and basic principles, and condemned class alliances and compromise politics. While the party's right advocated cautious moderation and cooperation with bourgeois groups and the center defended isolation and passivity, Düsseldorf and the emerging left elsewhere criticized the bureaucratization and the organizational fetishism of the SPD. In place of "mere trade unionism" and "mere parliamentarism," the left proposed a mixture of mass action and more traditional means and argued for more rank-and-file initiative. The Düsseldorf Social Democrats expressed not only the immediate concerns but also the revolutionary potential of the working class. The popularity of the movement and its radical policies is indicated by party membership, which increased from 3,067 to 5,484 between 1909 and 1911, and trade-union support, which rose from 11,881 to 22,032 in the same period.[130]

The radical movement in Düsseldorf reflected the position of workers whose commitment to the existing order was at the very least equivocal. It attracted workers who were not integrated positively or negatively into that order but who were isolated from it politically, socially, and culturally. In Düsseldorf, as well as in Prussia as a whole, the economic and political structures and class alliances prevented the working class from winning substantial gains. And this remained true despite the spectacular growth of the social democratic movement after the turn of the century. Indeed, the more powerful the movement became locally and regionally, the less willing the government and ruling classes were to make any concessions. This stalemated and repressive status quo encouraged radicalism in Düsseldorf and many other cities. A minimum of progress would have been necessary to make reformism plausible, achieve negative integration, or encourage passivity. That minimum was absent in Düsseldorf.

Yet the very structures and social forces that pushed the Social Democrats to the left made it extremely difficult to translate that radicalism into practice. The limits of trade-union and political success radicalized the movement but weakened it as well. The Social Democrats' isolation from the surrounding society increased their class consciousness but not necessarily their ability to wage class struggle. The isolation from Berlin provided the critical distance necessary to develop dissenting left-wing views but lessened their influence on the national party and their contacts with other radicals. Despite their dissatisfaction with the center and right, the Düsseldorf radicals were too weak to implement radical tactics alone, too sensible to continue the suffrage struggle without aid, and too committed to party unity to leave. After 1910 they turned back to the parliamentary arena once again. Their experiences in national and municipal politics were to erase any lingering doubts about the limits of parliamentarism and reformism.

9

The limits of reformism

After the disappointing demise of the Prussian suffrage campaign and the tactical disputes that accompanied it, the Düsseldorf Social Democrats devoted unprecedented energy to the upcoming Reichstag election on the one hand and continued to be active in municipal politics on the other. Resigned, isolated, and lacking other options, they retreated into electoral activity and practical work, albeit with ambivalence and low expectations. Their experiences were to convert skepticism about the possibility of reform into disillusionment.

On the municipal front, ten years of Social Democratic involvement in city politics yielded meager results. Although Social Democratic participation fundamentally altered the character of local government by politicizing it, the Social Democrats won few economic or political concessions and no representation. They were deeply disappointed in the fruits of their labor. Moreover, the Center Party and the Liberals took credit for what scattered reforms there were, and co-opted any new welfare institutions. Thus, far from promoting working-class integration and interparty cooperation, the Social Democrats' attempts to play reformist politics, to moderate their demands, and to cooperate with other parties and city hall intensified isolation and disaffection.

The long-desired Reichstag victory of 1911, repeated a year later, did not restore the Social Democrats' faith in parliamentarism. The Center Party fortress finally fell as a result of the growing conservatism of political Catholicism, the changing composition of the working class, the ideological, political, and organizational strength of the social democratic movement, and the absence of concessions to the working class. Nonetheless, after the initial euphoria wore off, the Social Democrats realized that the "red flag over Düsseldorf," however important as a symbol, had failed to change policies or power relations on the national and local levels. The emptiness of victory convinced the Social

Democrats that the limits of reformism were even narrower and more insurmountable than those of radicalism.

Participation and "positive work" in Düsseldorf

After the turn of the century, the Social Democrats greatly increased their involvement in municipal affairs as part of their effort to contest control of all political institutions and defend workers' material interests. Their reformist activities, which were sometimes a complement to more radical endeavors and sometimes a substitute for them, yielded results almost as negligible as noninvolvement, for the structural and political obstacles to reformism on the local level remained as strong as ever. In North German Protestant towns, the Social Democrats won some representation, despite inequitable suffrage systems, and extracted concessions for which they received credit. In the Catholic South German states of Baden, Württemburg, and Bavaria, the climate for reformism was even more favorable, for democratic institutions enabled the Social Democrats to win substantial representation and shape policy directly.[1] In Catholic Prussian cities such as Düsseldorf, however, authoritarian structures, a powerful liberal industrial elite, and a popular Catholic mass party combined to exclude the Social Democrats completely from city government and policy formation. Few concessions were granted to the working class, and the Center Party claimed credit for them. Participation, far from overcoming the Social Democrats' pessimism about municipal politics, increased it. Their experience convinced them that they had not missed any reformist opportunities, for there were no such opportunities to miss.

A checkered history of abstention and participation, cynicism and hope lay behind the Düsseldorf Social Democrats' final despairing dismissal of municipal politics in the immediate prewar years. Throughout the 1890s they had remained outside the municipal political arena, in contrast to their Catholic comrades in South Germany and their Protestant ones in the North. Making a virtue of necessity, leaders such as Schmitt, Gotthusen, and Grimpe praised isolation and noninvolvement. To be sure, the trade-union cartel and party participated in elections to the worker–employer mediation courts and the health insurance boards and agitated around unemployment in times of crisis.[2] But they did not run candidates for the city council, champion institutional reform, or demand particular social welfare measures. They were disdainful of the existing system and pessimistic about the possibility of "positive work" on however modest a scale.

Both the Social Democrats' ambivalence about participation and the limits of positive work had their roots in the institutions and ideologies that shaped local politics. Municipal government had extensive power in areas that directly affected workers' lives. Düsseldorf's elected city council and appointed mayor managed the police, education, health, sanitation, and public utilities. In 1900 the city employed 1,600 workers, by 1910 double that number. In addition, the city council voted the indirect taxes and special levies which supported these activities.[3] On the local level, policy making was most transparent and power most tangible. Yet working-class exclusion was most blatant.

Only respectable, politically experienced men, sympathetic to industrial interests, such as Ernst Lindemann and Wilhelm Marx, served as mayor. Only cautious liberals and some Catholics won places in a civil service that expressly forbade allegiance to social democracy. The city council was elected by a three-class suffrage that relegated 90 percent of the voters to the third class. Moreover, only those males over 25 who had resided in Düsseldorf for at least one year, owned a home, or earned at least 900 M a year and had received no poor relief were eligible. A large proportion of Düsseldorf's unskilled workers as well as highly mobile skilled ones were thereby disenfranchised. The vast majority of eligible voters, regardless of class, did not bother to exercise their right.[4]

The 36-member council was even more select than the electorate. The liberal coalition, called the Middle Party, was unchallenged in the first class, as was the Center Party in the third, and the second-class positions were divided in advance so as to secure a liberal majority. It was government by co-option more than election, and wealth was a prerequisite for prominence. At least half of the council members were legally required to be homeowners, and in practice 90 percent were.[5] As the Social Democrats noted with dismay in 1904, "of the twelve city fathers in the council who are supposed to represent the thoughts and feelings of the workers . . . five belong to the first, the millionaire class, four to the second class, and three to the third."[6]

Throughout the 1890s both Liberals and Centrists were deeply committed to the representation of interests rather than individuals and to the nonparty conduct of municipal politics. The National Liberals, who lacked a mass base, and the Center Party, which feared Social

Democratic competition, argued that politics had no place in local government. Although they competed ferociously in Reichstag elections, they avoided forming hard-and-fast party factions in the city council. Rather than mobilizing mass support, the Catholic and liberal middle and upper classes preferred to iron out differences in closed committee hearings.[7] On the local level, class united more than party or religion divided.

The Social Democrats began to challenge the closed and comfortable world of elitist local politics after the turn of the century. Berten, Erbert, Schmitt, and Laufenberg were both encouraged by the movement's successes in other cities and eager to challenge the Center in all spheres. Although they accorded primacy to national politics, they recognized the necessity of representing workers' interests in Düsseldorf if possible. They realized that industrialists not only used their local economic position to win political prominence but also used their municipal political power to enhance their economic stature. The Social Democrats had little choice but to respond simultaneously on both fronts. Pressure to win influence on the local level did not come from trade-union and party members who had become interested in municipal affairs because they were more stable and integrated into the community.[8] Rather, municipal involvement was part of the leaders' attempt to meet the social and economic needs of workers who were new to Düsseldorf and excluded from its dominant culture.

Although the reasons for participation were internal to Düsseldorf, the initial impetus came from outside. In 1900 the Lower Rhine party congress, which was dominated by the strongly social democratic cities of Barmen, Remscheid, and Solingen, ordered involvement in municipal elections. The Düsseldorf Social Democrats fought bitterly over this proposal. Proponents, such as Gotthusen and Schmitt, argued that because representation was the prerequisite for reform the struggle must begin, however discouraging prospects seemed. Opponents, such as Wessel, insisted that workers, demoralized by the three-class system, would avoid voting in an open election.[9] Unable to agree and preoccupied with organization and leadership crises, the party let the issue drop.

Then, two weeks before the 1902 municipal election, the Social Democrats suddenly announced that they were running a joint slate with the liberal Hirsch-Duncker trade unions. "It is high time that the working class expose the meaningless work of the gentlemen from the

National Liberal party and the glorious Center," they proclaimed.[10] The origins of this unlikely alliance are shrouded in mystery. Erbert, head of the trade-union cartel, described it now as "a first, entirely spontaneous attempt on the part of the working class to win influence on the municipal level," now as a carefully negotiated agreement, initiated by the liberal unions.[11] Each partner nominated half the candidates, and the hastily patched-together program demanded a municipal labor exchange, public libraries, baths, and sports facilities, as well as reforms in housing, education, and municipal utilities.[12] Although the program was unfocused and the campaign ill-managed, the joint slate won enough votes to force the surprised Center into a run-off. The Center triumphed easily, but recognized that "the municipal elections are a serious warning to us."[13]

Although encouraged by the result, the Social Democrats were ambivalent about the alliance, for it was most beneficial to the Hirsch-Duncker candidates and aroused distinctly critical reactions among regional comrades. The Lower Rhine agitation committee, for example, noted that "the behavior of the Düsseldorf comrades, who certainly cannot be accused of favoring compromises with bourgeois parties, was most strange."[14] In 1904, therefore, Düsseldorf revised its strategy by running a full-scale campaign, presenting a well-thought-out program, and avoiding all embarassing alliances.[15] A new era had begun.

The municipal program, which was drawn up by the regional organization, reflected the party's conception of local politics. It argued that "municipalities in the capitalist state can only operate on the basis of the existing relationships of dominance and exploitation. They are not in a position to eliminate existing social contradictions on their own." Despite these limitations, the Social Democrats asserted that "municipalities can become a very powerful means of working against the moral and physical misery that capitalism always brings to the working masses and can contribute to the intellectual and physical regeneration of the working class." The municipal program then outlined both the piecemeal improvements that were desired and the institutional reforms required to realize them. The maximum program called for a fundamental restructuring of municipal government and local power relationships, including complete municipal autonomy, universal suffrage for women as well as men, and free, secular, and equal education. Cities should adopt progressive labor, welfare, and housing policies, improve the situation of municipal workers, and expand the public sector. And all this was to be financed by direct, rather than indirect taxes.[16]

Both regional leaders, such as Grimpe and Gewehr, and their Düsseldorf counterparts, such as Berten and Arzberger, realized that the entire, quite radical program would not be passed in the foreseeable future. Nonetheless, they wanted to attempt to accomplish "positive work" in order either to win concrete gains for the working class or to prove that the system and its supporters, not the Social Democrats, were responsible for the failure of reform. The leaders thus focused on short-range, modest demands, aimed at bringing immediate benefits to the working class and forcing the Center to reveal its class biases. From 1904 to 1914 they fought for reform in the suffrage, the school system, and the city budget, for the establishment of a labor exchange, and for the rights of municipal workers.

The Düsseldorf Social Democrats accorded top priority to suffrage reform, for the current system disenfranchised many who supported the SPD in Reichstag elections and discouraged those who were eligible. Instead of fighting for universal suffrage, however, they merely sought improvements in the three-class system – and pursued those in a most moderate way. They wanted the income requirement lowered to 600 M, the residency requirement abolished, and elections scheduled for Sunday.[17] These modest proposals would not have radically altered municipal politics for, as the Social Democrats admitted, "the three-class suffrage in any case assures that the propertied classes will retain an oppressive preponderance in the city council."[18] At best, the Social Democrats might win a few third-class seats.

The proposed educational reforms were more extensive. The party wanted to end all fees, introduce free medical care for all school children, and supply free meals for needy ones. In a more radical vein, they called for the abolition of separate schools for university-bound middle- and upper-class children, for such schools, better funded and staffed than their proletarian counterparts, reinforced class differences and virtually eliminated mobility.[19] Working-class children "have the same right to education as better-off ones," argued a social democratic flyer. "If the children of the propertied classes had to go to the regular elementary schools, those schools would have all the necessary money and materials."[20]

The Social Democrats' preoccupation with questions of national finance carried over into the municipal arena. They urged the city to stop "throwing away money" on exhibitions, patriotic festivals, and bourgeois associations and spend it instead on "the important cultural tasks which concern the material welfare of the people."[21] In 1907, for example, they protested vigorously when the city claimed that it had no money for the unemployed but nonetheless donated more than 21,000 M to such causes as the chess club and the dog show.[22] Once again the Social Democrats were not making radical demands for preferential treatment or fundamental reform but were merely asking for some semblance of equality.

In other areas they did request not only the correction of existing abuses but also the creation of new institutions to serve explicitly proletarian needs. They called for a municipal workers' office, staffed by doctors, government officials, and elected workers, to investigate working and living conditions. Without such information, existing social legislation could not be enforced nor new measures instituted. They also proposed a municipal labor exchange, which would be managed jointly by business and labor and would provide free information.[23] Both demands spoke directly to the insecurities and inequities of working-class daily life; neither was exorbitant or unprecedented in the annals of German municipal politics. In the context of Düsseldorf, however, both were controversial, for they required that the city abandon benign neglect in favor of active intervention and allow political participation by elected worker delegates.

After 1904 the Social Democrats paid special attention to municipal workers, a particularly oppressed and defenseless group. Although in theory the city could provide better wages and working conditions because it was not concerned with profit, in practice municipal industries were far from being the "model firms" they claimed to be. In 1906, for example, wages for municipal workers were 1 M to 3 M a day less than those of most Düsseldorf trade unionists. Hours were equally abysmal. Gas, water, and electrical workers worked a twelve-hour day, whereas construction and streetcar employees suffered short winter hours with severe wage cuts. Job security, even for long-time employees, was virtually nonexistent. Municipal workers had no right to bargain collectively or strike, and had to obtain special permission to hold meetings or circulate petitions. No wonder the unemployed sought municipal work only as a last resort.[24] The Social Democrats, who repeatedly pointed out that white-collar civil servants received substantially better treatment, argued for an array of relatively modest reforms that would put municipal employees on a par with the rest of the working class.

The final area of Social Democratic activity on the municipal front concerned unemployment. Despite an inability to aid the jobless in the early 1890s, the party and cartel championed their cause in the crisis of 1900–3 and 1907–9. They urged the city to establish emergency public works programs, which would provide useful employment to all needy workers at union wages.

The issues chosen were popular with the rank and file, for they addressed workers' most basic needs in the crucial areas of jobs, political rights, health, and education. Although some workers objected that the goals were too limited, the tactics too cautious, most saw the struggle for municipal reform as a necessary component of the movement's multi-faceted economic and political strategy. They soon despaired of imple-menting their local program, however, for they ran into insurmountable structural and political obstacles.

The liberal Middle Party and the Center perceived the social demo-cratic demands, modest though they were, as a serious threat to the status quo. From 1904 on the Liberals, determined to retain their control of the city council, discouraged suffrage reform and broad participation and campaigned only reluctantly at election time, directing their agita-tion against the Center Party, which challenged them in the second class.[25] Occasionally, the *Düsseldorfer Zeitung* justified liberal local rule in glowing terms:

Everywhere the municipal ordinances have wisely given property and intel-ligence the decisive influence . . . The current majority has not failed to provide for the social welfare of the small and the many. Things would be very different if the wishes of the great mass, who contribute little to the cost of the municipalities, were dominant.[26]

At times the Middle Party warned against electing "men of revolution, of disorder and of anarchy . . . who want to trample all that has been holy to us for centuries: religion and morality."[27] By and large, however, the Liberals simply ignored the working class and social democracy.

The Center, recognizing that municipal politics had been incorpor-ated into the larger struggle between social democracy and political Catholicism, responded vigorously and vituperatively. It defended its own local social policies, claimed credit for any concessions made to the "workers' estate," and blamed the liberal majority for the city council's shortcomings. Although the Center argued for middle-class deputies, "who have experience with municipal politics and whose vision extends beyond the interests of a particular group," it did run a token worker or two.[28]

The Center vehemently denied that the Social Democrats were seriously interested in or capable of accomplishing anything constructive.[29] Their candidates were not "real workers" but movement functionaries, who simply "sought to arouse discontent."[30] Despite their promises, the Social Democrats "have so far achieved very little in terms of positive work . . . They are only good at bragging, rationalizing, and criticizing." The Center frequently accused the SPD governments of Mülhausen and Offenbach of incompetence.[31] Although the Center bitterly attacked demands for secular education, it otherwise preferred to discuss the motives and abilities of the Social Democrats rather than the substance of their proposals. In 1906, for example, the *Volksblatt* sarcastically dismissed a Social Democratic petition by noting that "the comrades reckon this way: If our request is fulfilled, then our friendliness to the working class will be clearly illustrated. If, however, the city council rejects the petition, then we have a good slogan for the next election."[32]

The SPD, the Center, and the Middle Party disagreed not only about the specifics of their municipal programs but also about the character of local government. The Social Democrats fought aggressively to politicize and publicize municipal affairs as well as to extend working-class participation in the electoral process and the city council. At the opposite extreme stood the liberal alliance, whose ideal remained a co-optive, relatively invisible government of the representatives of *Bildung und Besitz*. The Center occupied an ambiguous middle ground, for although it had no qualms about playing mass politics, it mobilized its followers in defense of an only slightly reformed status quo.

Measured in electoral terms, the liberal vision was gloriously triumphant. The Middle Party continued to monopolize the first class and maintained a majority in the second by successful appeals to artisans, civil servants, and white-collar workers. Although the Center made little progress against the liberal enemy above, it held its own against the Social Democratic challenge from below. The Social Democrats did not win a single seat and did not force the Center into a run-off until 1910. The situation in Düsseldorf was only slightly worse than in the rest of the Lower Rhine, where the party managed to elect only 144 deputies in twenty-two towns (see Table 9.1).[33]

Table 9.1. *Municipal election results: third class*

Year	Center slate	SPD slate
1904	6,480–6,531[a]	2,118–2,140
1906	8,034–8,133	3,914–3,998
1908	9,617–9,634	4,067–4,071
1910	13,311–13,326	9,577–9,582
1912	15,103–15,116	11,416–11,423
	14,422	9,722

[a]Indicates the highest and lowest vote received by candidates on each slate.
Source: Stadtarchiv Düsseldorf, III 10147–50, 1904–10. *Volkszeitung*, October 17, 1912.

Party leaders blamed workers for these defeats. Beginning in 1904, they lamented that "the damned lack of interest of the eligible voters, the workers' ignorance of the portentous importance of bourgeois class rule in the cities, was decisive for the continuation of the regime of wealthy snobs."[34] Many Social Democrats were migrants who had neither long-standing ties to the city nor knowledge of its problems and peculiarities. They often refused to take out Prussian citizenship, failed to register in Düsseldorf, or avoided the polls on election day. Although most workers endorsed the party's municipal aims, some claimed that "voting does no good"; others that "the party will win without me"; and a third group simply feared losing their jobs. Most disturbing, "a not insignificant group ended up voting for the Center or liberals."[35] Berten, Arzberger, Laufenberg, and Milow, as well as their district counterparts, threatened and cajoled, pleaded and punished, tried education and expulsion, but with little success.[36]

The SPD vote grew significantly, at least until 1912, but the Center electorate expanded more rapidly. The Social Democrats could not break out of the vicious circle. The longer they failed to win representation, the more futile electoral participation seemed. The more strongly they condemned the class character and structural flaws of municipal politics, the more absurd it seemed to join a contest that was rigged against them from the start. Despite their strength and accomplishments in other areas, the rank and file saw little hope for representation in the municipal system and preferred to condemn it from without rather than struggle futilely within the electoral arena.

Although the same parties and personalities ruled Düsseldorf in 1914 as in 1904, the style of municipal politics changed dramatically as a result of social democratic participation. The Social Democrats publicized, politicized, and factionalized local politics. They made city government a highly visible object of public interest. Although the Middle Party and the Center resented being put in the spotlight and refused to abandon secret committee meetings, they did patch together formal municipal programs, hold educational meetings, and discuss municipal affairs in the press. Every decision was now made with one eye on the public. Elections, once quietly managed by the elite, gradually became miniature replicas of the bitter Reichstag contests. In 1900 fewer than 1,000 voters, or 18 percent of those eligible, turned out in the third class; by 1910 nearly 27,000 or 49 percent did.[37] Instead of putting up third-class candidates drawn exclusively from the first and second classes, the Center ran the Christian trade-union functionary Bernard Meyer and several lower-middle-class candidates as well.

Of greater importance, after 1904 SPD participation disrupted the traditional alliance between the National Liberals and the Center and introduced party conflict into the council itself. Once the Social Democrats made a bid for the working-class vote, the Center sought to rally its proletarian and petty bourgeois supporters around mild social reform on the one hand and the defense of Catholicism on the other. Moreover, it began to contest liberal control of the second class. Whereas the Center had once cooperated harmoniously with the Liberals, it now attacked them for being dictatorial and anti-Catholic. Center deputies gradually formed a disciplined party group within the council, thereby ending the fluid, informal coalitions of the 1890s, which had been based on economic interest rather than political affiliation.[38] Class was able to triumph over religious and party differences only as long as municipal politics was restricted to an elite.

The Social Democrats had more difficulty extracting substantive concessions. Initially, the council rejected Social Democratic reform proposals in toto, but such intransigence, however much it corresponded to the deepest convictions of the Catholic and liberal council members, could not be maintained indefinitely.[39] As Social Democratic strength grew outside city government, the council made a series of half-hearted and belated concessions – concessions that angered the ruling parties but left the Social Democrats dissatisfied.

Suffrage reform illustrates this process. In 1906, 1908, and 1909 the council rejected Social Democratic petitions to enfranchise those who earned between 600 M and 900 M, even though cities such as Cologne, Elberfeld, and Barmen had done so. In 1910, however, the council abruptly reversed itself and passed the reform. It repeatedly claimed that it had not been swayed by the SPD's political arguments but rather by the need to bring local suffrage regulations in line with Prussian ones.[40]

Social democratic pressure also led the council to establish a social commission and municipal labor exchange. In 1906, after rejecting the social democratic request for a workers' office, the Center proposed a social commission, which was a watered-down version of the SPD demand. It was immediately approved, for, as Berten noted, the Liberals and Center were beginning "to discover the working class" before each election.[41] The labor exchange was a more significant victory. From 1900 to 1905 the Social Democrats negotiated with the city. The council repeatedly broke off talks and rejected proposals while the Christian unions first supported the Social Democrats and then withdrew under pressure from the Center. Not until the Social Democrats held large protest meetings in 1905 did the government seriously entertain the idea. By year's end, a municipally funded exchange, with a worker–employer advisory board, was in operation. Municipal workers also won some improvements in this period. The agitation of the SPD, the exposés of the *Volkszeitung*, and the abortive organizing drives of first the free unions and then of their Christian competitors forced the city to eliminate the worst abuses. Finally, Social Democratic pressure pushed the city to establish limited public works programs to deal with the severe unemployment of 1901–3 and 1907–9.[42]

Both movement leaders and members were highly ambivalent about these relatively meager concessions, which had been wrung from a reluctant government through so much effort. Occasionally, the Social Democrats paraded their accomplishments with great pride. In 1910, for example, Schotte announced to the yearly party conference that "the Düsseldorf Social Democrats can be satisfied with their previous municipal activity ... The little which has been accomplished in Düsseldorf in the area of social policy originated in the initiatives of the Social Democrats." These reforms, argued Berten, proved that the Social Democrats were genuinely interested in "positive work" and capable of achieving it even when they held no power.[43]

More often than not, however, the Social Democrats were struck by the inadequacy of the reforms and the durability of the old municipal system. They greeted each concession with cries of victory but quickly became disillusioned. Suffrage reform, for example, offered too little, too late to convince many Social Democrats that voting made sense.

Moreover, as many had predicted, minor reforms did not break the Center's monopoly on the third class. The social commission proved to be even more disappointing. As the *Volkszeitung* noted bitterly in 1910:

Our much praised social commission is only a decoration, from which the representatives of the free trade unions are intentionally excluded. It is only a toy for big children who think that their pretense and apparent good will are enough to allow Düsseldorf's "social policy" to appear in a favorable light. Even Bernard Meyer, the Center's working-class deputy, admits that the commission is simply a fifth wheel.[44]

The labor exchange also came under fire from both the Social Democrats and the working class. It did partially alleviate the chaos of the labor market and save Düsseldorf's highly migratory working class from expensive private exchanges. Yet even in its most successful years, it found work for only one-half to two-thirds of those seeking jobs. In addition, the Social Democrats held only two of the nine working-class seats, the remainder being distributed among a variety of small Catholic, Protestant, and liberal associations. The public works programs were a similarly mixed blessing. In times of crisis they saved a few thousand workers from destitution – no insignificant achievement – but they failed to aid many thousands more who were migrants, unmarried, or simply too far down on the list of applicants.[45]

During these years, social democratic failures with city government were not balanced by success with the worker–employer mediation court or health insurance boards. When the free trade-union slate won a majority in the 1902 court election, the government, pushed by the Center Party, introduced proportional representation and thereby assured a strong minority position for the Christian trade unions, even though the Social Democrats outpolled them two to one by 1910.[46] Workers were hindered by antiquated and discriminatory court procedures. Whereas employers could argue their cases persuasively, a worker, according to the *Volkszeitung*,

does not know court procedures ... He is unacquainted with the most important provisions of the commercial code ... He comes before the court with a sense of awe and reveals a certain shyness and anxiety. In arguing his case he often loses himself in details ... As a result he is frequently sharply reprimanded by the presiding officer. The worker then becomes upset ... This leads to more reprimands and conflicts.[47]

As a result, many cases were thrown out, and the majority of others were settled by compromise. Although the Center and employers favored such conciliation, the Social Democrats argued that the workers paid heavily for it. And working-class confidence in the court did gradually decline, with fewer and fewer cases being brought before it.[48]

The Social Democrats had a similar experience with the insurance system. After the turn of the century, they continued their conquest of the numerous health insurance boards, trouncing the Center so seriously that it stopped contesting most elections. Nonetheless, social democratic representation failed to bring any reform or inspire working-class confidence in the insurance system.[49] As in the 1890s, workers remained indifferent or hostile to the government's major welfare policy.

The results of a decade of strenuous work were meager indeed. The Social Democrats had changed the style more than the substance of municipal affairs. As the Chamber of Commerce noted with satisfaction. "in Düsseldorf – and in most other cities – a sufficient number of industrialists and merchants sit in the city council and in the special commissions . . . There is adequate opportunity to protect economic interests. Moreover, the current administration continually discusses transportation questions and even general economic issues with the Chamber of Commerce."[50]

The working class was still accorded a second-class status, whereas the Social Democrats were singled out for special discrimination. Involvement merely increased their isolation and intensified their conflict with the Center. It bred bitterness toward the city government and cynicism toward reformist arguments about the possibilities of substantive reform, material gains, and political alliances. Social democratic abstention in the 1890s had been based on weakness and bred passivity. Participation after 1904 was rooted in the movement's new strength and assertiveness. Its failure taught the Social Democrats the structural and political limits of reform. It made them receptive to radicalism despite the acknowledged difficulties of implementing a leftist strategy. Nothing sums up the party's pessimistic and angry attitude better than its 1912 municipal election flyer:

The class interests of the propertied, of big capitalists, large landlords, and speculators, impress their stamp on the municipal politics of Düsseldorf. No sum is too large for the special interests of the rich, for their comfort, their sport, and their entertainment.

When the interests of the broad mass of the population, of the poor, the worker, and the little man come into question, however, then the government haggles and bargains, negotiates and adjourns, and finally refuses. The government displays an ignorance of the true situation of the population such as is possible only when the propertied and wealthy rule. The council talks of a general improvement in the popular welfare and then recommends means which generally leave everything as it was.[51]

The fall of the Center fortress

As the Social Democrats were winding up their first discouraging decade of involvement in municipal affairs, they turned with renewed energy to national parliamentary politics. The Prussian suffrage campaign had convinced them of the limits of organization, agitation, and parliamentarism. "From the standpoint of the revolution," argued Berten in mid-1910, "all that is only preparatory work. The proletariat is still faced with the task of conquering power."[52] Nonetheless, once the national party had terminated the "suffrage storm" and directed attention to the 1912 Reichstag elections, Düsseldorf followed suit. "At some point," insisted the *Volkszeitung*, "the economic means of the proletariat, the mass strike, must be employed. Until then, it is a question of organization and agitation . . . and proper use of the Reichstag elections."[53]

The Düsseldorf Social Democrats' rather resigned return to electoralism came abruptly in mid-1911, for Center deputy Kirsch died and a special election was scheduled for September. "The decisive battle is impending," predicted the Center with noticeable anxiety. The transformation of the economy, the working class, and political Catholicism, the failure of reformism, and the growth of the movement were to contribute to a significant SPD victory.

Rather than developing new strategies against the Center, the Social Democrats relied on their most effective past maneuvers. They constantly criticized tariffs and inflation but accorded less importance to Prussian suffrage and scarcely mentioned social legislation. They avoided the treacherous issue of religion entirely, preferring to emphasize the strength of their own arguments. They mobilized their electoral machine on an unprecedented scale, distributing tens of thousands of flyers and papers, registering voters, and canvassing house to house. Noted Social Democrats, such as Liebknecht, Luxemburg, Lehmann, and Molkenbuhr, spoke at rallies, for the national party regarded Düsseldorf as a crucial test case for the upcoming regular election.[54]

The Social Democrats did pay more attention than usual to personalities rather than just issues. On the one hand, they needed to give maximum publicity to Karl Haberland, the regional party secretary, whom they were running in place of the deceased Grimpe. On the other hand, the new Center Party candidate, Johannes Friedrichs, was an irresistible target. As the Social Democrats pointed out on every possible occasion, in a district that was three-quarters working class, the Center had chosen a politically unknown, wealthy bank director. Friedrichs was an active member of the Hansabund, an alliance of economically diverse middle-class groups, ranging from small business and light industry through foreign trade and finance to some heavy industry. In comparison to the Conservative–right National Liberal alliance, the Hansabund advocated a much more moderate course. It sought to curb Junker economic and political power, lower tariffs, and establish a more thoroughly bourgeois order.[55] Nonetheless, the Hansabund was staunchly anti-socialist, and the SPD remained deeply suspicious of it. According to Berten and Haberland, Friedrichs "shows understanding for the capitalists," and "will follow the policies of big business."[56]

The Center Party, which had returned to the government fold by 1911, defended both its new candidate and its old policies. Even before Kirsch died, the Center had decided that although "one must no doubt give due consideration to the worker, in the Düsseldorf election district agriculture, heavy industry, art, and the middle classes are strongly represented, so that a neutral candidate is preferable."[57] The Center leaders then vigorously championed the hardly neutral Friedrichs in the face of social democratic censure and Christian trade-union qualms. Similarly, the Center endorsed existing tax and tariff policies as essential to national security and economic prosperity. Unconvinced of the persuasiveness of these arguments, however, Catholic leaders played on religious fears and nationalist aspirations to an unprecedented degree. The choice was between "Christianity and atheism," between "the fatherland and Haberland," to quote the Center's favorite election slogans.[58] Priests and politicians alike warned Catholic voters that the "unpatriotic international Social Democrats," who advocated "crass materialism ... class hatred, hatred of humanity, and atheism," would introduce "a time of the wildest rule of violence."[59]

In imitation of the Social Democrats, the Center had restructured its organization, hired a paid secretary, and given special training to the newly appointed district leaders and block captains. During the campaign, the Center held frequent rallies, agitated in all neighborhoods,

Table 9.2. *Düsseldorf Reichstag elections, 1911, 1912*

Year	SPD	Percent	Center	Percent	National Liberal	Percent	Other	Percent
1911	34,066	48.8	29,276	41.9			6,828	9.3
1911	39,283	52.3	35,894	47.4				
1912	36,561	43.4	31,522	37.4	11,475	13.6	4,775	5.6
1912	42,850	49.9	42,088	49.0				

Source: Stadtarchiv Düsseldorf, XXI 232, September 20, 30, 1911; January 13, 22, 1912.

and planned its election day activities in minute detail.[60] Political Catholicism, which had long been the organizationally superior mass movement, was now on the defensive, and like the Social Democrats in the 1890s, it responded by seeking organizational solutions to problems that were social and political.

In 1911 the red and black armies fought alone, for the National Liberals, who dismissed the election as "a very insignificant contest," ran no candidate, urging instead a boycott of the election.[61] To vote SPD would be politically suicidal, argued the *Düsseldorfer Zeitung*, but "the most honorable aversion of nationalistically inclined men toward seeing even a temporary victory of the Social Democrats does not provide an excuse for supporting the Center which is at least as anti-national."[62] Although the Center had run Friedrichs in part to woo Liberal voters, the latter believed that he would put party loyalty over economic interest. Of equal importance, by mid-1911 heavy industry had become disillusioned with the Hansabund and its more progressive tariff and social policies.[63] The Düsseldorf National Liberals thus preferred to retreat to their local bastions of economic and political power rather than become the Center's junior partner in national affairs. Only the miniscule Progressive group in Düsseldorf "viewed the Center as the greater evil" and urged its followers "to vote accordingly."[64]

When the ballots were counted, the Social Democrats' most optimistic predictions were fulfilled. They not only surged ahead in the first round but won the run-off by well over 3,000 votes. When the victory was announced at the Volkshaus, thousands of workers cheered. A banner *Volkszeitung* headline proclaimed that at last "the red flag flies over the industrial metropolis on the Lower Rhine!"[65]

In early 1912 the Social Democrats repeated their feat, as Table 9.2 shows. The Center had jettisoned the controversial Friedrichs in favor of the small manufacturer Jakob Schmitz, whereas the National Liberals ran their own candidate in the primary and then supported political Catholicism in the run-off. Such efforts whittled the SPD's final margin of victory to a mere 800 votes but did not reverse it. Düsseldorf was thus able to share in the SPD's nationwide triumph, which brought it more than 4 million votes and 110 seats and made it the largest party in the Reichstag. For Düsseldorf, although not for the other Catholic cities in the Ruhr, the long siege of the Center fortress had finally ended.

Neither the victory of social democracy nor the defeat of political Catholicism can be attributed to a single cause or a conjuncture of events particular to 1911 and 1912. Rather, both were the result of long-term transformations in the economic and social structures and political movements of Düsseldorf. The majority of workers supported social democracy because of who they were and what they experienced, because of the movement's successes and the limits of that success in a society still dominated by organized capitalism and political Catholicism.

The economic development of Düsseldorf in the first decade of the twentieth century greatly increased the city's wealth and the power of its industrial and commercial upper class without promoting the integration of the vastly expanded proletariat. The sharp and visible differences in housing, consumption, health, and education were more galling to workers than in the 1890s, not only because they were as large as ever but also because prosperity had raised expectations that crisis and inflation left unfilled. In addition, industrialists responded to both recessions and growing trade-union strength with rationalization and new organizations, thereby further diminishing workers' economic position.

The structural obstacles to working-class political integration were as great as the economic ones. The conservative and nationalistic alliance of heavy industry, Junker agriculture, and political Catholicism, however tenuous it periodically became, did consistently defend the authoritarian state and exclude social democracy. After the turn of the century, conservative indifference, industrial intransigence, and Catholic ambivalence blocked all further social reform. Industrial leaders in Düsseldorf, like their counterparts elsewhere, grudgingly accepted existing social legislation but adamantly opposed its extension on the grounds that new measures would be costly, unnecessary, and unlikely to pacify workers. On the last point, they were undoubtedly correct. Political discrimination and legal harassment lay at the heart of working-class disaffection with the Wilhelmian state, as even the Düsseldorf police admitted in 1911.[66] The Prussian suffrage system, paragraph 153, "class justice," the absence of ministerial responsibility, militarism, indirect taxes – these were the institutions and practices that the ruling alliance defended and that encouraged workers to become Social Democrats. The social question required a political answer. By 1911 the working class in Düsseldorf had learned that a positive political answer was not forthcoming. Several developments drove home that lesson.

In the months before the election, conflict between the Social Democrats and the state escalated markedly in Düsseldorf. During several bitter strikes the police protected scabs and harassed pickets with a diligence and disrespect for the law not previously shown. This was especially true in the labor disputes that plagued the harbor. When twenty-five workers struck the Cretschmar shipping firm to protest deteriorating working conditions and the custom of paying off foremen, the police, many of whom were mounted, charged a crowd of 400 to 600 pickets and supporters. During a subsequent strike of more than 600 longshoremen against fifty firms, there were several pitched battles between workers and the police in which the former threw rocks and bottles while the latter fired blanks. Sixteen workers were arrested and predictably convicted.[67]

At the same time, the Düsseldorf social democratic youth movement, an unofficial and ostensibly nonpolitical adjunct to the party, came under heavy attack. On orders from the Prussian Ministry of the Interior, the Düsseldorf police began to disrupt educational lectures, poetry readings, and recreational activities, arrest suspected leaders, and dissolve "nonexistent organizations." Their efforts at intimidation were hardly subtle. In early 1911, for example, sixteen policemen stormed into the Youth House and arrested the twenty-six boys and girls who were talking and playing cards. They gave no reason.[68] A few months later, when the youths sponsored a talk entitled "After Leaving School," the *Volkszeitung* reported:

It was like a state of war outside. There were large numbers of heavily armed police in front of the Volkshaus and even at the entrances to nearby streets. With their revolvers visible in their belts and a determined look on their faces, they waited impatiently for what would come if it pleased the powers that be to label the meeting political.[69]

The Social Democrats were upset but not surprised. "One has always known that the municipal police readily respond to pressure from interests which stand in the background," commented Berten.[70] The bourgeoisie openly approved of this new hard line, believing, in the words of the *Düsseldorfer Zeitung*, that "a strong fist is absolutely necessary against the ferment of Düsseldorf's red youths."[71]

The government, not content to repress, tried to integrate proletarian youths into bourgeois institutions and convert them to nationalistic ideologies. In 1909 the Prussian government launched a far-reaching youth welfare campaign. As the *Volkszeitung* noted with dismay in 1911, "a million and a half marks in tax revenues were spent in order to influence youth who left school in an anti-socialist manner and to attract soldiers and voters who will form a reliable defense force against the internal enemy."[72] The government established continuing education schools, attended primarily by working-class adolescents, as well as recreational and cultural associations. In addition, it subsidized the youth organizations of nationalist and religious groups. Not surprisingly, the Catholics were particularly active in this area, mobilizing the church, schools, and a variety of associations.[73]

Nothing revealed the unreformed and unreformable nature of the German economy and state more clearly than tariffs, the issue that dominated the 1911–12 Reichstag contest as it had the 1903 one. The full impact of the tariffs, which had been passed in 1902 and implemented in 1906, was felt after 1910. While tariffs preserved the inefficient, high-cost Junker agriculture and thus bolstered aristocratic political power, they discouraged agrarian innovation, diversification, and technological improvement. On the industrial front, tariffs promoted concentration, monopolization, and export-oriented heavy industry. The main victims of the tariff legislation were consumers, especially working-class ones, who were burdened by numerous indirect taxes and a cost of living that rose from 100 in 1900 to 113 in 1906 and on to 130 in 1912.[74]

Düsseldorf, always an expensive city, was especially hard hit. In 1908 working-class families, who spent roughly 50 percent of their budget on food, paid 2.50 M to 3.50 M more a week than comparable families in Dresden, Munich, or Berlin. Although the government-calculated average daily wage for Düsseldorf was 3.50 M, the highest in the Lower Rhine and among the highest in all of Germany, earnings could not keep up with the steep rise in prices over the next three years. Between 1908 and 1911 the price of ten eggs rose from 0.89 M to 0.96 M, a half-kilogram of butter from 1.29 M to 1.42 M, and a comparable amount of coffee from 0.99 M to 1.37 M. As meat supplies lagged behind population growth, those prices soared as well. A half-kilogram of mutton rose from 0.66 M to 0.96 M, beef from 0.75M to 0.81 M, and oxen from 0.79 M to 0.86 M. Only pork fell slightly. As a result, Düsseldorf workers spent one-third of their food money on meat as opposed to one-fourth nationally, and meat consumption dropped from 64 kilograms in 1908 to 54 kilograms in 1911 – considerably below the per-capita yearly consumption of many major cities.[75]

Many working-class families sought to keep abreast of inflation by taking in boarders, roomers, or *Schlafgänger*, that is, men who simply rented a bed. By 1911 more than 10,500 Düsseldorf households had more than 21,000 such extra-family inhabitants, who contributed to overcrowding and wives' work as much as to the family income. Others were forced to seek municipal aid. In 1908 just over 7,000 people received some form of poor relief, whereas in 1911 that figure passed the 10,000 mark.[76]

The precarious position of the average working-class family emerges clearly from a municipal survey of income and expenditures for twelve working-class families from mid-1908 to mid-1909. In nine of the twelve families the men were skilled workers. None of the wives was employed outside the home but instead took care of the children, who numbered two to five per family and ranged in age from 1 to 15. Incomes ranged from a low of 1,274 M for a mason's family to a high of 2,003 M for a carpenter's. Half of the families ended the year with savings of from 0.24 M to 171 M, whereas the other half amassed debts of 24 M to 368 M.

A look at three representative families illustrates the narrowness of proletarian life. The molder's family, which earned 1,857 M and saved 171 M, spent 53 percent of its income on food, 12 percent on clothing, and 16 percent on rent. Another 11 percent went for utilities and household expenses, with 5 percent for education, newspapers, and recreation. Families that went into debt skimped on necessities. The woodworker, who made more than 2,000 M, had four children and ended the year owing more than 260 M. His family spent only 40 percent of their income on food and 11 percent on clothing, but were forced to pay 28 percent for a large apartment. The carpenter's family, which broke even, could afford to spend nearly 60 percent on food because it gave only 14 percent for rent and had no school fees. Transportation, however, took nearly 5 percent.[77]

These sobering statistics outline the parameters of proletarian life in Wilhelmian Düsseldorf, a life marked by enormous insecurity and relative austerity at best, deprivation at worst. They suggest why tariffs had such economic and symbolic importance for Düsseldorf workers. Tariffs illustrated as no other issue could the nexus of economic and political relationships that relegated the working class to an inferior and isolated position.

The success of the Social Democrats and the failure of the Centrists, the radicalism of the former and the conservatism of the latter, were two sides of the same coin. As a government observer noted in late 1911:

According to circles whose members can in no way be considered followers or fellow travelers of the Social Democrats . . . the Center's policies in recent years, whether viewed nationally or in relationship to local conditions, were not suited to increase the party's popularity. In truth, the Center in Düsseldorf has lost ground.[78]

At one crucial juncture after another, the Center had opted for policies that discriminated against the working class and thereby eroded political Catholicism's credibility and claim of "equalizing justice." In the previous decade and a half, political Catholicism, of both the liberal and conservative varieties, had abandoned its opposition to the state and ruling parties as well as its critique of industrial capitalism. It had joined the government, allied with National Liberals and Protestant Conservatives, supported military spending, endorsed colonialism – although not colonialist excesses – and pledged allegiance to the fatherland with unprecedented enthusiasm. On the domestic front, the Center had voted for grain tariffs, opposed direct taxes, and remained utterly passive on the central question of suffrage reform. In order to maintain a pivotal parliamentary position and tenuous social equilibrium, Center leaders, whether lay or clerical, catered to the interests of the Catholic upper classes, peasantry, and traditional petty bourgeoisie.

Political Catholicism recognized the need to retain the loyalty of industrial workers but refused to grant them parity within the Center Party or to fight for their equality within the larger society. Although the Center did try to lessen its dependence on parishes and subsidiary associations, it retained its oligarchic character, and its new institutional structures failed to function either democratically or effectively.[79] The

Center offered the working class integration – but on separate and subordinate terms. And the ever more cautious and nationalistic Christian trade unions hardly provided workers compensation for what the party failed to give them. The Center was no longer able to play mass politics more effectively than the Social Democrats. Even if it had corrected its organizational weaknesses, it would not have defended its Düsseldorf fortress successfully, for by 1911 political Catholicism lacked an analysis and a program that met the needs of the majority of Düsseldorf workers.

Industrialization, urbanization, and migration had transformed the working class in Düsseldorf and steadily eroded the Center's proletarian base. In Düsseldorf, as in other Catholic areas, economic development and Center strength moved inversely. In the government district of Düsseldorf, 86 percent of all Catholics had supported the Center in the 1880s, 75 percent in 1890. By 1903 support had dropped to 68 percent, and it stood at 61 percent in 1912.[80] In a city like Düsseldorf, which remained two-thirds Catholic, such losses were extremely serious, especially because they occurred primarily among workers. As previously shown, the Center held on to large numbers of Catholic workers who were born and raised in Düsseldorf, although the Social Democrats made inroads even there after 1905. Neither the Center nor the ostensibly interconfessional Christian trade unions attracted the growing Protestant contingent. Most important, they did not win the enormous number of migrant Catholics, who had weaker ties to the Catholic culture and traditional authorities.[81] Catholic and Protestant migrants, many of whom were skilled or semiskilled, could not be pacified by traditional paternalism or by the newer company unions that made virtually no headway in Düsseldorf.[82] Migrant workers were more receptive to social democratic overtures and recognized that social democracy could best represent their interests. By 1911 the SPD, free trade unions, and workers' cultural associations were much larger than their Christian counterparts. The Social Democrats dominated the worker–employer mediation court, the health insurance boards, and the journeymen's committees in the guilds. Political Catholicism could no longer compete with social democracy politically, ideologically, or organizationally.

Between 1902 and 1912 the social democratic movement in Düsseldorf had undergone as dramatic a transformation as had the Center. It had mobilized and politicized a working class that had once been disorganized, apathetic, and often openly hostile to the left. Party membership rose from 530 to more than 7,000, while trade-union strength increased from just under 4,000 to nearly 25,000. In 1912, when the SPD received a record 36,561 votes in the primary, one in every seven voters was a party member and two in every three were in a union. That was a far cry from 1903, when the ratios were one to twenty-one and one to four, respectively.[83]

The Social Democrats articulated the economic and political dissatisfactions of a working class that was excluded from the dominant society and ignored by the national movement. They singled out the deprivations and discriminations most immediate to proletarian life, analyzed their economic and political origin, and advocated both short- and long-run policies for dealing with them. The Social Democrats provided an analysis of workers' experiences, a program for action, and a promise of social transformation. They accorded a centrality and dignity to the working class that no other party did.

Social democracy offered workers an alternative to an environment still predominantly controlled by political Catholicism and industrial capitalism as well as a means of combating both. The party, unions, and cultural, recreational, and service associations helped workers cope with an urban, industrial world and secure some of the opportunities denied them by the dominant society. And that associational network reached beyond the committed to the ambivalent and unorganized. It provided the bridge that many crossed on their way to the party and unions. Finally, the organizations of the movement and the rich life they engendered provided the structural supports necessary to enable workers to withstand the dominant society's pressure to conform and submit.[84]

Through a variety of economic and political strategies, of organizational and ideological means, the Social Democrats thus became the spokesmen for Düsseldorf's workers. Indeed, the movement played a central role in forging those diverse and divided workers into a cohesive class with a shared political outlook, cultural experiences, and goals. The Social Democrats provided a common language and created a dissenting tradition where none had existed. In mediating between workers on the one hand and the state and society on the other, the Social Democrats not only created a powerful movement but a working class as well. The Reichstag victories were testaments to their success on both counts.

Those victories were also to illustrate the limits of that success – the limits of parliamentarism in general. As early as 1903 Kremser had warned the Düsseldorf Social Democrats that "the influence of parliament on policy is slight and even if we had socialist representatives, we would still be powerless."[85] In 1910 Berten had reiterated that view, cautioning that "even with the most spectacular electoral victory, we remain as far removed from true victory as ever."[86] The 1912 election fulfilled these dismal prophecies. Although the Social Democrats conquered the Center Party fortress in Düsseldorf and became the largest party in the Reichstag, they were unable to alter the fundamentals of the Wilhelmian economic and political order. They were unable to alter anything at all. When this realization dawned, it created first paralysis and stagnation, then further radicalization. In the wake of their greatest success, the Düsseldorf Social Democrats were to move still further to the left until they finally became revolutionaries outside the party rather than simply radicals within it.

PART III

Radicals become revolutionaries: 1912–1920

During the optimistic decade from 1903 to 1912 the Düsseldorf Social Democrats had created a party and union movement, a workers' culture, and most important, a cohesive working class. On the shop floor and in the political arena, social democracy had gained visibility and power that neither political Catholicism nor national liberalism nor Prussian authoritarianism could ignore. Despite these accomplishments, however, the Social Democrats were not able to reform, let alone transform, the economic and social structures of Wilhelmian Germany nationally or locally. They were not able to disrupt the conservative ruling coalition of Junkers, national liberal industrialists, and Catholics.

After 1912 the Düsseldorf Social Democrats confronted both the limits of reformism and the national party's reluctance to develop radical alternatives more strongly than ever before. From 1912 to 1920 the movement in Düsseldorf, as elsewhere, experienced first stagnation and a loss of direction, then war and schism, and finally revolution. Each of these experiences contributed to the learning process through which workers in Düsseldorf had been going. Each was to convince them of the impossibility of reformism and the necessity of implementing militant tactics. Each strengthened their commitment to Marxism and intensified their critique of the national party leadership. Part III will explore this process, which led the Düsseldorf Social Democrats from being radicals within the movement to being revolutionaries outside it.

Chapter 10 will analyze the immediate prewar crisis, which was a product of economic recession, political stalemate, and paralyzing divisions within social democracy, and which culminated in the outbreak of World War I and national party support for war credits. Chapter 11 will explore the impact of prolonged total war on economics and politics, on the working class and the workers' movement in Düsseldorf. Both chapters will trace the growing radicalization of the Düsseldorf Social Democrats, which led them to break with the SPD and join the

Independent Social Democratic Party (USPD) en masse in 1917. Chapter 12 will examine the Düsseldorf revolution of 1918–19, which enjoyed wide popular support, was extremely radical, and assumed a highly political and organized character, distinguishing it from uprisings elsewhere in Germany.

Part III argues that the roots of the post–1914 radicalism lay as much in the prewar years as in the war itself. To be sure, from 1914 to 1919 the deprivations of war and the policies of the national SPD influenced Düsseldorf workers more than political Catholicism or local politics. Nonetheless, the economic and social structures and the political alignments and policies of the earlier era profoundly shaped the later options and actions of the Social Democrats. War was the catalyst to revolution, but it was the strengths and weaknesses of the earlier radical tradition that determined what kind of revolution the socialist working class made. Likewise, it was not only the national SPD and the right in Germany that defeated the revolution but also the Düsseldorf socialists' ongoing uncertainty about how to merge economic and political struggles, how to translate their radicalism into practice.

10

Things fall apart

In the enthusiasm of the 1911 Reichstag campaign the Düsseldorf Social Democrats proclaimed that "this [electoral] struggle is a preparation for the still greater struggles to come in which the final decision between socialism and capitalism will be the issue." Reaffirming their commitment to working-class emancipation, they insisted that "only the indissoluble bond between our daily struggles and this powerful goal gives the former greatness and meaning."[1]

By mid-1912 that bond seemed tenuous indeed, for the Reichstag victory had not increased the Social Democrats' real power one iota. Rather, the structural and political obstacles to reform multiplied. The National Liberals failed to move to the left, while the Center Party continued on its conservative course and the military expanded steadily. There were renewed attempts at anti-socialist legislation and the onset of yet another recession. The limits of parliamentarism were reached just as the limits of radicalism had been two years earlier.

In the ensuing stalemate, the patient work of a decade unraveled and the movement stagnated. Leaders lost their sense of direction politically and organizationally; members became apathetic, and new recruits failed to materialize. After years of intensive activism, the Social Democrats were tired. Tired of meetings and demonstrations. Tired of hard work and responsibility. Tired most of all of great hopes and small rewards.

The more the Social Democrats' practice floundered, the more radical their theory and their tactical prescriptions became. The more disillusioned they grew with the national party leadership, the more strongly they articulated their critique of reformism and bureaucratization. The movement's renewed commitment to radicalism in response to crisis and malaise was both the logical culmination of its previous development and the preparation for its wartime opposition and further radicalization.

227

Shift to the right

The right within the SPD had long pinned its hopes on an alliance between progressive middle-class elements and moderate working-class ones. At first glance 1912 seemed favorable for this. Within the National Liberal Party the more progressive wing was in the ascendancy. At the same time the Hansabund, the League of Industrialists, and sectors of the Progressive Party were criticizing both the hegemony of the Conservative Party agrarians and talk of intensified repression against the working class. In recent years, the Reichstag had shown more initiative, even if it had failed to secure greater control over policy. To be sure, significant disagreements over political and financial reform and nationalism precluded any coalition among National Liberals, Progressives, and Social Democrats. Nonetheless, the right of the SPD believed that major concessions were possible, indeed probable given the magnitude of the party's 1912 victory. Their less optimistic comrades on the left maintained that at least a bulwark against reaction had been created.[2]

The anticipated "shift to the left" did not occur, for the SPD victory frightened the aristocratic and bourgeois right into action more readily than it pushed the liberal middle into concessions. It promoted polarization rather than conciliation. Instead of jarring Wilhelmian Germany out of its stalemate, it further immobilized it. The greatest triumph of social democratic reformism made reform all but impossible.

The first indications of the resurgence of the right came in the parliamentary arena. Shortly after the election Berten had warned his comrades that the hope of a liberal–social democratic coalition policy was "an illusion, which must necessarily end in disappointment." The very expectation, he continued "is only possible where one focuses exclusively on the parliament, does not see the classes which back the parties, and judges these parties by their rhetoric and not by their position in the great societal class struggle."[3] Class did reassert itself with a vengeance. By the late spring of 1912 the right National Liberals had dismissed the more progressive leaders, curbed the youth organization, condemned any left coalition policy, and restored the alliance with Conservatives and Centrists.[4] The SPD was once again pushed to the margins of German politics.

On the local level, industry and commerce renewed their complaints about inadequate representation and governmental excesses. The Düsseldorf Chamber of Commerce claimed that only those "estates" that controlled "masses of voters" had influence in parliament and the parties. Both the Reichstag and the government consistently "neglected" industrial and financial interests when shaping economic and especially social policy.[5] The right was shifting the locus of debate from progressive reform to reactionary restructuring.

Although there was ruling-class agreement on the illness, there was not unanimity about the cure. The most extreme right groups, such as the Pan German League, proposed a coup to abolish universal male suffrage and pave the way for repressive legislation. The Agrarian League and the Central Association of German Industrialists wanted to supplement existing parliamentary bodies with an economic chamber organized along corporatist lines. The Düsseldorf Chamber of Commerce, dissenting from the position of Ruhr mining and metal magnates, viewed these proposals as impractical, even dangerous, and offered a more moderate solution. Both the government and the Reichstag should institute regular consultations with industry and commerce at all stages of the legislative process. Capitalist interest associations would, in effect, become the semiofficial advisors of the state. To translate some of these ideas into practice, heavy industry, the Junkers, significant segments of the Center Party, and the traditional *Mittelstand* formed a "cartel of the productive estates" in mid-1913. This recreation of the turn of the century alliance sought to influence economic policy, maintain authority and hierarchy, "protect national work" (a euphemism for nonunion labor), and, of course, fight social democracy.[6] Although industrial interests in Düsseldorf disagreed with the cartel's most reactionary domestic proposals, they shared its enthusiasm for imperialism.

Industrial interests also shared an aversion to new social welfare measures. Although the right had no hope of retracting the long-established insurance programs, it vetoed all new protective legislation and condemned proposals for semiofficial workers' chambers, comparable to those for industry and artisan production.[7] It denounced unemployment insurance as a threat to the competitiveness of the German economy and the moral fiber of the working class. The Düsseldorf Chamber of Commerce, summarizing the position of industry, argued:

The worker does not need to make any provisions for cases of illness or invalidism because he is insured. He receives a pension when he is old. He does not need to pay school fees for his children. He is exempt from taxes if his income is low. Thus, one can certainly demand that in exceptional cases – and it is a question of exceptional cases when a diligent worker is unemployed – he save emergency funds. That is most definitely possible, especially here in the west where wages are high.[8]

The *Volkszeitung* reprinted this view from above with an angry commentary that undoubtedly found a strong echo among working-class readers.[9]

Industrialists were equally determined to curtail trade-union rights. They strengthened employers' organizations on the local and sectoral levels and formed a national Union of German Employers' Associations, which consolidated the separate organizations of light and heavy industry. The Central Association of German Industrialists and the Agrarian League advocated outlawing picketing, whereas the League of Industrialists, the Center, and National Liberals shunned such a confrontation course in favor of limiting strike activity by administrative means. The Düsseldorf Chamber of Commerce was apparently divided on the best tactic, for it failed to answer a government survey on the question. Caught between these conflicting forces, the government, which sided with the far right, was unable to pass measures "protecting the right to work."[10]

In Düsseldorf scabs were protected with unusual thoroughness during a series of bitter strikes.[11] "Class justice" continued to be meted out as well. When workers brought charges against the local Metal Employers' Association for blacklisting those who left with notice, the provincial court ruled that the association's action was not "morally reprehensible" because it was not aimed "at completely undermining the opponent's economic position and making him permanently unemployed and impoverished." It simply – and according to the court, justifiably – tried "to make him temporarily unemployed in order to force him to submit to the wishes and conditions of his opponents."[12]

Not content to limit existing working-class organizations, large industrialists throughout the Lower Rhine and Ruhr established company or yellow unions, which were hierarchical, anti-socialist, and strongly nationalistic. Such organizations, which assumed their most conservative character in this region, sought to prevent unionization, rally the unorganized, and secure working-class support for authoritarian policies on the shop floor and in society at large. Scarcely a month after the 1912 election, the first yellow union in Düsseldorf was established at the metalworking firm of Haniel and Lueg. Scheiss, Oecking, and the Oberbilker steel works immediately followed suit. In each case foremen were co-opted to recruit those under them. By late 1912 six metal firms and the streetcar company had yellow unions, but according to the police their membership scarcely topped the 1,000 mark and was drawn from the previously unorganized who were motivated by fear more than enthusiasm.[13]

Düsseldorf, unlike Bochum and Dortmund, never became a stronghold of the company union movement. On the one hand, its work force was highly skilled, mobile, heterogeneous and young, that is, composed of those least likely to join a yellow union. On the other hand, Düsseldorf's largest industrialists preferred either more direct repressive measures or slight concessions to socialist unions, which were, by 1912, well established even in metal. Nonetheless, the yellow union movement, which won the enthusiastic endorsement of the Chamber of Commerce, did curb the expansion of the free and Christian unions in the immediate prewar years.[14]

The Center Party, having undergone its fundamental transformation more than a decade before, did not move significantly further to the right. It continued to defend vigorously the traditional *Mittelstand* and cooperate with the Conservatives in defense of agrarian interests. In response to the chorus of capitalist complaints about neglect, the Lower Rhine party organization did establish an industrial advisory committee. But the need to hold the remains of its working-class base precluded official support for abolishing picketing or universal suffrage. As the Berlin wing of the Center Party gained strength and a 1912 papal encyclical announced the church's preference for Catholic Workers' Associations, the Christian trade unions became ever more pacific, nationalistic, and anti-socialist. They retreated from reluctant and rare collaboration with social democratic unions to a total condemnation of them.[15] The social democratic working class felt more beleaguered and isolated than ever.

In the aftermath of 1912 there were thus few indications that German domestic politics were gradually evolving in a parliamentary direction. Although the forms of mass politics were more prevalent, the content was increasingly anti-liberal and anti-democratic.[16] Chancellor Bethmann-Hollweg, having "pushed meek measures meekly" and nonetheless antagonized all sides in his first years in office, retreated into inactivity.[17] From 1912 to 1914 there was polarization and quasiparalysis in German political life.[18] And the Social Democrats, far from overcoming that situation, replicated it in their own ranks.

Stagnation and confusion

The Düsseldorf Social Democrats did not know how to combat the resurgent right. Although they had long criticized the assumptions of reformism, they had not anticipated a stalemate that would leave them virtually no economic or political options. Although they had spent decades besieging the Center Party fortress, they had not thought beyond the victory celebration. For a decade they had been making steady progress in their organizational, educational, and cultural activities and rather facilely assumed that the momentum would continue. It most definitely did not. In the dramatically altered situation after 1912, all aspects of movement life stagnated, and the efforts of local and national leaders to combat this deterioration were confused and counterproductive.

Membership provides one indication of the seriousness of the problems besetting the Düsseldorf movement. From 1902 to 1911 the party had expanded from a mere 530 workers to nearly 5,500. Thereafter, as Table 10.1 shows, recruitment slowed and then virtually stopped. The young skilled male migrants, who had formed the majority of recruits, failed to join in large numbers. Complete stagnation was averted only by the growing number of women who turned to the SPD once they were allowed to join political parties in 1908. The vast majority were married, usually to Social Democrats, but it is not known whether they worked in factories and shops or were housewives. The presence of these women, along with that of settled, skilled male workers, made party membership substantially more stable than in previous years.[19] But for a party that equated organizational success with recruitment, stability alone was inadequate.

Trade-union membership figures were even more discouraging and partially account for the slump in the party. In 1913 the economy entered a recession that, though milder than previous crises, nonetheless increased unemployment, dampened shop-floor militancy, and decreased union strength from a peak of 24,920 in 1912 to 23,093 in 1914. The DMV was especially hard hit, losing nearly 10 percent of its 10,000 members as a result of unemployment, lost strikes, and perhaps competition from yellow unions. To be sure, there were a few encouraging trends. By 1913 one in every three trade unionists had joined the party, testifying to the growing political commitment of the working class. Both the unions and the party were making steady inroads into the

Table 10.1. *Party membership, 1910–14*

Year	Total	Growth rate	Men	Growth rate	Women	Growth rate
1910	3,579		2,997		582	
1911	5,484	53.2	4,487	49.7	997	71.3
1912	7,166	30.6	5,722	27.5	1,394	39.8
1913	7,388	3.0	5,893	2.9	1,495	7.2
1914	7,793	5.4	5,918	0.4	1,875	20.2

Source: Volkszeitung, July 21, 1910; July 26, 1912; April 22, 1914; April 23, 1915.

increasingly industrialized county. Nonetheless, the Center, which in the words of SPD leader Zöllig, "made the confessional into a battleground for political struggles," held its own, and the Catholic Workers' Associations continued to have more than 10,000 members.[20]

While the Center press gloated over the "decline" of the social democratic movement, Berten, Arzberger, Agnes, and other local leaders denied that the situation was serious. They never analyzed their own recruitment problems or those of the national party in depth, preferring to blame the "regrettable slump" on economic crisis or "Center terrorism," even though they had weathered both much more effectively in the past.[21] When they finally did act in early 1914, launching, in conjunction with the national party, a massive recruitment drive called Red Week, they won nearly 1,000 members as well as additional subscribers to the *Volkszeitung*. Yet Red Week was a politically unfocused effort, whose rather empty slogan was "We must organize everything down to the smallest detail."[22] This attempt to find organizational solutions to problems that had social and political causes was reminiscent of the 1890s and testifies to the disorientation of the Düsseldorf Social Democrats.

Growth problems were only one aspect of a more general malaise affecting movement life in these years. The inevitable post-election lull gave way not to renewed activity but to apathy. By early 1913 leaders such as Berten were frequently complaining that "some of our comrades seem to be of the opinion that since we won the Reichstag election everything has been achieved ... Most believe that they have fulfilled their responsibilities if they pay their dues and attend an occasional meeting."[23] Many failed to do even that.

Attendance at meetings dropped precipitiously as their content and function became ever more amorphous. In early 1912, for example, the local leadership transformed the citywide general meetings into business affairs, with no educational component. Few members bothered to come. Simultaneously the district meetings, which had been the cornerstone of party life in recent years, lost their vitality. Although leaders such as Erbert, Milow, and Schmitt shifted from one orientation to another, they were unable to arouse the members' interest. In 1912, for instance, district speakers concentrated on socialist theory. Although fifty to sixty workers occasionally turned out, crowds of twenty or thirty were more common. When municipal politics were discussed, audiences of a dozen were normal. The rank and file showed scarely more interest in 1913, when current events dominated the agenda.[24]

The movement's educational program, which had once effectively promoted political awareness and activism, was also in disarray. Instead of courses on socialist theory, history, and economics, there were offerings on art, science, health, and basic German. In trying to touch all bases, the program covered none adequately. Leaders such as Fischer and Arzberger blamed this ineffective eclecticism alternately on worker apathy, the Reichstag election, and the regional education commission.[25] The causes lay deeper.

Neither the leaders nor the rank and file knew where the party should go nor how to get there, and this loss of a sense of direction lay at the root of the pervasive demoralization. Since 1890 the Düsseldorf Social Democrats had focused all their attention on the Center. For years they had been the scrappy underdog, fighting relentlessly for the victory they were convinced would someday be theirs. Now that they were on top, they did not know whom to attack next or by what means. Once popular issues lost their viability, and once promising tactics seemed unproductive.

Although the Social Democrats still viewed political Catholicism as a principal enemy, their struggle against it lost momentum. Unless the suffrage laws were altered, they could not challenge Catholic power on the provincial and municipal levels. In opposition to their comrades elsewhere, they would not attack religion for, as the *Volkszeitung* insisted, the SPD "is an organization which fights the ruling, exploiting and oppressive classes, not . . . the church." Although Berten, Agnes, Schmitt, Schotte, and at least two dozen other leaders had severed their connections with the established churches, they recognized that many workers were still religious and others feared repercussions if they left the church. Therefore, the leaders argued, the SPD should encourage religious indifference rather than overt hostility, "for such indifference represents a much higher stage of development. It is an expression of a materialistic world view; to be sure not a theoretical but nonetheless a practical materialism."[26]

Unable to move forward, the Düsseldorf Social Democrats turned back to issues that had once been effective. In mid-1912, as meat prices rose steeply and working-class consumption fell still further, the party once again condemned the tariff system and demanded special municipal food programs. Although more than 3,000 workers turned out for the initial protest meetings, the campaign quickly dwindled. The government simultaneously turned a deaf ear to the workers' protests, thus driving home to them the powerlessness of social democracy, and refrained from increasing existing tariff rates and thereby fueling the flames of protest.[27]

The Social Democrats had no more success with anti-militarism. When the Balkan war broke out in 1912, the workers, according to the Düsseldorf police, "set in motion an unusually vehement anti-nationalistic and strongly anti-militaristic agitation for world peace. It culminated in a peace demonstration at the Apollo Theater, attended by 5,000 to 6,000 persons."[28] But the Social Democrats, who had never accorded anti-militarism a central place in their agitation, did not know how to sustain the campaign once the immediate crisis had subsided. A similar scenario was played out in 1913. Several large meetings protested the military's illegal arrest of civilians in the Alsatian village of Zabern and the subsequent acquittal of the officers involved. "We will make clear to every member of the working class that every day this system of militarism continues to exist is an outrage and a danger," declared the Social Democrats in a fiery resolution. Then they limply added, "however, this system can only be eliminated when the existing capitalist state, with all its other horrors, is eliminated."[29]

On three different occasions the Düsseldorf Social Democrats raised the question of Prussian suffrage. In October 1912 they held several large protest meetings, but by November the agitation was dead, for the leaders were uncertain about tactics and the workers were indifferent after the abortive 1910 effort. The following spring Berten and Schmitt avoided public meetings and street demonstrations in favor of quiet preparations for the impending Landtag election. Few workers bothered to attend election meetings, however, and fewer still were willing to distribute flyers or register voters. On election day, only 10,831 Social Democrats turned out for a contest that was lost before it began. The results vindicated apathy. The SPD won a mere 206 electors, while the Center Party, with 16,567 votes, won 647 electors, and the liberal alliance, with only 5,002 votes, got 260.[30]

In the late spring of 1914, when the Prussian party leaders suggested resuming suffrage agitation, the Düsseldorf Social Democrats were ambivalent, for they were convinced that the national leadership would shun the radical tactics required to win reform. In a statement echoed by others in Düsseldorf, Berten argued that "the authority of the party with the masses as well as with the enemy will suffer more if we call forth a misleading impression of our indecisiveness through half-hearted actions and paper resolutions than if we temporarily remain inactive."[31] Despite this conviction, and in the absence of assurances that comrades elsewhere shared it, Düsseldorf took action. On June 8, 5,000 to 6,000 workers packed a protest meeting and cheered Conrad Hänisch when he declared that "the proletariat must accept the idea that at the appropriate time it must employ the mass strike." But the time was not appropriate, and the protest began and ended there. Provincial and national leaders strongly discouraged militant action, confirming Düsseldorf's worst fears.[32]

Nothing symbolized the movement's malaise more than the demise of May Day. In 1910 and 1911 between 10,000 and 14,000 workers had attended the rallies and festivities. In 1912, however, a mere 500 turned out for the march and meetings, and only construction workers struck in large numbers.[33] In 1913 the police prohibited a parade on the grounds of public safety; in 1914 because "large segments of the population of Düsseldorf see the international demands and goals of the Social Democrats . . . not only as a serious danger to the existing order but also as an insult to their own national feelings."[34] The Social Democrats were too demoralized to respond to these blatant provocations.

Trade unions suffered no less than the party did. As unemployment rose, membership dropped, and in the face of economic crisis, government harassment, and employer organization, fewer and fewer unions risked confrontation. Following the 1907–9 depression the level of militancy had risen significantly, and both traditionally strong occupations, such as woodworkers, and more recently organized ones, such as longshoremen, had waged vigorous offensive struggles.[35] After 1912, however, the size, frequency, and success rate of strikes dropped sharply.

According to the Chamber of Commerce, whose figures were lower than those of the trade-union cartel, from mid-1911 to mid-1912 more than 2,600 workers were involved in thirty-two strikes against 312 firms. By contrast, from mid-1913 to mid-1914 only 637 workers participated in sixteen, mainly defensive strikes, against 84 employers. In only one instance did a handful of employers lock out sixteen workers.[36] A decade of capitalist rationalization, concentration, and mechanization, as well as the proliferation of employers' associations and lockouts, had made effective union struggles difficult in times of prosperity and nearly impossible in times of recession.

Some unions held their own or made progress. In early 1912, for example, a six-week citywide strike of more than 300 tailors forced the multitude of small firms, which were organized either in the guild or the employers' association, to raise wages. The carpenters, who had extracted a contract from the compulsory guild in 1909, renewed it and won the closed shop as well. In 1913 the tinsmiths won a contract after the guild failed to lock out its 200 journeymen, but the terms were poor and a large minority voted against it. The roofers union was more successful, winning both a wage increase and union recognition from the guild despite the slowdown in construction.[37] Traditionally strong unions in sectors with numerous small employers were thus still able to fight with some prospect of success. Larger factories and state enterprises, however, proved invincible.

In mid-1912, to the surprise of the Social Democrats, the Christian streetcarmen's union walked off the job to demand higher wages. Although the activism was heartening, the response of the city-owned transportation system was not. The mayor refused any financial concessions and posted policemen on all streetcars and at major stops as well. Despite the union's strong protests, the justice minister defended the government's actions.[38] The union stood no chance against such opposition.

The DMV continued to fare badly against major employers. In 1911 it launched a campaign for the 9½-hour day in Düsseldorf's vast machine-making industry. Many small firms gave in without resistance, others after short strikes, and by the fall 3,500 workers in thirty-two firms had won their demand. The twenty-eight companies in the Düsseldorf Employers' Association for the Machine, Iron and Steel Industry, however, refused any concessions, and they employed more than 20,000 workers. In subsequent years the DMV had little success extending the limits of reform. By late 1912, 7,200 workers in fifty-two firms were working the 57-hour week, but the largest and most powerful industrialists still refused to budge. Finally, 1,200 metalworkers struck four large plants, but to no avail. The longer workday remained in effect, and factories such as Indem, which had 500 employees, fired all trade-union leaders, thereby destroying the organization. In 1913 the DMV campaign ground to a halt.[39] The metal industrialists were as secure and intransigent as ever, their position as *Herr-im-Haus* undiminished.

Most unions did not experience such overt setbacks, for they did not risk strikes at all. Where possible they tried to bargain about hours and wages; where unavoidable, they stood by helplessly as unemployment diminished their membership while rising food costs eroded the meager gains of previous years. This quiescence on the shop floor was both discouraging in its own right and increased political demoralization. The Social Democrats could find no options for action on either the economic or the political front.

The only area of social democratic life that displayed vitality and initiative in these years was the women's movement. As we saw earlier, prior to 1905 it had been impossible to establish a women's organization because of the economic structure and cultural climate of Düsseldorf and because of political persecution and the indifference if not hostility of male Social Democrats. Even when the party and union expanded after 1903, male Social Democrats, concerned with political questions traditionally defined, made no effort to organize women. The wives of party leaders, such as Gotthusen and Agnes, however, took it upon themselves to establish a Women's Organization, which was officially independent of the party because women could not legally join political associations.[40] From 1905 until 1908 the Women's Organization held monthly meetings, attracting women who had previously shunned involvement. It discussed women's issues, such as child rearing, and more general questions, such as religion, but ignored the political and theoretical debates that preoccupied the male comrades.

Although women were formally SPD members after 1908, they continued to run their own activities in addition to participating in some party ones. From 1909 until 1914 both membership and activism expanded steadily. Women sponsored small reading evenings and large public lectures with nationally noted social democratic women. Rather than supporting the party's general Reichstag campaigns in 1911 and 1912, the women organized their own agitation.[41] In 1911 Düsseldorf women, like their comrades elsewhere, celebrated the first women's day. Fifteen hundred enthusiastic women attended an open meeting to demand the vote, and afterwards "a street demonstration developed entirely spontaneously." The male Social Democrats were as surprised as the police. "A street demonstration of women and girls!" remarked the *Volkszeitung* in a most condescending manner. "Who would have considered that possible?"[42] In 1913 and 1914 several hundred women again took to the streets, supported this time by the men. The police called the women "a damned bunch of swine," broke up the demonstration, and arrested the leaders. The women were nonetheless elated by their own militancy and the grudging admiration of their male comrades.[43]

The flourishing women's section did not revitalize the movement as a whole. Although every fourth party member was female by 1914, women continued to occupy a relatively marginal position in Düsseldorf's economy and union movement. Unskilled, poorly paid, and transient, they were trapped in the least organized sectors or in domestic service, if they did paid labor at all.[44] They lacked the vote not only locally but nationally as well. In addition, Catholic working-class women were much more involved in the church than their male counterparts. All these factors combined to make many women indifferent to social democracy. Of equal importance, they fed the antifeminism of the men, most of whom seem to have remained convinced that it was neither feasible nor desirable to devote too much attention to politicizing women. Women were still considered to be a negative factor to be neutralized more than a positive one to be mobilized. Thus the *Volkszeitung* seldom discussed either women's activities or women's issues. The male-dominated membership selected men as leaders and functionaries, congress delegates, and speakers. And the audiences at party and union meetings were overwhelmingly male.[45]

The influence of the women's movement was further diminished by the roles that women and men alike assigned to women. Considering women primarily as housewives, rather than workers, they emphasized women's contribution as good social democratic wives, mothers, and helpers. In 1906, for example, Berten claimed that "women are becoming auxiliaries to the party, whose importance should not be underestimated." Milow encouraged women to fight for the vote, but urged them even more strongly to rear their children as good Social Democrats.[46] The leading social democratic women, such as Agnes and Weitz, accepted and propagated this image. Neither the men nor the women questioned traditional sex roles and family patterns. The male Social Democrats did not want to undermine their position and power in the family. They did not intend to give political Catholicism a pretext for claiming that social democracy undermined the family. They insisted that the family, like religion, was "a private affair." Nor did the women, who were aware of their weak economic position, reject the nuclear family, for they saw no alternative. Moreover, they had to direct their agitation to Catholic women, who were strongly oriented to home and church. Women thus remained helpers rather than becoming equal comrades. They could supplement the male movement but not stimulate it.

Women compensated for their minimal influence on the movement by trying to maximize their autonomy from it. Although male Social Democrats favored an end to all vestiges of separatism after 1908, women, fearing that their interests would be neglected by the male-dominated party, continued to hold separate meetings and activities. They preferred to serve the special educational needs of women and create a space where women could develop their talents, rather than participate in the concerns of the party as a whole. They defended the division of labor in the districts, which assigned female leaders the task of dealing exclusively with female members, for this gave women a small sphere of power.[47]

The women, unlike the men, knew in what direction they wanted to move in the immediate prewar years. But that separatist direction, however understandable and temporarily useful, made it all too easy for the men to ignore the women's movement and virtually impossible for the women to help alleviate the stagnation and confusion of the movement as a whole.

A left alternative

The problems of the Düsseldorf SPD found parallels throughout Germany, and the more severe the stalemate became, the more vigorously the Social Democrats debated means to break out of it. National party leaders, such as Kautsky and Ebert, clung to the centrist combination of radical rhetoric, isolation, and passivity. Reformists renewed their pleas for compromises and class alliances. The Düsseldorf Social Democrats, however, sided with their radical comrades elsewhere in urging a definitive swing to the left.

This further radicalization of social democracy in Düsseldorf was a response both to the shift to the right in German politics and to the ongoing structures and class alliances that underlay it. Radicalization resulted not from weakness in the movement, comparable to the situation in the 1890s, but rather from the movement's inability to translate organizational strength into material gains and political power. If political Catholicism played a less significant role in shaping the movement's ideology in these years, internal party debates and national party policies assumed a proportionately greater one. The left alternative articulated in Düsseldorf reflected the lessons learned between 1906 and 1912 and represented an attempt to apply them to the altered situation within Germany and within the SPD after 1912.

The Düsseldorf Social Democrats developed a most pessimistic assessment of the situation. As the *Volkszeitung* wrote in late 1913, "throughout the International reformism and bureaucratization are widespread, and there is an effort to suffocate all revolutionary strivings. Sometimes it seems like the entire movement is gradually being bogged down, while the bourgeoisie feels itself strengthened and inspired by the new perspectives opened to it by imperialism."[48] An escape into parliamentarism would never reverse these trends, for "only where the entire party unanimously leads a sharp class struggle in a revolutionary way – that is, with a clear recognition that the great goals stand over momentary advantages and can only be reached through the sole power of the proletariat – will the spirit of struggle be awakened in the masses."[49]

Düsseldorf's analysis, like that of the left elsewhere, emphasized mass action over organization and working-class self-reliance over political alliances. As befit its past orientation, Düsseldorf focused on domestic questions rather than imperialism, which was of primary concern to national radical leaders, such as Luxemburg and Liebknecht.[50] The Düsseldorf Social Democrats articulated their position most clearly in the course of the acrimonious debates over militarism and the mass strike, which absorbed the SPD in 1913 and 1914.

The divisive problem of taxes and militarism reappeared in early 1913 when Bethmann-Hollweg proposed a revised version of Bülow's 1909 finance-reform plan. This time the SPD's Reichstag delegation agreed to support a vast expansion of the notoriously conservative army in return for some direct taxes. The left was irate. A vote for taxes was a vote for militarism, argued the *Volkszeitung* editors without hesitation, and "we cannot agree with it." Düsseldorf was convinced that the SPD had become bogged down in a meaningless parliamentary debate over whether the agrarians would pay a little more or a little less. In so doing, they abandoned "the truly revolutionary educational struggle among the masses." They appeared "uncertain" and thereby increased the apathy of the working class.[51]

Throughout the summer and fall of 1913 the Düsseldorf press, the leadership, and large sections of the membership were embroiled in the dispute. In mid-July, for example, Düsseldorf's Reichstag deputy Haberland came to town. A former leftist who was gravitating toward the party's center, he vigorously defended the tax vote by ignoring the issue of militarism and arguing on the grounds of practicality. If a property tax had not been passed, the working class would have had to pay more. Berten, representing the more radical local leadership, insisted that indirect tax sources had been exhausted and that even if they had not been, "a principled policy" of absolute opposition to militarism was necessary to win respect from the masses. Although some members of the large audience supported Haberland, most maintained that "the comrades in the factories and workshops share Berten's opinion." There was no vote, for when someone proposed a pro-tax resolution, Haberland requested that it be withdrawn.[52] One suspects he feared defeat.

At the 1913 Jena party congress, which endorsed the Reichstag delegation's tax position by a vote of 336 to 140, Berten, Westkamp, and Lore Agnes sided with the radicals, as did Müller, who was representing another constituency. Arzberger and Spiegel, who attended because he was a member of parliament, supported the national executive.[53] In the heated debate, Berten argued that "when the army bill was proposed, the party should have emphasized that militarism in its entirety had to be combatted, that all means had to be used to defeat the measure."[54] Only the radicals shared his critique.

The Jena majority angered the Düsseldorf Social Democrats without persuading them. "Even if the party congress is the highest organ of the party, the comrades in the country still have the last word," remarked the *Volkszeitung* defiantly.[55] At three large meetings held to discuss Jena, those last words were spoken with a bitterness seldom heard among the Düsseldorf comrades. Five of the fifteen speakers defended both the Reichstag delegation and the congress resolution, using the same pragmatic arguments as Haberland had. Only Thielemann regarded the vote as proof of the party's strength. The radical majority viewed the issue more broadly. Support for militarism was a perversion of the idea of positive work and an affront to working-class internationalism. "We cannot change our principles like we change our clothes," declared Obuch indignantly.[56] The tax vote forced the Düsseldorf Social Democrats to recognize how thoroughly reformism had penetrated the party. The radicals' simultaneous defeat on the mass strike issue dispelled any lingering doubts as to the power of the right.,

The revival of the Prussian suffrage campaign in 1912 and 1913 inevitably brought with it discussion of the mass strike. Although both the national and Prussian leadership took a negative stance, local organizations were much more receptive.[57] The *Volkszeitung* consistently argued that "the mass strike is the method of struggle which is most suited to the social position of the proletariat."[58] It should be employed not only to achieve specific goals but also to halt the party's internal disintegration, which was a direct result of the fear of mass action. According to local leaders, the current policy of seeking petty reforms or waiting passively for revolution

cannot possibly inspire and sweep along the masses. Only great goals can waken enthusiasm and a willingness to sacrifice. Only a revolutionary tactic, which always builds on the reality of class conflict and appeals to the elemental power of the masses, can waken the energy, activism, and enthusiasm of the exploited proletariat.[59]

Drawing heavily on the analysis of Luxemburg, Berten and his fellow editors envisioned the mass strike not as a one-shot affair but as a series of actions of ever increasing size and power.[60] They would strengthen the fighting spirit and solidarity of organized workers and draw in the unorganized. "What the proletariat possesses, in addition to its chains," argued the *Volkszeitung*, "is power that does not disappear through struggle. Rather it grows until it suffices to break the chains."[61]

In the spring and summer of 1913 the *Volkszeitung* was not a voice crying in the wilderness. Berten and several other functionaries were the most vociferous proponents of the mass strike, but their ideas found a sympathetic echo among comrades locally and regionally. Although many districts avoided the issue, probably from a belief that no action would be taken, those that discussed it were most favorable. Wersten, an industrial suburb of Düsseldorf, even submitted a resolution to the regional party congress, asking that the national executive and the trade-union general commission prepare for a general strike in conjunction with the Prussian suffrage campaign. When the Lower Rhine congress met in June, the delegates, recognizing that previous tactics had proven ineffective, unanimously endorsed this viewpoint.[62]

At the Jena party congress, the Lower Rhine was the only region to submit a mass strike resolution, and Berten gave an impassioned speech on its behalf.[63] He insisted that:

People are in error if they believe that the recent discussion of the mass strike is the work of a few individuals. With us the discussion of this issue was demanded by workers in the factories and shops. I was surprised by the enthusiasm for the mass strike shown by comrades from whom I least expected it.[64]

Berten, who believed that the leaders came out of the masses and were always subject to recall by them,[65] urged his comrades to draw the appropriate lesson.

The organized workers demand sharper action. We cannot pacify them with meaningless resolutions. For the worker, it is a question of more than Prussian suffrage. It is a question of winning political equality and political power, of overcoming capitalism in general . . . It is damaging to suppress the utterances of party comrades.[66]

Berten, Westkamp, and Agnes supported Luxemburg's pro–mass·strike resolution whereas Arzberger opposed it, but the left-wing position was defeated by a vote of 333 to 142.[67]

In Düsseldorf the votes of the delegates reflected the views of the members.[68] The majority of Social Democrats agreed with Müller that the position of the executive and party congress was "an expression of complete helplessness." The SPD needed to regain a clear sense of its goals and overcome its cowardly fear of mass action. The minority followed Haberland, who maintained that the weakness of the party, the conservatism of the unions, and the immobility of the unorganized made it impossible even to talk of a mass strike. Organization should be the movement's first priority.[69] The minority view neither spoke to the party's deep strategic problems nor appealed to workers who acknowledged the necessity of organization but recognized the need to move beyond it.

After Jena the debate subsided, but Düsseldorf continued to attack both the recent congress decisions and the general prevalence of reformism and bureaucratization in the SPD and the International.[70] Berten and his fellow leaders argued that "the tactic of being morally right, of only agitating in order to appeal to the moral consciousness of the people, may be necessary for a movement in its early stages." Social democracy was hardly in its infancy, however, and its current crisis required a different strategy. "What keeps the masses from us now is not a belief in capitalism but a disbelief in the proletarian cause. The masses do not doubt the justice of our demands, but rather our power to gain them . . . What we need is an energetic, offensive tactic in all areas." Only such a course could overcome "the contradiction between the disgraceful offensive of our enemies and the immobility of the organized workers' movement." If it were not adopted, organization, which should be a prerequisite for action, would remain a hindrance to it. The rank and file would continue to complain that the leaders put a brake on all action, while the leaders would wait fatalistically for the masses to act spontaneously.[71]

The Düsseldorf Social Democrats understood the party's dilemma with painful clarity, but their alternative strategy was not without its difficulties. Around what issues should the party launch the much-needed offensive? When could it begin? And most important, how could the loosely organized radical minority of which Düsseldorf was a part convince the party's mainstream that such a course was not merely desirable but absolutely necessary? As Jena had shown, disaffection was rampant not only in the party itself but also in such trade unions as the DMV, and radical views could not be dismissed as the preserve of a mere handful of bourgeois intellectuals. Yet the leftist locals remained isolated from one another, with no practical leadership or rudimentary organization. Düsseldorf, for example, played a leading role in the Lower Rhine but had few contacts outside. Some leftists looked to Luxemburg for guidance, others to Liebknecht or Ledebour, and many relied on their own, often inadequate resources.[72] Of equal seriousness, the left had a short-run tactical prescription but no long-run strategy for seizing power and transforming society. Radicals saw the mass strike as a way out of the current impasse, but did not conceptualize its broader implications clearly. They had not even put these issues on the discussion agenda.

In short, radicalism was more pervasive in 1914 than in 1910 and its critique of the status quo more fully elaborated, but its strategic prescriptions were not better developed. The strengths and weaknesses of the left in Düsseldorf and throughout Germany were to determine its reaction to the outbreak of war in mid-1914.

War

Although both social democracy and German society had long considered war a possibility, neither was prepared when it became a reality.
As the Europe-wide conflict began, industrialists, agrarians, the diverse
strata of the old and new middle classes, and the peasantry quickly
rallied behind the flag. Most surprisingly, the SPD and the trade-union
general commission endorsed the war effort as well. The working class
and leftist Social Democrats were much more divided on the issue,
however, and nowhere was dissent more vocal than in Düsseldorf.
August 1914 precipitated the last round of struggle between the Düsseldorf Social Democrats and the national party.

Throughout the spring of 1914 the Düsseldorf Social Democrats had
been preoccupied with recruitment drives and suffrage agitation. When
Archduke Franz Ferdinand of Austria was assassinated at Sarajevo in late
June, they staged no protest, for they did not foresee the possibility of
war. In July the *Volkszeitung*, like its bourgeois counterparts, paid
scarcely any attention to the diplomatic negotiations among Austria,
Serbia, and Germany about the recent troubles in the Balkans. Local
leaders such as Berten and Arzberger were busy promoting a lecture
series on socialist education in the family by Otto Rühle of Berlin.[73] The
members, so far as they were active at all, were preparing for the late
summer trade-union festival.

Not until July 21 did the Düsseldorf Social Democrats recognize the
danger of a conflict involving Germany. The *Volkszeitung* immediately
called for "a flaming protest against the war."[74] Düsseldorf had little
sympathy with the analyses of war that distinguished between offensive
and defensive wars and promised to participate in the latter, especially if
autocratic Russia were the enemy. The anti-militarism of the radicals was
tinged with pacifism, and many believed that Germany was deliberately
encouraging a Russian mobilization.[75] Leaders such as Berten felt that
the state was plunging into war for quite reactionary domestic purposes–a
view shared by many historians.[76] As Berten wrote in his memoirs:

It is remarkable that apparently no one in the social democratic Reichstag
delegation wondered whether the war enthusiasm of the ruling class could not
be traced back to the giant electoral success of the SPD in 1912. A future social
democratic majority in the Reichstag seemed so dangerous to the powerful
factory owners and banking magnates that they preferred to purify the people by
means of a fresh and jolly war.[77]

Local leaders urged "the class-conscious proletariat to express its will to peace," and maintained that the vast majority of organized workers in Düsseldorf shared the anti-war sentiment of the *Volkszeitung*.[78] Certainly the mammoth protest demonstrations lent credence to this assertion. Although there may well have been "frenzied enthusiasm" for the war on the part of many social democratic functionaries and workers elsewhere,[79] this was not the case in Düsseldorf. On July 29, when Austria and Serbia had already declared war, 15,000 to 20,000 workers packed twelve giant social democratic rallies and later marched and sang through the streets. "It was a day of honor for the working class in Düsseldorf," proclaimed the *Volkszeitung* proudly. The proletariat had protested a war that "would bring unending misery and new burdens to the workers of all lands" and "had warned those who desire war not to play with fire or they could get burned."[80]

The protest gave eloquent testimony to the radicalism of the Düsseldorf working class. But it achieved nothing. On August 1 Germany declared war on Russia. On August 4 the SPD voted for war credits, agreed to suspend all political and union activity for the duration, and applauded enthusiastically when William II announced that "I no longer recognize parties. I only recognize Germans."[81]

Various explanations have been offered for the SPD's behavior, which stunned all and was condemned by many within the movement. Some Social Democrats believed that the war was defensive; others hated Czarist Russia. Most, however, were probably influenced by the movement's past experiences and actions – or inaction. Since 1907 center and right Social Democrats, with the strong backing of the trade unions, had moderated the party's internationalism and anti-militarism while flatly refusing to make concrete preparations for resisting war. Neither the SPD nor the International had a strategy to implement if war broke out.[82] As a result of the anti-socialist laws and subsequent harassment and discrimination, movement leaders feared massive repression if they resisted the call to arms. Having spent two and a half decades painstakingly building a vast and wealthy organization, they were reluctant to risk it in defense of a position of total opposition in which only the radicals still believed. For many, support for the war seemed a means to end the isolation of the working class and the second-class status of the movement.[83] For the center and right cooperation with the government opened a possible escape from the stalemate in which the party, like

German society as a whole, found itself. For the party, as for the state and ruling classes, war was a weapon to be wielded against the left.

Radicals were effectively disarmed and temporarily silenced. Like its counterparts elsewhere in Germany and abroad, the left in Düsseldorf had no concrete strategy for resisting war because it had failed to win previous approval for a mass strike, the only possible weapon against mobilization.[84] Nothing testifies to this unpreparedness more clearly than the resolution passed at the July 29 protest meetings in Düsseldorf. Workers were not urged to protest or strike or resist but simply to join the SPD, "which is the only party which works expressly and tirelessly for peace."[85] In addition, war preparations and then martial law greatly intensified the isolation of the Düsseldorf radicals from like-minded comrades. Finally, the Düsseldorf Social Democrats still believed in the primacy of party unity and the need for party discipline. They were opposed to the war, bitter about the party's vote for war credits, and angry that Haberland, contrary to local sentiment, had supported both. They refused to heed the advice that national party leader Phillip Scheidemann gave to the *Volkszeitung*: "You must adjust to the given circumstances."[86] The paper continued to protest the war vigorously until August 4, when it was confiscated and pre-censorship imposed. But in August 1914 the Social Democrats were not yet prepared to leave the SPD.

The first months of war profoundly disrupted Düsseldorf's economic life and the social democratic movement. Ten thousand men were drafted almost immediately, and another 6,000 were thrown out of work as the economy jerked to a halt. Neither the military nor the government, which expected the troops home by Christmas, nor industry, which could not predict military needs, organized war production. Employment at Rheinmetall, for example, dropped from 8,000 in early 1914 to 3,400 at the end of August, and armaments production did not pick up until year's end. All major construction projects, including the large Prussian centennial exhibition site, were suspended – as it turned out, permanently. Firms not producing war-related goods shortened shifts, work weeks, and, of course, pay.[87]

The ranks of the social democratic movement were severely depleted. By November more than 1,500 party members, including many leaders, had been drafted, and those remaining curtailed their activities. The trade-union cartel suffered even more, losing 41 percent of its membership. The construction workers union, for example, lost 1,438 supporters, 1,035 of them to the army. Twenty-nine hundred metalworkers were drafted, and another 1,000 either lost their jobs or left the city. Nearly one in every three subscribers to the *Volkszeitung* was in uniform, and many others were unemployed. The families of both soldiers and the unemployed received free copies, but as the burden grew and the ad section shrank, the paper's finances became ever more precarious.[88]

The movement struggled to maintain a minimum of activity in the face of martial law and continued harassment. Although national leaders urged workers only to devote themselves to organizational tasks, those in Düsseldorf tried to promote education and strengthen adherence to principles as well.[89] Berten, Schotte, and Pfeiffer concentrated on publishing the *Volkszeitung*, which was subject to thorough precensorship. White spots dotted every page. Sometimes there were so many that Pfeiffer assembled them together and left an entire page blank, to the great annoyance of the censors.[90] As the content became, of necessity, ever more bland, the editors urged their readers to turn to Marx Engels, and Lassalle, noting that "the study of scientific socialism was somewhat neglected of late due to the multitude of practical tasks."[91] They reminded workers "to apply to the current situation all that you have learned in your years of educational work about the economic and social causes of historical events."[92]

In order to maintain their visibility and retain the confidence of the working class, the Social Democrats participated in the fall city council election. Although permitted to hold election meetings, they were forced to limit their critique to inadequacies in the city's food, housing, and welfare programs. They acknowledged the "need" to deemphasize the conflict of world views that had pervaded previous elections, but nonetheless insisted that only the SPD could represent working-class interests and secure reform. Because of severe demoralization in the movement, however, barely 2,700 voted as opposed to nearly 10,000 in 1912. The Center – liberal alliance won all seats handily and made no effort to bring the Social Democrats into the war effort on the local level. The Düsseldorf Social Democrats were as isolated as ever in an unreformed system.[93]

In the first six months of World War I the gamble of the German ruling classes seemed to have paid off. The SPD and trade-union leadership, calculating that cooperation would be rewarded with substantial political reforms, had actively endorsed the war.[94] The left, though unconverted, was quiescent. The calm was to be short lived, however, for the anticipated reforms did not materialize, but the deprivation and dislocation of prolonged total war did. The left began to regroup its forces, articulate its critique, and engage in active resistance. Ultimately, the war that had been begun to prevent revolution was to precipitate one. And the Düsseldorf Social Democrats were to be active participants in all these events.

11

War

The impact of war on the economy and society in Düsseldorf was similar to that in other industrial cities central to war production. There was a restructuring of the economy and the labor force, marked by rationalization, the recruitment of young and female workers, and extensive state intervention. As demands for munitions and manpower increased, hours lengthened and the workpace intensified while unsafe working conditions proliferated. Food shortages and inflation led to a significant deterioration in workers' standard of living. On the political front, concessions to social democracy were not forthcoming. Yet this common war experience affected a working class and a social democratic movement with a quite uncommon prewar history, and the interaction between the two accounts for both the strength of radicalism in Düsseldorf and its particular character.

Although the outbreak of war temporarily stabilized Wilhelmian Germany, its continuation precipitated the disintegration of both the social and political order and the social democratic movement. Military mobilization, economic reorganization, and national social democratic adherence to the *Burgfrieden*, or political truce, increased the Düsseldorf workers' disaffection with the state, their employers, and the national SPD and trade-union confederation. The war, which was to polarize German society as well as social democracy, confirmed the Düsseldorf radicals' previous analysis of the intractability of German economic and political structures and the unreliability and animosity of other social classes. War transformed their previous preoccupation with political Catholicism into one with the state on the one hand and the national party and unions on the other. It strengthened their commitment to Marxism and militant tactics and convinced them that they would have to leave the SPD in order to conduct the class struggle according to their principles.

Once the Düsseldorf Social Democrats had left the SPD, the strengths

251

and weaknesses of their radicalism were fully revealed. Throughout 1917 and 1918 the vast majority of leaders, party members, and trade unionists supported the USPD and continued their agitation for peace and political reform. They enthusiastically endorsed the Russian Revolution, and by mid-1918 many spoke of the need for a German republic on the Bolshevik model. In short, they remained true to their radical tradition with its emphasis on working-class autonomy, mass action, and fundamental reform. Because the socialist party and unions moved in step with the working class – indeed, at times they moved more quickly to the left – the ties between workers and their traditional institutions remained close. New organizations and leaders did not appear.

Yet the Düsseldorf Social Democrats failed to develop either a strategy for seizing power or a concrete picture of the society to be created. As in the past, political goals had top priority, while both economic programs and the economic wing of the movement remained relatively weak. Finally, Düsseldorf was unable to overcome the negativism and passivity that had long characterized the social democratic movement.

The battle from within, 1915–1916

The tense truce that had prevailed in Düsseldorf in late 1914 began to unravel in 1915 and 1916. As the military and economic situation of Germany deteriorated, so too did the social and political position of the working class. Efforts to reorganize economic and political life in order to meet the needs of a prolonged, two-front war exacerbated class divisions, while SPD and national trade union support for these policies heightened tensions within the labor movement. In Düsseldorf the Social Democrats protested the inequitable burdens of war and criticized the national leadership's endorsement of "the policy of August 4." They played a highly visible role in the emerging left opposition, which sought to reform the party from within, not attack it from without.

During the first months of war neither economic nor political life had been fundamentally restructured, for military and civilian leaders alike anticipated a quick victory. By early 1915, however, it was clear that business-as-usual could not continue, for munitions, manpower, and food were in increasingly short supply. The state and the military, with the active collaboration of industry and social democracy, intervened in production, distribution, and labor relations. War industries companies were established to secure raw materials; labor allocation schemes were developed, and research and plant expansion were funded.[1]

This restructuring, which both the left and the right misleadingly called "war socialism," sought to limit prices and wages but did not interfere with profits and property relations. Although it temporarily alleviated the munitions and manpower shortages, it increased existing economic and social inequities. It greatly strengthened the large-scale metal, mining, chemical, and electrical industries at the expense of light industry and artisan production.[2]

In Düsseldorf the vast, diversified metal sector converted totally to war production and expanded still further. Rheinmetall, for example, which had employed 3,400 workers in 1914, had more than 30,000 by 1916, and all firms cried out for skilled craftsmen. In "nonessential" sectors, however, hundreds of factories and workshops closed, either because their owners were drafted or because they lacked raw materials and orders.[3] The Düsseldorf Chamber of Commerce, spokesmen for the prospering metal firms, smugly recommended that "we must accept that the burdens and benefits of the war economy are distributed very differently within industry and commerce."[4] The government's policies also favored the city over the country, the private sector over the public, and munitions workers above all others. And the state paid no heed to cost in its efforts to increase productivity. As a result, the war industries charged exorbitant prices and made huge profits, which in turn were paid by the printing press rather than by loans or taxes. The tax system could be reformed no more easily in war than in peace. The ensuing inflation made the burdens of war still heavier, more inequitable, and more visible. Although most Düsseldorfers complained bitterly, the Düsseldorf Chamber of Commerce vigorously denied that its members were war profiteers, claiming instead that inflation inevitably accompanied war.[5]

For the working class the war economy was at best a mixed blessing. On the positive side, it ended unemployment, brought high money wages to munitions workers, and opened thousands of jobs in war-related industries to women and the unskilled. Between January 1915 and January 1917, for example, nearly 30,000 workers, two-thirds of them women, found positions in Düsseldorf. More than 7,000 women were employed at Rheinmetall, formerly a male bastion. The rationalization of production, which created these opportunities for the unskilled, however, threatened the security and craft culture of the skilled.[6]

Of more immediate importance, even the best-paid workers could not keep up with the soaring cost of living, and those in non-war industries suffered acutely. Because the government had failed to solve the food problem, even temporarily, bread was rationed in Düsseldorf and potatoes were in short supply from early 1915 on. The city's efforts to regulate prices and procure extra supplies failed, and the prices of other goods rose steeply. A half-kilogram of beef cost 0.88 M in 1914 and 2.80 M in late 1916. Pork rose from 1.03 M to 2.50 M, eggs from 1.38 M to 3.20 M, and milk from 0.23 M to 0.41 M in the same period. Often these basic foods were not available at all.[7]

Labor relations scarcely improved. Although the state consulted with trade-union leaders and urged industrialists to adopt a more conciliatory policy toward workers, only small-scale and light industry, always more vulnerable and tractable, did so. Heavy industry, above all the metal firms in the Ruhr and Lower Rhine, refused to recognize unions or engage in collective bargaining. They were fighting the war to preserve the conservative status quo and did not want to do anything that would enhance workers' power when the inevitable conflict resumed after the war.[8]

Despite this, national SPD leaders continued to cooperate with the state, disciplining their dwindling and disaffected ranks as much as possible. Some were moved by arguments of patriotism and national defense. Others were seduced by the slight recognition they were accorded by the powers that be. Most had lost contact with the rank and file in the factories and battlefields and made no effort to mobilize the thousands of new workers flocking into the war industries. All hoped that their quiesence and collaboration would be rewarded with political reforms.[9]

In the first two years of war there was little evidence that such reform would be forthcoming. There was slight progress on the social policy front and minor improvements in the organization law, but no movement in the direction of parliamentarism.[10] Quite the opposite. The *Burgfrieden* had reduced "the Bismarckian state to its ideal form."[11] The parties had suspended their conflicts, and both the chancellor and the military increased their power at the expense of an already weak parliament. Although both civilian and military leaders recognized that the war could not be waged without the cooperation of the working class, neither wanted to alter the existing system substantially.[12] As

Bethmann-Hollweg so trenchantly put it, "the leaders of the Social Democratic Party must understand that the German Reich, and particularly the Prussian state, can never permit any weakening of the firm foundations on which they are built."[13] Nationally, social democratic parliamentary deputies and trade-union functionaries alike ignored the message and adhered to the *Burgfrieden* more stringently than any other group. In Düsseldorf, however, the Social Democrats could neither comprehend nor condone such behavior.

Signs of disaffection appeared in several areas of Düsseldorf party life from early 1915 on. Despite pre-censorship, the *Volkszeitung*, under Berten and Pfeiffer's editorship, printed a running critique of food prices and supplies, of war profiteering and inadequate state aid for soldiers' families. The paper followed Luxemburg's anti-war activities with rapt attention and carried a detailed and sympathetic account of the Copenhagen conference entitled "Socialists for Peace."[14] When the prominent local leader Hoch was killed in battle, a strongly pacifist obituary called for "an era in which men will consider other men, regardless of nationality, as brothers and comrades."[15] On one occasion Berten even ran a scathing editorial condemning any annexations and blaming Germany for ruining its relations with Britain. But the paper was summarily shut down for three days by the military and avoided such intemperate critiques thereafter.[16] The *Volkszeitung* was more reticent about attacking the national executive and parliamentary party, both out of obedience to the SPD's rigid conception of discipline and out of fear of harassment from the police and military.[17] But silence did not mean support.

Throughout the spring of 1915, the Düsseldorf Social Democrats met regularly to discuss ongoing national party support for the war and *Burgfrieden*. According to the Düsseldorf police, "there have been several stormy scenes . . . Haberland and the entire social democratic Reichstag delegation, with the exception of Liebknecht, have been called traitors, Judases, and the like for their approval of war credits."[18] More than a hundred members, some of whom had been in the party for ten or twenty years, quit in disgust. In April Haberland came to defend himself at the annual local party conference. After he and Berten had fought a bitter verbal duel over the national party's policy and the *Volkszeitung*'s refusal to support it, all but four members voted in defense of Düsseldorf's dissenting position.[19] The local party refrained from formally condemning Haberland, but the police assumed that he could never run again in Düsseldorf and predicted "that a split in the party is probably unavoidable at the end of the war."[20]

Although the war disrupted the tenuous connections among radical Social Democrats in Germany, Düsseldorf was intimately involved in the opposition efforts of the left from their inception. In September 1914 Berten attended a meeting in Frankfurt with Luxemburg, Liebknecht, Mehring, and a few others to plan agitation against the war and war credits. In early 1915 he printed the group's brochure, *Die Internationale*, at the *Volkszeitung* press and distributed 9,000 copies in Düsseldorf and throughout Germany. A loophole in the law saved Berten from jail but not from the military, which drafted him as punishment a few months later. The response from the national executive was equally quick and unequivocal. They circulated a ringing denunciation of the Gruppe Internationale, which was to become the core of the Spartacists and the Communist Party (KPD), and then approved supplementary war credits in the late spring.[21]

The opposition answered on a much larger scale than previously. Seven hundred sixty functionaries from throughout Germany signed a letter to the national executive that labeled the party's policies "a retreat from principle" and "the cross on the grave of the class struggle." The manifesto insisted that the imperialist character of the war was clear for all to see and condemned the leaders' blindness. In Düsseldorf thirty-five functionaries, including the entire local executive, the editorial board of the *Volkszeitung*, several district leaders, the trade-union secretary, and the officers of the tailors union, signed. Although the local party leadership was as solidly behind the opposition cause as the rank and file, trade-union functionaries were more divided. In neighboring Benrath, an industrial suburb of Düsseldorf, four SPD city councilmen and the head of the DMV endorsed the protest. Only Berlin, Hanau, and Potsdam had more signatories than Düsseldorf, but several other Lower Rhine cities did support the letter in large numbers.[22] The Bochum party paper, securely in the hands of rightist Social Democrats, remarked disparagingly that Düsseldorf was "the center of the extreme elements."[23]

Protest soon spilled over from the party to the unions. Although Düsseldorf was a prosperous munitions center, its thousands of metal-workers were by no means enthusiastic supporters of the war. Beginning in early 1915 the formerly quiescent Düsseldorf DMV, along with its counterparts in Hanau, Leipzig, and Jena, began protesting the national leadership's endorsement of the war and cooperation in the war economy. At the yearly congress Düsseldorf introduced a resolution censuring the content and tone of the *Metallarbeiter Zeitung*.[24] The DMV policies violated the political principles of the Düsseldorf metalworkers, whereas the war economy had done nothing to improve either factory conditions or union power. Even if the demand for munitions workers brought a slight wage increase in the short run, rationalization threatened the position of the skilled in the long run. Fitters and turners and the other craftsmen who dominated the Düsseldorf DMV were in a contradictory position and acted out of mixed motives. But craft consciousness and solidarity with the semiskilled, economic self-interest, and political principle all pushed them steadily to the left.

Throughout late 1915 and early 1916 the Düsseldorf Social Democrats followed the growing dissension in the national movement closely. The national majority, which continued to defend the war and the *Burgfrieden* while refusing to reject annexations, came under heavy attack not only from the radical left but from the left center as well. The radicals were led by Liebknecht, who had broken party discipline and voted against war credits. They opposed the war unequivocally, insisting that "the chief enemy is at home" and that the struggle for socialism must begin immediately. The left center, led by Haase and Ledebour, condemned annexations but not national defense, and advocated a restoration of civil liberties but not revolutionary agitation. By late 1915 the two groups comprised a full third of the SPD's parliamentary delegation. These forty-four Social Democrats urged the party to veto further credits, and when twenty broke discipline and did so, both the Düsseldorf party and the Lower Rhine district leadership enthusiastically applauded the action.[25] Summing up the local mood, the *Volkszeitung* stated confidently that "we are fully conscious of the responsibility which we assume when we urge the minority to act independently . . . We are also convinced that such action does not mean the division of the party."[26]

Like radicals elsewhere, the Düsseldorf Social Democrats were deeply committed to maintaining party unity. They were not only optimistic that they would soon become the majority, but also convinced that a formal division would pave the way for working-class demoralization and defeat. The national majority, however, was increasingly willing to force a split if the left did not submit.[27] In March 1916 it expelled the opposition from the social democratic Reichstag delegation, although not yet from the party. Düsseldorf was incensed. "What a sensation!" exclaimed the *Volkszeitung*. "The majority of the social democratic Reichstag delegation has declared that the minority is unworthy to sit at the same table . . . The majority has crowned its war work and slammed the door on the representatives of a principled socialism."[28] Closer to home, the national executive attempted to curb the spread of oppositional attitudes by closing the Düsseldorf press bureau, which supplied agitational material to the entire region.[29]

The intransigence of the majority had a predictably radicalizing effect on the Düsseldorf Social Democrats. By a nearly unanimous vote the annual party conference resolved "to prevent the further use of party dues in support of the policy of August 4." A second resolution praised Liebknecht "for his brave support for a truly social democratic policy" and "declared a willingness to work further in the sense of this policy."[30] Although local union leaders hesitated to endorse the extreme left, the trade-union cartel did vote 36 to 15 to condemn the trade-union general commission and its *Korrespondenzblatt* for supporting the war and the SPD executive's attack on the opposition.[31]

By mid-1916 relations between the majority and minority had degenerated into a polarized stalemate that no faction knew how to break – least of all the left radicals. Neither in Düsseldorf nor elsewhere did they have a positive strategy to complement their total rejection of the war and the *Burgfrieden*. Thus, in the second half of 1916 attention turned from interparty conflicts about foreign and domestic politics to economic problems.

The food situation in Düsseldorf, as throughout Germany, had deteriorated markedly by 1916. Despite grain tariffs, Germany had been far from agricultural self-sufficiency in 1914 and suffered heavily from the blockade. In addition the conscription of men and animals cut agrarian production significantly. The predictable results were acute shortages, high prices, and a flourishing black market. Bread was severely rationed in 1915, and the following year potatoes were no longer an abundant substitute. Nearly half the households in Düsseldorf were short of them, and by June the ration for the 30,000 Rheinmetall workers was only $\frac{1}{2}$ pound per day. When only a small portion of the supplies expected for the Pentacost holiday arrived, angry crowds stormed the city's wholesale potato outlets and took all that was available while the police looked on. Immediately thereafter, ration cards were introduced, but supplies did not increase. Between October and December the weekly ration dropped from 5 to 1.5 kilograms in the wake of a disastrous harvest.[32]

Munitions and manpower were equally inadequate, despite more extensive state intervention in those areas. To satisfy the army's voracious appetite for armaments and soldiers, the Supreme Command and the war economy were reorganized in late 1916. Generals Ludendorff and Hindenburg, both staunch conservatives and strong proponents of annexations, took over the Supreme Command and de facto control of the civilian government as well. With the aid of industrial interests they introduced the Hindenburg Program, a total mobilization of the economy for munitions production, which promoted rationalization and concentration while "silencing" nonessential industries. It was an unequivocal triumph for heavy industry and the military.[33]

To cope with the manpower crisis brought on by the demands of trench warfare and munitions production, the Auxiliary Service Law introduced industrial conscription for all men from 17 to 60. The national SPD and ADGB supported the law, as they had the Hindenburg Program, in return for a provision requiring the establishment of workers' committees in large factories.[34] The rank and file, however, was considerably less enthusiastic. In Düsseldorf the open meeting called by the trade-union cartel to discuss the situation was extremely disorderly. The right-wing Social Democrat Brey praised the law for actually improving the workers' position, whereas Ostertag and Jäker regarded it as inevitable but only partially positive. Ochel and Müller, however, claimed that the law brought "new chains which force the workers to drag the capitalist wagon forward." Their resolution, condemning the law and SPD support of it, passed but with a sizable minority dissenting.[35]

The skepticism of the left proved justified. In Düsseldorf, factories were slow to establish the much-heralded workers' committees.[36] And these committees never became the nucleus of protest during the war or of revolutionary activity after it. Of greater importance, the Hindenburg Program failed to alleviate the munitions, manpower, and food shortages. By early 1917 these economic and military problems were compounded by the Russian Revolution and growing domestic unrest. The resulting crisis of 1917 was to destroy the *Burgfrieden*, divide the SPD, and radicalize the working class, especially in Düsseldorf.

The battle from without, 1917–1918

1917 was a year of crisis for Germany, as for all the belligerents. The crisis was brought on by Germany's inability to solve the military, economic, and political problems of prolonged war, but it raised issues extending far beyond the war itself. The crisis reactivated and intensified all the disputes that had existed prior to 1914 and showed that they could not be solved within the framework of the old order. The societal crisis was paralleled by that of the social democratic movement, which could no longer contain the conflicts between supporters and opponents of the war, between reformist practice and revolutionary theory, between a right-wing leadership and a radicalized working class. The *Burgfrieden* in both politics and the party disintegrated. In response to the dual crisis, the Düsseldorf Social Democrats were to leave the SPD for the USPD en masse, while the workers, organized and unorganized alike, engaged in demonstrations and strikes. The arduous task of building a left alternative, a task for which they were so ill prepared, began.

The failure of the Hindenburg Program and the Auxiliary Service Law was manifested in all areas of economic life. Even though night shifts, overtime, and Sunday work were the norm in industry, the demands of trench warfare could not be satisfied, and the military and heavy industry fought constantly over workers. Coal shortages and inadequate transportation, which were exacerbated by the sudden attempt at total economic mobilization, worsened conditions on both the home and battle fronts. In Düsseldorf, as throughout the country, the food situation went from serious to catastrophic, for the potato harvest had been abysmal. Rations were cut, prices soared, and the turnip became the mainstay of the German diet. Munitions firms, such as Rheinmetall, frantically sought supplementary food for their workers, and the black market flourished, for virtually no one could survive without some recourse to it. In the face of such deprivation, the birthrate sank, infant mortality rose, and crime proliferated.[37]

The military news was no more encouraging. The stalemate continued on the Western front, while the decision to engage in unlimited submarine warfare precipitated American intervention rather than British and French capitulation. Although the Russian Revolutions of February and October were ultimately to give Germany a victory in the East, their initial impact proved quite disruptive.

The February Revolution in Russia, which established both a liberal parliamentary government and a socialist workers' soviet, did not spark similar protests in the West, but it did force all parties in Germany to confront two problems surpressed since 1914 – war aims and domestic reform. The Petrograd soviet issued a public call for "a peace without annexations and indemnities," published the secret treaties signed by the Entente, and touched off a bitter debate about war aims in Germany. Whereas previously those on the left had criticized expansion, now the SPD and some Progressives questioned the grandiose designs for *Mitteleuropa* and *Mittelafrika* that Junkers, industrialists, and the military harbored. The Russian Revolution also raised the issue of domestic reform, because it showed that the old order was fragile, that war was not always a successful antidote to revolution. Furthermore, it eliminated the repressive Czarist autocracy, which provided the SPD with its principal justification for supporting the war.[38]

The economic and military crises lessened divisions within the working class by decreasing wage differentials, increasing geographic and occupational mobility, and homogenizing working and living conditions. At the same time, the war economy and the ramifications of the Russian Revolution increased conflict between classes. Growing proletarian deprivation, the visibly unequal distribution of the burdens of war, and the disappointing results of the *Burgfrieden* heightened working-class discontent and led to protests not only for more food and higher wages but also for peace without annexations, suffrage reform, and parliamentary government.[39]

But the forces that precipitated this radicalization also promoted intransigence on the part of the ruling classes. Ludendorff vowed to make no concessions "to the spirit of the times."[40] Heavy industry and Junker agriculture held out "for farreaching territorial gains . . . to ensure through a successful peace settlement the continuation of the existing order to their own advantage and to the political and economic detriment of the German people."[41] Those, such as Bethmann-Hollweg and the national SPD leaders, who hoped that a modicum of political reform could be achieved in order to placate the working class without arousing the ire of the old order, proved powerless to stop the escalating conflict within German society and social democracy.

The first casualty of the crisis of 1917 was the SPD itself. In January left radicals and left centrists held their first conference, aimed at strengthening the opposition but not splitting the party. The majority, eager to rid itself of uncomfortable critics, expelled them. Düsseldorf's sympathies were predictable. A large general meeting refused to take any action against the opposition, that is, against itself, and decided to withhold all funds from the national party. Throughout February and March the *Volkszeitung*, under Pfeiffer, and the party, led by Schmitt, Agnes, and Obuch, avoided forcing a final break with Berlin or giving the national executive a pretext to take over the press, as it had done elsewhere.[42] But local leaders did nothing to stop the leftward drift; indeed, "in secret they encouraged it." According to the police, by mid-March "almost the entire membership" of the Düsseldorf SPD consisted of "convinced supporters" of Liebknecht and the Spartacists, and 150 to 200 were loosely organized in the Gruppe Internationale.[43]

When the national opposition leaders announced a congress at Gotha to establish a new party, 77 of 81 Düsseldorf functionaries and 561 of 600 members voted to send a delegate. In late April the Düsseldorf Social Democrats joined the USPD en masse, in order, as they put it, "to uphold the old principles and decisions."[44] They retained control of the *Volkszeitung* and all party funds and associations. Although a few leaders, such as Ostertag, Arzberger, and Walbrecht, established a branch of the Majority Social Democratic Party, they found only a handful of followers. As the police noted, "almost the entire working class, those who are politically organized as well as those in trade unions, have joined the left radical wing."[45] The workers' movement and the working class were thus radicalized at the same time and in the same way, and the ties between workers and their institutions remained close. The same was true in Elberfeld-Barmen, Remscheid, Solingen, and Hagen, making the Lower Rhine, together with Berlin and Leipzig, one of the major centers of the new party. In the Ruhr mining towns, however, workers' radicalism, though directed against the SPD and social democratic miners' union, developed outside of the USPD and ignored that party's politics and goals.[46]

The USPD to which the Düsseldorf socialists pledged such enthusiastic allegiance was a most ill-defined affair. Due to the exigencies of war, internal diversity, and the reaction against SPD centralization, the USPD was a collection of semiautonomous local units. And these locals had followed very different routes to their current radicalism – a radicalism that they defined in very different theoretical and strategic terms. The USPD's supporters ranged from anti-war reformists through cautious left centrists to committed revolutionaries. As a result, the national party was not able to develop either a new program or clear tactics. It saw the defense of principle as its primary function. Born of opposition, it never transcended the negativism inherent in its origins. The Düsseldorf socialists, together with the Spartacists, the Berlin revolutionary shop stewards, and the local organizations in Leipzig, Halle, Bremen, Braunschweig, and Stuttgart, belonged to the left wing of the USPD.[47] But that left, despite its relative clarity about goals, shared the strategic uncertainty and organizational weakness of the rest of the USPD.

Throughout the remainder of 1917 the Düsseldorf Independents devoted themselves to recruitment, organization, and finances rather than to new forms of activism. They expanded steadily, largely because the radical metalworkers in the Düsseldorf DMV, which played a leading role in the left of the national union, strongly supported the party. Although the Independents endorsed demonstrations and strikes, they did not initiate or orchestrate them. On the political front, they knew quite well what they disliked and where they wanted to go. They denounced weak SPD peace resolutions and demanded immediate peace, democratization, and the freeing of political prisoners.[48] But they did not know how to achieve these goals. The weakness of their radical tradition – its failure to unite economic and political struggles, to plan the seizure of power, to develop an activist conception of revolution – came back to haunt them. Thus, although the left in Düsseldorf benefited organizationally from the wave of militancy that swept over Germany in 1917, it was not able to harness it for a concerted attack on the old order.

The new militancy, which began in early 1917, was precipitated by acute food shortages, but political demands soon surfaced. Although the city sought to buy extra potatoes, and the large metal firms dealt on the black market to secure food supplements for their undernourished workers, the situation continued to deteriorate. In February there were strikes and unrest throughout the Düsseldorf munitions industry, as there were in several other cities. Metalworkers staged a rally at city hall, and 400 men and women struck the Freundlich machine factory over food shortages. Twenty thousand Rheinmetall workers planned a

massive street demonstration, but municipal and trade-union intervention averted it.[49] According to the police, "the trade-union leaders
unanimously condemned public demonstrations ... but explained that
the bitterness about the lack of potatoes was currently so great that they
could not guarantee orderly behavior, especially since these demonstrations usually broke out spontaneously, before the working-class leaders
knew anything about them."[50]

Although this statement accurately portrays the initiative from the
rank and file, it is not clear whether the condemnation of their
spontaneity reflected the leaders' reformism or their duplicity toward
government officials. Oehler, the mayor of Düsseldorf, blamed the
discontent not on economic factors but on the agitation of "the
extremist Social Democrats" whose ranks were augmented "by foreign
forces."[51] He did not specify the role of the USPD. The police, however,
recognized both that wages and food had touched off the protest and
that "far-reaching political demands and hopes" drove it forward. "The
outbreak and success of the Russian Revolution had a considerable
impact on the attitudes of the radically inclined portion of the working
class," they noted with dismay.[52] Because anti-war sentiment was
pervasive and further outbursts likely, they concluded that "the mass of
workers who are very revolutionary can only be calmed without violent
means if political rights are granted and food is supplied."[53]

The government did not want to concede the former and could not
provide the latter. From April to July the food shortages worsened
dramatically. Düsseldorfers had no potatoes at all for nine weeks, and
many could not afford substitutes. The obvious inability of civilian and
military officials to manage food supplies undermined their authority
and legitimacy, whereas the flourishing black market highlighted the
class-specific character of wartime suffering.[54]

Although Düsseldorf was not involved in the big metalworkers' strikes
that affected Berlin and Leipzig in April, there were numerous short
strikes about food and wages. In addition, women staged regular
demonstrations in the market. While the municipal government urged
patience and understanding, the working class remained convinced that
the city was suffering more than rural areas and that employers could do
more to procure food. Workers wanted to strike en masse, but the trade-
union leaders opposed the idea and tried in vain to negotiate shorter
hours. Finally, from June 26 to June 29, "serious unrest" erupted in
Düsseldorf. Food stores were plundered, property was destroyed, and

thousands of workers struck Rheinmetall and other large firms. The role of the USPD and DMV in sparking or directing these demonstrations is unclear. The government responded with swift repression. The police made numerous arrests. and the special war courts handed down very stiff sentences, especially to women and adolescents. In addition, many men were drafted. According to the police, such severe action calmed the situation but caused deep resentment in the working class.[55]

Both the relative calm and the resentment were to persist for the next year. The talk of political reform and the brief show of parliamentary initiative that occurred on the national level in 1917 found no echo in Düsseldorf. When the Kaiser, in an effort to maintain the disintegrating *Burgfrieden*, issued his Easter Proclamation, promising universal suffrage in Prussia at war's end, the left considered it too little, the right too much. The Düsseldorf Independents demanded reform immediately, the Center maintained its usual silence, and Ehrhard, the head of Rheinmetall, expressed astonishment "that our industrial workers, who enjoy more than adequate wages far from enemy fire, could suddenly be so stirred up about such a dumb and insignificant thing as parliamentary suffrage."[56] The July Peace Resolution, which the SPD, Center, and Progressive Party sponsored and which called for a vague peace of understanding and reconciliation, met a similar response.

There was no collaboration among parties on the local level comparable to that nationally. According to Mayor Oehler, the municipal government was committed "to fulfilling the needs of industry," and fostering interparty cooperation was not necessary. The city did not even put working-class representatives on the municipal food commission until after the June demonstrations. The USPD would have nothing to do with the SPD, let alone with any party farther to the right. And by the time the Center had overcome its deep aversion to the SPD, the latter hardly existed in Düsseldorf.[57]

Düsseldorf, like the Lower Rhine as a whole, was scarcely involved in the massive anti-war strikes of January 1918. Whereas hundreds of thousands of workers struck elsewhere, only 4,000 did so in Benrath and a mere 250 at Rheinmetall. The USPD attributed this quiesence to a lack of leadership, and certainly the arrest of Pfeiffer, Agnes, and others, as well as the draft and harassment of earlier protesters, had taken their toll. The police stressed the workers' justified fear of military and police repression and the leaders' belief that the time was not ripe for mass action. Both Independents and officials warned, however, that discontent seethed beneath the surface calm. As the *Volkszeitung* asserted repeatedly, the war was continuing to raise workers' class consciousness and expose the contradictions of capitalism.[58]

The discontent continued to have both an economic and a political component. Although the food shortages eased somewhat, the more than 90,000 industrial workers in Düsseldorf were far from well nourished. Fruits, vegetables, and most meats were not available. The price of eggs was 250 percent above prewar levels, beef was 200 percent higher, and milk 140 percent. The black market continued to expand, and even though party and union leaders condemned it, workers insisted that their employers secure extra rations by that means. In Düsseldorf as elsewhere, real wages fell by nearly a quarter in war industries and by almost half in non-war ones.[59]

The end of fighting on the Eastern front had merely increased political tensions at home, for the Independents were adamantly opposed to the treaty of Brest-Litovsk, which imposed extensive territorial losses on Russia, as well as to the SPD's endorsement of it. Anger over the continued existence of the three-class Prussian suffrage, the most galling symbol of working-class inequality, mounted, and the police predicted "catastrophic results" if it were not changed. But as long as military victory seemed possible, the ruling classes would not grant political reform.[60] Nor would they make concessions in the economic sphere.

In early January the Düsseldorf DMV began a campaign for the 53-hour week in the munitions industry. The government and the Supreme Command responded with wage cuts, and for the next ten months of agitation and negotiation industrialists refused to shorten the workday.[61] Throughout this struggle the Düsseldorf DMV complained bitterly that the national union had "given up its class standpoint and fighting character." It demanded that "the banner of class struggle be held high" while ridiculing those union functionaries who acted "as if the working class would secure its rights without class struggle, and the bourgeoisie in union with the workers would bring about the social revolution."[62] Their skepticism proved more than justified. As late as October, when defeat was certain and armistice negotiations were underway, employers agreed to recognize the union but refused to bargain collectively, terminate their support for yellow unions, or grant the eight-hour day.[63]

The persistent economic crisis, the absence of domestic reform, and the failure of the German spring offensive all rebounded to the benefit of the USPD. Throughout 1918 the police noted that more and more workers were enlisting in the USPD while SPD influence on the unions, whose membership had increased from just over 9,000 in 1917 to nearly 13,000 in mid-1918, was "disappearing." Although both the Christian and Hirsch-Duncker unions, overcome by war weariness, abandoned their efforts to stem the radical tide, the miniscule local SPD made a final attempt to win back its lost prestige.[64] Through a bitter court battle the majority Socialists took control of the *Volkszeitung*. It was a pyrrhic victory, however, for the Independents boycotted the paper, and most of the delivery women quit. In addition, the USPD-controlled trade-union cartel fired the workers' secretary, Arzberger, who was a leading spokesman for the SPD. The paper's staunch defense of the SPD's wartime policies fell on deaf ears, and few workers endorsed the party's proposed alliance with the Center and National Liberals in the upcoming municipal elections.[65] To workers the USPD was the only party truly concerned with peace. Moreover, they had learned that the *Burgfrieden*, far from lessening ruling-class intransigence, had strengthened it.[66]

The forces that enhanced the popularity of the USPD in Düsseldorf also pushed it to the left. In addition to demanding immediate peace and democratization, the Independents endorsed the October Revolution in Russia. The government responded by drafting some leaders and arresting others, but repression radicalized more than it disrupted.[67] The police were anxiously reporting that elements of the Düsseldorf working class could "without exaggeration be described as German Bolsheviks."[68] Moreover, those to the left of the USPD, such as supporters of the Bremen radicals and syndicalist members of the newly founded General Workers' Union, were also active and in contact with the Independents.[69]

According to the police, in October, when the end of the war was imminent, the Düsseldorf USPD looked with satisfaction on the "collapse of militarism and imperialism." When Lundendorff staged a revolution from above by handing over power to the coalition government of Prince Max von Baden and granting universal suffrage in Prussia, the workers remained dissatisfied. They believed that the government had conceded too little, too late, and out of necessity rather than conviction. The Düsseldorf Independents began agitating for a German republic along Bolshevik lines.[70] Like their comrades elsewhere, they lacked a clear conception of what such a socialist republic would be like, for they had neither much concrete information about Russia nor their own well-developed plans for an alternative society. Nonetheless, the agitation reflected their desire for a far-reaching transformation of the existing order rather than a superficial reshuffling of political power in Berlin.[71]

In the last years of the war the Düsseldorf socialists thus broke definitively with the SPD, whose thoroughly reformist character they could no longer deny. They moved decisively to the left, for the war experience confirmed their previous analysis of Wilhelmian politics and economics and reinforced their isolation from the dominant society. Unlike their reformist comrades, the Düsseldorf socialists had not changed their self-image or their image of society anymore than society had changed its image of social democracy.[72] This spared them the illusions that crippled the Majority Socialists and made them eager for a social and political revolution. They were nonetheless ill prepared to make that revolution, as the events of late 1918 and early 1919 were to show.

12

Revolution

In the wake of economic dislocation and deprivation, military defeat, and the government-sponsored "revolution from above," a revolution from below swept over Germany in early November 1918. The Düsseldorf socialists, long bitter opponents of authoritarian politics and organized capitalism in Germany, wholeheartedly supported the revolution, which they had so long desired but for which they were so ill prepared. The revolution they made in the ensuing six months was an improvisation – at times brilliant, at times tragic. It was an improvisation that had both strong similarities and striking differences with the revolution elsewhere. It was a widely popular revolution that took a particularly radical turn and that ended not only with the triumph of the counterrevolution but also with the deep disillusionment and division of the socialist working class.

There were three phases to the revolution in Düsseldorf, and with each successive one the working class had more radical political and economic aspirations and less real power. In November and December the USPD-dominated Workers' and Soldiers' Council sought to democratize the government and begin economic reform. After the Independents failed to implement this left course, the Communists took over in early January. Their two months of tenuous rule, which ended when government troops invaded Düsseldorf, was marked by demonstrative actions and growing support for a social revolution but no substantial economic and political reforms. From March to May 1919 the USPD-controlled Workers' Council and a still more radicalized working class attempted unsuccessfully to regain the offensive in order to secure socialization and a permanent role for the councils. By summer the revolution was over. Its failure brought the demise not only of the old social democratic movement but of the new Independent one as well and intensified the powerlessness and isolation of the Düsseldorf working class.

269

Düsseldorf's pattern of revolution, like its wartime road to radicalism, was shaped by certain types of political behavior and forms of political consciousness that had developed in the prewar years. Both before World War I and during the revolution the Düsseldorf socialists were preoccupied with, and more certain about, political as opposed to economic issues. Radical action was advocated to achieve democratization. Workers' control was conceived in political terms, whereas socialization was defined as a gradual transformation to be imposed from above by political means. Shop floor militancy and spontaneous protests were virtually absent, and workers acted through socialist organizations and unions, remaining loyal to their radical local leaders. This combination of strong organization, traditional leaders, and radical political goals and actions but relatively weak economic ones distinguished the revolution in Düsseldorf from the equally structured but much more conservative upheavals in cities such as Hamburg and Remscheid as well as from the very radical but more spontaneous and economically focused uprisings in the Ruhr mining towns.

These prefigurative institutions and preexisting patterns of behavior were, as we have seen, a product of Düsseldorf's economic and political structures, which marginalized the ever-growing working class. They were developed by a relatively skilled yet highly diversified working class, which was united by the social democratic movement rather than by work, culture, or community. They reflected the close integration of the working class and the socialist movement and the centrality of the latter in working-class politics and association life. Finally, these institutions and patterns had been forged first in the long battle between social democracy and political Catholicism and then in the bitter struggles between Düsseldorf and the national SPD on the one hand and the state on the other. The goals of the revolution in Düsseldorf, the role of the parties and unions in the council movement, and the attitude toward socialization were all shaped – and limited – by this prewar experience.

The failure of the revolution was due in part to national SPD opposition and military intervention, which sealed the fate of the revolution in Düsseldorf as in many other areas. But the Düsseldorf socialists contributed to their own demise. They were willing to act in 1918, developed strong organizations and effective leadership, and had an initially clear vision of political revolution. After December, however, they could not push the revolution forward on the political and above all on the economic front, despite the fact that the working class remained remarkably united. Although they looked to their comrades in Russia and Germany for inspiration, they could neither find a model for action nor overcome their previous isolation from radicals elsewhere. The absence of a revolutionary strategy that merged economic and political struggles, and of tangible progress, that fulfilled radical aspirations, bred militancy among both leaders and the highly mobilized workers. But it also created frustration, dissension, and ultimately despair. In the revolutionary situation of 1918–19 the Düsseldorf socialists were thus crippled by the theoretical and strategic uncertainty that had plagued them for decades.

The political revolution

On November 8 a hastily established Workers' and Soldiers' Council seized political power almost effortlessly in Düsseldorf and inaugurated the most dynamic, productive, and optimistic phase of the revolution. For six weeks the council and the left Independents who exercised undisputed hegemony within it, as well as within the working class, tried to take full advantage of the revolutionary situation to democratize the government, build alternative institutions, and initiate economic reform while maintaining order and broadening their base of support. These first revolutionary months revealed the strengths of the Düsseldorf left and its pattern of revolution – the flexibility of traditional organizations, the prominence of prewar and wartime leaders, the clarity of political goals, and the willingness to act decisively.

By late December, however, it was clear that the USPD's innovative yet pragmatic program could not be realized. The SPD and the institutions and classes of the old order opposed it on the one hand, and the radical socialists had no conception of how to complete the political revolution and organize a social one on the other. The first phase of the revolution thus marked the culmination of the prewar radical tradition, exposed its limits, and inaugurated the search for a new pattern of radicalism.

The revolution from below broke out a few weeks after the armistice had been signed and the military, anxious to avoid the onus of defeat, had given power to Prince Max von Baden and a coalition of Social Democrats, Catholics, and Liberals. It began with the sailors' mutiny in Kiel on November 4 and quickly won wide support from hungry and demoralized workers and soldiers, who profoundly mistrusted the bourgeois democracy so hastily granted in the face of defeat and potential unrest. Unwilling to settle for superficial political change at the top of the governmental system, they wanted a thoroughgoing democratization of the bureaucracy, the army, and the economy. Although the SPD opposed the revolution and the USPD and Spartacist groups, which wanted and half expected it, were unprepared for it, the uprising spread rapidly throughout northern, central, and western Germany, carried by emissaries of the Kiel sailors. On November 7 they reached Cologne, where, following the pattern elsewhere, a Workers' and Soldiers' Council was established. This signaled the beginning of the revolution in the Rhineland.[1]

In Düsseldorf socialist leaders and government officials, eager workers and an anxious bourgeoisie, watched these events with avid interest. The miniscule SPD, led by Arzberger, endorsed the government of Max von Baden and officially ignored the disturbing developments in northern Germany. Although Pfeiffer, Agnes, Obuch, Ochel, and other prominent Independents and Spartacists had long pleaded for revolution and workers' councils, there is no indication that they laid any concrete plans for seizing power in these chaotic days. The municipal government and the local military, however, feared the worst, and when the USPD scheduled a meeting at the large Apollo Theater for November 10, they assumed that revolution was on the agenda.[2]

On November 6 Mayor Oehler and police commissioners Blase and Gauer, shocked by the lack of resistance elsewhere and convinced that the revolution could be stopped by force, stockpiled machine guns, hand grenades, and carbines and prepared to occupy key points in the city. One day later these plans were abandoned. Neither the civilian government in Berlin nor the military command in Münster endorsed armed struggle – in part because they lacked the requisite loyal troops. As the Düsseldorf police subsequently explained, isolated efforts to stem the tide of revolution "would undoubtedly have aroused considerable indignation in wide circles of the working class and led to unavoidable serious damage to the life and property of the bourgeoisie."[3] Moreover, industrialists were reluctant to launch a last-ditch defense of the old order, for they were negotiating with the national trade unions to defuse militancy with material concessions and union recognition.[4] The way for revolution was clear.

On the evening of November 8 revolutionary sailors and soldiers arrived at Düsseldorf's main railroad station. Joined by a large crowd of workers and soldiers, they immediately disarmed the troops there and then moved through the city, relieving officers and policemen alike of their weapons and insignia. The demonstration stopped in front of city hall, where an emergency session of the city council agreed to discuss demands for disarming the police and freeing political prisoners. A hastily chosen delegation of workers, soldiers, and sailors, consisting of Korte, Lützenkirchen, Heyer, Sturm, and others, none of whom had previously played a prominent role in the socialist movement, began negotiations with Oehler, Police Commissioner Lehr, and several lesser officials. Within a few hours the police and these self-appointed representatives of the recently elected Workers' and Soldiers' Council issued a joint proclamation explaining that the police were responsible for maintaining order and were empowered to shoot looters on sight and that workers should refrain from striking. The powers of the council remained unclarified, and no reforms were implemented.[5]

Revolution by negotiation had produced meager results, and a process of radicalization set in immediately. While the delegation was still in city hall, workers and soldiers continued to disarm the police and military and then stormed the Derendorf prision, freeing all the inmates. As soon as the joint proclamation was issued, Lore Agnes, Erdmann, the Reichstag deputy from Cologne, and Schmitt, the head of the consumer cooperative, appeared at city hall. These well-known figures, whom the police described as "the real leaders of the revolution," demanded that negotiations be broken off and a meeting of the Workers' and Soldiers' Council convened. The council quickly proceded to appoint Weimann and Baues to control the police and a committee to manage food supplies and then freed the remaining political prisoners.[6] During the night of November 8/9, thousands of soldiers, who were in Düsseldorf on their way back from the Western front, went over to the revolution with virtually no resistance.

By November 9, when the national social democratic leaders Ebert and Scheidemann reluctantly proclaimed the republic in Berlin, the first act of the revolutionary drama was over in Düsseldorf. The military, the police, and the bureaucracy had either temporarily collapsed or accepted the authority of the Workers' and Soldiers' Council. The Chamber of Commerce, which was later to complain so vociferously about revolutionary excesses, accommodated itself to the seizure of power in silence. Even the Center accepted the change in government as a fait accompli and pledged to help maintain order and food supplies. On November 10 the triumphant USPD held a rally, replete with bands and red flags, to celebrate the "new order."[7]

At the center of the revolution was the Düsseldorf Workers' and Soldiers' Council, a new institution, which, like its counterparts elsewhere, had been set up in a revolutionary situation that required new forms of organization and struggle. Although the Düsseldorf socialists looked to Russia for inspiration, they did not regard the soviets as a model, both because they had little information on them and because they regarded German conditions as sui generis.[8] Although the German councils had been formed partly in reaction to the previous failures of the SPD and the unions, the Düsseldorf council, unlike its counterparts in Ruhr mining towns, was closely tied to the political parties. It was elected not by factory councils, but by the USPD and SPD, which initially cooperated as a result of revolutionary euphoria and working-class pressure for unity. This new institution sustained and benefited from traditional leaders and forms of organization; it strengthened the ties between the working class and the preexisting workers' movement. In Düsseldorf, as in neighboring industrial cities, but not in mining towns, the Workers' and Soldiers' Council was temporarily able to bridge the gap between Majority Socialists and Independents, between the parties and the unions, between the political and economic struggles. And it did so on terms beneficial to the left, for the Düsseldorf council, like that of Mülheim and a handful of other German cities, was dominated by the radical Independents and the Spartacists.[9]

Initially both the council members and the workers who enthusiastically supported them lacked a clear conception of this new institution. Neither prewar SPD practice nor Marxist theory helped them determine the character of the councils and their relationship to the parliament and bureaucracy, the party and the unions, or one another.[10] On one level, the absence of a blueprint made the councils open and flexible; on another, it left them susceptible – consciously or not – to the formative influence of prefigurative institutions and patterns of behavior. The socialists lacked as well a revolutionary theory that assigned the working class an active role, and a revolutionary strategy, that aimed at seizing state power. They thus had little guidance in dealing with the ambiguous situation created by economic dislocation, military defeat, and the collapse of the old order. On the one hand, this situation helped produce a mass movement, carried it to power, and opened the way for radical change; on the other, it intensified class divisions and economic chaos, created strategic confusion, and potentially limited action.[11]

In early November the Düsseldorf socialists, eager to overcome the traditional social democratic passivity, were undaunted by these obstacles to revolution. Unlike the SPD-dominated provisional government, which conceived of itself as a transitional, caretaker regime with no mandate to institute reform, the Workers' and Soldiers' Council in Düsseldorf was not inhibited by a narrowly legalistic mentality or by fear of creating chaos. Certain of what it opposed in the old regime, it sought to transform as much as possible in the politically and structurally open situation of November 1918.

The Workers' and Soldiers' Council was faced with the immediate political task of democratizing local government and the pressing practical one of maintaining order, securing food supplies, and overseeing demobilization. It tackled both by taking control of the existing administration rather than building a new one from scratch.[12] The city council was simply circumvented, rather than reformed or deposed, for the Independents did not want to reestablish institutions with bourgeois representation until fundamental change had been achieved. Whereas the socialists had defined democratization in terms of universal suffrage and ministerial responsibility before the war, they now realized that more was necessary. But that "more" centered on politics rather than economics. On November 11 the council called for immediate peace and "political rights and freedoms on a democratic and social basis," and asked all civil servants who supported the new order to remain on the job. A few days later it appointed representatives of the council to supervise every municipal government office. (The provincial government in Düsseldorf was, in turn, to be controlled by the regional Workers' and Soldiers' Council.)[13]

Mayor Oehler and all department heads immediately urged their subordinates to cooperate with the council, and there is no evidence of resistance from lower-echelon bureaucrats. Indeed, in the first weeks of the revolution, civil servants and businessmen, economic organizations and political parties turned to the Workers' and Soldiers' Council for advice and aid.[14] As the Independents realized, this initial cooperation enabled the council to deal effectively with the immediate problems that would otherwise have undermined the regime. Nonetheless, they found it politically uncomfortable at best, potentially dangerous at worst.

In one vital area, that of security, the Düsseldorf council went beyond controlling existing institutions. Although the provisional government took no steps to form a militia and SPD leader Ebert even entered an unholy alliance with General Groener to preserve the Prussian army, the Düsseldorf council immediately formed its own security force. By mid-November 1,500 reliable Independents and Spartacists, supplemented by some demobilized soldiers, patrolled the streets and supervised the police. In addition, the council abolished the political police, which had harassed the Social Democrats for decades. These actions suggest that the socialists on the local level had a broader, more realistic conception of democratization than did their comrades in Berlin, for they did not assume that the temporarily weakened old order had been permanently destroyed. Yet even the Düsseldorf independents argued that it would be politically immature and disruptive to disarm the military and police completely, as returning soldiers demanded in late November. Moreover, other councils were not pursuing such a radical course.[15] As so often in the past, the left in Düsseldorf failed to act fully on its convictions, for it was crippled by its isolation on the one hand and its lack of a revolutionary strategy on the other.

During the first weeks of the revolution the Independents and Spartacists were most concerned with political reforms, but they were forced to deal with economic questions as well, not only because the war economy had to be converted to peacetime production but also because economic reform was beginning to be viewed as an integral part of political democratization.[16] From late October on, workers and industrialists were preoccupied with unemployment, for 61 percent of Düsseldorf's labor force worked directly in munitions, and many others were indirectly dependent on war production. The Chamber of Commerce and the city government predicted that 40,000 workers, or one-third of all blue-collar workers, would lose their jobs by January. Officially, 18,000 or 13 to 15 percent did, for the national government continued some contracts to ease the transition. Yet even that number, astronomical by prewar standards, created enormous dislocation and deprivation.[17]

The Workers' and Soldiers' Council's economic interventions involved reform and relief, not steps toward socialization. In mid-November the council required that all jobs be registered with the municipal labor exchange and forbade employers to fire workers without giving two weeks notice. Later in the month it introduced the eight-hour day in metal, both to assert the principle and to share the available work. These measures were admittedly inadequate, but there was little more the council could do in the absence of aid from the provisional government and of an economic program of its own.

During this period both the Chamber of Commerce and leading industrialists were quiet and cooperative, even accepting in silence the agreement between ADGB head Legien and steel magnate Stinnis, which required employers to recognize unions, stop subsidizing yellow organizations, and establish *Arbeitsgemeinschaften* or union–management committees.[18] Perhaps they saw accommodation with the SPD and abandonment of the Junkers as the only viable strategy for maintaining their power. Perhaps they realized that the Düsseldorf unions, firmly in the hands of the left, would never agree to the planned cooperation between capital and labor.

Although the Düsseldorf Workers' and Soldiers' Council and the local USPD did not demand socialism when the revolution first broke out, they moved in that direction more quickly than their comrades elsewhere, for in the process of controlling the bureaucracy they came to mistrust their bourgeois collaborators and recognize the limits of purely political reform.[19] As early as November 16, the *Volkszeitung*, which was once again in the hands of the USPD, argued that workers must "begin the task of clearing away the rubble of the old order, of building anew, of erecting on firm ground the free people's state, the socialist republic."[20]

This strong desire for socialism was not matched by a clear conception of how "to clear away the rubble" and "build anew." The Düsseldorf Independents supported the regional Workers' and Soldiers' Council's demand for gradual socialization, beginning with mines and banks. They adamantly opposed the Majority Socialists' plan to convene a national assembly as soon as possible, arguing that capitalists should not be given a political role until substantial structural reform had been achieved in the administration and the economy. As they correctly realized, the bourgeoisie could come to terms with the republic, but socialism, or even a social republic, would be an entirely different matter.[21] Yet they took few actions on the local level to achieve their goal. The Düsseldorf Workers' and Soldiers' Council proposed that special taxes be levied against the middle and upper classes, that unoccupied housing be given to the needy, and that superfluous government offices be eliminated. Neither the council nor the local USPD, however, believed that Düsseldorf's diversified economy was ripe for immediate socialization. Neither defined workers' control as control of production on the shop floor. Even the workers themselves did not try to assert such power. Rather, socialization was to be imposed from above by political means. And this Düsseldorf could not achieve alone.

By late November the initial revolutionary euphoria had worn off, and the divisive questions about the future of the revolution could not be avoided. Although the tenuous alliance between right and left socialists was to last until late December on the national level, it collapsed earlier in Düsseldorf. Leading Independents, such as Erdmann, Pfeiffer, Agnes, and Schmitt, were angry that the provisional government had not reformed the bureaucracy and military or instituted partial socialization.[22] According to Berten's subsequent assessment, which coincided with his actions and statements at the time:

> The Majority Social Democrats in the provisional government had made a common war policy with the capitalist, militaristic ruling classes for too long. They were not able to take a fighting stance toward them. They did not trust themselves to write a constitution that would give power to manual and mental laborers. They lacked a revolutionary program.[23]

The SPD, for its part, was dismayed that the Workers' and Soldiers' Council, on which it held one-third of the seats, and the local USPD called for socialization and council government and condemned plans "to save capitalism" by convening a National Assembly. Independents and Social Democrats also fought bitterly over more mundane issues, such as control of the *Volkszeitung*.[24]

Simultaneously, relations between the left and the middle class worsened. On November 28 soldiers from the Thirty-ninth Regiment attacked workers who were distributing leaflets. Pfeiffer blamed not the soldiers, who had just returned from the front, but "the open and hidden campaign against the revolution, instigated by the bourgeois press and other circles."[25] One day later, the *Volkszeitung* published police reports from early November, which detailed the city's plans to defeat any uprising by force. While the Independents' mistrust of the bourgeoisie was growing, the Social Democrats insisted that middle-class representatives be included on the Workers' and Soldiers' Council, a demand seconded by the Center. When the USPD and the soldiers' delegates refused, the SPD resigned from the council.[26]

In contrast to 1917, the Independents broke from the Majority Socialists without anguish or hesitation. Their criticism of the Majority

Socialists, whom they frequently referred to as "the dependents," gave way to contempt for their timidity and collaboration with the old order. Schmitt, Obuch, Pfeiffer, and other leaders had viewed their alliance with the SPD with a certain cynicism and opportunism and seemed relieved when it ended. Because the Düsseldorf SPD had only a small following, some of which was probably drawn from the middle and lower middle classes, the USPD considered it perfectly feasible to govern alone.[27] The break with the SPD did, in fact, enhance the popularity of the Independents with the working class, but it did not help them develop a positive political or economic program.

Initially it was the strengths of the USPD that were most evident. By early December the Düsseldorf council had become an established institution that was capable of supervising the bureaucracy, even though its long-run role had not been decided. And the USPD was in uncontested control of it, for after the SPD members resigned, the military representatives left because all troops were withdrawn from Düsseldorf under the terms of the armistice. The Independents' situation in Düsseldorf, which was similar to that in Mülheim and a few other Lower Rhine cities, compared favorably to that in most places. In Elberfeld-Barmen, for example, the SPD and USPD continued to struggle for hegemony; in Dortmund the SPD was dominant from the first days of the revolution; and in Hamburg the initial weeks of USPD ascendency had been followed by a resurgence of the SPD and a diminution of the council's power by old economic and political elites.[28]

Many prominent prewar radicals played a leading role in the Düsseldorf council, thereby providing both expertise and continuity. Schmitt, jokingly referred to as "Wilhelm III" by his comrades, was responsible for general business; Berten, who returned from military duty in Rumania in early December, took over agitation and external relations; Schotte dealt with the press, and Lore Agnes handled food, health, and welfare. Others who had become active during the war, such as Schmidtchen, Obuch, and Ochel, managed relations with the local government and economic matters.[29] It was, in short, skilled workers and party functionaries with years of experience in the movement and an intimate knowledge of politics and society in Düsseldorf who led the revolution in its first phase. A similar pattern emerged in other cities where the socialist movement had been strong in the prewar years and supported the revolution in its moderate or radical forms. Where the movement was weakly organized or firmly opposed to the revolution, as in Ruhr mining towns, workers were forced to rely on young, inexperienced leaders.[30]

Building on its wartime popularity, the USPD was able to mobilize the trade-union movement on behalf of both the party and the council, thus preventing any significant division between traditional and new forms of organization. Düsseldorf's highly skilled workers, who had long been able to express their radicalism through the party and unions, did not abandon them during the revolution. Even the new semiskilled, who lacked a tradition of organization, accepted the USPD's leadership, including its emphasis on politics and its curtailment of strikes, rather than developing a more syndicalist strategy as they did in nearby mining towns such as Hamborn.[31]

There was no appealing alternative to the USPD in December 1918. As a result of its wartime behavior, the SPD had lost all credibility in Düsseldorf. Its call for a National Assembly and claim that "you cannot socialize a ruin" fell on deaf ears, for, as Berten noted, workers realized that capitalists would hardly grant socialization voluntarily once reconstruction was completed.[32] The Spartacist group, with a membership of 300 or 400, offered a program for socialization and continued council rule that scarcely distinguished itself from that of the USPD.[33] As long as the Spartacists and left Independents remained within the USPD and agreed on tactics, and as long as the revolution seemed to be making progress, the vast majority of Düsseldorf workers would continue to rally behind the USPD.

By late December, however, signs of progress were few and far between. In Düsseldorf the Workers' Council continued to control the bureaucracy and manage, albeit with difficulty, the economic situation, but the Independents did not know how to advance the political revolution or initiate the social one of which they spoke with increasing frequency.[34] The Lower Rhine Workers' Council, in which the recently radicalized Ruhr miners played a dominant role, demanded socialization and council power even more vociferously than Düsseldorf did, but was equally powerless to achieve them.

Most disturbing, while politics were moving to the left in Düsseldorf and the Lower Rhine, they were going in the opposite direction – or at least in an ambiguous one – nationally. The SPD, led by Ebert, Noske, and Scheidemann, believed that the provisional government could not and should not attempt substantial political change. Eager to hand over power to a constitutional assembly based on universal suffrage, it scheduled elections for January 1919 and opposed all efforts to prolong the councils' political role. It rejected as well all demands for socialization, citing economic chaos and allied opposition as the justification. For the Majority Socialists, blind to the resurgence of the old military and economic elites, the danger came from the left, and they were prepared to defeat it by force if necessary.[35] The national USPD leadership, divided about the SPD, the National Assembly, councils, and socialization, alternated between bouts of erratic action and paralysis. The membership, without central guidance, moved left to varying degrees, depending on local traditions and circumstances. The council movement, which most accurately reflected working-class atitudes, was unsure how to push the revolution forward and under whose guidance, as the Congress of Workers' and Soldiers' Councils showed.

The first national Congress of Councils, held in Berlin from December 16 to December 21, took quite contradictory decisions on the three major issues before it. By an overwhelming majority the congress endorsed the SPD's plan to hold early elections and thus undermined the position of the councils themselves. With equal enthusiasm, however, the several hundred workers passed resolutions favoring gradual socialization and substantial military reform. Delegates Berten and Schmitt, reflecting the revolutionary aspirations of their Düsseldorf constituents, were distinctly dissatisfied with the results of the congress, which, Berten claimed, was characterized by "confusion and indecision." To his dismay, "there was no talk of some sort of thoroughgoing measures to take power from large owners in industry and agriculture." By approving early elections, the congress opened the way for continued Junker and capitalist influence and thereby "lost the game from the start." Even though the Düsseldorf USPD bowed to the decision of the majority and participated in the election campaign, Berten, who was himself a candidate, maintained that "a great opportunity was missed."[36]

Although the congress was much too conservative for the Düsseldorf Independents, it was much too radical for the national Majority Socialists, who continued their preparations for the impending election but refused to act on the economic and military resolutions of the Congress of Councils. In the last week of December they moved against the left, using the Prussian army to attack the People's Naval Division when it staged a large demonstration in Berlin. Although the sailors' behavior verged on mutiny, Independents and Social Democrats throughout Germany were enraged by the SPD's use of troops against leftists, regardless of the merits of the case. The USPD members of the provisional government resigned in protest and with the strong support of locals such as Düsseldorf, which accused the SPD of trying to provoke civil war and of "sacrificing the accomplishments of the revolution to the counterrevolution." The Düsseldorf Independents vowed "not to rest until the working class is united again under the old, undefiled banner of socialism and led to victory."[37]

Neither unity nor victory were to be achieved. No sooner had the SPD split off on the right than the Spartacists did so on the left, forming the Communist Party of Germany (KPD) on December 31. The Düsseldorf USPD, hoping to avoid such a schism, had refrained from censuring the Spartacists for their relentless criticism of the Independents. Nonetheless, the 300 or so Spartacists, whom Ochel, a stone mason and activist in the city since 1913, had organized, joined the new party en masse.[38] Although they did not disagree with the goals of the Düsseldorf USPD, the Communists felt that its tactics were inadequate – a tragically correct assessment.

The Düsseldorf Independents lacked a vision of the councils' future role and a strategy for defending them once parliamentary government was established. They were unwilling to go beyond controlling the government to restructuring and restaffing it, even though they were increasingly aware of the need for this. They did not know how to channel the revolutionary energy of the working class into a struggle for socialization. Much as they criticized the national SPD, they were unable to alter its course or diminish its influence. The Düsseldorf Independents were hindered not by reformism, timidity, or internal divisions – if anything, they underestimated the obstacles to revolution – but by the lack of a revolutionary strategy and by their isolation from like-minded radicals elsewhere. The Communists, however, were no better prepared to save the floundering revolution.

The social revolution

In the first months of 1919, while the SPD consolidated its power nationally and the old economic and military elites reasserted their power, the working class became progressively more radicalized. While parliamentary institutions were being established in Weimar, the revolution was moving from its predominantly political to its more economic phase elsewhere. Socialization replaced democratization as the first item on the working-class agenda. Events took a particularly radical turn in Düsseldorf, where the KPD staged a successful putsch and proceeded to rule for two months.

Yet the pattern of revolution in Düsseldorf remained largely the same. Although the KPD-dominated Workers' Council behaved more militantly in the political arena than its predecessor had, it was unable to cope with the economic crisis or initiate an active campaign for socialization that would directly affect the city's industries. Although Düsseldorf's Communists and Independents enthusiastically endorsed the Ruhr miners in their campaign for socialization, they did not share the latter's emphasis on controlling the workplace through economic struggles. Socialization continued to mean state ownership to be imposed from above by political means. Similarly, the parties and unions with their established leaders continued to dominate the Workers' Council, which in turn, remained far more important than the factory councils. The Communists were as unsuccessful as the Independents in finding new forms of struggle and ending the isolation of Düsseldorf from radicals elsewhere.

By early 1919 the limitations of Düsseldorf's radical heritage outweighed the benefits. The very frustrations and tactical divisions that had led to the KPD putsch were intensified by demonstrative actions that neither produced concrete results nor stemmed the tide of reaction nationally. By the time the Free Corps invaded Düsseldorf in late February, the Independents and the bulk of the working class had abandoned the KPD but not their own revolutionary goals.

The second phase of the Düsseldorf revolution was played out in a national context marked by bitter struggles among the working-class leaders and pervasive but uncoordinated radicalization among workers. After the Congress of Councils, the withdrawal of the UPSD from the provisional government, and the founding of the KPD, the SPD was more determined than ever to curb the councils, prevent socialization, and steer the revolution into safe parliamentary channels. The national USPD, which was moving to the left under pressure from its base, nonetheless remained paralyzed by divisions between a right-wing that favored temporary council power in order to implement democratization and socialization and a left that advocated a permanent council regime. The national KPD, which shared many of the goals of the left

Independents, was likewise divided between leaders, such as Luxemburg and Liebknecht, who considered an immediate and violent seizure of power to be impossible, and a rank and file that pushed for militant action whatever the risks.[39]

No party gave adequate guidance to those workers who were disappointed with the emerging parliamentary regime, stunned by Majority Socialist collaboration with the military, and threatened by unemployment, inflation, and the resurgence of employer power. Workers in large cities, such as Berlin, Bremen, and Munich, and in the industrial centers of Middle Germany and the Lower Rhine and Ruhr were convinced that without much more thoroughgoing democratization and at least partial socialization, their economic and political power would not be substantially increased nor would their social isolation be lessened. But the goals and forms of their radicalism were diverse, at times even contradictory. All cried out for socialization and councils, but few defined these elusive terms in the same way. Some workers supported left Independents; others participated in Communist putsches; whereas a third group was involved in militant strikes and factory councils. Many eventually came into conflict with the military.[40] Within this chaotic context, Düsseldorf workers were to combine all these elements into a massive but unsuccessful protest against the existing order.

The ill-planned offensive of the Düsseldorf left began in early January. In conjunction with massive demonstrations in Berlin, the Düsseldorf KPD, which had virtually no organization of its own but which enjoyed growing support in the Workers' Council and the Security Force, occupied the city's bourgeois newspapers, which had become increasingly critical of the left.[41] Believing that "the revolution is in danger as a result of indecisiveness," the Communists, led by Ochel, decided to act without orders from the party leadership in Berlin or cooperation from the local USPD.[42]

On January 8 the KPD and the Security Force occupied the railroad station, the telegraph offices, and the police headquarters. Mayor Oehler, Government President Kruse, and County President von Renvers fled across the Rhine to Belgian-occupied territory, and several "notable citizens," including city councilmen Brandt and Siebel, were arrested. Oehler confidently assumed that the putsch would collapse within a few hours. Instead, the Communists immediately dissolved the city council, took over the municipal transportation system, and seized the city treasury in order to pay the Security Force. The next day the

Workers' Council, in which the USPD still had a majority, elected a new executive council to run the city, and the KPD began publishing its own organ, *Rote Fahne vom Niederrhein*, on the presses of the bourgeois *Düsseldorfer Nachrichten*.[43]

On January 10 the new regime met its first serious opposition. The SPD and the German Democratic Party (DDP) staged a joint protest that ended in a pitched battle between demonstrators and the Security Force, which shot into the crowd, killing 14 and wounding 25. In response the Workers' Council prohibited all demonstrations, closed hotels such as the Breidenbacher Hof, which were known meeting places for the right, shut down the *General Anzeiger*, and ordered the bourgeoisie to surrender their arms. To fill the power vacuum at the top, Schmidtchen was appointed mayor and Seidel became chief of police. In conjunction with the SPD–DDP protest, the civil servants and postal workers had called a strike but by the 11th resistance ceased, for the government leaders had fled, and no military aid was forthcoming from the SPD government in Berlin.[44] To the surprise of many workers and the dismay of the middle classes, the new regime had survived its difficult birth.

The KPD was carried to power on a wave of frustration and fear – frustration over the meager accomplishments of the revolution and fear of a bourgeois resurgence. In its initial weeks, it was by no means an unpopular minority government. Prussian officials estimated that in January two-thirds of Düsseldorf's industrial workers supported the left parties, and their willingness to rally to the defense of the new regime in its first days lends credence to this estimate.[45] Although food supplies were marginally lower in January and unemployment and inflation slightly higher, economic factors were not decisive in creating support for the new government. Rather, workers endorsed the Spartacists' street tactics because organization and mobilization alone had neither sustained the momentum of the revolution nor prevented the broad socialist alliance from disintegrating. They took over the government from within because merely controlling it from without had not brought sufficient democratization. They favored council rule because parliament was restoring the old order.[46]

There is little indication that the new regime had substantially different support than the old. Certainly, it was not the creation of lumpen elements. Although younger, less skilled, and more recently politicized workers may have been most enthusiastic in their support of the KPD, they neither acted alone nor against the wishes of those who had previously formed the core of the Düsseldorf workers' movement.

Skilled and unskilled, old and young, those with long organizational experience and those recently politicized, seemed initially to have backed the new regime with equal strength. Indeed, one suspects that most of the working class saw little difference between the KPD and the USPD in these weeks, for they shared the same goals despite tactical differences. Of equal importance, they cooperated, whatever their reservations, in day-to-day politics.[47]

Although the Spartacists had been extremely critical of the USPD, they made every effort to work with them in January, both because they needed material support and because they gave priority to democratization and socialization, not the interests of their party, narrowly conceived.[48] Both Independents and Communists were convinced, to quote Seidel, that "the disputed issues involve not the goal but the way." By January the Independents, whose way had been tested and found wanting, were willing to endorse the Communists' alternative, for, as Pfeiffer argued at a Workers' Council meeting, "there is no possible orientation toward the right." Podtevin insisted that the council had "a moral right" to take over the government since the officials had fled. Berten was instrumental in setting up the new executive council, consisting of the Communists Ochel, Seidel, and Schmidtchen, the Independent Birkenmeyer, and Melcher, whose affiliation is unknown.[49] This political and organizational support from the USPD compensated for the KPD's lack of structure and small membership.

In its internal organization the communist phase of the revolution distinguished itself little from its predecessor. In contrast to the Ruhr mining areas, the Workers' Council remained more important than either factory councils or spontaneous strike movements, and within the council, the political parties continued to play the leading role. As in the past, it was not work or community but rather the organized workers' movement that united the working class and served as the locus and vehicle for protest. Workers in other metal towns, such as Remscheid and Mülheim, were also loyal to the parties and unions, but neither leaders nor the rank and file became as radical as in Düsseldorf. This institutional continuity strengthened the leadership and organization of the revolution, but it also preserved divisions between leaders and members and limited flexibility.[50]

It was in its relations to bourgeois society that the Communists tried to distinguish their rule. But they were more certain about the organizational and personnel changes they wanted to make than about the policies they would implement. The goal of the Communists and their left Independent allies was a much more radical form of dual power, verging on pure council rule. The executive council of the Workers' Council assumed ultimate political power and supplied the mayor and police chief, thereby consolidating new and old offices at the top. The city council was dissolved – whether temporarily or permanently was left open – and even the Security Force was partially disbanded and partially merged with the police, perhaps because the Communists considered it superfluous, perhaps because they feared a repeat of the January 8 shootings. Despite this dramatic restructuring, the entire municipal bureaucracy remained intact, for the workers' movement lacked trained personnel on the one hand and continued to assume that control, rather than replacement, was an adequate safeguard on the other. Only one new institution, a summary court of justice was created, but there are no records to indicate the uses to which it was put. No effort was made to reform the provincial government, for both Independents and Communists assigned the regional Workers' Council sole jurisdiction over that body.[51] Like radicals elsewhere, those in Düsseldorf had an excessively local focus.

Although Ochel subsequently claimed that the new government had taken "truly revolutionary measures," one looks in vain through the minutes of the council for any indication of this. Of necessity the council devoted most of its efforts to mundane questions of food supplies, public order, and unemployment. Preoccupied with these problems and increasingly beset by internal divisions, it failed to launch the extensive political education program that both Independents and Communists regarded as essential. Instead, it engaged in demonstrative actions, such as periodically closing bourgeois papers, removing Imperial emblems from public buildings, and naming the elegant Königsallee Karl Liebknechtstrasse. On January 18 the council held a successful one-day strike to protest the murders of Luxemburg and Liebknecht but did not otherwise attempt to rally its supporters publicly.[52] Like its predecessor – indeed, like the German left as a whole – the new regime had a detailed negative critique but no positive vision to galvanize the working class and win broader support.

A mere ten days after the Communists came to power, the controversial elections to the National Assembly were held. Despite the left's shortcomings, the USPD's ambivalence about running, and the Communists' refusal to vote, the Independents did remarkably well in

Düsseldorf. The provisional government had redrawn the electoral map when it introduced proportional representation, and most of Düsseldorf city and county fell into the Düsseldorf-East district, which also included Elberfeld-Barmen, Solingen, and Essen. There, the USPD received 18.7 percent of the vote and elected Lore Agnes and party secretary Brass from Remscheid, whereas the SPD won 25.7 percent and elected three candidates; the Center and Liberals shared the remaining seven seats. This compared favorably with the national averages of 7.6 percent for the USPD and 37.9 percent for the SPD. In Düsseldorf-West, which included more rural areas and the textile towns Mönchen-Gladbach and Krefeld, the USPD won only 0.8 percent, whereas the SPD had 26.9 percent.[53] These results indicate the relative strength of the USPD as well as the dwindling appeal of the SPD and the inability of the KPD to persuade workers to abstain en masse.

The vote in Düsseldorf itself was even more encouraging to the left, as Table 12.1 shows. The USPD and the left liberal DDP were unquestionably the beneficiaries of the postwar political realignment, whereas the Center Party held its own and the SPD lost votes absolutely even though the electorate was nearly three times larger than in 1912. The USPD support undoubtedly came almost exclusively from the more than 120,000 workers in the city. Many organized socialist women, who had been on the party's left in the prewar years, probably voted for the USPD, which placed women's movement leader Agnes at the head of its list. Although the SPD's proletarian electorate may have been diluted by petty bourgeois supporters, as the Independents claimed, the startling growth of the left liberals suggests that most disaffected members of that strata voted DDP. In line with prewar trends, the Center Party probably drew increasingly from the heterogeneous Catholic middle classes as well as from newly enfranchised women.

Underlying the left's strong showing, however, were some disquieting trends that suggested how costly the division of the socialist movement and the disillusionment of the working class had been. Electoral participation dropped to 77 percent, and most of the abstainers were probably radical workers. More troubling still, the SPD and USPD combined captured a smaller percentage of the vote than had the SPD in 1912, and the drop was most marked in Düsseldorf-city, the former bastion of the socialist movement, where the SPD won more than 56 percent in 1912 and the SPD–USPD got just over 40 percent in 1919. Overall, the prewar electoral balance, or more accurately stalemate, in Düsseldorf did not change, for the smaller liberal parties picked up what the working-class

Table 12.1. *Reichstag elections in Düsseldorf, 1912 and 1919*

Parties	1912		1919	
	Votes	Percent of total	Votes	Percent of total
USPD			58,637	24.9
SPD	36,561	43.4	33,931	14.4
Center	31,522	37.4	91,420	38.9
NL	11,475	13.6		
DNVP			22,490	9.5
Other	4,775	5.6		
DDP			28,391	12.0

Source: *Volkszeitung*, February 2, 1919.

ones lost. But in the face of socialist divisions, the Center Party reemerged as the largest single party at the polls.

After the election the situation in Düsseldorf became increasingly polarized. In early February a variety of middle-class groups, angered by the executive council's behavior and encouraged by the electoral victory of the SPD, DDP, and Center Party nationally, launched an offensive against the Communist regime. Stoffers, the editor of the National Liberal *Düsseldorfer Zeitung*, insisted that the local government was "a reign of terror," subsidized by the Russians, and called for a civil servants' strike against it. This "bourgeois putsch," as the *Volkszeitung* derisively labeled it, met a mixed response. Policemen, railroad workers, and employees of the telegraph and food offices all struck, while postal workers were locked out, but neither municipal employees nor the Christian trade-union cartel would support the action. Several thousand attended a rally to endorse the strike committee's demands for complete freedom of the press and assembly, immediate municipal elections, and a restructuring of the executive council to give equal representation to the USPD-dominated Workers' Council, the SPD, and the bourgeois strike committee.[54] Given the workers' obvious allegiance to the left, the middle classes could only envision reforming the council, not eliminating dual power.

Although the Workers' Council did not agree to new elections for the executive, it scheduled municipal ones, and the strike committee, whose support was rapidly dwindling, accepted the compromise.[55] The government had weathered the storm, yet the Independents were increasingly pessimistic. In a February 8 *Volkszeitung* editorial, entitled "Counterrevolution in Germany," Berten argued:

The German revolution is suffering from a great mistake. The first assault was not strong enough to destroy fundamentally the old regime with all its excesses. The bourgeoisie and its organizations were preserved more fully than the interests of the revolution dictated ... And the resurgent forces of reaction, whose task is facilitated by the exhaustion which is making itself felt in the ranks of the revolutionaries, is throwing the German revolution back to the bourgeois, plutocratic stage.[56]

Economic developments, even more than political ones, were to prove this pessimism justified.

The economic situation in Düsseldorf worsened in January and February. Of a working class of more than 120,000 between 17,000 and 20,000 were officially unemployed, and the Workers' Council feared their number could rise to 50,000 or 60,000. Large firms, such as Rheinmetall, Hohenzollern, and Oberbilker Stahlwerk, were refusing government contracts in order to lower wages and destabilize the national government. And the SPD-led national government had no economic policy. Faced with this critical situation, the Düsseldorf Workers' Council proposed a multifaceted economic program. The provisional government should publicize all available contracts, so that the Workers' Council could encourage – and if necessary force – firms to accept them. In addition, the government should build roads, begin construction of the Middle Canal, and sponsor much-needed repair work on railroad equipment and machine tools. The Workers' Council tried in vain to pressure individual firms, even suggesting that if they could not convert to peace production, as the workers wanted, they should produce munitions and sell them to the Entente powers.[57]

As the Independents and Communists realized, their very modest and practical program could only be implemented with aid from the provisional government. But the Majority Socialists lacked a plan for conversion to peacetime production, feared to alienate the victorious powers by supporting the left, and viewed the Communists as their principal enemy. According to Podtevin, the government in Berlin actually "refused contracts for political reasons, in order thereby to pressure the Workers' Council, i.e., the Independent movement."[58] It was, Düsseldorf believed, "sabotage" plain and simple.[59] Whether the SPD acted this consciously is unclear; that they gave no aid is beyond doubt. The very isolation that fostered radicalism in Düsseldorf had once again begun to cripple the left.

By early February workers throughout the city were becoming increasingly restive in the face of these setbacks. Political rights meant little without economic power. The eight-hour day and higher wages were of slight value when there were few jobs, high inflation, and inadequate food and coal.[60] Losing faith in the Workers' Council and the USPD, the formerly disciplined metalworkers began to engage in spontaneous strikes. The factory council at Rheinmetall, with its numerous newly organized, less skilled workers, even demanded that the leading Independents resign from the council so that it would adopt more militant policies. Schmitt responded to these actions with an angry condemnation of "the masses," claiming, with a quote from Lenin, that they were "70 percent idiots, 28 percent criminals, and 2 percent idealists." Others, such as Ochel, roundly criticized such judgments.[61] But no one had a solution, for the discontent was a response not only to the immediate economic situation but also to the absence of an effective campaign for socialization.

Düsseldorf lay at the geographic heart of the 1919 socialization movement. Although the Ruhr miners had been relatively quiet and moderate in the political phase of the revolution, they subsequently spearheaded the drive for economic change and council rule. In early January, 80,000 of the region's more than 350,000 miners struck not only for higher wages and shorter hours but also for socialization of the mines, by which they meant above all direct workers' control. This spontaneous mass movement caught all three leftist parties by surprise, but within a week, local and regional Workers' and Soldiers' Councils, with representatives of the SPD, USPD, and KPD, as well as delegates from the provisional government, endorsed the call for socialization, at least in the form of nationalization. After a month of negotiations, however, the SPD abandoned its conciliatory posture and sent troops into the Ruhr. More than 180,000 miners, embittered by this betrayal, struck for three days and then continued their campaign by more peaceful means, even though the military remained.[62]

Despite its proximity to these dramatic events, Düsseldorf was only tangentially involved in them, for neither the leadership nor the rank and file initiated a socialization campaign that would affect local industry. Although prominent Independents and Communists spoke explicitly, emphatically, and repeatedly about the necessity of socialization – or more accurately, nationalization – none of them believed that Düsseldorf's metal sector was "ripe" for it.[63] Unlike the mines or basic heavy industry of the Ruhr, metal in Düsseldorf was relatively unconcentrated and highly diverse in terms of products, plant size, and work force. Coordinating production and creating a community of interests among workers would have been extremely difficult. Moreover, Düsseldorf was not a single-industry town, and other sectors, such as construction and wood, were structurally even less suited for nationalization and workers' control. The Workers' Council, which had representatives from all these industries, never even discussed socialization as part of the solution to the economic problems besetting Düsseldorf. Whereas in the Ruhr mining centers leaders abandoned their hesitations about socialization in response to the strike wave, in Düsseldorf the caution of union and party officials was reinforced by the lack of pressure from below.[64]

The character of the labor process, the forms of capitalist control, the composition and expectations of the working class, and its previous political experience all militated against any spontaneous socialization movement. Unlike Rhur mining centers, which were socially homogeneous, single-industry towns, Düsseldorf was very heterogeneous. Although the war had greatly increased the prominence of metal, other industries, such as construction, wood, and chemicals, as well as commerce, were still large and prospering. Although the socialist movement had gone far toward creating a unified working class, migratory peasant workers, the unskilled, women, and native Catholics still remained apart from it. Neither work nor community provided the basis for spontaneous local protest as they did in the Ruhr.

The more skilled and stable Düsseldorf workers, who were permanently committed to industrial work and urban life and had led the movement before 1914, continued to provide the structure and strategies for the whole working class during the war and revolution. These workers, with their relative security, greater job autonomy, and ability to plan somewhat for the future, were unquestionably radical, but their radicalism differed from that of the less skilled and secure miners. Düsseldorf's radicalism focused on political issues and the Workers' Council, not on economic questions and factory councils. It manifested itself through political parties and the party-dominated Workers' Council rather than through works councils in which traditional organizations and leaders played a minor role. These workers preferred disciplined protests to spontaneous strikes and regarded city hall, not the factory, as the center of action. They strove to control the state, not the shop floor directly.[65]

For Düsseldorf workers socialization was not on the immediate agenda. Woodworkers, for example, who were not threatened by technological change, made no effort to restructure the scattered, artisan sector in which they worked. Seasonal, migratory construction labor, unaffected by dequalification, considered workers' control equally implausible.[66] Even metalworkers failed to develop socialization plans, despite the fact that wartime rationalization threatened skills and brought an influx of semiskilled and that the DMV was an all-grades industrial union. Conditions in the metal industry remained very diverse and the skill level relatively high. Some workers were employed in small and medium-sized shops with patriarchal and personal modes of supervision and little hierarchy, whereas others worked in large plants with an extensive division of labor, omnipresent foremen, and ruthless discipline. The labor process alone did not bring forth a spontaneous movement for workers' control.[67] Nor was there a tradition of struggling around working conditions, as was the case in mining.[68] Although skilled and semiskilled collaborated in defense of wages and hours and formed factory councils in the larger plants, such as Rheinmetall, they do not appear to have made far-reaching demands for co-determination or socialization. The skilled channeled not only their own militancy but also that of the unskilled into political issues beyond the shop floor.

If social and cultural factors distinguished Düsseldorf radicals from their comrades in the Ruhr, it was political circumstances that separated them from the skilled metalworkers in Berlin, who did actively demand workers' control. The Berlin shop stewards and their followers had left the SPD without the support of either their party or union leaders, and they subsequently strove to build socialism not through political means but from the factory up.[69] In Düsseldorf the prewar leaders had been in the forefront of the split, and both the political and union organizations moved left en masse. As a result. Düsseldorf workers continued to operate within their traditional organizations and to follow a strategy of first seizing power and then socializing. This was both the strength and weakness of the Düsseldorf movement.

Whatever the merits of the case against beginning socialization in the Düsseldorf metal industry – and there were many – the policy bred frustration among workers. They were unable to push the revolution forward on either the political or the economic front and unable to channel their militancy toward a goal that was both feasible and immediately relevant. To be sure, the Düsseldorf workers cheered the Ruhr miners from afar, but they were not directly involved in the struggle until the February general strike, called to demand socialization and an end to the military occupation. Then, they went out with a kind of desperate enthusiasm, born of confusion and despair more than optimism. Isolated and on the defensive, they were fighting as much to regain momentum and boost their morale as to win concrete change for their comrades in the mines. And the Düsseldorf workers stayed out long after the miners had gone back, and even after the Düsseldorf Workers' Council had ordered them to do so. They returned only when employers, perhaps hoping that revolutionary fervor could be deflated or redirected by economic concessions, agreed to pay the strikers 75 percent of the previous weeks' wages.[70]

Impressive though it was, the general strike was the last act of the Communist regime. In late February support for the Spartacists eroded. Like the USPD before it, the KPD floundered on its inability to push the political revolution forward, initiate fundamental social transformation, and break out of its isolation from radicals elsewhere. Like the USPD, it paid the price for faults that stemmed as much from Düsseldorf's radical tradition and the national situation as from its own shortcomings. But this time failure brought not more militant action but division and demoralization into the heart of the revolutionary movement. Workers' Council meetings were poorly attended, discussions grew chaotic and indecisive, and personal accusations against individual members flew fast and thick. Although the council, at the insistence of the USPD, agreed to hold municipal elections on February 23, the KPD, which feared a bourgeois majority, first closed all non-socialist papers and then seized and destroyed the ballots. Furious over these actions, the Independents argued that the Communists had betrayed the ideas of Luxemburg and Liebknecht, and insisted that it would be suicidal for the USPD to continue the alliance.[71]

Simultaneously, bourgeois opposition to the regime mounted. Outside banks, upset by political developments in Düsseldorf, refused all future loans and demanded payment of outstanding debts. Whether this financial attack was spontaneous or orchestrated is not known. But its impact was devastating. Düsseldorf banks could not step into the breach, for the middle classes and industry had recently withdrawn approximately 8 million M. The Workers' Council was thus without the needed funds for unemployment insurance, veterans payments, and its own expenses.[72] Finally, the right-wing troops, dispatched by the SPD government, continued to approach Düsseldorf.

On February 28, before financial disaster or internal division toppled the regime, the Free Corps Lichtenstrahl marched into Düsseldorf. The Workers' Council immediately dissolved the KPD executive council and elected a USPD–SPD one, composed of Peter Agnes, Weinzieher, and Potdevin, while the leading Communists fled. Berten, Gerlach, and Spiegel telegraphed the SPD minister Hirsch in Berlin, urging him to recognize the new Workers' Council and not reinstate the old municipal government, lest "great unrest" break out. But the Majority Socialists and their bourgeois allies, having thrown the revolution on the defensive, had little interest in substantive concessions.[73]

Counterrevolution

By early March all prospects for social transformation had vanished, but the struggles between the military and the left, between capitalists and workers, and among the three socialist parties persisted. Rather than capitulating to what they regarded as a counterrevolution, the Düsseldorf working class moved still farther to the left. The Workers' Council and the USPD that dominated it as well as the working class, became increasingly vociferous proponents of pure council government and continued to support the Ruhr miners' socialization campaign. Although the Düsseldorf revolution retained its political focus, new forms of struggle emerged. As the Workers' Council lost ground to the resurgent municipal government, the military, and industrial interests, the factory councils played an increasingly important role in defining goals and initiating action. As the traditional leaders succumbed to uncertainty and demoralization, the rank and file provided direction and energy. But in the face of military intervention and national government opposition, the isolated Düsseldorf workers were doomed to defeat.

Berten, Schmitt, Pfeiffer, and the other Independents who took back control of the Workers' Council had hoped to return the revolution to a more fruitful but no less militant course. Before they had an opportunity to analyze the mistakes of the Sparticists and develop a new strategy, however, they ran into stiff opposition from the military, which had assumed control itself instead of reinstating the prerevolutionary municipal government. The USPD insisted that the council be allowed to exercise its previous functions and the Düsseldorf SPD seconded the request, perhaps in an effort to regain working-class support, perhaps out of anger about the national party's use of military force. Within a few days Berlin did give the requisite permission, even though it was systematically dismantling councils elsewhere, but no troops were withdrawn, thereby nullifying the left's power. In addition, the military repeatedly attacked workers, searched houses, and stood by when the recently improvised bourgeois security force behaved in a similar manner.[74] Within a week the Independents were demanding the immediate withdrawal of government troops and the dissolution of the Free Corps, as well as amnesty for all recent political prisoners, an end to factory firings, and the replacement of the Ebert–Scheidemann government, whose "so-called socialization law in no way corresponds to the proletariat's demand for a socialist ordering of our economic life."[75] Even the local SPD endorsed all but the last demand, for the SPD's policies were abhorrent even to the more conservative Düsseldorf socialists.[76]

The USPD's position was grounded in an extremely pessimistic analysis, which mixed self-criticism with attacks on other socialists and the bourgeoisie. Some Independents focused their attack solely on the Majority Socialists. Flormann, for example, insisted that they were responsible for the military occupation of Düsseldorf, and Zöllig argued that "the line to the right must be drawn with all possible clarity, for an unbridgeable gap separates us from those people." Taking a broader view, Winnen claimed that "the fruits of the revolution were taken from us by Ebert and Scheidemann and by the capitalists but also by self-interested elements on the extreme left." And the USPD shared the blame for allowing that to happen, for as Podtevin correctly pointed out, "we did not act radically enough from the first day of the revolution." According to Ficks, the revolution failed because "the vast majority of the German working class lacked the necessary theoretical education," on the one hand, and because "the bourgeoisie had unconsciously known how to act more effectively in its own class interests" on the other. He and Berten no longer believed that democracy was possible under capitalism, that there was a middle road between the National Assembly and proletarian dictatorship. They, together with Quirl, argued that "if no other means is available, the general strike must once again be resorted to."[77]

There was widespread support for a general strike, especially in the metal sector, and once again skilled, older workers who had a tradition of organization, supported militant action as readily as did younger, less skilled ones, who had been more recently politicized. While various factory councils put pressure on the Workers' Council, the DMV held three large meetings to protest military repression and mass firings and urge a strike. Before the Workers' Council acted, however, the military did, proclaiming martial law to prevent an impending USPD demonstration. When 200 workers nonetheless appeared, soldiers shot one and wounded several.[78]

Stunned and angered, both the Workers' Council and the factory councils met to deliberate about a general strike. Kaster, speaking for the trade-union cartel, favored an immediate protest, and Pfeiffer warned that "if the proper measures are not taken, the working class will simply shoot over the heads of the leaders. The mood in workers' circles is completely different than among the leaders." But Berten and Agnes, fearing a bloodbath, favored negotiating with the National Assembly for an end to martial law, the withdrawal of troops, the creation of a militia, an amnesty for political prisoners, and an end to politically motivated firings. The factory councils agreed to back these demands, albeit with misgivings, and the temporary rift between leaders and the rank and file was healed.[79]

For a few weeks the situation relaxed. Martial law was lifted, the military, though present, was less visible, and on March 18 the elections to the city council were held peacefully. They provided one of several indications that the left's popularity was growing. The USPD won nearly 27 percent of the vote, an increase over January, and elected twenty-three councilmen, while the SPD, which lost still more ground, won only eleven seats and the Center Party held its own. The Düsseldorf city council finally lost the dubious honor of being "free of socialists."[80] In the Workers' Council elections, which were open to a bourgeois slate at the insistence of the SPD, the Independents won 22,048 votes, the bourgeois bloc 20,959, and the Majority Socialists a mere 6,500. In the last weeks of March more than 2,000 workers joined the KPD, and the membership of the USPD topped 12,000.[81]

In a situation that was painfully reminiscent of the Imperial era, the left was unable to translate organizational strength into concrete policies or power. The national government continued to attack the councils and collaborate with the right while the military occupied not only Düsseldorf but the entire Ruhr. And industrialists, who had been quiet in the first months of the revolution, fired workers en masse in the largest factories and severely criticized the revolution. According to the Düsseldorf Chamber of Commerce, industry could accept the eight-hour day as well as moderate wage demands in a time of inflation. Adjusting to the new post-war conditions, the chamber even endorsed the *Arbeitsgemeinschaften*, as long as they promoted the cooperation between industry and unions on terms favorable to the preservation of capitalism. But the chamber resoundingly rejected any plans for socialization, factory councils, workers' control, or a Workers' Chamber, comparable to the employers' one.[82] If the revolution could be transformed into a wage movement, that was accceptable. If not, it must be repressed.[83]

Repression won the upper hand in the final bloody showdown, which occurred in the Ruhr in April. On March 30 the miners called for a general strike on behalf of council government, socialization, a militia, and the six-hour shift. Within a few days more than 300,000 miners, or 75 percent of the total, walked out of the pits.[84] On April 6 Düsseldorf joined in. Although the Workers' Council had opposed the strike by a vote of 42 to 8, it agreed to organize the protest if the workers favored it, which they emphatically did by a vote of 14,707 to 5,272 in the factories. The strike demands – the resignation of the SPD government, a council republic, the release of all political prisoners, the abolition of class justice, and recognition of the Soviet government – reflected the ongoing political orientation of the revolution in Düsseldorf and its inability to develop an economic program. But the strike was nonetheless enormously popular and shut down not only industry but the press and the municipal gas and electrical works as well. Despite several battles between workers and the Free Corps, which claimed the lives of thirty-nine men, women and children, the strike lasted nearly two weeks.[85]

As the Workers' Council proudly noted, the April strike was more effective than the previous one and the workers in the factories played a much larger role in the decision-making process.[86] Certainly the strike confirmed the Düsseldorf socialists' long-held faith in the militancy of the masses and their receptivity to the general strike. It illustrated clearly that leaders and members alike had undergone not only a process of radicalization but also of reevaluation. They had clarified and expanded their goals, developed new institutions, and experimented with tactics that would overcome the traditional division between economic and political struggles. But the lessons had been learned incompletely and too late.

Of equal importance, the Düsseldorf socialists lacked the necessary resources and allies to withstand the military force used against them. In late April the general strike ended, the Workers' Council was dismantled, and the military reasserted control over Düsseldorf and the entire Ruhr. The Majority Socialists, with the approval of the Entente powers and the aid of the military and industrial interests they had opposed for decades, had won the civil war. But they lost the allegiance of radical workers in Düsseldorf and throughout the region.

Despite defeat and demoralization, the Düsseldorf workers engaged in sporadic resistance throughout the remainder of 1919.[87] There were demonstrations of war veterans, attacks on soldiers, wildcat strikes about wages and food shortages and in July a 24-hour general strike, involving 75,000 workers, to protest intervention in Russia and the Versailles treaty. The government responded with continued military occupation, renewed martial law, and a virtual outlawing of the KPD.[88] As the danger from the left diminished, industrialists reasserted their position yet more forcefully. The Düsseldorf Chamber of Commerce rejected all wage increases, rescinded its acceptance of the eight-hour day, and demanded the reintroduction of piece rates. It condemned the USPD and KPD for risking chaos and destruction because "they were furious that capitalism was not dead and the dictatorship of the proletariat could not be achieved." It accused the workers of under-mining the authority and hierarchy that were economically necessary and of engaging in "wild, violent strikes, extensive corruption, and boundless pleasure seeking."[89]

Faced with this intransigence from Majority Socialists and capitalists alike, the Düsseldorf workers moved still farther to the left. In the fall of 1919 the local DMV was instrumental in helping the Independents take over the national union and reassert "the principle of class struggle." The Düsseldorf USPD, still led by Berten and Pfeiffer, voted overwhelmingly to send a delegate to the Third International meeting in late 1919. In the June 1920 parliamentary elections, the USPD won nearly a third of the vote in Düsseldorf-East and 14 percent in Düsseldorf-West, soundly trouncing the SPD in both.[90]

But this radicalization was the last gasp of the revolution, not the beginning of a new phase. It heralded not the resurgence of the left, but its demise. In October 1920 the Düsseldorf USPD, after weeks of anguished debate, split nearly evenly over the 21 Points that Moscow made a precondition for admission into the Third International. Berten,

Pfeiffer, Schmitt, Schotte, Agnes, and most lower-echelon functionaries, fearing excessive centralization and Russian domination, rejected the conditions, but much of the membership, moved by enthusiasm for the successful Russian Revolution rather than by the points themselves, favored acceptance. The USPD never recovered from this split. Nationally and locally it struggled on for a few years before its remaining members either returned to the SPD or withdrew from politics altogether. In Düsseldorf the majority of workers who had joined the KPD remained in it, and nearly 25 percent of the electorate supported that party throughout the 1920s.[91]

Düsseldorf workers remained radical in the postwar period, for the economic structures and social isolation that had first shaped their consciousness persisted and the new political institutions and alignments of Weimar fell far short of their expectations. But the working class was more powerless than ever because it was now divided not only by occupation, religion, and culture but by socialist political allegiance as well. The workers' movement, bitterly factionalized by the failed revolution and ensuing civil war, was no match for either the resurgent Center Party or the power of organized capitalism.

The revolution had shown the strengths and the enduring limits of the Düsseldorf radical tradition. Düsseldorf workers created strong organizations, effective and responsive leaders, and a clear political analysis and goals. They could sustain action even if they could not give it adequate direction. But they were unable to find a strategy for economic reform, let alone revolution, unable to overcome the diversity of their work situations in economic as opposed to political and cultural ways. They sought to solve the problems of economic power by seizing control of the state. But as in the past, they lacked the necessary radical allies to accomplish the task they set for themselves.

Conclusion

The period from 1890 to 1920 witnessed the making and the unmaking of the Düsseldorf working class. In the 1890s Düsseldorf's workers were divided by occupation and skill, culture and religion, age and sex, birthplace and commitment to urban life and industrial work. They shared neither common experiences nor similar attitudes and goals. Many were loyal to political Catholicism, some to liberalism, and a few to social democracy, but most, whatever their dissatisfactions and needs, remained unpolitical and passive. Neither the workers nor the weak social democratic movement presented a serious challenge to existing power structures and values.

From the turn of the century until World War I a cohesive working class emerged, formed primarily by young, skilled and semiskilled migrant workers, Catholic as well as Protestant, but including an increasing number of unskilled, women, and native Catholics. Although continued industrialization and migration as well as the growing conservatism of political Catholicism laid the groundwork for this, the changes they wrought in work, culture, and community did not suffice to create a common consciousness or common action. The social democratic movement was necessary for that. The party, unions, and cultural and service associations provided the physical and social space in which an alternative community could develop and a vehicle through which workers could challenge the existing economic and political order. They offered a common vocabulary in which workers could understand society, and a vision, however ill defined, toward which they could strive. Subject to the same structural and political constraints as the workers, social democracy articulated and reshaped their frustrations and aspirations. Society could still exclude the working class and the workers' movement, but it could no longer ignore the challenge they presented to capitalist economic power or political Catholicism.

War and revolution solidified the working class and expanded its boundries to include more women, youths, and unskilled, who had been drawn into the war economy. Both the workers' movement and the skilled who formed its core continued to dominate and unify the culture and politics of the working class. But the defeat of the revolution brought the dissolution of the working class. Politics and the workers' movement which had first united the class, came to divide it. To the divisions between Catholics and socialists, between the politicized and the unpolitical, were added those among the SPD, USPD, and KPD, as well as that between the politically involved and the disillusioned nonparticipants. Workers could no longer challenge Catholic cultural and political hegemony, nor capitalist economic and political power as they had when united.

In these same tumultuous decades the working class and the social democratic movement developed a strong radical tradition in Düsseldorf. Their analysis of society stressed the importance of class, the impossibility of reform, and the necessity of revolution. They rejected theoretical revisionism and practical reformism, criticized the bureaucratization and passivity of the SPD, and advocated the unequivocal defense of Marxist principles and an active strategy of confrontation with the state and capital. The radicalism of the Düsseldorf Social Democrats stressed political goals, such as universal suffrage, antimilitarism, democratization, and ultimately council government. It preferred political means, such as demonstrations, the political mass strike, and finally, the seizure of state power, and expressed itself through political organizations and structured struggles rather than through workplace associations and spontaneous protests. The working class and the workers' movement alike saw political power and transformation as the prerequisites for social change.

Radicalism was not an ideology imposed on the Düsseldorf working class from without and accepted with ambivalence. Rather, it represented a logical and rational attempt to grapple with the economic and political realities in which workers were embedded. It spoke to the needs of a working class whose dominant element, the young, skilled migrant worker, was committed to urban life and industrial work and was central to the economy but who was marginalized politically, excluded socially, and hard-pressed economically. The political orientation of Düsseldorf radicalism reflected the situation of workers who did not share a common work experience and who both encountered extremely strong opposition in struggles at the workplace and recognized the necessity of organizations that extended beyond the factory and shop. Radicalism was articulated by a thoroughly proletarian local social democratic movement, which lacked entrenched leadership and close ties to either the national party or bourgeois society in Düsseldorf. The radicalism of Düsseldorf's social democratic working class developed in three phases. In each a somewhat different combination of structural and political factors was most important in radicalizing workers; in each the working class and the workers' movement learned different lessons, which both deepened and limited their radicalism.

In 1890s the weak social democratic movement was isolated not only from the dominant society in Düsseldorf but also from the local working class and the national workers' movement. Frustrated in their attempts to make headway against the power of organized capitalism, authoritarian government, and above all political Catholicism, the Social Democrats developed a deep mistrust of parliamentarism, class collaboration, and political alliances, which were either unfeasible or unproductive in the Düsseldorf context. They developed an equally deep commitment to Marxism because it provided both an analysis of the reality that they confronted and the prospect of its transformation. But their Marxism was strongly imbued with economic determinism, for the Düsseldorf movement, too weak to act vigorously, preferred to await the expected ripening of the contradictions of capitalism.

From 1903 to 1914 the social democratic workers of Düsseldorf retained their allegiance to Marxism and their mistrust of reformism but became advocates of much more activist and militant tactics. In this period the movement had unprecedented success in recruiting workers, building political, union, and cultural organizations, and successfully defeating political Catholicism in the Reichstag elections. Yet, as the workers learned, institutional expansion and visibility, even electoral victory, did not bring real power. Despite the successful siege of the Center fortress, capitalist control and inflation weakened the workers' ecomomic position, restrictive regulations excluded them from municipal politics, and the Reichstag seat proved no more than an empty symbol. Even after the power of political Catholicism was significantly weakened, the structural and political realities of Düsseldorf thus continued to radicalize workers. They became convinced that the limits of reformism could be transcended only by radical tactics, by the use of the mass strike and reliance on rank-and-file militancy. Advocacy of such leftist positions embroiled the Düsseldorf Social Democrats in bitter conflicts with the increasingly reformist national party. It intensified their isolation – an isolation that provided the critical distance necessary to develop a radical analysis on the one hand and inhibited action on the other.

After 1914 Düsseldorf's workers moved from being radicals within the social democratic movement to being revolutionaries outside of and against it. War aims, wartime repression, and the war economy greatly increased not only their hostility to the state and capitalism but also their willingness to protest openly against both. Simultaneously, national party and trade-union support for the war created unprecedented disillusionment and active opposition to the movement's right and center. As a result, by 1917 Düsseldorf was a stronghold of the left USPD and by 1918 was advocating democratization and a social republic. The revolution of 1918–19 tested the Düsseldorf workers' commitment to radicalism and the viability of their goals and strategies. It showed their willingness to act, their clarity about what democratization entailed, and the strength of the ties between workers and their traditional leaders and organizations. But it also revealed their inability to develop new forms of action, merge economic and political struggles, break out of their isolation, and make a social revolution.

In all three periods the very factors that promoted radicalism in Düsseldorf also limited its effectiveness. The predominance of large-scale industry and the power of organized capitalist interests, the lack of democratic rights and the weakness of parliamentary institutions, the repressive apparatus of the state and the political power and cultural hegemony of Catholicism made reformism impossible. But they also made organization and mobilization difficult and militant confrontation dangerous. The rapid growth and geographic mobility of the working class, which prevented integration and provided ready recruits for the social democratic movement, made it difficult to build a stable organization with experienced and educated members. The Düsseldorf Social Democrats' isolation from the movement's headquarters in Berlin created the space within which radical ideas could develop, but that same isolation relegated Düsseldorf to the margins of the movement, limited its contacts with radicals elsewhere, and inhibited action. After 1914, when the Düsseldorf Social Democrats finally risked radical action, the combined opposition of the SPD, the national trade unions, the military, and industry first thwarted opposition to the war and then defeated the revolution. Düsseldorf fought valiantly, but it fought in isolation from workers elsewhere.

The Düsseldorf Social Democrats were not simply victims of forces beyond their control, however, for the strengths of their radical tradition were also its weaknesses. There were certain constant aspects of their consciousness and behavior that crippled them. Although they broadened their appeal, they were unable to mobilize women, native Catholics, and peasant workers in large numbers. Although they built extremely effective political organizations, they were unable to develop a comparable power base within Düsseldorf's most important factories. Despite their persistent criticism of the national social democratic movement, they bowed to reformist decisions in the name of proletarian unity until forced to leave during the war. Düsseldorf's radicalism emphasized political goals and actions, but at the expense of economic ones. The radical movement was built around and benefited from the institutional pattern established at the turn of the century, but it was unable to transcend or modify significantly traditional organizations and forms of action when the situation required. Düsseldorf's radicalism was not informed by a theory of revolution that assigned the working class an active role and provided a strategy for building socialism. When Düsseldorf's radical tradition was put to the test in 1918–19, its limits were tragically exposed.

In several ways the experience of Düsseldorf challenges the prevalent image of a reformist social democratic movement, integrated, if only negatively, into German society. It questions the validity of sweeping generalizations about the social democratic movement or the German working class. History from above has ignored the autonomy of local movements, overestimated the ability of Berlin to enforce one pattern of thought and action on Social Democrats, and abstracted the local movement from its formative local context. Marked regional variations in politics and culture and the highly uneven development of the German economic and social structure have been overlooked. These regional variations helped produce not only radicalism but, as the contrast between Düsseldorf and Ruhr mining centers suggests, different patterns of radicalism. They helped produce as well different patterns of reformism, which historians have barely begun to examine.

This study suggests that large numbers of workers (one thinks of the entire Lower Rhine and Ruhr as a start) were not negatively integrated into German society. Rather they were actively excluded and felt themselves to be. Indeed, the concept of negative integration, with its emphasis on political institutions and the combination of political legality and powerlessness, proves to be an excessively narrow category, which ignores both the social and economic reality of working-class life and society's and social democracy's perceptions of one another.

Most directly, the Düsseldorf experience indicates that reformism was not always and everywhere the dominant ideology and practice of German workers. It was not always and everywhere a possibility. By examining the birth and development, the strengths and weaknesses of one radical tradition, this study argues that social democracy had other options than those chosen. Radicalism was not the preserve of a handful of intellectuals before 1914, nor an aberration brought on by the war thereafter. Rather, radicalism had deep social and political roots in important segments of the German working class. The tragedy of German social democracy was not only that the leaders ignored or suppressed the left. It was also that the left was unable to overcome its isolation and the limits of its radicalism to present a successful alternative to reformism.

On the methodological front, this study rejects monocausal explanations of working-class radicalism and the prevalent tendency to downplay politics, parties, and ideology. Although it argues that neither work nor community nor culture alone can explain working-class behavior or consciousness, it insists on the importance of structure. People make their own history but not, as Marx noted, under circumstances of their own choosing. The circumstances they encountered on the job, in their community, in civil society, and in the state need to be analyzed in all their complexity. The Düsseldorf experience also shows the importance of political movements to the process of class formation in one complex industrial city and to the particular pattern of radicalism that emerged. It argues that politics and ideology are not outside of or imposed on the working class but are often an integral part of it.

This study has not regarded structure or politics as absolute givens, imposed on the working class from without and inevitably determining its attitudes and actions. Rather, the essence of this endeavor has been to re-create the learning process through which the working class and the workers' movement went in confronting society and politics in Wilhelmian Düsseldorf. It has sought to unravel the logic of the attitudes and actions not of a working class abstractly conceived but of specific groups of workers, such as skilled migrants, peasant workers, and women. And these groups are unique neither to Düsseldorf nor to the period. This study has explored the interaction between these workers' backgrounds and expectations on the one hand and their experiences on the other. It has investigated how social democracy (and for some workers, political Catholicism) mediated that interaction. By analyzing the categories through which workers perceived their world and the institutions and patterns of action by which they sought to change it, it has reconstructed how workers made their own history and how they became imprisoned by it.

The Düsseldorf experience has raised questions about class formation, political movements, and the possibility of social transformation in more advanced capitalist societies. Comparable studies of workers elsewhere in Germany, in Europe, and in the United States are needed in order to re-create the complex totality of working-class history in this period. They are needed because the questions raised by the Düsseldorf experience are still with us. The tasks that the Düsseldorf working class set for itself have yet to be accomplished, and there is much to learn from its successes and failures.

Appendix: Statistical tables

Table A.1. *Party membership, 1898–1915*

Year	Number	Growth rate (%)	Men	Growth rate (%)	Women	Growth rate (%)
1898	350					
1899	—					
1900	—					
1901	346					
1902	530	53.1				
1903	950	79.2				
1904	1,000	5.2				
1905	987	−1.3				
1906	1,534	55.4				
1907	2,560	66.8				
1908	2,783	8.7				
1909	3,067	10.2	2,621	−5.8	446	
1910	3,579	16.6	2,997	14.3	582	30.4
1911	5,484	53.2	4,487	49.7	997	71.3
1912	7,166	30.6	5,722	27.5	1,394	39.8
1913	7,388	3.0	5,893	2.9	1,495	7.2
1914	7,793	5.4	5,918	0.4	1,875	20.2
1915	4,581	−41.2				

Sources: Niederrheinische Volkstribune, January 14, 1899; January 25, 1902; *Volkszeitung*, November 12, 1903; September 24, 1904; October 5, 1906; September 30, 1907; October 10, 1908; July 28, 1909; July 21, 1910; July 26, 1912; April 22, 1914; April 23, 1915.

Table A.2. *Trade-union membership, 1896–1914*

Year	Number of unions	Membership	Growth rate (%)	Trade unionists: party members
1896	27	1,312		
1897				
1898	27	2,251		6.4:1
1899				
1900		4,672		
1901	26	4,467	−4.3	12.9:1
1902	32	3,944	−11.7	7.4:1
1903	30	5,403	36.9	5.7:1
1904	34	6,622	22.5	6.6:1
1905	37	9,465	42.9	9.6:1
1906	40	13,807	45.8	9.0:1
1907	41	13,030	−5.6	5.1:1
1908		10,299	−20.9	3.7:1
1909		11,881	15.3	3.9:1
1910	38	15,034	26.5	4.2:1
1911	39	22,032	46.5	4.2:1
1912	37	24,920	13.1	3.5:1
1913		23,207	−6.8	3.1:1
1914[a]	37	23,093	−0.4	2.9:1
1914[b]	36	13,398	−41.9	2.9:1

[a]Second quarter.
[b]Fourth quarter.
Sources: Stadtarchiv Düsseldorf, III 5911, 1896. *Niederrheinische Volkstribune*, February 12, 1902. Bericht des Gewerkschaftskartell, 1902, 1903, 1904, 1906. *Volkszeitung*, July 23, 1908; July 28, 1909; November 21, 1914. Bericht des Gewerkschaftssekretariat, 1911, 1912.

Table A.3. *Düsseldorf Reichstag elections, 1890–1912*

Year	Soc. Democrats	Center	Nat. Liberals	Other
1890	7,573	12,476	5,616	1,125
1890	8,228	16,511		
1893	9,367	15,214	5,384	2,358
1893	9,123	17,017		
1898	10,712	17,874	4,715	2,864
1898	12,657	22,756		
1903	20,375	21,628	7,866	823
1903	23,762	27,084		
1907	25,389	29,259	14,664	861
1907	25,233	33,317		
1911	34,066	29,276		6,828
1911	39,283	35,894		
1912	36,561	31,522	11,475	4,775
1912	42,850	42,088		

Source: Stadtarchiv Düsseldorf, III 10104, 1890; 10105, 1893; 10106, 1898; 10107, 1903; 10109, 1907. Stadtarchiv Düsseldorf, XXI 232, Sept. 20 and 30, 1911; Jan. 13 and 22, 1912.

Table A.4. Social Democratic vote, 1890–1912

Year	Total	Growth rate (%)	City	Growth rate (%)	County	Growth rate (%)	Percent total vote	Ratio A[a]	Ratio B[b]
1890	7,573	—	5,701		1,872		28.2	—	—
1890	8,228	—	6,251		1,977		33.2	—	—
1893	9,367	23.7	7,342	28.7	2,025	8.1	28.2	—	—
1893	9,123	10.8						—	—
1898	10,712	14.4	8,404	14.4	2,308	13.9	29.6	30.6:1	4.8:1
1898	12,657	35.1	10,013	36.3	2,644	30.5	35.7	36.2:1	5.6:1
1903	20,375	90.2	15,018	78.7	5,357	132.1	39.8	21.4:1	3.8:1
1903	23,762	87.7	17,663	76.4	6,099	130.6	46.5	25.0:1	4.4:1
1907	25,389	24.6	18,658	24.2	6,731	25.6	36.1	9.9:1	1.9:1
1907	25,233	6.2	18,333	3.7	6,900	13.1	42.9	9.8:1	1.9:1
1911	34,066	34.2	28,704	53.8	5,362	−20.3	48.8	6.2:1	1.5:1
1911	39,283	55.7	32,842	79.1	6,441	−6.6	52.3	7.2:1	1.8:1
1912	36,561	7.3	30,779	7.2	5,782	7.8	43.4	7.6:1	1.5:1
1912	42,850	9.1	36,365	10.7	6,485	0.7	49.9	8.8:1	1.7:1

[a]Ratio of voters to party members (only male members in 1911, 1912).
[b]Ratio of voters to trade unionists.
Sources: Stadtarchiv Düsseldorf, III 10104, 1890; 10105, 1893; 10106, 1898; 10107, 1903; 10109, 1907. Stadtarchiv Düsseldorf, XXI 232, September 20 and 30, 1911; January 13 and 22, 1912.

Table A.5. New membership classified by economic category: 1896–1908

	1896		1897		1898		1899		1900		1901	
	No.	%	No.	%	No.	%	No.	%	No.	%	No.	%
Gardening	0	0.0	0	0.0	0	0.0	0	0.0	0	0.0	0	0.0
Industry	34	94.4	24	85.7	19	82.6	95	73.6	27	81.8	101	87.0
Trade	1	2.8	0	0.0	0	0.0	2	1.6	0	0.0	1	0.9
Unclassifiable												
Skilled	0	0.0	0	0.0	0	0.0	0	0.0	0	0.0	1	0.9
Unskilled	1	2.8	4	14.3	4	17.4	32	24.8	6	18.2	12	10.3
White-collar	0	0.0	0	0.0	0	0.0	0	0.0	0	0.0	1	0.9

	1902		1904		1905		1906		1907		1908	
	No.	%	No.	%	No.	%	No.	%	No.	%	No.	%
Gardening	0	0.0	0	0.0	5	1.4	5	0.6	6	0.7	4	1.8
Industry	44	84.7	20	82.7	314	86.1	682	79.4	680	74.9	170	73.6
Trade	2	3.8	1	4.3	12	3.3	25	2.9	24	2.7	4	1.8
Unclassifiable												
Skilled	6	11.5	2	8.7	7	1.9	14	1.6	17	1.9	3	1.3
Unskilled	0	0.0	0	0.0	27	7.3	131	15.3	179	19.7	47	20.6
White-collar	0	0.0	1	4.3	0	0.0	2	0.2	1	0.1	2	0.9

There is no occupational information for 1903.
Source: Stadtarchiv Düsseldorf, III 6923–33, 1896–1908.

Table A.6. Distribution of the working class by economic group and sex

	1895						1907					
	No. men	% men[a]	No. women	% women[a]	Total no.	% total[b]	No. men	% men[a]	No. women	% women[a]	Total no.	% total[b]
Gardening	1,285	81.0	303	19.0	1,588	4.0	1,113	67.6	534	32.4	1,647	2.6
Animal breeding	11	100.0	0	0.0	11	0.0	16	100.0	0	0.0	16	0.0
Smelting	2,505	98.9	28	1.1	2,533	6.4	4,138	99.6	18	0.4	4,156	6.5
Stone and earth	1,032	97.9	23	2.1	1,055	2.7	1,027	95.1	53	4.9	1,080	1.7
Metal working	6,544	98.3	119	1.7	6,663	16.9	7,243	97.5	192	2.5	7,435	11.6
Machine-making	2,082	98.9	25	1.1	2,107	5.3	8,795	99.4	57	0.6	8,852	13.9
Chemicals	536	83.5	106	16.5	642	1.6	569	66.7	285	33.3	854	1.3
Fat, lighting	224	98.3	4	1.7	228	0.6	548	89.3	66	10.7	614	1.0
Textiles	1,397	60.6	910	39.4	2,307	5.8	792	50.7	773	49.3	1,565	2.5
Paper	486	72.7	183	27.3	669	1.7	696	76.3	217	23.7	913	1.4
Leather	482	93.1	36	6.9	518	1.3	678	97.3	19	2.7	697	1.1
Woodworking	2,420	99.4	15	0.6	2,435	6.2	3,365	98.0	71	2.0	3,436	5.4
Food	1,983	90.1	218	9.9	2,201	5.6	2,743	80.1	682	19.9	3,425	6.0
Clothing	1,480	48.3	1,588	51.7	3,068	7.8	1,404	37.0	2,400	63.0	3,804	6.0
Cleaning							481	47.4	534	52.6	1,015	1.6

Construction	5,920	99.8	17	0.2	5,937	15.0	8,064	100.0	6	0.0	8,070	12.6
Printing	551	90.5	58	9.5	609	1.5	1,043	80.8	248	19.2	1,291	2.0
Artistic products	242	99.2	2	0.8	244	0.6	283	96.6	10	3.4	293	0.5
Trade	2,162	66.0	1,114	34.0	3,279	8.3	4,194	58.5	2,981	41.5	7,175	11.2
Insurance	19	100.0	0	0.0	19	0.0	27	100.0	0	0.0	27	0.0
Transportation	1,943	99.9	3	0.1	1,946	4.9	4,562	99.2	38	0.8	4,600	7.2
Hotels	647	44.9	794	55.1	1,441	3.6	1,581	55.2	1,287	44.8	2,868	4.5
	33,951		5,546		39,497		53,355		10,478		63,833	
Casual labor	1,006	49.3	1,034	50.7	2,040	50.7	516	18.6	2,255	81.4	2,771	
Domestics	76	1.2	6,078	98.8	6,154	98.8	72	0.8	8,903	99.2	8,975	

[a]Percentage of the economic group.
[b]Percentage of the working class in economic categories A–C.
Source: Statistik des deutschen Reiches, n.s. 108:85–91; 207, 2nd part: 478–81.

Table A.7. *Percentage of the labor force in firms of different sizes, 1907*

Economic group	1-5 employees	6-20 employees	21-50 employees	51-100 employees	101-500 employees	500-1,000 employees[a]
Entire economy	22.9-24.1	13.0-22.0	10.2-13.6	8.6-12.0	18.2-35.6	11.0-18.8
Gardening	32.1-33.8	10.9-18.5	0.0	14.0-18.5	37.1-39.4	0.0
Smelting	0.0	0.1	0.9-1.1	1.6-2.2	21.1-45.7	49.4-74.1
Stone and earth	3.0-3.3	10.2-17.9	36.3-48.8	9.6-13.5	21.9-32.5	0.0
Metalworking	7.7-8.3	7.0-12.2	6.7-9.1	6.4-9.1	41.5-89.7	11.2-22.0
Machine making	3.9-4.2	4.8-8.4	7.7-10.2	10.3-14.5	26.7-54.3	24.9-41.4
Chemicals	7.7-8.5	15.6-27.4	16.1-21.0	11.6-16.0	32.3-45.8	0.0
Fat, lighting	2.3-2.5	5.3-9.2	10.4-14.2	0.0	25.2-54.3	41.9
Textiles	4.0-4.1	5.9-10.6	7.4-9.7	20.4-27.5	25.6-44.5	21.2-42.4
Paper	6.1-6.6	11.3-19.8	9.0-11.8	20.1-27.7	36.0-51.5	0.0
Leather	73.3-77.8	19.8-34.0	0.0	0.0	0.0	0.0
Woodworking	23.0-24.6	16.7-29.0	19.3-25.2	12.2-17.0	15.2-21.4	0.0
Food	38.9-42.4	21.5-37.1	11.6-15.5	8.1-11.3	8.6-12.3	0.0
Clothing	61.0-62.8	15.6-27.3	5.0-6.5	4.4-6.2	6.8-9.6	0.0
Cleaning	55.5-56.8	11.0-19.1	7.4-10.3	6.9-9.5	10.9-27.3	0.0
Construction	11.8-12.6	11.7-20.5	10.1-13.2	12.9-18.3	23.6-47.3	8.0-15.9
Printing	12.4-13.1	15.6-27.5	19.0-25.5	10.0-14.7	29.7-55.7	0.0
Artistic	58.2-59.6	15.2-26.9	12.4-16.4	7.6-14.9	0.0	0.0
Trade	44.1-46.1	20.6-35.8	13.6-18.2	7.0-9.9	3.6-7.4	0.0
Insurance	31.9-33.2	30.0-52.7	21.8-29.0	0.0	0.0	0.0
Transportation	20.6-22.0	16.0-28.2	5.1-6.8	6.9-9.5	17.9-26.0	13.7-27.4
Hotels	40.6-42.4	21.6-37.6	17.3-23.0	8.6-12.4	0.0	0.0

[a]The two smelting mills and one chemical plant with more than 1,000 workers have been included in this category.
Source: Mitteilungen, No. 3, pp. 2-3.

Notes

Abbreviations used in notes

AZ	*Düsseldorfer Arbeiterzeitung*
JdH	*Jahresbericht der Handelskammer zu Düsseldorf*
JdHW	*Jahresbericht der Handwerkskammer zu Düsseldorf*
JdSA	*Jahresbericht des Statistischen Amt Düsseldorf*
MdH	*Monatsschrift der Handelskammer zu Düsseldorf*
Mitteilungen	*Mitteilungen zur Statistik der Stadt Düsseldorf*
NV	*Niederrheinische Volkstribune*
Parteitagen	*Sozialdemokratische Parteitagen für die Rheinprovinz und den Niederrhein*
Protokoll der SPD	*Protokoll über die Verhandlung der Parteitages der sozialdemokratischen Partei Deutschlands*
Reg. Dd.	Akten der Regierung zu Düsseldorf
SADd	Stadtarchiv Düsseldorf
SdR	*Statistik des deutschen Reiches*
SM	*Statistische Monatsberichte der Stadt Düsseldorf*
StADd	Staatsarchiv Düsseldorf
StAK	Staatsarchiv Koblenz
VZ	*Volkszeitung*
WdH	*Wochenschrift der Handelskammer zu Düsseldorf*

Introduction

1 E.P. Thompson, *The Making of the English Working Class* (New York: Vintage Books, 1966), p. 11.

2 For recent theoretical discussions of this, see Harry Braverman, *Labor and Monopoly Capital* (New York: Monthly Review Press, 1974), and Charles F. Sabel, *Industrial Conflict and the Sociology of the Labor Market* (Cambridge: Cambridge University Press, in press).

3 Antonio Gramsci, *Prison Notebooks* (New York: International Press, 1971), pp. 123–320. Hans-Ulrich Wehler, *Das deutsche Kaiserreich, 1871–1918* (Göttingen: Vandenhoeck und Ruprecht, 1973).

4 Much current working-class history in the United States and Great Britain pays relatively little attention to working-class parties and unions. This reflects in part their relative weakness in those countries and in part the previous overemphasis on institutions. For a review of the study of working-class movements, see Georges Haupt, "Why the History of the Working-Class Movement?" *New German Critique* 14 (Spring 1978);7–27.

5 See, e.g., Robert Michels, *Political Parties* (New York: Free Press, 1962); Carl Schorske, *German Social Democracy, 1905–17* (New York: John Wiley & Sons, 1955); and Hans-

Josef Steinberg, *Sozialismus und deutsche Sozialdemokratie* (Hannover: Verlag für Literatur und Zeitgeschehen, 1967). Although DDR historians have worked on the social history of the working class, their findings have not been integrated into the political history of working-class movements. See Dieter Fricke, *Die deutsche Arbeiterbewegung, 1869–1914* (Berlin: Dietz, 1976). Jürgen Kuczynski, *Die Geschichte der Lage der Arbeiter unter dem Kapitalismus*, Vols. 4, 18 (Berlin: Akademie, 1967).

6 Guenther Roth, *The Social Democrats in Imperial Germany* (Totowa, N.J.: The Bedminster Press, 1963). Dieter Groh, *Negative Integration und revolutionärer Attentismus* (Frankfurt: Ullstein, 1973).

7 See, e.g., Karl-Ernst Moring, *Die Sozialdemokratische Partei in Bremen, 1890–1914* (Hannover: Verlag für Literatur und Zeitgeschehen, 1968).

8 Two recent studies have made significant progress in this direction: Erhard Lucas, *Zwei Formen von Radikalismus in der deutschen Arbeiterbewegung* (Frankfurt: Roter Stern, 1976); Wilhelm Heinz Schröder, *Arbeitergeschichte und Arbeiterbewegung* (Frankfurt: Campus, 1978).

9 Gramsci, p. 151.

1. The hostile environment

1 Hugo Weidenhaupt, *Kleine Geschichte der Stadt Düsseldorf* (Düsseldorf: Verlag L. Schwann, 1968), p. 131.

2 For an introduction to Imperial Germany, see Richard J. Evans, ed., *Society and Politics in Wilhelmine Germany* (London: Croom Helm, 1978); Eckert Kehr, *Primat der Innenpolitik* (Berlin: Walter de Gruyter, 1965); Fritz Stern, *The Failure of Illiberalism* (Chicago: University of Chicago Press, 1976); and Wehler, *Das deutsche Kaiserreich*.

3 Josef Wilden, *Grundlagen und Triebkräfte der Wirtschaft Düsseldorf* (Düsseldorf: Deutsche Kunst und Verlagsanstalt, 1923), p. 7 SADd, III 6933, October 23, 1907.

4 *VZ*, March 11, 1914.

5 *AZ*, October 2, 1890.

6 Wilden, *Grundlagen und Triebkräfte*, p. 20.

7 For an introduction to German economic and social history, see Helmut Böhme, *Prolegomena zu einer Sozial- und Wirtschaftsgeschichte Deutschlands im 19. und 20. Jahrhundert* (Frankfurt: Suhrkampf, 1968); Tom Kemp, *Industrialization in Nineteenth-Century Europe* (London: Longman, 1969); and David Landes, *The Unbound Prometheus* (Cambridge: Cambridge University Press, 1969).

8 *Mitteilungen*, No. 3, *Industrie und Handelsgewerbe in Düsseldorf nach der Betriebszählung von 12. Juni 1907* (Düsseldorf: Statistisches Amt, 1908), pp. 2–3.

9 Wilden, *Grundlagen und Triebkräfte*, pp. 12 and 20.

10 Ibid., pp. 68–71. Hubertus Beckers, "Entwicklungsgeschichte der Industrieunternehmungen in Düsseldorf, 1815–1914" (Ph.D. diss., University of Cologne, 1958), pp. 69–72, 78, 99–102, and Appendix 8.

11 Wilden, *Grundlagen und Triebkräfte*, pp. 134, 137–8. *Rheinisch-Westfälische Wirtschaftsbiographien*, ed. die historische Kommission des Provinzialinstituts für Westfälische Landes- und Volkskund des Rheinisch-Westfälische Wirtschaftsarchiv und der Volkswirtschafliche Vereinigung im Rheinisch-Westfälische Industriegebiet (Münster: Aschendorffsche Verlag, 1974), 3:115–32, passim, and 4:172–8.

12 Kehr, *Primat der Innenpolitik*, pp. 219–28.

13 Beckers, pp. 69–72, 78, 99–100.

14 From the 1840s to the 1860s Düsseldorf, benefiting from the newly built railroads, became a commercial and transportation center for the Wuppertal region, but its

manufacturing sector remained underdeveloped. Otto Brandt, "Düsseldorfs Wirtschaftliche Entwicklung," in Hans Arthur Lux, ed., *Düsseldorf* (Düsseldorf: Deutsche Kunst und Verlagsanstalt, 1921–2), pp. 58, 118.

15 Weidenhaupt, pp. 114–17. Beckers, p. 51.

16 *Mitteilungen*, No. 3, p. 5*.

17 *Mitteilungen*, No. 3, p. 18*.

18 Hans Seeling, *Geschichte der Gerresheimer Glashütte, Ursprung und Entwicklung, 1864–1908* (Düsseldorf: Ed. Lintz, 1964), pp. 30–2, 51, 73–4.

19 *Mitteilungen*, No. 3, pp. 13*, 17. Beckers, pp. 131–2.

20 *Mitteilungen*, No. 3, p. 1. Otto Brandt, *Studien zur Wirtschafts- und Verwaltungsgeschichte der Stadt Düsseldorf im 19. Jahrhundert* (Düsseldorf: n.p., 1902), pp. 120–1.

21 *Mitteilungen*, No. 3, pp. 9*, 14*.

22 Hans Winkels, "Die Entwicklung des Handwerks in Düsseldorf seit dem Jahre 1816" (Ph.D. diss., University of Cologne, 1933), pp. 21–7.

23 *MdH*, October 1910, p. 259.

24 Ibid., p. 260.

25 Wilden, *Grundlagen und Triebkräfte*, p. 26. *Mitteilungen*, No. 3, pp. 19*, 20*, 22*.

26 Weidenhaupt, pp. 129–31. Brandt, *Studien*, p. 403. *Mitteilungen*, No. 3, p. 20.

27 Essays by Jürgen Kocka and Hans-Ulrich Wehler in *Organisierter Kapitalismus*, Heinrich August Winkler, ed., (Göttingen: Vandenhoeck and Ruprecht, 1974), pp. 19–57.

28 Ernst Heinson, "Düsseldorf als Sitz wichtiger industrieller Verbände," in Lux, p. 56; Wilden, p. 33.

29 Wolfgang Köllmann, "Die Bevölkerung Rhineland-Westfalens in der Hochindustrialisierungsperiode," *Vierteljahresheft für Sozial- und Wirtschaftsgeschichte* 58 (1971): 359. In the government district of Düsseldorf, which included Barmen, Elberfeld, Krefeld, Duisburg, and Essen, only 7% of the population lived in rural areas, whereas 37% dwelt in towns of more than 100,000. National figures were 42% and 19%, respectively. *Mitteilungen*, No. 4. *Die Nichteinheimischen in Düsseldorf nach der Volkszählung vom 1. Dezember 1905* (Düsseldorf: Statistisches Amt, 1912), pp. 4*–5*, 9*. *MdH*, October 1910, p. 256.

30 *Mitteilungen*, No. 4, p. 12*.

31 Wolfgang Köllmann, "Industrialisierung, Binnenwanderung und die 'soziale Frage'," *Vierteljahrescheft für Sozial- und Wirtschaftsgeschichte* 46 (1959):53.

32 Köllmann, "Die Bevölkerung," pp. 363–7. *Mitteilungen*, No. 4, pp. 10*, 18*–19*. *JdSA*, 1902, pp. 2 and 5. Rudolf Heberle and Fritz Meyer, *Die Grossstädte im Strom der Binnenwanderung* (Leipzig: Verlag von F. Hirzel, 1937), p. 119.

33 Köllmann, "Industrialisierung," p. 66.

34 Hans Meydenbauer, *Die Stadt Düsseldorf und ihre Verwaltung im Ausstellungsjahr 1902* (Düsseldorf: August Bagel, n.d.), p. 94.

35 *SdR*, n.s. 108:183; 207, Pt. 2:477. Köllmann, "Industrialisierung." p. 66.

36 Helmuth Croon, "Die wirtschaftlichen Führungsschichten des Ruhrgebiets in der Zeit von 1890–1933," *Blätter für deutsche Landesgeschichte* 108 (1972):143. Wolfgang Köllman, *Sozialgeschichte der Stadt Barmen im 19. Jahrhundert* (Tübingen: J. G. B. Mohr, 1960), pp. 108–9.

37 Georg Renard, *Struktur- und Konjunkturtendenzen im Düsseldorfer Wirtschaftsraum* (Essen: Essener Verlagsanstalt, 1939), p. 11.

38 Rudolf Eberstadt, *Rheinische Wohnungsverhältnisse und ihre Bedeutung für die Wohnungswesen in Deutschland* (Jena: G. Fischer, 1903), pp. 33–4.

39 Wilden, *Grundlagen und Triebkräfte*, p. 30.

40 *JdSA*, 1906, p. 9. *Beiträge zur statistischen Monatsbericht der Stadt Düsseldorf*, July 1909, p. XXXIX, Meydenbauer, p. 100.

41 Heinrich Ehrhardt, *Hammerschläge* (Leipzig: Koehler, 1922), pp. 41–52, 56–62. Lutz Hatzfeld, *Die Handelsgesellschaft Albert Poensgen, Mauel-Düsseldorf* (Cologne: Rheinisch-Westfalisch Wirtschaftsarchiv, 1964), passim. *75 Jahre Mannesmann, 1890–1965* (Berlin: Tempelhof, 1965), pp. 16–35, 40–2, 55–60.

42 Josef Wilden, *100 Jahre Düsseldorfer Wirtschaftsleben* (Düsseldorf: Kommissionsverlag A. Bagel, n.d.), pp. 86, 96, 120–1. *JdH*, 1890–1903, passim.

43 Ehrhardt, pp. 117–19.

44 Friedrich Zunkel, "Industriebürgertum in Westdeutschland," in Hans-Ulrich Wehler, ed., *Moderne Deutsche Sozialgeschichte* (Cologne: Kiepenheuer and Witsch, 1966), pp. 312–15, 328–30, 333.

45 Hatzfeld, p. 215.

46 Ehrhardt, p. 54.

47 Zunkel, "Industriebürgertum," pp. 318–19. *VZ*, May 2, 1902. *Mitteilungen*, No. 8, *Die Grundbesitz- und Wohnungsverhältnisse in Düsseldorf und ihre Entwicklung seit 1903* (Düsseldorf: Statistisches Amt, 1912), p. 98*.

48 Hansjoachim Henning, *Das westdeutsche Bürgertum in der Epoche der Hochindustrialisierung, 1860–1914* (Wiesbaden: Franz Steiner, 1972), pp. 331, 334, 366–71, 473, 483–5.

49 Kehr, *Primat der Innenpolitik*, pp. 220–33. Hans Jaeger, *Unternehmer in der deutschen Politik, 1890–1918* (Bonn: Ludwig Röhrscheid, 1967), p. 176.

50 Zunkel, "Industriebürgertum," pp. 321, 334–5. Kehr, *Primat der Innenpolitik*, pp. 31–63. Jaeger, p. 291.

51 Henning, pp. 185, 188–92. Wehler, in Winkler, ed., *Organisierter Kapitalismus*, pp. 36–57. David Blackbourn, "The *Mittelstand* in German Society and Politics, 1871–1914," *Social History* 4 (January 1977):409–33. Robert Gellately, *The Politics of Economic Despair: Shopkeepers and German Politics, 1890–1914* (London: Sage, 1974), pp. 148–96.

52 *JdSA*, 1906, p. 9. *SdR*, n.s. 108:183; 207, Pt. 2:477.

53 Werner Conze, "Sozialgeschichte 1850–1918," in Hermann Aubin and Wolfgang Zorn, eds., *Handbuch der deutschen Wirtschafts- und Sozialgeschichte* (Stuttgart: Ernst Klett, 1976), 2:626. Blackbourn, pp. 420–2.

54 Blackbourn, "The *Mittelstand*," p. 422. *JdHW*, 1902/3–1906/7, 1910/11.

55 *JdHW*, 1902–3, Winkels, pp. 43–4, 47–9.

56 *JdHW*, 1920–3, p. 37.

57 Paul Adam, *Lebenserinnerungen eines alten Kunstbuchbinders* (Stuttgart: Max Hettler, 1951), p. 133.

58 *VZ*, July 30, 1907; December 16, 1909. The problem was not unique to Düsseldorf. Blackbourne, "The *Mittelstand*," pp. 423–9.

59 *SdR*, n.s. 108:183. *Mitteilungen*, No. 4, pp. 10*, 18*–19*. See Table A.6, Appendix.

60 Domestics are not counted as part of the labor force in German statistics. *SdR*, n.s. 108:85–91.

61 Ibid. *Mitteilungen*, No. 3, pp. 2–3.

62 Brandt, *Studien*, p. 403. *JdSA*, 1904, p. 15.

63 *SdR*, n.s. 108:85–91.

64 Eckhard Brockhaus, *Zusammensetzung und Neustrukturierung der Arbeiterklasse vor dem ersten Weltkrieg* (Munich: Trikont, 1975), pp. 42–67. Heidrun Homburg, "Anfänge des Taylorsystem in Deutschland vor dem Ersten Weltkriege," *Geschichte und Gesellschaft*, 4, No. 2 (1978):170–227. Schröder, *Arbeitergeschichte*, pp. 78–192.

65 Peter Berten, *Lebenslauf eines einfachen Menschen* (Düsseldorf: Selbstverlag, 1958), pp. 7–8, 23–7, 39–50.

66 The term *elite* has been chosen deliberately and is used as a description of the workers' position, not as an explanation of their consciousness and behavior. The concept of a labor aristocracy is too fraught with inconsistencies and polemics and relates too closely to the peculiarities of British working-class development to be useful in this context.

67 Hans Berlepsch, *Sozialpolitische Erfahrungen und Erinnerungen* (Mönchen-Gladbach: Volksvereinsverlag, 1925), pp. 19–20.

68 Ibid., p. 20. Lawrence Schofer, *The Formation of a Modern Labor Force in Upper Silesia, 1865–1914* (Berkeley, Calif.: University of California Press, 1975), pp. 137–64.

69 Eduard Bernstein, *Die Berliner Arbeiterbewegung* (Berlin: Dietz, 1924). Richard Comfort, *Revolutionary Hamburg* (Stanford, Calif.: Stanford University Press, 1966). Moring.

70 For discussions of craft consciousness, see James Hinton, *The First Shop Stewards Movement* (London: Allen and Unwin, 1973). Joan Wallach Scott, *The Glassworkers of Carmaux* (Cambridge, Mass.: Harvard University Press, 1974).

71 See especially Brockhaus; and Karl Heinz Roth, *Die "andere" Arbeiterbewegung* (Munich: Trikont, 1976).

72 For discussions of this theme, see Robert Q. Gray, *The Labour Aristocracy in Victorian Edinburgh* (Oxford: Clarendon Press, 1976). Gareth Stedman Jones, "Working-Class Culture and Working-Class Politics in London, 1870–1900," *Journal of Social History* 7 (1973–4): pp. 460–508. Sabel, pp. 1–49. Jonathan H. Zeitlin, "Rationalization and Resistance: Skilled Workers and the Transformation of the Division of Labor in the British Engineering Industry, 1830–1930" (B.A. thesis, Harvard University, 1977).

73 Barrington Moore, *Injustice: The Social Bases of Obedience and Revolt* (New York: M. E. Sharpe, 1978), p. 196.

74 The average working-class family spent 50 to 60 % of its income on food, most of the remainder on rent, clothing, insurance, and the like. *Beiträge zur statistischen Monatsberichten der Stadt Düsseldorf,* July 1909, pp. XL–XLII.

75 SADd, III 5739, 1893; III 5742, 1896; III 5389, 1892. *AZ,* November 22, 1890. *NV,* November 29, 1892; November 29, 1899.

76 *Mitteilungen,* No. 8, p. 30*. Wilhelm Kieber, "Stadtentwicklung und Wohnungsfrage in Düsseldorf" (Ph.D. diss., University of Münster), pp. 146–7.

77 SADd, III 6931, 1906; III 10154, December 25, 1905.

78 Moore, pp. 185–216.

79 See Helmut Böhme, *Deutschlands Weg zur Grossmacht* (Cologne: Kiepenheuer und Witsch, 1966). Arthur Rosenberg. *Entstehung der Weimarer Republik* (Frankfurt: Europäischer Verlagsanstalt, 1961). Hans Rosenberg, "Political and Social Consequences of the Great Depression of 1873–96 in Central Europe," *Economic History Review,* 13 (1943):58–73. Alexander Gerschenkron, *Bread and Democracy in Germany* (Berkeley, Calif.: University of California Press, 1943).

80 Kehr, *Primat der Innenpolitik,* pp. 31–52. Gordon A. Craig, *The Politics of the Prussian Army, 1640–1945* (Oxford: Oxford University Press, 1955), pp. 217–54.

81 Wolfram Fischer, *Wirtschaft und Gesellschaft im Zeitalter der Industrialisierung* (Göttingen: Vandenhoeck und Ruprecht, 1972), pp. 194–213. Hartmut Kaelble, *Industrielle Interessenpolitik in der Wilhelmischen Gesellschaft* (Berlin: Walter de Gruyter, 1967), pp. 114–46. Thomas Nipperdey, *Die Organisation der deutschen Parteien vor 1918* (Düsseldorf: Droste, 1961), pp. 375, 383, 387. Wehler, *Kaiserreich,* p. 90.

82 Wehler, *Kaiserreich,* p. 79.

83 Böhme, *Deutschlands Weg*, p. 420.

84 Dirk Stegmann, *Die Erben Bismarcks* (Cologne: Kiepenheuer und Witsch, 1970), pp. 13–15.

85 Rosenberg, *Entstehung*, pp. 28–31, 50.

86 Many workers who earned more than the 900 M minimum were nonetheless disenfranchised, for they had large families and thus paid less than the required 6 M in taxes. Brandt, *Studien*, pp. 141, 143, 451. Otto Most, *Die deutsche Stadt und ihre Verwaltung*, Vol. 1 (Berlin: G. J. Goschensche Verlagshandlung, 1912), pp. 26–30.

87 M. Rainer Lepsius, "Parteiensystem und Sozialstruktur: zum Problem der Demokratisierung der deutschen Gesellschaft," in Gerhard A. Ritter, ed., *Die deutschen Parteien vor 1918*, (Cologne: Kiepenheuer und Witsch, 1973), pp. 66–8.

88 Josef Hansen, *Preussen und das Rheinland von 1815–1915* (Bonn: A. Marcus und E. Webers, 1918), pp. 186–7. Jaeger, p. 112.

89 Ehrhardt, p. 108. Jaeger, pp. 112–19. Kaelble, pp. 52–3, 57–61. *75 Jahre Mannesmann*, passim.

90 Gerhard Adelmann, "Führende Unternehmer im Rheinland und in Westfalen, 1850–1879," *Rheinische Vierteljahresblätter*, 35, 1971, p. 351. Jaeger, p. 157. Stegmann, pp. 97–128. Wehler, *Kaiserreich*, pp. 90–105.

91 Weidenhaupt, p. 131.

92 Adelmann, pp. 351–2. Jaeger, pp. 87–94. James Sheehan, "Liberalism and the City in Nineteenth Century Germany," *Past and Present* 51 (May 1971):131.

93 Hatzfeld, pp. 54, 215. According to Hatzfeld, Poensgen ran consciously as a representative of the emerging metal sector, whose leaders cooperated closely to influence municipal politics. p. 54.

94 Weidenhaupt, p. 136. Josef Wilden. *Gründer und Gestalter der Rhein-Ruhr Industrie* (Düsseldorf: August Bagel, 1951), p. 135. Jaeger, pp. 87–90. *AZ*, November 25, 1890.

95 Weidenhaupt, p. 136.

96 Gisbert Knopp, *Die preussische Verwaltung des Regierungsbezirks Düsseldorf in den Jahren 1897–1919* (Cologne: Grote, 1974), pp. 54–5.

97 Wehler, in Winkler, ed., *Organisierter Kapitalismus*, pp. 40–50.

98 Nipperdey, *Organisation*, pp. 86–175.

99 Sheehan, "Liberalism," pp. 119–20.

100 Fischer, *Wirtschaft*, pp. 194–6.

101 *JdH*, 1899–1903, passim.

102 Thomas Nipperdey, "Interessenverbände und Parteien in Deutschland vor dem ersten Weltkrieg," in Wehler, ed., *Moderne deutsche Sozialgeschichte*, p. 375.

103 Peter Maslowski, *Was ist die deutsche Zentrumspartei? Klerikalismus und Proletariat* (Berlin: Vereinigung Internationaler Verlagsanstalten, 1925), p. 19. Heinrich Karl Schmitz, *Anfänge und Entwicklung der Arbeiterbewegung im Raum Düsseldorf* (Hannover: Verlag für Literatur und Zeitgeschehen, 1968), pp. 115–29.

104 SADd, XXI 232, August 26, 1911.

105 Lepsius, p. 70. Maslowski, pp. 7–12. Ronald J. Ross, *Beleagured Tower: the Dilemma of Political Catholicism in Wilhelmine Germany* (Notre Dame, Ind.: University of Notre Dame Press, 1976), pp. 63–4.

106 John K. Zeender, *The German Center Party, 1890–1906* (Philadelphia: American Philosophical Society, 1976), p. 36.

107 Ross, pp. 48–56.

108 August Erdmann, *Die christliche Gewerkschaften, insbesondere ihr Verhältnis zu Zentrum und Kirche* (Stuttgart: Dietz, 1914), pp. 29–30, 108–116.

109 Ross, pp. 42–5, 72–4.

110 August Erdmann, *Die christliche Arbeiterbewegung in Deutschland* (Stuttgart: Dietz, 1909), pp. 205–10. Erdmann, *Gewerkschaften*, pp. 108–16. Ross, pp. 79–105.
111 Zeender, pp. 4, 14–15.
112 Ross, p. 135.
113 Wehler, *Kaiserreich*, p. 122.
114 Sheehan, "Liberalism" pp. 133–5.
115 Ross, pp. 134–7.
116 *VZ*, August 27, 1903.

2. Social democracy and political Catholicism

1 Schmitz, pp. 13–30. For the early history of the socialist movement, see Ulrich Boettcher, *Anfänge und Entwicklung der Arbeiterbewegung in Bremen von der Revolution 1848 bis zur Aufhebung des Sozialistengesetzes 1890* (Bremen: Carl Schünemann, 1953). Hugo Eckert, *Liberal-oder Sozialdemokratie, Frühgeschichte der Nürnberger Arbeiterbewegung* (Stuttgart: Ernst Klett, 1969). Franz Mehring, *Geschichte der deutschen Sozialdemokratie*, Part 2 (Stuttgart: Dietz, 1898). Hans Pelger, "Zur sozialdemokratischen Bewegung in der Rheinprovinz vor dem Sozialistengesetz," *Archiv für Sozialgeschichte* 5 (1965):377–406.
2 Schmitz, pp. 43, 70, 116–18, 126. Erdmann, *Arbeiterbewegung*, p. 118. Only Essen and Aachen had larger Catholic workers' associations.
3 Schmitz, pp. 123–7, 131–4.
4 *VZ*, October 27, 1906. SADd, III 6704, early 1890s.
5 SADd, III 6915, August 30, 1886; January 1, 26, 27, 1887. Berten, p. 83. Schmitz, p. 150.
6 StADd, Reg. Dd. 8843, March 15 and September 12, 1888. *NV*, September 3, 1899.
7 SADd, III 6918, September 11, 1890.
8 Ibid.
9 *VZ*, October 27, 1906. Hermann Herberts, *Zur Geschichte der SPD in Wuppertal* (Wuppertal: Molkenbuhr, 1963), p. 126.
10 SADd, III 5816, n.d. The quotes are from the lead editorial of the first issue.
11 In areas where the laws were applied leniently, the unions became depoliticized in an effort to survive. Boettcher, p. 151.
12 For comparable developments elsewhere, see Moring, p. 18, and Vernon Lidtke, *The Outlawed Party: Social Democracy in Germany, 1878–1890* (Princeton, N.J.: Princeton University Press, 1966), p. 331.
13 Karl Erich Born, *Staat und Sozialpolitik seit Bismarcks Sturz* (Wiesbaden: Franz Steiner Verlag, 1957), pp. 7–30. Gerhard A. Ritter, *Die Arbeiterbewegung im Wilhelmischen Reich* (Berlin: Colloquium Verlag, 1959), pp. 15–26, 79–82, 97–9.
14 *NV*, February 12, 1898.
15 *NV*, January 2, 1898. StAK, 403 7159, January 1, 1893. The Catholic press was the main political competitor of the social democratic one and dated back to the 1870s. Catholic efforts to establish a special workers' paper in Düsseldorf failed repeatedly. Friedrich Schubert, *Düsseldorfer Zeitungswesen in Vergangenheit und Gegenwart* (Düsseldorf: Mathias Strucken, 1932), p. 14. Hans Stöcker, *250 Jahre Düsseldorfer Presse* (Düsseldorf: Rheinische-Bergische Druckerei und Verlagsgesellschaft, 1962), p. 26.
16 *NV*, October 6, 1900. The strict application of the anti-socialist laws in the Rhineland enabled the *General Anzeiger* press to gain an insurmountable lead over the SPD

papers. Kurt Koszyk, *Anfänge und frühe Entwicklung der sozialdemokratischen Presse im Ruhrgebiet, 1875–1903* (Dortmund: Fr. Wilhelm Ruhfus, 1953), pp. 51–2.

17 Arguments about the Social Democrats' organizational fetishism and passivity are made by Ritter, *Die Arbeiterbewegung im wilhelmischen Reich*, p. 98. Peter Nettl. "The German Social Democratic Party, 1890–1914 as a Political Model," *Past and Present* 30 (April 1965):66–7, 70, 91. Guenther Roth, pp. 165–9, 269, 283. Steinberg, passim.

18 Lepsius, pp. 66–70.

19 Adolf Braun, *Die Gewerkschaften vor dem Kriege* (Berlin: Dietz, 1925), p. 60. Ludwig Kantorowicz, *Die sozialdemokratische Presse Deutschlands* (Tübingen: Mohr, 1922), pp. 9–11.

20 Eric Hobsbawm, "Class Consciousness in History," in Istvan Meszaros, ed., *Aspects of Class Consciousness and History,* (New York: Herder and Herder, 1972), p. 14.

21 *NV*, January 5, 1891.

22 SADd, III 6918, March 18, 1891. StAK, 403 6836, September 1892; 403 9048, February 11, 1895. StADd, Reg. Dd. 8845, October 31, 1894; Reg. Dd. 9044, February 13, 1895. *NV*, January 5, 1893.

23 SADd, III 6918, March 18, 1891.

24 Ritter, *Die Arbeiterbewegung im wilhelmischen Reich*, p. 124. SADd, III 6224, July 1, 1893.

25 SADd, III 6224, 1893–5.

26 *NV*, November 25, 1893.

27 *NV*, January 5, 1891.

28 Ritter, *Die Arbeiterbewegung im wilhelmischen Reich*, pp. 107–27.

29 SADd, III 4590, II and IV Quartels, 1890; III 4591, I and IV Quartels, 1892; 1893. *JdH*, 1890, p. 3; 1891, pp. 4, 62, 66. Renard, p. 143. *NV*, December 15, 1892.

30 *NV*. January 13, 20, November 30, 1893. SADd, III 6224, January 6, October 8, 1893. passim.

31 Ritter, *Die Arbeiterbewegung im wilhelmischen Reich*, pp. 69–70, 110–11.

32 The country had a few industrial towns such as Gerresheim, Benrath, and Hilden, several artisan villages, and some small farms.

33 Moring, pp. 20–3. Ritter, *Die Arbeiterbewegung im wilhelmischen Reich*, p. 71.

34 *NV*, September 24, 1892; March 3, 1896. StAK, 403 9048, July 12, 1891; March 13, 1893.

35 Ritter, *Die Arbeiterbewegung im wilhelmischen Reich*, pp. 71, 134ff. Moring, pp. 20–1.

36 *NV*, September 24, 1892. StADd, Reg. Dd. 9028, November 2, 1893.

37 *NV*, March 3, 1896.

38 The Prussian organization law prohibited the national affiliation of political groups. Therefore the *Vertrauensmänner* were formally independent of the local Social Democratic Association.

39 SADd, III 6918, March 18, 1891; III 6924, September 11, 1898. *NV*, January 25, 1895.

40 *AZ*, October 4, 1890. *VZ*, August 27, 1909. SADd, III 6925, October 23, 1899. Between 1892 and 1901 Düsseldorf received only 900 M of the more than 500,000 M given by the national executive to the press. *VZ*, January 28, 1902.

41 *AZ, NV*, passim. Koszyk, pp. 137, 141.

42 *NV*, January 25, 1895; April 9, 1896.

43 NV, January 5, 1891; November 1, 1894.

44 Ritter, *Die Arbeiterbewegung im wilhelmischen Reich*, pp. 47–8, 68–70.

45 *VZ*, August 27, 1909.

46 Ibid. *NV*, January 12, 13, 1892. SADd, III 5934, 1899; III 6224, January 1, 1897.

47 *NV*, January 12, 13, 1892; January 17, November 1, December 18, 1894; October 3, December 31, 1895.

48 *NV*, November 26, 1895; April 3, 1896. SADd, III 6556, 1891 passim; III 6918, March 18, 1891.
49 *NV*, October 3, 1895; April 1, 9, 1896. StAK, 403 6836, May 13, 1892. StADd, Reg. Dd. 9045, September 15, 1896; September 12, 1899. SADd, III 6924, June 17, 1899.
50 See Chapter 3.
51 *NV*, January 9, 1898.
52 SADd, III 4590, I Quartel 1891; III 6918, December 19, 1893; III 6918, February 1896. *NV*, February 28, 1895.
53 *NV*, January 10, 22, 23, 30, February 19, 1895; December 9, 1898. SADd III 6224, July 8, 25, 1896. John Foster's study of Oldham, England, has shown that a cohesive working-class community can use boycotts successfully: "Nineteenth Century Towns: A Class Dimension," in H. J. Dyos, ed., *The Study of Urban History* (New York: St. Martin's, 1968), pp. 281–90, 295–6.
54 *NV*, November 16, 1894; December 9, 1898. Klaus Saul, *Staat, Industrie und Arbeiterbewegung im Kaiserreich* (Düsseldorf: Bertelsmann, 1974), pp. 188–91.
55 *Düsseldorfer Zeitung*, March 30, 1892.
56 StADd, Reg. Dd. 9028, October 25, 1893.
57 *AZ*, October 14, 1890. *NV*, May 25, 1892; February 7, April 19, October 7, 1893; September 21, October 23, 1895; January 1, 1898; September 3, 1899.
58 *NV*, October 11, 1895.
59 Gerhard A. Ritter, *Arbeiterbewegung, Parteien und Parlamentarismus* (Göttingen: Vandenhoeck und Ruprecht, 1976), pp. 17–18.
60 Heiner Grote, *Sozialdemokratie und Religion* (Tübingen: J. C. Mohr, 1968), p. 231, points out that the Social Democrats were aware of the complexity of Catholicism's appeal from the 1870s on.
61 Nipperdey, *Die Organisation*, pp. 270–1. Peter Molt, *Der Reichstag vor der improvisierten Revolution* (Cologne: Westdeutscher Verlag, 1963), pp. 266–7. Lepsius, p. 70.
62 Maslowski, p. 8. Knopp. p. 183, notes that missions "sharply attacked the Social Democrats and warned workers about the aims of this party."
63 Erdmann, *Gewerkschaften*, p. 20.
64 Zeender, p. 77.
65 SADd, III 6396, 1896.
66 *Jahresbericht des Bezirks Verbandes katholischer Arbeiter Vereine von Düsseldorf Stadt und Land von das Jahr 1912*, n.p.
67 Erdmann, *Arbeiterbewegung*, p. 155.
68 Erdmann, *Gewerkschaften*, pp. 23–4. The quotes are from the founding statement of the People's Association.
69 Ibid., p. 21, 30. Ross, pp. 62–3. Molt, pp. 267–8.
70 Emil Ritter, *Die katholisch-soziale Bewegung Deutschlands im 19. Jahrhundert und der Volksverein* (Cologne: J. P. Bachem, 1954), pp. 188–200, 203–7.
71 Erdmann, *Gewerkschaften*, pp. 34–5, 169–70. At least 90% of the union members were Catholic. Ross, p. 45.
72 StADd, Reg. Dd. 9052, September 1, 1901.
73 Erdmann, *Arbeiterbewegung*, p. 508. Ross, pp. 93–4. Michael Berger, "Arbeiterbewegung und Demokratisierung. Die wirtschaftliche, politische und gesellschaftliche Gleichberechtigung der Arbeiter im Verständnis der katholischen Arbeiterbewegung im Wilhelmischen Deutschland zwischen 1890 und 1914" (Ph.D diss., University of Freiburg, 1971), pp. 93, 110–11, 119.
74 *VZ*, April 13, 1905.
75 Georg Eckert, *Aus den Lebensberichten deutscher Fabrikarbeiter*. (Braunschweig: Alfred Limbach, 1953), pp. 58, 65.

76 See Chapter 6.
77 Ross, pp. 42–8.
78 Berger, pp. 161, 209–11.
79 Emil Ritter, pp. 29–42.
80 SADd, III 5740, 1893. *NV,* March 5, 1896. Clemens Bauer, "Wandlungen der sozialpolitischen Ideenwelt im deutschen Katholizismus des 19. Jahrhunderts," in Sektion für Sozial- und Wirtschaftswissenschaft der Görres-Gesellschaft, ed., *Die soziale Frage und der Katholizismus* (Paderborn: Ferdinand Schöning, 1931), pp. 11–46.
81 Ibid., pp. 15, 26–30. Born, p. 48. Emil Ritter, pp. 120–5. Zeender, p. 36.
82 Bauer, p. 45. Born, pp. 48–51. Maslowski, pp. 77–9.
83 Born, pp. 47–53.
84 Ibid., pp. 51–2. Zeender, p. 38.
85 *Düsseldorfer Volksblatt,* February 10, 1890.
86 Ibid., April 29, 1893; June 1893, passim.
87 Ibid., June 5, 1893. The liberal *Düsseldorfer Zeitung* made the same charge. June 10, 14, 1893; May 2, 1895.
88 Zeender, p. 75.
89 Saul, p. 213. Stegmann, p. 101.
90 *JdH,* 1889, p. 7; 1892, p. 8; 1893, pp. 5–6; 1894, p. 7; 1895, p. 13; 1896, pp. 13–14. Wilden, *100 Jahre,* pp. 120–1. Berlepsch, p. 167. Born, p. 232.
91 *Düsseldorfer Volksblatt,* June 5, 1893.
92 Ibid., February 18, 1890. Italics in original.
93 Ibid., February 10, 1890.
94 Ibid., February 17, 1890. Italics in original.
95 *NV,* February 4, 1892. SADd, III 6923, July 27, 1897.
96 Grote, pp. 8–123, passim. Vernon Lidtke, "August Bebel and German Social Democracy's Relation to the Christian Churches," *Journal of the History of Ideas,* 27, No. 2 (April–June 1966):250, 255–8.
97 *NV,* March 17, 1894.
98 Ibid. Adolf Levenstein's survey of several thousand free trade unionists confirms this indifference but not hostility to religion: *Die Arbeiterfrage* (Munich: Rheinhardt, 1912), pp. 324–6, 334–5, 342–3, 352–3.
99 *AZ,* October 4, 1890. *NV,* February 13, August 6, 1892; June 8, 11, 24, 1893. Grote, pp. 167, 177.
100 *NV,* June 24, 1898.
101 *NV,* May and June 1898, passim.
102 *NV,* September 13, 1898.
103 *NV,* February 18, 1898.
104 StADd, Reg. Dd. 9044, 1895.
105 Ernst-Detlef Broch, *Die katholische Arbeitervereine in der Stadt Köln, 1890–1901* (Wentorf/Hamburg: Einhorn Presse, 1977), p. 31*. Wilhelm Spael, *Das katholische Deutschland im 20. Jahrhundert, 1890–1945* (Würzberg: Echter Verlag, 1964), p. 21.
106 *NV,* July 27, 1893; December 12, 1895; March 5, 1896. SADd, III 5740, 1893. Accident rates rose from 1,200 to 1,600 injuries and 4 or 5 deaths in the early 1890s to 2,400 to 2,600 injuries and 25 to 30 deaths at the turn of the century, a rate much higher than that of the expansion of the labor force. SADd, III 4590–4596. 1890–1903.
107 Gaston Rimlinger, *Welfare Policy and Industrialization in Europe, America and Russia* (New York: John Wiley & Sons, 1971), pp. 123–5.
108 Heinrich Herkner, *Die Arbeiterfrage,* Vol. 1, *Arbeiterfrage und Sozialreform* (Berlin: Walter de Gruyter, 1922), pp. 378–9.
109 Ritter, *Die Arbeiterbewegung im wilhelmischen Reich,* p. 41.
110 StAK, 403 9048, December 3, 1890. Moritz W. T. Bromme, *Lebensgeschichte eines*

modernen Fabrikarbeiters. Ed. Paul Göhre (Jena: Diederichs, 1905). Franz Louis Fischer, *Arbeiterschicksale* (Berlin: Buchverlag der *Hilfe*, 1906). Wenzel Holek, *Lebensgang eines deutsch-tschechen Handarbeiters* (Jena: Diederichs, 1930); and *Vom Handarbeiter zum Jugenderzieher* (Jena: Diederichs, 1921). Eugen May, "Mein Lebenslauf, 1889–1920," in Eugene Rosenstock, ed., *Werkstattaussiedlung* (Berlin: Julius Springer, 1922), pp. 12–72.

111 *NV*, October 9, 1898; October 15, 1899.

112 *NV*, May 23, 1893. Zeender, pp. 28–34, 53–4.

113 Although the electoral statistics are available for every district in the city, the occupational statistics are not. Therefore it is possible to estimate the percentage of the social democratic electorate that was working class and Catholic but not to do more refined analysis.

114 The percentage of Catholics voting for the Center Party was higher in the government district of Düsseldorf than nationally but was dropping everywhere. Johannes Schauff, *Die deutschen Katholiken und die Zentrumspartei* (Cologne: Bachem, 1928), pp. 74, 80.

115 Roughly 19,000 of urban Düsseldorf's 33,951 male workers were over 25 and hence eligible to vote. Assuming that they turned out in the same proportion as the total electorate, 73%, then 14,000 voted in 1893. Seventy-two percent of the population was Catholic. Thus, there were approximately 10,000 working-class Catholic voters and 3,900 Protestant ones. The total SPD vote in the city was 7,324 in the first election.

116 R. Blank, "Die soziale Zusammensetzung der sozialdemokratischen Wählerschaft Deutschlands," *Archiv für Sozialwissenschaft und Sozialpolitik*, n.s. 4 (1905):p. 529.

117 Lepsius, p. 69. Schauff, p. 84.

118 SADd, III 4591, II Quartel 1893.

119 Frank Parkin, *Class Inequality and Political Order* (New York: Praeger, 1971), pp. 90, 96–9, on the role of parties in creating radical consciousness.

120 Guenther Roth, p. 201.

121 This is the contention of Arthur Rosenberg, *A History of the German Republic* (New York: Russell and Russell, 1965), p. 12.

122 *NV*, March 1, 1892.

123 *AZ*, November 13, 1890. *NV*, January 16, 1892; April 28, 1894; April 3, 19, 1895.

124 *NV*, January 2, 1896.

125 Guenther Roth, pp. 199–203.

126 *AZ*, November 20, 1890.

127 *NV*, November 25, 1893.

128 *NV*, July 6, 1892.

129 Lidtke, *The Outlawed Party*, pp. 285–6, 289.

130 *NV*, January 19, 1893.

131 *NV*, November 8, 1892.

132 Ibid., and October 10, 1893.

133 *NV*, October 10, 1893.

134 *NV*, August 30, 1892.

135 *NV*, November 8, 1892; October 10, 1893.

136 *NV*, November 8, 1892.

137 Lidtke, *The Outlawed Party*, pp. 305–8.

138 Hans Manfred Bock, *Geschichte der "linken Radikalismus" in Deutschland* (Frankfurt: Suhrkamp, 1976), pp. 30–49, 58–62.

139 StAK, 403 9048, November 30, 1892. Ritter, *Die Arbeiterbewegung im wilhelmischen Reich*, pp. 83–6.

140 Parkin, p. 90.

3. A false start

1 Theodor Cassau, *Die Gewerkschaftsbewegung. Ihre Soziologie und ihr Kampf* (Haberstadt: H. Meyer, 1925), p. 2. Ritter, *Die Arbeiterbewegung im wilhelmischen Reich*, p. 150.

2 *NV*, December 12, 1898. *VZ*, April 13, 1905.

3 See Table A.2, Appendix.

4 *NV*, February 12, 1901. SADd, III 5745, November 1898; III 5981, 1898–1903.

5 *NV*, September 3, 1899. According to the chamber of commerce, the guilds "had a most questionable side effect. . . . The Social Democrats have used them to break into artisan circles. It used to be very difficult for them to organize journeymen, but now the journeymen's committees provide them with a legal form of organization which they use." *JdH*, 1899, p. 37.

6 *NV*, July 4, 1893; March 2, July 23, 1894; February 12, 1896; September 4, 1899.

7 *NV*, March 14, 1896.

8 SADd, III 6712, 1894, 1896; III 6713, 1897–8.

9 SADd, III 6225, June 18, 1901; III 5743, 1896.

10 Moore, pp. 257–69. Ritter, *Arbeiterbewegung, Parteien*, p. 93.

11 SADd, III 7027, June 3, 1897, and flyer, n.d. Ritter, *Arbeiterbewegung, Parteien*, p. 85.

12 *NV*, February 12, 1901.

13 SADd, III 6224, December 23, 1896.

14 Patrick de Laubier, "Esquisse d'une théorie du syndicalisme," *Sociologie du Travail* 10 (1968):364–5, 374.

15 Fritz Klein, *Deutschland von 1897/8 bis 1917* (Berlin: VEB Deutscher Verlag der Wissenschaft, 1961), pp. 74–5. SADd, III 5381, 1891–5, passim.

16 Klein, p. 72.

17 SADd, III 4594, III Quartel, 1897; III 6224, July 10, 1897. *NV*, January 9, 1898.

18 StADd, Reg. Dd. 24690, July 1898. SADd, III 5381, May 11, 13, August 8, October 1, 1898. *NV*, June 18, July 29, 1898.

19 StADd, Reg. Dd. 24690, July 1898. SADd, III 5381, October 7, 1896. *NV*, August 16, December 7, 1898.

20 SADd, III 4593, III Quartel 1896.

21 Edward Shorter and Charles Tilly, *Strikes in France, 1830–1968* (Cambridge: Cambridge University Press, 1974), p. 68.

22 Douglas A. Hibbs, "Long-Run Trends in Strike Activity in Comparative Perspective," (Cambridge, Mass.: MIT, 1976), p. 26.

23 Roland Trompe, cited in Shorter and Tilly, p. 68.

24 SADd, III 6224, August 25, 1896.

25 SADd, III 6225, July 31, 1898.

26 Authors such as Stearns play down the meaning of personal strikes. Peter Stearns, "The European Labor Movement and the Working Classes, 1890–1914," in Harvey Mitchell and Peter Stearns, *Workers and Protest* (Itasca, Ill.: Peacock, 1971), pp. 175–6.

27 SADd, III 4594, IV Quartel 1897. *NV*, September 29, October 3, November 2, 1894. *VZ*, June 28, July 12, August 12, 1901.

28 SADd, III 5381, 1896–9, passim.

29 *NV*, May 21, 1898.

30 SADd, III 5381, letters to police from Blasberg and Co., June 30, 1898, and from employers' association in woodworking, September 30, 1898.

31 Karl-Gustav Werner, "Gründung des deutschen Arbeitgeberbundes für das Baugewerbe 1899 und seine Entwicklung bis 1910," in Heinz Josef Varain, ed.,

Interessenverbände in Deutschland (Cologne: Kiepenheuer und Witsch, 1973), pp. 197–206.

32 Braun, *Die Gewerkschaften vor dem Kriege*, p. 389.

33 Norma N. von Ragenfeld, "The Attitude and Behavior of the Prussian Civil Service Toward the Working Class in the Rhineland, 1889–1905" (Ph.D. diss.; University of Connecticut, 1976), pp. 136, 233.

34 Cassau, pp. 254–5.

35 Under the Prussian organization law, the police were entitled to attend the meetings of political organizations and demand membership lists from them.

36 SADd, III 6224, January 28, 1897.

37 *NV*, January 21, 1898.

38 Ibid. SADd, III 5381, December 24, 1898.

39 SADd, III 4593, IV Quartel 1896.

40 SADd, III 5381, February 16, 24, 1898; June 7 and July 1899.

41 SADd, III 5381, September 30, 1898.

42 Ritter, *Arbeiterbewegung, Parteien*, p. 94. Cassau, p. 291.

43 Scott's study of Carmaux offers an example of workers who could influence municipal politics once they realized its importance to their lives and their relationships with their employers. Pp. 115–18.

44 Ritter, *Die Arbeiterbewegung im wilhelmischen Reich*, pp. 212–13. Herkner, p. 539. *Parteitagen*, p. 32.

45 *AZ*, November 1, 1890.

46 Cassau, p. 106. Rimlinger, p. 126. Heinz Josef Varain, *Freie Gewerkschaften, Sozialdemokratie und Staat: Die Politik der Generalkommission unter der Führung Carl Legiens, 1890–1920* (Düsseldorf: Droste, 1956), p. 55.

47 SADd, III 6224, October 10, 1893; III 6225, February 10, 12, 1901. *NV*, March 24, 1896.

48 Born, pp. 106–8. Herkner, pp. 152–3. *NV*, March 15, 1892.

49 *JdH*, 1895, p. 54; 1898–9, pp. 232–3. SADd, III 6224, January 5, 10, 1894. *NV*, May 4, 1893; November 22, 1897.

50 *NV*, November 19, 1899.

51 SADd, III 5739, 1891. *NV*, March 26, 1892.

52 *NV*, March 26, 1892.

53 *NV*, April 14, 1892; April 8, 1893; February 28, 1894.

54 *NV*, November 18, December 4, 9, 11, 23, 28, 1895; January 13, 1896. The Hirsch-Duncker slate got 250 votes.

55 *Düsseldorfer Volksblatt*, January 17, 1898.

56 *NV*, December 16, 1899.

57 Paul Gerlach, "Die Düsseldorfer Arbeiterbewegung," in Lux, ed., *Düsseldorf*, p. 69. SADd, III 5744, July 25, 1897. *NV*, April 23, 26, 1896; November 26, December 6, 1899.

58 SADd, III 6224, January 6, October 8, 1893. *NV*, January 24, 1893.

59 Helmut Albrecht, "Die Entwicklung der Düsseldorfer Arbeiterwohnungen" (medical diss., University of Düsseldorf, 1939), p. 7. Kieber, pp. 118–19, 146–07.

60 *NV*, October 14, 1899.

61 *NV*, September 16, October 9, 10, 14, November 5, 18, 1899; October 23, 1900.

62 *NV*, January 19, October 24, 1899.

63 Ritter, *Die Arbeiterbewegung im wilhelmischen Reich*, p. 41. Moring, pp. 33, 57–8.

64 *NV*, October 6, 1900.

65 Berten, pp. 85–6. Köllmann, *Barmen*, pp. 52–3.

66 *NV*, March 29, 1896.
67 Studies of the party elsewhere do not indicate whether the press covered the movement better than in Düsseldorf.
68 *NV*, January 21, 1895.
69 StAK, 403 7158, July 1898. Because of financial and time constraints, workers bought only one paper.
70 *NV*, September 19, 1900.
71 StAK, 403 7158, July 1898.
72 SADd, III 6923, October–November 1897, passim.
73 *NV*, October 8, 1895; October 6, 1900.
74 Gottfried Mergner, *Arbeiterbewegung und Intelligenz* (Starnberg: Werner Raith, 1973), p. 28
75 There are no attendance figures available for the early 1890s.
76 *NV*, August 30, September 10, 1892; January 5, 1893; August 16, 21, November 1, 2, 1894.
77 Ibid. Steinberg, pp. 140–1.
78 *NV*, August 8, October 10, 1895.
79 SADd, III 6923, April 19, September 7, 1896.
80 SADd, III 6923, September 7, 1896. Michels, *Political Parties*, pp. 86–7. Steinberg, p. 141.
81 SADd, III 6557, February 8, 1892.
82 SADd, III 6923, June 6, July 28, November 22, 1897; III 6924, April 5, May 20, June 11, August 29, September 27, 1898; February 20, June 8, 22, 1899.
83 SADd, III 6923, April 19, 1896; III 6924, August 30, 1898.
84 *NV*, January 14, 1899. StADd, Reg. Dd. 9052, August 1901. The police claimed that the 1898 figure was inflated by 100.
85 SADd, III 6225, June 18, 1901.
86 SADd, III, 6225, September–December 1899, passim.
87 Emil Ritter, pp. 228–45.
88 *Düsseldorfer Volksblatt*, May 26, 1898.
89 *NV*, December 12, 1898.
90 SADd, III 10106, 1898. *NV*, June 19, 1898.
91 *Düsseldorfer Volksblatt*, May 23, 1898.
92 *NV*, June 3, 1898.
93 According to Blank's calculations, 13,286 workers participated in the 1898 election, of whom roughly 9,500 were Catholic. P. 592.
94 The Center Party destroyed its records for the pre–World War I period in 1921. The Catholic press does not indicate whether the Center Party and its affiliates realized that they were losing migrant workers.
95 Eckert Kehr, *Schlachtflottenbau und Parteipolitik, 1894–1901* (Vaduz: Kraus Reprint, 1965), pp. 374–5.
96 Zeender, p. 78.
97 Ibid., pp. 45–7. Kehr, *Schlachtflottenbau*, p. 287.
98 Kehr, *Schlachtflottenbau*, p. 205.
99 *NV*, March 27, 29, April 10, 1898. SADd, III 6924, May 12, 1898.
100 *NV*, March 26, 1898.

4. Ideological unity and organizational disarray

1 Ritter, *Die Arbeiterbewegung im wilhelmischen Reich*, pp. 134–7.
2 Cora Stephan aus Strang, "Das Verhältnis von Strategie und Theorie in den Debatten der deutschen Sozialdemokratie von den Anfängen bis zum Sozialistengesetz" (Ph.D.

diss., University of Frankfurt, 1976), pp. 22–55.
3 Gerschenkron, pp. 41–50. Paul Massing, *Rehearsal for Destruction* (New York: Harper & Bros., 1949), pp. 60–113.
4 Ritter, *Die Arbeiterbewegung im wilhelmischen Reich*, pp. 139–42.
5 *NV*, November 27, 1894; July 22, 1895.
6 *NV*, August 27, 1895. The provincial party congress took a similarly hard line. *Parteitagen*, p. 19.
7 *NV*, October 16, 1895.
8 *NV*, August 3, 1898. With the exception of Elberfeld and Barmen, Social Democrats throughout the region opted for abstention. *NV*, December 25, 1898.
9 *NV*, September 1, 1900. The 1900 Mainz party congress had required that all Social Democrats participate in Landtag elections. Ritter, *Die Arbeiterbewegung im wilhelmischen Reich*, p. 182.
10 SADd, III 6923, May 2, 1897.
11 *NV*, April 1, 1893; June 30, 1894.
12 Steinberg, p. 43.
13 *NV*, August 31, 1895.
14 *NV*, March 19, 1898.
15 *NV*, November 12, 1892. Italics in original.
16 *NV*, September 16, 1895. Italics in original.
17 *NV*, March 20, 1895.
18 SADd, III 6926, March 24, 1902.
19 SADd, III 6923, March 21, 1897.
20 SADd, III 6925, March 19, 1900.
21 Steinberg, p. 61.
22 Nettl, "The German Social Democratic Party," p. 67.
23 *NV*, March 20, 1895.
24 SADd, III 6924, March 19, 1899.
25 *NV*, March 19, 1896.
26 Steinberg, p. 142.
27 SADd, III 6924, March 19, 1899.
28 *AZ*, October 2, December 6, 1890. *NV*, March 1, July 6, 1892; February 23, August 19, 1893; September 14, 1894; May 4, 1898, Nettl, "The German Social Democratic Party," p. 73.
29 SADd, III 6926, May 2, 1902.
30 Moore, pp. 185 216. Peter N. Stearns, *Lives of Labor* (New York: Holmes and Meier, 1975), pp. 335–53.
31 Haupt, "Working-Class Movement," p. 11.
32 SADd, III 6925, March 19, 1900.
33 *VZ*, March 18, 1904.
34 Haupt argues that history as tradition must do both: "Working-Class Movement," p. 23.
35 Groh, *Negative Integration*, p. 58. Guenther Roth, pp. 170–1. Steinberg, p. 60.
36 Stephan aus Strang, p. 295.
37 Levenstein, pp. 213–43. Moore, pp. 208–16.
38 Steinberg, pp. 138–9.
39 *NV*, February 23, 1893.
40 Steinberg, pp. 89–96. Peter Gay, *The Dilemma of Democratic Socialism* (New York: Collier Books, 1962), pp. 166–252, passim.
41 SADd, III 6924, April 21, 1899, *NV*, September 6, 1899.
42 *NV*, September 6, 1899. Italics in original.
43 *VZ*, June 9, 1902, SADd, III 6927, March 23, 1903.

44 *JdSA*, 1901, p. 14; 1903, p. 12, SADd, III 4596, IV Quartel 1902. *VZ*, September 14, October 24, 1901; January 24, 1902.
45 Strikes did not decline nationally. Georg Frey, *Die Streikbewegung in Deutschland 1900 bis 1910* (Bamberg: St. Otto Verlag, 1927), p. 6. Seeling, p. 69. *VZ*, June 9, 10, 1900; January 25, 1902; August 13, 14, and 17, 1903.
46 *NV*, September 6, 1899.
47 SADd, III 6924, April 21, 1899.
48 Nettl, "The German Social Democratic Party," pp. 68–9. Grimpe, the Reichstag candidate who worked for the Elberfeld *Freie Presse*, was the only "practical man," and he received little support when he pleaded for more lenient attitudes toward intellectuals. *VZ*, October 23, 1903.
49 Moring, pp. 63ff.
50 Haupt, "Working-Class Movement," p. 23.
51 *NV*, September 6, 1899.
52 SADd, III 6926, October 9, 1901.
53 Ibid. SADd, III 6927, October 10, 1902.
54 *VZ*, September 21, 1901.
55 Steinberg argues that *Praktizismus* dominated the SPD after the turn of the century. Pp. 124–5.
56 *VZ*, September 21, 1901.
57 SADd, III 6928, October 15, 1903. *VZ*, October 23, 1903. Michels, *Political Parties*, pp. 298–302.
58 SADd, III 6928, October 15, 1903.
59 *VZ*, October 23, 1903.
60 *VZ*, October 14, 1903.
61 *VZ*, October 23, 1903. This conception was widespread in the SPD. Massimo L. Salvadori, *Kautsky e la revoluzione socialista 1880/1938* (Milan: Feltrinelli, 1978), pp. 70–1.
62 *VZ*, May 5, 1904.
63 Salvadori, pp. 67–83. Eric Matthias, "Kautsky und Kautskyanismus," *Marxismusstudien* 2 (1957):170–2.
64 *NV*, November 27, 1894. *VZ*, October 14, 1903.
65 *NV*, August 25, 1900.
66 *VZ*, September 21, 1901.
67 SADd, III 6928, October 12, 1903.
68 Nettl, "The German Social Democratic Party," pp. 68–70, 88, 91. Ritter, *Die Arbeiterbewegung im wilhelmischen Reich*, pp. 206–7.
69 Matthias, p. 165. Guenther Roth, p. 283. Stephan aus Strang, p. 295.
70 Tables A.1 and A.2, Appendix.
71 *VZ*, May 28, 1902.
72 *VZ*, December 14, 16, 1901. *Bericht des Gewerkschaftskartell*, 1902, pp. 2–4.
73 See Chapter 7.
74 StADd, Reg. Dd. 9050, September 12, 1899. SADd, III 6925, September 4, 1899.
75 SADd, III 6924, September 15, 1898.
76 Ibid. SADd, III 6924, March 6, July 10, 1899. *NV*, September 6, November 10, 1899.
77 StAK, 403 6867, n.d.
78 *NV*, November 1, 6, 1900. SADd, III 6925, March 12, November 12, 1900; III 7776, February 22, 1906.
79 Berten, p. 87. SADd, III 6925, February 24, March 12, November 12, 1900. *NV*,

February 1, November 1, 6, 1900.
80 *NV*, November 14, 1900.
81 SADd, III 6926, October 23, 1901.
82 *NV*, January 30, 1901. SADd, III 6925, January 16, 1901. *VZ*, February 5, 1902.
83 *VZ*, April 1, 1901.
84 SADd, III 6925, July 4, 9, 1901; III 6926, October 17, 1901; III 5748, January 1, 1902. StADd, Reg. Dd. 9052, September 1, 1901, *VZ*, January 25, 1902.
85 *VZ*, January 27, 1902.
86 *VZ*, January 27, 28, 1902. *Parteitagen,* p. 36.
87 SADd, III 6926, July 17, 30, 1901; January 5, 9, 12, 22, February 8, March 25, April 23, August 1, 1902; III 6927, September 9, 1902; September 21, November 8, 1903.
88 *VZ*, October 11, 1904.
89 Berten, p. 95.
90 *VZ*, May 28, 1902.
91 *VZ*, July 28, 1902; January 12, 1904. SADd, III 6926, August 1, 1902.
92 SADd, III 6927, August 6, 14, 23, 1902. *VZ*, September 9, 1903; January 12, 1904.
93 *VZ*, July 10, 1902; February 14, March 30, 1903. SADd, III 6927, August 23, 1902; III 6928, December 1, 1903.
94 SADd, III 6927, September 11, December 9, 1902; September 8, 1903; III 6226, November 17, 19, December 20, 1902, StADd, Reg. Dd. 9055, September 8, 1903; September 1, 1904. *VZ*, September 16, 1903.
95 *VZ*, October 13, 1903.
96 SADd, III 6927, September 22, 1903. Berten, pp. 89–90.
97 *VZ*, January 12, 1904.
98 *VZ*, February 8, 1904.
99 *VZ*, April 9, 1904. SADd, III 6928, March 8, 1904.
100 *VZ*, September 9, 24, 1903; May 5, 1904, SADd III 6748, March 29, 1904. StADd, Reg. Dd. 9054, August 31, 1903.
101 *VZ*, January 8, 1904. These reforms brought local statutes in line with those drawn up by the 1903 provincial party congress.
102 *VZ*, October 10, 1904.

5. Skilled migrants, peasant workers, and native Catholics

1 See Tables A.1 and A.2, Appendix.
2 The national government conducted occupational censuses in 1895 and 1907. Local party records have been destroyed, but police records survive. Under the terms of the Prussian organization law, valid until 1908, the Social Democrats were required to submit party membership lists to the police, and they generally complied. Either the party, relying on information from its members, or the police, using their registration forms, indicated the birthplace, occupation, and birthdate for most, but not all, of the new members.
3 For critical discussions of monocausal and reductionist approaches, see Sabel, pp. 1–22, and Thompson, pp. 9–14, 189–212. For a critical review of the production-oriented theories of K. H. Roth and other contemporary Germans, see Rudi Schmidt, "Die Geschichtsmythologen der 'anderen' Arbeiterbewegung," *Internationale Wissenschaftliche Korrespondenz zur Geschichte der deutschen Arbeiterbewegung* 11, No. 2 (June 1975):178–99.

4 Sabel, pp. 25–49.

5 As women and minors could not legally join political organizations until after 1908, they are analyzed separately.

6 Gray, *Labour Aristocracy*, pp. 170–80. Sabel, pp. 41–2.

7 SADd, III 6923–33, 1896–1908. *VZ*, July 23, 1908.

8 Berten, p. 105. Robert Michels, "Die deutsche sozialdemokratische Parteimitglied- schaft und soziale Zusammensetzung," *Archiv für Sozialwissenschaft und Sozialpolitik*, n.s. 5 (1906):504–9. Moring, passim.

9 Ralf Lützenkirchen, *Die sozialdemokratische Verein für den Wahlkreis Dortmund-Hörde* (Dortmund: Verlag des Historischen Vereins Dortmund, 1970), pp. 122–3. Michels, "Die deutsche Sozialdemokratie," pp. 504–9.

10 See Chapter 4.

11 SADd, III 6923–33, 1896–1908. *SdR*, n.s. 207, Pt. 2:477–81. Schröder, *Arbeitergeschichte*, pp. 68–9. See Table A.5, Appendix.

12 Comparable statistics are available for Dortmund in Lützenkirchen, pp. 124–5. Dieter Fricke provides occupational statistics for the membership in Berlin and Hamburg but not for the working class. *Die deutsche Arbeiterbewegung*, pp. 256–71.

13 See note 11. *VZ*, July 13, 1906; February 14, 1907; July 23, 1908.

14 Brockhaus, pp. 12–26.

15 Vorstand des Deutschen Metallarbeiter Verbandes, ed., *Die Schwereisenindustrie im deutschen Zollgebiet. Ihre Entwicklung und ihre Arbeiter*. (Stuttgart: Schlicke, 1912), p. 70.

16 Ibid., pp. 477, 484–6. Dieter Groh, "The Relationship Between the Intensification of Work and Industrial Conflict in Germany, 1896–1914," *Politics and Society* 8, No. 3–4 (1978):357–8.

17 Groh, "Relationship," pp. 360–3. Homburg, pp. 170–80. Moore, pp. 265–6. Heinrich Reichelt, "Die Arbeitsverhältnisse in einem Berlin Grossbetrieb der Maschinenindustrie (Ph.D. diss., University of Berlin, 1900), p. 46.

18 Reichelt, p. 46. *Vorstand des Deutschen Metallarbeiter Verbandes*, pp. 327, 333, 340–9.

19 Schröder, *Arbeitergeschichte*, p. 197.

20 Ibid., pp. 46–8. Brockhaus, pp. 17, 32–4.

21 Braun, *Die Gewerkschaften vor dem Kriege*, pp. 197–8. Hinton, pp. 56–99. Sabel, pp. 125–46.

22 Otto Hommer, *Die Entwicklung und Tätigkeit der DMV* (Berlin: Carl Heymanns, 1912), p. 38–9. Sabel, pp. 187–9. Schröder, *Arbeitergeschichte*, pp. 42–3. Walter Timmermann, *Entlohnungsmethoden der Hannoverschen Eisenindustrie* (Ph.D. diss., University of Berlin, 1906), pp. 10–11.

23 See Table A.7, Appendix.

24 Moore, p. 265.

25 Hermann Beck, *Lohn- und Arbeitsverhältnisse in der deutschen Maschinenindustrie am Ausgang des 19. Jahrhundert* (Berlin: Leonhard Simion, 1902), p. 13, Jochen Loreck, *Wie man früher Sozialdemokrat wurde* (Bonn-Bad Godesberg: Verlag neue Gesellschaft, 1977), pp. 247–9. Schröder, *Arbeitergeschichte*, p. 160.

26 Kaelble, pp. 54–61.

27 SADd, III 6225, June 18, 1901. *VZ*, June 28, July 12, August 12, 1901; September 28, 1905; June 1, 1906.

28 *Rheinisch-Westfälische Wirtschaftsbiographien*, p. 185. Ehrhardt, passim.

29 SADd, III 5389, 1892. See also Piedboeuf, Dawans, and Co., Oberbilker Stahlwerk, and Ferd. Möllau und Söhne, III 5389; Bachem and Co., III 5391.

30 *Vorstand des Deutschen Metallarbeiter Verbandes*, pp. 488–90.

31 *NV*, March 21, 1900. *VZ*, May 6, 1910. *JdH*, Pt. 2, 1903, pp. 262–3. *Mitteilungen*, No. 8, pp. 110*–11*. Hommer, pp. 34–5. Schröder, *Arbeitergeschichte*, p. 25.

32 Brockhaus, pp. 60–2. *Vorstand des Deutschen Metallarbeiter Verbandes*, pp. 501–3.
33 Moore, p. 261.
34 Fricke, *Die deutsche Arbeiterbewegung*, pp. 256–71. Lützenkirchen, p. 124.
35 *VZ*, July 23, 1907.
36 Hinton, pp. 56–99. Schröder, *Arbeitergeschichte*, pp. 97–101. Zeitlin, pp. 11–15.
37 Karl Anders, *Stein für Stein* (Hannover: Verlag für Literatur und Zeitgeschehen, 1969), pp. 9–109. August Bringmann, *Geschichte der deutschen Zimmerer-Bewegung* (Stuttgart: Dietz, 1905), 2:1–198, passim.
38 Berten, pp. 5–9, 23–7, 39–52.
39 See Chapter 1.
40 Bingmann, 1:82–4. Franz X. Habersbrunner, "Lohn-, Arbeits- und Organisationsverhältnisse im deutschen Baugewerbe" (Ph.D. diss., University of Regensburg, 1903), p. 52.
41 See Table A.7, Appendix. Between 1895 and 1907, firms increased 70%, employees 140%. *Mitteilungen*, No. 8, p. 13*.
42 Braun, *Die Gewerkschaften vor dem Kriege*, p. 204. Cassau, pp. 203–4. Schröder, *Arbeitergeschichte*, pp. 43–4. Karl-Gustav Werner, *Organisation und Politik der Gewerkschaften und Arbeitgeberverbände in der deutschen Bauwirtschaft* (Berlin: Duncker und Humblot, 1968), pp. 38–41. Winkels, p. 21.
43 *JdHW*, 1899, Pt. 1, p. 37; 1903–4, pp. 130–1. *VZ*, July 30, 1907.
44 Groh, "Relationship," p. 369.
45 Werner, *Organisation*, pp. 52–69. Also Chapter 3 and Chapter 7.
46 "Statistik des Jahres 1906 über Lohn- und Arbeitsverhältnisse der Arbeiter in Düsseldorf," *Bericht des Gewerkschaftskartell*, 1906, pp. 100–1. Anders, pp. 130–1.
47 SADd, III 5385, November 24, 1906.
48 Michels, "Die deutsche sozialdemokratiche Parteimitgliedschaft," p. 514. *VZ*, July 23, 1907.
49 *VZ*, July 27, 1902; January 18, 1906.
50 *Bericht des Gewerkschaftskartell*, 1906, p. 10.
51 See Tables A.6 and A.7, Appendix. *Mitteilungen*, No. 3, pp. 2–3. Schröder, *Arbeitergeschichte*, pp. 141–2.
52 *VZ*, July 23, 1907. *Bericht des Gewerkschaftskartell*, 1906, n.p. See Chapter 7.
53 *VZ*, June 27, 1902; July 23, 1907. Michels, "Die deutsche Sozialdemokratie," p. 514.
54 Köllmann, "Industrialisierung," pp. 64–9. See Chapter 1.
55 *NV*, February 1, 1900.
56 *VZ*, July 31, 1907; July 26, 1908.
57 *Mitteilungen*, No. 4, pp. 13*, 14*, 23*, 24*, 26*, 5, 22. *JdSA*, 1902, p. 5; 1912, p. 16. Köllmann. "Industrialisierung," p. 66. Peter Schöller, *Die deutschen Städte* (Wiesbaden: Franz Steiner Verlag, 1967), p. 19.
58 Steve Hochstadt, "Rural Migrants and Urban Population in Nineteenth Century Germany" (Paper delivered at the American Historical Association Annual Convention, Dallas, 1977), p. 7.
59 Köllmann, "Industrialisierung," pp. 64–9. *Mitteilungen*, No. 4, p. 26*. StADd, Reg. Dd. 9058, August 27, 1906.
60 SADd, III 6928, June 27, 1908.
61 Sabel, p. 185. Schröder, *Arbeitergeschichte*, pp. 42–6. Hochstadt, p. 7.
62 *NV*, June 12, 1898; January 19, 1899. *VZ*, June 26, 1908. Braun, *Die Gewerkschaften vor dem Kriege*, p. 124.
63 Sabel, pp. 193–7.
64 Schröder, *Arbeitergeschichte*, pp. 42–8. See Chapter 2, note 110. *Mitteilungen*, No. 4, p. 5. Laubier, pp. 364–7.

65 StADd, Reg. Dd. 9058, August 27, 1906; Reg. Dd. 42810, September 1, 1908; Reg. Dd. 42813, 1912. SADd, III 6160, January 10, 1905. Spael, p. 29.

66 In Dortmund the SPD recruited primarily from migrants who had come from confessionally mixed regions. Lützenkirchen, p. 127. Loreck, pp. 145–50.

67 *VZ*, July 10, 1903.

68 *VZ*, July 23, 1907. Düsseldorf was by no means exceptional. Fricke, *Die deutsche Arbeiterbewegung*, pp. 247–8. Lützenkirchen, p. 132. Dieter Langewiesche, "Wanderungsbewegungen in der Hochindustrialisierungsperiode," *Vieteljahresschrift für Sozial- und Wirtschaftsgeschichte* 64, No. 1 (1977):40. Michels wrongly attributed the high turnover to a psychological lack of commitment. *Political Parties*, pp. 90, 105–6.

69 Langewiesche, p. 40. Lützenkirchen, p. 133. See Chapter 6.

70 SdR, n.s. 207, Pt. 2, p. 477. SADd, III 6923–33, 1896–1908. Erdmann, *Arbeiterbewegung*, p. 241.

71 See Chapter 2, note 110. Adelbert Koch, "Arbeitermemorien als sozialwissenschaftliche Erkenntnisquelle," *Archiv für Sozialwissenschaft und Sozialpolitik* 61 (1929): 128–67. These autobiographies were written by skilled and unskilled workers, who were either politically unimportant or inactive. They describe their upbringing, education, work histories, and life-styles in remarkably similar ways.

72 Cassau, p. 194.

73 Karl Korn, *Die Arbeiterjugendbewegung*, Parts I, II (Berlin: Arbeiterjugend Verlag, 1922, 1923), pp. 27–30, 33, 47, 61–9, 83, 202–42, passim. StADd, Reg. Dd. 42813, September 1, 1912.

74 Braun, *Die Gewerkschaften vor dem Kriege*, p. 196. Moore, pp. 200–1. In 1905–6, 3.7% had joined elsewhere and 8.4% were over 40. By 1907–8 the figures were 18.3 and 11.5%, respectively. See Table 5.3.

75 Fricke, *Die deutsche Arbeiterbewegung*, p. 272. In Bremen more than 50% of the party was over 35 by 1909. Moring. p. 222.

76 StAK, 403 6867, n.d., and 403 6870, n.d. Robert F. Wheeler, "German Labor and the Comintern: Problem of Generations," *Journal of Social History* 7 (Spring 1974):307, 311–14.

77 Jürgen Kuczynski, *Geschichte der Lage der Arbeiter unter dem Kapitalismus*, Vol. 18, *Studien zur Geschichte der Lage der Arbeiterin in Deutschland von 1700 bis zur Gegenwart* (Berlin: Akademie, 1963), pp. 107, 110. See Table A.6, Appendix.

78 *SdR*, n.s. 107:183; 207, Pt. 2:477. *JdSA*, 1904, p. 17.

79 *Bericht des Gewerkschaftskartell*, 1902, p. 40. "Statistik über Lohn- und Arbeitsverhältnisse," 1906, pp. 100–1. Kuczynski, Vol. 18, pp. 134–5.

80 *Mitteilungen*, No. 4, p. 27*. The Social Democrats made only one short-lived attempt to organize domestics in 1907. *VZ*, June 22, July 4, 9, 1907.

81 *VZ*, August 10, 1904.

82 Braun, *Die Gewerkschaften vor dem Kriege*, pp. 191–2. Kuczynski, Vol. 18, pp. 116–39. Werner Thönnissen, *Frauenemanzipation* (Frankfurt: Europäische Verlagsanstalt, 1969), pp. 1–62, passim.

83 SADd, III 6000, December 21, 1891; January 23, May, and July 20, 1892; III 6188, December 23, 1892; January 24, 1893. *NV*, March 3, 15, 1891; May 11, July 22, October 21, 1893. The women's agitation committees elsewhere in Germany were also suppressed. Thönnessen, p. 52.

84 *NV*, November 1, 1900.

85 StAK, 403 6864, December 1905. *VZ*, October 5, 1905; July 16, 1906.

6. Party building and popular culture

1 See Table A.2, Appendix.
2 SADd, III 6929, June 20, 1905.
3 Berten, p. 98. *NV*, March 20, 1900; January 20, 1901. *VZ*, June 29, July 30, 1901. StADd, Reg. Dd. 9052, August 31, 1901.
4 *VZ*, June 29, 1901.
5 SADd, III 6929, June 20, 1905.
6 *NV*, February 1, 1900.
7 Berten, pp. 102–3.
8 In many respects the districts replicated the Social Democratic Association activities of the 1890s. SADd, III 6929, November 12, 1905; III 6930, March 11, July 17, 1906.
9 *VZ*, July 23, 1907.
10 *VZ*, July 23, 1908; July 28, 1909.
11 *VZ*, December 21, 1907.
12 *VZ*, March 27, 1909.
13 Loreck, pp. 32–6, 247–54.
14 Nettl, "The German Social Democratic Party," pp. 76–7.
15 SADd, III 6928, June 13, 1904.
16 SADd, III 6928, October 26, 1904.
17 *VZ*, July 10, 1905.
18 SADd, III 6929, January 16, 20, February 11, 12, 21, 24, May 20, August 12, 1905; III 6930, July 28, 1906; III 6931, October 17, 1906. Both police and party reports on district meetings are less thorough than on general meetings.
19 Nipperdey, *Die Organisation der deutschen Parteien*, p. 326. A. Braun, in his article, "Bildungsprobleme in der Arbeiterbewegung," also argues that the lack of discussion encouraged authoritarian beliefs, discouraged young workers from joining the party, and inhibited the training of new leaders. *Der Kampf*, 8 (1915):345–6.
20 Attendance was disappointingly low in the eyes of the leaders in 1904 and 1905 but picked up thereafter as the district organizations became more viable and the speakers more skilled. *VZ*, February 9, 1905; June 25, 1909; May 27, 30, July 21, 1911. SADd, III 6929, November 11, 1908.
21 *VZ*, August 27, 1908.
22 SADd, III 6932, July 31, 1907. Social Democrats elsewhere still clung to the illusion that the press was an effective means of winning new workers. Loreck, pp. 36–7.
23 StADd, Reg. Dd. 9058, August 27, 1906; Reg. Dd. 9041, December 23, 1906.
24 *VZ*, September 13, 1905.
25 STAK, 403 6864, December 1905; 403 6867, n.d. StADd, Reg. Dd. 9041, December 23, 1906, December 13, 1907; Reg. Dd. 9069, December 22, 1905; Reg. Dd. 42810, September 1, 1908; Reg. Dd. 42781, September 1, 1910. SADd, III 6931, September 23, 1906. *VZ*, April 2, 1904; January 12, 1906; January 10, 1907; April 1, 1908; October 18, 1909; November 6, 1911.
26 StADd, Reg. Dd. 9069, December 22, 1905; Reg. Dd. 42781, September 1, 1910. SADd, III 6929, October 26, 1905; III 6930, March 25, 1906. *VZ*, July 21, 1911.
27 Schröder, *Arbeitergeschichte*, p. 41.
28 Michels, *Political Parties*, pp. 117–67, passim, 254–64.
29 StAK, 403 6867, n.d., and 403 6870, n.d. Wheeler, "German Labor," p. 307.

30 Martin Martiny, "Die politische Bedeutung der gewerkschaftliche Arbeiter-Sekretariat vor dem ersten Weltkriege," in Heinz Oskar Vetter, ed., *Vom Sozialistengesetz zur Mitbestimmung* (Cologne: Bund Verlag, 1975), pp. 160–6.

31 See Chapters 4, 8, 11, and 12.

32 *VZ*, July 4, 1905; October 22, 1906; October 17, 1910. Laufenberg ran in Mönchen-Gladbach in 1907, Berten in 1912. In addition, Arzberger ran in Neuss in 1912. StADd, Reg. Dd. 9058, August 27, 1906.

33 Erdmann, *Arbeiterbewegung*, pp. 534–6. See Chapter 7 for the Christian trade-union critique.

34 Wolfgang Stump, *Geschichte und Organisation der Zentrumspartei in Düsseldorf, 1917–1933* (Düsseldorf: Droste, 1971), p. 130. StADd, Reg. Dd. 9052, September 1, 1901. *VZ*, June 26, 1908.

35 Erdmann, *Arbeiterbewegung*, pp. 458–86, passim. Ross, pp. 86–91.

36 Ross, p. 84.

37 Hans-Jürgen Puhle, "Parlament, Parteien und Interessenverbände," in Michael Stümer, ed., *Das kaiserliche Deutschland, Politik und Gesellschaft, 1870–1918* (Kronberg: Athenäum, 1977), p. 356.

38 Dieter Dowe, "The Workers' Choral Movement Before the First World War," *Journal of Contemporary History* 13, 'No. 2 (April 1978):269–70.

39 For discussions of the culture of the skilled and unskilled in Britain, see Robert Q. Gray, "Styles'of Life, the 'Labour Aristocracy' and Class Relations in Late Nineteenth Century Edinburgh," *International Review of Social History* (1973):428–52. Hinton. Jones. For France, see Scott. Comparable work has not been done for Germany.

40 Frank Parkin, "Working-Class Conservatives: Theory of Political Deviance," *British Journal of Sociology* 18, No. 3 (September 1967):282.

41 *VZ*, October 17, 1910.

42 StAK, 403 6870, n.d.

43 *VZ*, October 1, 1904.

44 *VZ*, July 23, 1909.

45 *VZ*, February 25, 1902; September 29, 1908. *Bericht des Gewerkschaftskartell*, 1906, p. 8. Gerlach, in Lux, ed., *Düsseldorf*, p. 72.

46 *VZ*, December 31, 1909.

47 *VZ*, November 26, 1904.

48 SADd, III 6226, November 26, 1904.

49 *VZ*, March 1, 1905; October 3, 1908. *Bericht des Gewerkschaftskartell*, 1905, pp. 37–8.

50 *VZ*, October 17, 1910. For comparison, see Alfred Zeitz, *Zur Geschichte der Arbeiterbewegung der Stadt Brandenburg vor dem ersten Weltkrieg* (Potsdam: Veröffentlichungen des Bezirksmuseum Potsdam, 1965), p. 4697. Braun, "Bildungsprobleme," pp. 243–4.

51 *VZ*, April 2, 1906.

52 *VZ*, September 6, 1910.

53 Eric J. Hobsbawm, "Inventing Traditions in the nineteenth Century," in *Past and Present Society Annual Conference* (Oxford: Past and Present Society, 1977), pp. 8–9.

54 *VZ*, February 10, 1906.

55 Hobsbawm, "Inventing Traditions," pp. 8–9.

56 SADd, III 6923, May 2, 1897.

57 *AZ*, October 2, 1890. *NV*, May 2, 1892; April 10, 1894; May 1, 3, 1895; May 5, 1896; May 4, 1898; January 14, March 31, 1900. StAK, 403 6832, May 1, 1890. StADd, Reg. Dd. 8867, May 2, 1892; Reg. Dd. 8868, May 2, 1894; Reg. Dd. 9043, May 2, 1895; Reg. Dd. 9045, May 2, 1896; Reg. D. 9046, March 31, May 3, 1897.

58 *NV*, April 26, 1900.

59 *VZ*, May 2, 1902.
60 *VZ*, April 30, 1904; September 28, 1905.
61 *VZ*, April 29, 1905.
62 SADd, III 6929, May 2, 1905. *VZ*, May 2, 22, September 28, 1905.
63 *VZ*, April 10, 24, 1906.
64 *NV*, August 31, September 11, 13, 1893; September 3, 1895; September 1, 1900. SADd, III 6225, June 16, August 29, 1901.
65 *VZ*, August 26, 1905.
66 *VZ*, August 28, 1905; August 4, 1906; July 6, 1908.
67 *VZ*, April 6, 1901.
68 *AZ*, November 27, 1890. *VZ*, July 30, 1908. SADd, III 6225, October 29, 1898. StADd, Präsidialbüro 28, November 2, 1911.
69 Michael Klöcker, *Die Sozialdemokratie im Regierungsbezirk Aachen vor dem 1. Weltkrieg* (Wentorf/Hamburg: Einhorn, 1977), p. 173.
70 The Social Democrats were obviously not the only ones to idealize the dead, but the political character of their eulogies was unique. *NV*, February 18, July 29, 1895; June 13, 1898; November 25, 1900. *VZ*, February 23, 1909. SADd, III 6916, June 9, 1896; III 6930, December 11–14, 1905.
71 As Geoff Eley has noted, it is far from clear that the nationalist associations made significant inroads into the working class. "Defining Social Imperialism: Use and Abuse of an Idea," *Social History* 3 (October 1976):270–7. Nonetheless, the very fact that they made overtures to the working class spurred the Social Democrats into action.
72 *VZ*, June 21, 1909; September 12, 1910. *Jahresbericht des Bezirksverbandes katholischer Arbeitervereine von Düsseldorf Stadt und Land für das Jahr 1912*, p. 12. *Jahresbericht des christlichen Gewerkschaftskartell Düsseldorf*, 1911, 1912.
73 *NV*, March 24, 1892. *VZ*, July 20, 1905. It is not clear how many such associations there were. The police kept loose tabs on two. SADd, III 5931, 1877–1902; III 5933, 1887–98. In 1905 the DMV in Düsseldorf considered such organizations so prevalent and popular that it passed a resolution forbidding members from joining. *VZ*, July 20, 1905.
74 *VZ*, January 16, 1906.
75 StAK, 403 9048, May 26, 1898. *VZ*, May 11, 1910; January 25, October 6, 1911.
76 *VZ*, March 11, 1910.
77 *VZ*, May 11, 1910; January 25, March 2, October 6, 1911. Schröder, *Arbeitergeschichte*, pp. 75–6.
78 Maslowski, pp. 7–47. Ross, pp. 79–119.
79 Boris Goldenberg. "Beiträge zur Soziologie der deutschen Vorkriegssozialdemokratie" (Ph.D. diss., University of Heidelberg, 1932), pp. 35–6. Nettl, "The German Social Democratic Party," p. 66. Guenther Roth, pp. 203, 221.
80 Klöcker, p. 173.
81 *VZ*, April 8, 1911.
82 *VZ*, April 19, 1900. StAK, 403 9048, May 26, 1896. StADd, Präsidialbüro 28, November 2, 1911.
83 Gerhard A. Ritter, "Workers' Culture in Imperial Germany," *Journal of Contemporary History* 13, No. 2 (April 1978):173.
84 See Gray, *The Labour Aristocracy*, and "Styles of Life," for useful insights on this.
85 Parkin, pp. 90–1.
86 See Michael Mann, *Consciousness and Action Among the Western Working Class* (London: Macmillan, 1973), p. 13, for a discussion of opposition and conception of an

alternative society as elements of class consciousness.

87 *NV*, February 10, 1896.
88 Vernon Lidtke, "Songs of the German Labor Movement, 1864–1914," (unpublished paper), p. 3.
89 *NV*, October 11, 1892. *VZ*, January 16, 1906.
90 Dowe, p. 269.
91 Vernon Lidtke, "Social Democratic Cultural Organizations in Imperial Germany" (Paper delivered at the American Historical Association Convention, Chicago, December 1974), p. 21.
92 Laubier, pp. 364–6.
93 Dowe, p. 274.
94 Gray, *Labour Aristocracy*, pp. 136–9.
95 *VZ*, April 19, 1900. SADd, III 6224, December 24, 1896.

7. Expansion and optimism

1 *MdH*, March 1905, p. 1; February 1906, p. 1; February 1907, p. 21. SADd, III 4598–9, 1905–6, I Quartel, 1907.
2 *JdSA*, 1903, p. 14; 1904, p. 16; 1906, p. 25. *VZ*, February 16, 1904.
3 Loreck, pp. 178–84.
4 SADd, III 5382, March 1, April 5, June 1904. *VZ*, March 5, 1904.
5 SADd, III 5382, April 9, June 4, 1904; list of 1904 court cases. *VZ*, May 30, 1904. See Cassau, p. 266, on police behavior nationwide.
6 *JdHW*, 1904–5, p. 229. *VZ*, March 7, 11, April 19, 1904.
7 Schorske, p. 29.
8 SADd, III 5382, August 1, 2, 4, 11, September 5, 13, 1904.
9 *NV*, October 19, 1899. *VZ*, June 20, August 8, October 17, 1900; November 2, 1901; May 9, 27, 1902. SADd, III 6925, May 8, 1901.
10 Erdmann, *Arbeiterbewegung*, pp. 465, 499, 568. Erdman, *Gewerkschaften*, pp. 187–92. Berger, pp. 110–12, 119.
11 SADd, III 4596, I and III Quartel, 1904, *JdHW*, 1904–5, p. 225.
12 *VZ*, July 29, 1904. *Düsseldorfer Tageblatt*, August 3, 1904.
13 *VZ*, August 4, 11, 1904. Georg Frey, p. 46.
14 SADd, III 5382, *Gewerbezeitung*, August 21, 1904.
15 SADd, III 5382, August 1, 1904; February 11, 14, 1905. *VZ*, July 28, August 2, 16, 23, September 2, 8, 11, 16, October 11, 20, 1904.
16 Schorske, pp. 31–7. See Chapter 8.
17 *JdSA*, 1906, p. 89.
18 *NV*, March 21, June 10, 1900, on employers associations. *VZ*, August 14, 1904; August 22, 1905. SADd, III 5383, September 12, 15, 1905. *Bericht des Gewerkschaftskartell*, 1905, p. 43.
19 *VZ*, April 12, 1905. SADd, III 5383, March 28, April 11, 1905.
20 *Bericht des Gewerkschaftskartell*, 1905, p. 28. SADd, III 4598, II Quartel, 1905; III 5384, April 19, 1905.
21 *VZ*, April 22, 1905.
22 SADd, III 5383, leaflet from employers.
23 *VZ*, April 19, May 13, 25, 1905.
24 SADd, III 5384, April 22, 28, May 5, 6, 1905.
25 *VZ*, May 29, June 10, July 13, 1905. SADd, III 5384, June 20, 1905. In twelve breweries

surveyed, only 21 of 135 strikers had gotten their jobs back. *Bericht des Gewerkschafts-kartell,* 1905, p. 28.
26 *VZ,* February 16, June 7, 10, 17, 24, November 23, 24, 1905. *Bericht des Gewerkschafts-kartell,* 1905, p. 27. SADd, III 5383, February 15, November 15, 29, 1905.
27 *VZ,* January 6, 1901; February 23, July 3, 1905. *JdH,* 1901, p. 38. *Bericht des Gewerkschaftskartell,* 1905, p. 29. SADd, III 5384, June 28, July 1, 1905.
28 *VZ,* July 4, 5, 7, 8, 11, 12, August 9, 1905. SADd, III 5384, July 11, 15, 1905, and clippings from the *Düsseldorfer Zeitung* and the *Westdeutsche Gewerbezeitung.*
29 SADd, III 5384, July 25, 26, 29, 1905.
30 StADd, Reg. Dd. 30411, September 11, 1905. SADd, III 5384, July 21, 1905.
31 SADd, III 5384, July 25, August 17, 1905.
32 StADd, Reg. Dd. 30411, July 27, September 22, 1905.
33 SADd, III 5384, July 28, 29, October 1905.
34 *VZ,* October 4, 1905.
35 *JdSA,* 1906, p. 26. *VZ,* June 21, September 15, December 17, 1906.
36 SADd, III 5385, April 7, May 17, 19, July 17, 19, 29, August 4, 11, 15, 22, 23, 1906. *VZ,* July 11, 21, September 10, 13, 1906.
37 "Statistik über Lohn- und Arbeitsverhältnisse, pp. 95–107. *Mitteilungen,* No. 4, p. 23*. *VZ,* August 22, 1906. *JdSA,* 1906, p. 26.
38 *NV,* June 10, 1892; May 24, 1894. *VZ,* September 14, 1901. Jürgen Kuczynski, *Geschichte,* Vol. 4, p. 358.
39 "Statistik über Lohn- und Arbeitsverhältnisse," p. 105.
40 *VZ,* September 20, 1905; May 14, 1906. Excerpts from the factory inspectors' reports.
41 See Chapter 8.
42 Guenther Roth, pp. 277–8. *JdHW,* 1906–7, pp. 135–6, 141–2, 169–71. Saul, pp. 74–86.
43 *Bericht des Arbeitersekretariats,* 1905, p. 3.
44 Kenneth D. Barkin, *The Controversy over German Industrialization, 1890–1902* (Chicago: University of Chicago Press, 1970), pp. 37–9, 44–50, 60–7, 95–102. J. H. Clapham, *Economic Development of France and Germany* (Cambridge: Cambridge University Press, 1966), pp. 209–15, 319–22. Gerschenkron, pp. 42–50, 56–64. Klein, p. 95
45 Barkin, pp. 219–20. Gerschenkron, pp. 60–1.
46 *Protokoll der SPD,* 1902, pp. 223–36. *Die Sozialdemokratie in München* (Berlin: Verlag von Wilhelm Baensch, 1902), pp. 17–20.
47 *NV,* July 25, 1900.
48 SADd, III 6925, leaflet 1901, March 4, 6, 10, 14, 1901; III 6926, August 28, 1901; March 18, 1902; III 6927, August 30, December 12, 1902; January 7, 1903.
49 SADd, III 6927, December 12, 1902.
50 SADd, III 6927, December 22, 1902.
51 SADd, III 6927, October 27, 1901. Gerschenkron supports this contention. P. 26.
52 SADd, III 6925, 1901 pamphlet, *Fort mit den Brodwucher. NV,* February 22, 1902.
53 SADd, III 6927, 1902 pamphlet, *Schwarz oder Roth?*
54 SADd, III 6925, February 28, 1901. According to Gerschenkron, the minimum 1902 rate would cost the worker 13.1 workdays, the maximum rates 17.9 days. P. 64.
55 SADd, III 6925, March 10, 1901.
56 SADd, III 6927, December 22, 1902.
57 SADd, III 6927, 1902 pamphlet, *Schwarz oder Roth?*
58 *VZ,* April 16, 1901.
59 *Die Sozialpolitik der deutschen Zentrumspartei 1907, Gesammelte sozialpolitische Flug-blätter des Volksverein für das katholische Deutschland nach dem Bestande des Jahres 1907* (Mönchen-Gladbach: Volksverein Verlag, 1910), pp. 133–40.

60 Ibid. SADd, III 6397, 1903 pamphlet, *Herunter mit der Maske! Eine praktische Abrechnung mit der Sozialdemokratie.*
61 *Düsseldorfer Volksblatt,* April 23, 29, May 10, June 8, 12, 15, 1903. SADd, III 6397, 1903 pamphlet, *Herunter mit der Maske!.*
62 *Die Sozialpolitik,* pp. 15–18, 27–30. Zeender, p. 90.
63 *Die Sozialpolitik,* pp. 19–22.
64 Barkin, pp. 229–30.
65 Wehler, *Kaiserreich,* pp. 102–3.
66 Kehr, *Schlachtflottenbau,* p. 205.
67 Wehler, *Kaiserreich,* p. 69.
68 Berger, pp. 20–1, 73–8, 83, 152. Puhle, pp. 356–7.
69 Heinrich Brauns, "Die politische Betätigung der Arbeiter," in Berger, p. 161.
70 Erdmann, *Arbeiterbewegung,* pp. 541–8, 552.
71 *VZ,* April 24, 1902.
72 Erdmann, *Arbeiterbewegung,* p. 552.
73 *VZ,* November 12, 1903. The Christian trade-union candidate won only 823 votes. SADd, III 10107, 1903.
74 Schauff, pp. 74, 80.
75 SADd, III 10107, 1903.
76 Berger, pp. 120–1.
77 *Düsseldorfer Volksblatt,* June 24, 1903.
78 *Düsseldorfer Volksblatt,* June 18, 1903.
79 *Düsseldorfer Zeitung,* June 26, 1903.
80 *VZ,* August 18, 1905.
81 *VZ,* August 17, 1905.
82 Gray, *Labour Aristocracy,* p. 173.
83 *VZ,* June 16, 1905.
84 Ibid.
85 Heinrich Laufenberg, *Lug und Trug oder christliche Reaktion und christliches Geschäft* (Düsseldorf: A. Gerisch, 1906); *Kann ein Katholik Sozialdemokrat sein?* (Düsseldorf: Düsseldorfer *Volkszeitung,* 1905); *Die Legende vom Arbeiter-Pabst* (Düsseldorf: A. Gerisch, 1905).
86 Wilhelm Gewehr, *Kann ein Christ Sozialdemokrat sein?* (Elberfeld: Molkenbuhr, 1903).
87 Berger, pp. 121, 139–41, 196–7.
88 *Lug und Trug der Sozialdemokratie im Kampfe gegen das Zentrum* (Mönchen-Gladbach: Verlag der *Westdeutsche Arbeiterzeitung,* n.d.), p. 1. SADd, III 6397, Center flyer, *Der entlarvte Programmsatz: Religion ist Privatsache.*
89 Saul, pp. 13–16, 32–3. *MdH,* 1903–6, passim. Stegmann, pp. 47–8.
90 Saul, pp. 17–18.
91 *VZ,* August 27, 1903.
92 SADd, III 6928, December 17, 1903.
93 SADd, III 6929, January 8, 1905.

8. Move to the left

1 These are the 1903 figures. StADd, Reg. Dd. 9067, 1903.
2 *VZ,* January 8, 1908.
3 *VZ,* November 13, 1903. See Chapter 4.
4 Schorske, pp. 45–7. *MdH,* October 1910, p. 312.

5 StADd, Reg. Dd. 9067, flyer, *Aufzum Kampf gegen das elendeste aller Wahlsysteme* SADd, III 6930, March 19, 1906.
6 StADd, Reg. Dd. 9067, flyer, *Aufgepasst! Lesen und selbstständig urteilen*, pp. 4, 10.
7 StADd, Reg. Dd. 9067, flyer, *Auf zum Kampf.*
8 *Düsseldorfer Zeitung*, January 6, 21, 1906.
9 Ross, pp. 137–8.
10 SADd, III 6930, January 22, 1906. Richard Reichard, "The German Working Class and the Revolution of 1905," *Journal of Central European Affairs* 13 (July 1953):144–6.
11 *VZ*, July 19, 1905.
12 SADd, III 6930, January 21, 1906.
13 *VZ*, June 1, 1906.
14 StADd, Reg. Dd. 9067, January 9, 1906.
15 *VZ*, January 13, 1906. SADd, III 5758, January 1906, passim.
16 *VZ*, January 20, 1906.
17 *Düsseldorfer Zeitung*, January 15, 1906.
18 SADd, III 6930, January 22, 1906. *VZ*, January 22, 1906.
19 *VZ*, January 22, 1906.
20 Berten, p. 108. SADd, III 6930, January 22, 1906.
21 Reichard, p. 147
22 *VZ*, July 19, 1905.
23 *VZ*, May 23, June 28, 1905.
24 *VZ*, September 26, 1905. SADd, III 6929, July 27, 28, 30, August 12, September 5, 8, 1905.
25 Schorske, pp. 37–9, 48–9. Manfred Scharrer, *Arbeiterbewegung im Obrigkeitsstaat* (Berlin: Rotbuch, 1978), pp. 68–79.
26 *VZ*, August 16, 1906. SADd, III 6931, August 16, 1906.
27 *VZ*, August 16, 1906.
28 *VZ*, October 3, 1906. Moring, p. 87.
29 SADd, III 6929, October 6, 1905; III 6931, October 11, 1906.
30 *VZ*, July 7, 11, November 1, 1906; September 10, 1911.
31 SADd, III 6930, June 7, 1906.
32 Schorske, pp. 60–1. Hedwig Wachenheim, *Die deutsche Arbeiterbewegung 1844 bis 1914* (Cologne: Westdeutscher Verlag, 1967), pp. 430–1.
33 Schorske, pp. 59–62, 75. Wachenheim, p. 435.
34 See George Lichtheim, *Imperialism* (New York: Praeger, 1971), pp. 100–24.
35 Guenther Roth, pp. 212–20. See Chapter 2, note 110.
36 SADd, III 6928, March 25, 1904; III 6929, May 1, 1905.
37 SADd, III 6929, May 2, 1905.
38 Wachenheim, p. 430.
39 *Düsseldorfer Tageblatt*, January 10, 1907.
40 SADd, III 6932, December 21, 22, 24, 25, 1906. *VZ*, January 28, 1907.
41 *VZ*, January 24, 1907. See also SADd, III 6932, January 2, 3, 1907.
42 SADd, III 6932, January 1, 2, 3, 5, 16, 22, 23, 24, February 3, 5, 6, 1907.
43 Zeender, pp. 104, 114. Erdmann, *Arbeiterbewegung*, p. 499.
44 *Düsseldorfer Tageblatt*, January 11, 15, February 1, 1907.
45 *VZ*, January 28, 1907. See Tables A.3, A.4, Appendix.
46 Klöcker, pp. 109–11.
47 Ibid., pp. 26, 41.
48 See Table A.3, Appendix.
49 Moring, pp. 100–2. Lützenkirchen, pp. 47–9.

342 *Notes to pp. 167–199*

50 *Protokoll der SPD*, 1907, pp. 167, 329–30.
51 *VZ*, September 24, 1907.
52 *VZ*, October 22, 1907.
53 Schorske, pp. 64–5. Wachenheim, p. 435.
54 *VZ*, October 22, 1907.
55 SADd, III 6933, October 23, 1907.
56 *VZ*, October 22, 1907.
57 SADd, III 6932, September 6, 1907.
58 *VZ*, October 22, 1907.
59 *VZ*, September 11, 1907. SADd, III 6932, September 6, October 4, 1907.
60 SADd, III 4600, I Quartel, 1908, 1909. *MdH*, February 1909, p. 25. *JdSA*, 1907, p. 19; 1908, pp. 23, 25; 1909, p. 3. *VZ*, July 16, 1908.
61 Groh, "Intensification," pp. 361–3. Fr. Selter, *Ueber die Einführung von Tarifverträgen in den Grossbetrieben der Maschinenbau und verwandter Industrien* (Berlin: A. Seydel, 1911), pp. 6–8.
62 Groh, "Intensification," pp. 374–5. See also Saul, pp. 112–15.
63 *MdH*, October 1910, p. 312.
64 Kuczynski, Vol. 4, p. 331. Gerhard Bry, *Wages in Germany, 1871–1945* (Princeton, N.J.: Princeton University Press, 1960), p. 73.
65 *VZ*, April 4, 17, 20, 1907. SADd, III 5385, March 23, 1907; III 5386, 1908, passim.
66 *VZ*, March 14, 1907.
67 *VZ*, April 17, 1907. *MdH*, April 1909, p. 125. SADd, III 5385, flyers, 1907.
68 Alfred Tischer, *Der Kampf im deutschen Baugewerbe, 1910* (Leipzig: Duncker and Humblot, 1912), pp. 65–6, 76–7, 87–91, 150–2. Groh, "Intensification," p. 383.
69 SADd, III 5386, June 27, 1910.
70 SADd, III 5386, July 20, 1910.
71 SADd, III 5385, May 31, July 17, October 10, 1907, *VZ*, March 18, April 4, 20, 26, July 8, 9, 30, August 7, 1907.
72 SADd, III 5386, August 14, December 3, 1908; January 11, 12, February 9, March 1909.
73 SADd, III 5385, April 11, 1907; III 5386, August 10, 17, 1907.
74 SADd, III 5386, 1908, passim. Saul, p. 213.
75 *VZ*, February 26, March 12, 1910.
76 SADd, III 5386, September 27, 1910.
77 Saul, p. 265.
78 Groh, "Relationship," pp. 386–7.
79 Berghahn, in Stürmer, ed., p. 378.
80 Schorske, pp. 158–61. Peter Nettl, *Rosa Luxemburg* (London: Oxford University Press, 1969), p. 280.
81 Wachenheim, p. 458.
82 *VZ*, August 28, 1908.
83 *VZ*, November 23, 1908.
84 V. R. Berghahn, *Germany and the Approach of War in 1914* (New York: St. Martins Press, 1973), p. 76. Annelies Laschitza, *Deutsche Linke im Kampf für eine demokratische Republik* (Berlin: Dietz, 1969), p. 48. Schorske, p. 48.
85 *VZ*, October 5, 1909.
86 *VZ*, July 21, 1909.
87 StADd, Reg. Dd. 42811, August 31, 1909.
88 *VZ*, July 7, September 6, 1909.
89 *VZ*, September 22, 1909.
90 *VZ*, October 9, 1909.

91 Schorske, p. 168.
92 *VZ*, November 27, 1907.
93 *VZ*, January 10, 1908. SADd, III 6933, January 11, 12, 1908.
94 *VZ*, January 13, 1908.
95 *VZ*, January 14, 1908.
96 SADd, III 6930, March 18, 1906; III 6933, March 19, 20, 1908. *VZ*, March 18, 1906; March 18, 1908.
97 *VZ*, May 5, 7, 8, 25, 30, June 2, 1908.
98 *VZ*, April 6, 1908. SADd, III 6933, February 9, 24, 1908. After mid-1908 the police could no longer legally attend party meetings, and the *Volkszeitung* did not give exact attendance figures.
99 *VZ*, March 25, 30, 1909; April 1909, passim; August 26, 27, 28, October 13, 30, November 26, 27, 1909.
100 *VZ*, February 9, 1909.
101 *VZ*, June 1, 1909; August 3, 1910.
102 StADd, Reg. Dd. 42812, August 31, 1911.
103 Schorske, pp. 171–5. Groh, *Negative Integration*, pp. 128, 131–4. Nettl, *Rosa*, p. 281. *VZ*, January 15, 21, 23, 24, 1910.
104 Berghahn, pp. 88–90. *VZ*, February 7, 8, 10, 1910.
105 StADd, Reg. Dd. 42788, February 13, 14, 1910.
106 *VZ*, February 14, 1910.
107 StADd, Reg. Dd. 42788, February 18, 1910.
108 *VZ*, March 1, 1910.
109 Berger, pp. 170–2, 177. Zeender, p. 118.
110 *VZ*, February 28, 1910.
111 *VZ*, March 7, 1910.
112 SADd, III 6933, March 17, 1910.
113 *VZ*, April 9, 1910.
114 Berten, p. 110.
115 *VZ*, April 9, 1910. Italics in the original.
116 *VZ*, March 26, 1910.
117 *VZ*, March 3, 1910.
118 *VZ*, April 12, 1910.
119 SADd, III 4601, I Quartel, 1910.
120 That is the view of Groh, *Negative Integration*, p. 144.
121 *VZ*, October 19, 1910.
122 Nettl, *Rosa*, p. 204. Fricke, *Die deutsche Arbeiterbewegung*. pp. 235–8.
123 *VZ*, April 11, 1910. SADd, III 6933, April 10, 1910.
124 *VZ*, September 1, 1909.
125 *VZ*, July 20, 1910.
126 *VZ*, July 27, 1910.
127 *VZ*, August 1, October 8, 1910. Groh, *Negative Integration*, pp. 176–8. Schorske, p. 194. Laschitza, pp. 262–4.
128 *VZ*, October 19, 1910.
129 The Bremen radicals had similar views. Bock, pp. 80–1.
130 See Tables A.1 and A.2, Appendix.

9. The limits of reformism

1 Ritter, *Die Arbeiterbewegung im Wilhelmischen Reich*, pp. 208–17.
2 See Chapter 4.

3 Most, *Die deutsche Stadt,* pp. 19–21, 61–3. Brandt, *Studien,* p. 403. *JdSA,* 1910, p. 29.
4 Brandt, *Studien,* pp. 413, 415. Hansen, p. 225. Most, *Die deutsche Stadt,* pp. 26–7, 31. SADd, III 10143–6, 1890–8.
5 Brandt, *Studien,* p. 141. Most, *Die deutsche Stadt,* pp. 28–31. *AZ,* November 25, 1890. *NV,* November 10, 1894. SADd, III 6928, October 4, 1904.
6 SADd, III 6928, October 4, 1904.
7 Comfort, pp. 18–19. Sheehan, "Liberalism," pp. 129, 136. Most, *Die deutsche Stadt,* pp. 31–2. *Düsseldorfer Volksblatt,* November 22, 1902.
8 In other cities, stability was the prerequisite for involvement in municipal affairs. See, for example, Scott, p. 118.
9 *Parteitagen,* p. 32. SADd, III 6925, September 12, November 8, 1900; January 30, 1901.
10 *Düsseldorfer Volksblatt,* October 29, 1902. Copies of the Social Democratic press for these months were not available. Thus it is necessary to rely on the Center Party paper and subsequent Social Democratic explanations.
11 *Bericht des Gewerkschaftskartell,* 1902, p. 5. *VZ,* October 12, 1912.
12 *Düsseldorfer Volksblatt,* November 3, 1902.
13 *Düsseldorfer Volksblatt,* December 1, 1902. SADd, III 10147, 1902.
14 SADd, III 6927, October 10, 1903.
15 SADd, III 6928, June 26, 1904; III 6929, May 31, 1905.
16 *VZ,* August 25, 1905.
17 SADd, III 6929, May 28, 1905; III 6931, September 23, 1906. *VZ,* November 26, 1910.
18 SADd, III 10154, December 25, 1905.
19 SADd, III 6929, May 28, 1905; III 6931, election flyer, 1906.
20 SADd, III 10154, December 25, 1905.
21 *VZ,* October 12, 1906. SADd, III 6933, October 23, 1907.
22 *VZ,* October 3, 1908.
23 See note 19.
24 "Statistik des Jahres 1906," pp. 100–1. *VZ,* October 14, 1904; August 31, September 7, 9, 16, 1905; October 6, 1906.
25 This was typical of Liberal behavior throughout Germany. Sheehan, pp. 119–20, 129, 135.
26 *Düsseldorfer Zeitung,* October 11, 1908.
27 *VZ,* November 1, 1904.
28 *Düsseldorfer Tageblatt,* October 30, 1908.
29 SADd, XXI 232, Center Party election flyer, 1910.
30 *Düsseldorfer Tageblatt,* October 5, 1912. The SPD did run functionaries, because workers who ran or were elected were generally fired. *VZ,* July 26, 1910.
31 SADd, XXI 232, Center Party election flyer, 1910.
32 *Düsseldorfer Tageblatt,* January 16, 1906.
33 *VZ,* November 5, 1904. Ritter, *Die Arbeiterbewegung im wilhelmischen Reich,* pp. 233–4.
34 *VZ,* September 30, 1904.
35 *VZ,* October 10, 1912. See also *VZ,* December 11, 1904; November 5, 1908; November 11, 1910; December 9, 1911.
36 *VZ,* December 10, 1904; October 21, November 5, 1908; October 22, 23, 1910; March 10, 1913.
37 *VZ,* November 3, 10, 1910.
38 SADd, XXI 232, election flyers, 1908, 1910. StADd, Präsidialbüro 28, October 25, 1912. Sheehan, p. 129.
39 *VZ,* February 14, 1906. SADd, III 6930, July 18, 1906.
40 *VZ,* October 4, 1906; October 1, 1908; December 3, 1909; February 25, March 2, 1910.

41 SADd, XXI 232, September 9, 1906. *VZ*, September 25, 27, 1906.
42 *VZ*, March 9, May 10, June 3, 1905; January 3, 1906. *Mitteilungen*, No. 1. *Die städtische Arbeitslosenbeschäftigung im Winter 1901/2 in Düsseldorf*, n.d., pp. 3–5. SADd, III 9372a, 1903. *JdSA*, 1908, p. 25.
43 SADd, III 6933, July 24, 1910.
44 *VZ*, October 3, 1910.
45 *JdSA*, 1905, p. 19; 1906, p. 23; 1911, p. 28; 1912, p. 32. SADd, III 5518, statutes of labor exchange, 1905–6; III 9372a, May 25, 1908. *VZ*, December 28, 1908; January 15, 20, 1909; January 13, October 3, 1910.
46 *VZ*, December 3, 1901; January 16, 27, 1905; March 10, 1913. *Bericht des Gewerkschaftskartell*, 1902, p. 4.
47 *VZ*, July 3, 1914.
48 *VZ*, December 9, 1910; July 31, 1912. *Bericht des Gewerkschaftskartell*, 1911, p. 9. *Die Sozialpolitik*, p. 39. *MdH*, October 1910, p. 309; October 1913, pp. 293–4.
49 *Bericht des Gewerkschaftskartell*, 1902, p. 5; 1905, p. 31; *VZ*, March 6, 1907; April 7, 1908; December 24, 1910; March 7, 1911. StADd, Reg. Dd. 42813, 1912. Schorske, pp. 224–5.
50 *MdH*, April–May 1914, p. 35.
51 *VZ*, October 12, 1912.
52 *VZ*, June 21, 1910.
53 *VZ*, July 6, 1911.
54 *VZ*, June 30, July 1, 11, 21, September 22, October 5, 1911; July 26, 1912. StADd, Präsidialbüro 28, July 24, 1911.
55 Kaelble, pp. 84–93. Dieter Fricke, ed., *Die bürgerlichen Parteien in Deutschland*, Vol. II (Berlin: das europäische Buch, 1970), pp. 201–7.
56 *VZ*, July 13, 18, 1911.
57 *Düsseldorfer Tageblatt*, July 12, 1911.
58 *Düsseldorfer Tageblatt*, August 23, 1911. *VZ*, September 10, 22, 1911; July 26, 1912.
59 *Düsseldorfer Tageblatt*, September 29, 1911; SADd, XXI 232, Center Party flyer, 1911.
60 SADd, XXI 72, 1909, 1910; XXI 73, 1911.
61 *Düsseldorfer Zeitung*, July 7, 1911.
62 *Düsseldorfer Zeitung*, September 29, 1911.
63 Jaeger, pp. 154–5. Stegmann, pp. 201–7.
64 *Düsseldorfer Zeitung*, July 18, 1911.
65 *VZ*, September 30, 1911. StADd, Präsidialbüro 28, November 2, 1911.
66 Herkner, pp. 438, 449. Saul, pp. 32–4, 49–50. SADd, III 4596, III Quartel, 1904; III 4601, II Quartel, 1911. *JdH*, 1900, Pt. 2:40–2; 1901, Pt 2:107–9; 1902, Pt 1:61–2, Pt 2: 14–18, 96–9. *MdH*, June 1905, pp. 4–5.
67 *VZ*, June 17, September 26, 1911. SADd, III 5386, August 1911. StADd, Präsidialbüro 28, November 2, 1911; Reg. Dd. 30412, January 25, 1912.
68 *VZ*, August 9, December 16, 1910; January 11, March 16, October 4, 1911. Korn, pp. 206–9, 226.
69 *VZ*, October 4, 1911.
70 *VZ*, January 11, 1911.
71 *Düsseldorfer Zeitung*, August 28, 1911.
72 *VZ*, March 2, 1911.
73 Korn, p. 195. *VZ*, May 11, 1910; January 25, March 31, October 6, 1911; November 27, 1912. *Bericht der katholischen Arbeitersekretariat zu Düsseldorf für das Jahr 1909, 1910. Jahresbericht des christlichen Gewerkschaftskartell, Düsseldorf*, 1911.
74 Barkin, p. 267.
75 *Beiträge zur statistischen Monatsberichten der Stadt Düsseldorf*, July 1909, pp. XL–XLIII.

Kuczynski, Vol. 4, p. 338. *JdSA*, 1907, p. 15; 1909, p. 20; 1911, pp. 22–3; 1912, p. 27.

76 *Mitteilungen*, No. 8, p. 99*. *JdSA*, 1908, p. 28; 1911, p. 34.

77 *Beiträge zur statistischen Monatsberichten*, July 1909, pp. XL–XLIII.

78 SADd, III 4602, IV Quartel, 1911.

79 *Düsseldorfer Tageblatt*, January 27, 1907. SADd, XXI 73, October 5, 1911. XXI 74, 1912, passim.

80 Schauff, pp. 74, 80, 84.

81 It is impossible to break down the SPD vote by religion for 1911. The 1907 occupational statistics for Düsseldorf city cannot be adjusted for 1911 because several surrounding towns were incorporated in 1908 and 1909, and information on the composition of their working class is unavailable.

82 Ehrhardt, pp. 103–4. Saul, p. 147.

83 See Table A.4, Appendix.

84 Parkin, "Working-Class Conservatives," p. 282.

85 SADd, III 6928, December 17, 1903.

86 *VZ*, June 21, 1910.

10. Things fall apart

1 *VZ*, October 26, 1911.

2 Puhle, p. 350. Schorske, pp. 234–5.

3 *VZ*, March 6, 1912.

4 Schorske, pp. 238–41.

5 *MdH*, No. 5–6, May–June 1913, pp. 162, 164–6. Saul, p. 324. Stegmann, pp. 360–1.

6 Hartmut Pogge von Strandmann and Imanuel Geiss, *Die Erforderlichkeit des Unmöglichen. Deutschland am Vorabend des ersten Weltkrieges* (Frankfurt: Europäischer Verlagsanstalt, 1965), pp. 10–11. Stegmann, pp. 283–92, 366–7. *MdH*, No. 5–6, May–June 1913, pp. 165, 174–5.

7 Saul, pp. 368–71.

8 *MdH*, No. 3, March 1914, p. 70.

9 *VZ*, March 11, 1914.

10 Jaeger, p. 157. Saul, pp. 323, 333, 350–5, 385.

11 *VZ*, July 22, August 12, 24, 1912. StAK, 403 13534, January 9, 1911.

12 *VZ*, February 27, 1912.

13 Klaus J. Mattheier, "Werkvereine und wirtschaftsfriedlich-nationale (gelbe) Arbeiterbewegung im Ruhrgebiet," in Reulecke, ed., pp. 179–90. *VZ*, February 14, March 1, 30, April 6, 1912. StADd, Reg. Dd. 42813, September 1, 1912; Reg. Dd. 15923, October 1, 1912.

14 Mattheier, p. 190. *MdH*, No. 2–3, February–March 1912, p. 36. SADd, III 4206, II Quartel, 1913.

15 David Blackbourn, "The Problem of Democratisation: German Catholics and the Role of the Center Party," in Evans, ed., p. 248. *VZ*, November 11, 1913. *Christliche Metallarbeiter Verband Deutschlands, Ortsverwaltung Düsseldorf*, 1912, pp. 17–19.

16 Puhle, p. 350.

17 Fritz Stern, "Bethmann-Hollweg and the War: The Limits of Responsibility," in Krieger and Stern, eds., p. 276.

18 Wehler, *Kaiserreich*, p. 104.

19 StAK, 403 6864, December 1905; 403 6867, n.d.; 403 6870, n.d. Jean Quataert, "The Social Basis of Socialist Feminism" (Paper delivered at the Berkshire Women's History Conference, South Hadley, Mass., August 1978).

20 *JdSA*, 1914, p. 3. SADd, III 4206, 1913, passim. *VZ*, July 21, 1910; July 24, 1911; July 1, 1913; January 26, 1914. *Jahresbericht des Bezirksverbandes katholisher Arbeitervereine*, 1912, Table 1, n.p.

21 *VZ*, April 28, 29, June 28, July 1, October 13, 1913.

22 *VZ*, March 14, 15, 1914.

23 *VZ*, April 25, 1913.

24 *VZ*, April 1, 22, 23, May 7, 27, 30, June 25, July 2, 26, 1912; January 21, February 2, March 7, October 26, 28, November 5, 1913.

25 *VZ*, June 11, October 3, 1911; April 16, July 23, 1912; July 7, 1914.

26 *VZ*, January 20, 1914.

27 *VZ*, August 26, 1912; April 25, 1913.

28 SADd, III 4602, IV Quartel, 1912.

29 *VZ*, January 12, 1914.

30 *VZ*, October 20, 1912; April 3, 6, 25, 30, May 7, 22, 1913. SADd, III 4602, II Quartel, 1913.

31 *VZ*, May 26, 1914.

32 *VZ*, June 8, 1914.

33 *VZ*, May 2, 1910; April 30, 1912. StADd, Reg. Dd. 42813, September 1, 1912.

34 *VZ*, April 16, 1914.

35 *Bericht des Gewerkschaftskartell*, 1911, p. 19. SADd, III 5386, 1911, passim.

36 *MdH*, No. 12, December 1914, p. 506.

37 *VZ*, February 22, March 2, 7, 13, 16, 22, April 18, 1912; May 7, July 12, 15, August 1, September 11, 1913.

38 *VZ*, July 22, 1912. StADd, Reg. Dd. 30412, July 27, 1912.

39 *VZ*, July 28–30, August 14, October 9, 1911; July 22, August 3, 5, 12, 24, September 14, October 24, November 30, 1912; January 26, 1914.

40 See Chapter 5.

41 *VZ*, March 24, 1909; July 21, 1911.

42 *VZ*, March 20, 1911.

43 *VZ*, March 3, April 25, 1913; March 9, 1914. StADd, Präsidialbüro 28, April 28, 1913.

44 See Chapter 5.

45 *VZ*, July 23, 1908; August 4, October 30, 1909; January 2, May 2, July 25, August 1, 1910; January 31, 1911.

46 StADd, Reg. Dd. 9058, August 27, 1906.

47 *VZ*, July 9, 1908; August 4, 1909; July 25, 1910.

48 *VZ*, December 29, 1913.

49 *VZ*, July 5, 1913.

50 Schorske, p. 249.

51 *VZ*, June 4, 1913.

52 *VZ*, July 5, 1913.

53 *Protokoll der SPD*, 1913, pp. 337–8.

54 Ibid., p. 364.

55 *VZ*, September 23, 1913.

56　*VZ*, October 6, 7, 10, 1913.

57　Groh, *Integration*, pp. 461, 486. Klöcker, pp. 164–5.

58　*VZ*, March 31, 1913.

59　*VZ*, July 5, 1913.

60　*VZ*, August 25, 1913.

61　*VZ*, September 1, 1913.

62　StADd, Reg. Dd. 42809, December 18, 1913. *VZ*, May 28, June 4, 30, 1913.

63　Groh, *Negative Integration*, p. 489.

64　*Protokoll der SPD*, 1913, p. 321.

65　Berten, p. 133.

66　*Protokoll der SPD*, 1913, p. 321.

67　Groh, *Negative Integration*, p. 596. *VZ*, October 7, 1913.

68　Schorske assumes that this was always the case. Pp. 276–8. Lützenkirchen, p. 147, suggests that it was not.

69　*VZ*, October 6, 7, 10, 1913.

70　*VZ*, September 13, 22, December 29, 1913.

71　*VZ*, July 8, 1914.

72　Dick Geary, "The German Labor Movement, 1848–1919," *European Studies Review* 6, No. 3(1976):307, 314–15. *VZ*, October 17, 1910; October 10, 1911. StADd, Reg. Dd. 42809, July 1912.

73　*VZ*, July 1, 2, 14, 1914.

74　*VZ*, July 21, 27, 1914.

75　Schaarer, pp. 104–6.

76　Fritz Fischer, *World Power or Decline* (New York: W. W. Norton, 1974), p. 82. Elie Halévy, *The Era of Tyrannies* (Garden City, N.Y.: Anchor Books, 1965), pp. 215–16. Arno Mayer, "Domestic Causes of the First World War," in Krieger and Stern, eds., pp. 312–20.

77　Berten, p. 140.

78　*VZ*, July 21, 27, 1914.

79　Guenther Roth, p. 288.

80　*VZ*, July 30, 1914.

81　Suzanne Miller, *Burgfrieden und Klassenkampf* (Düsseldorf: Droste, 1974), pp. 33–74.

82　Georges Haupt, *Socialism and the Great War: The Collapse of the Second International* (Oxford: Oxford University Press, 1972), pp. 11–29.

83　Moore, pp. 221–6. Schorske, pp. 288–90. Robert Wheeler, *USPD und Internationale* (Frankfurt: Ullstein, 1975), p. 9.

84　Haupt, *Socialism*, pp. 213–15, 222–3.

85　*VZ*, July 30, 1914.

86　Berten, p. 144.

87　Adalbert Oehler, *Düsseldorf im Weltkrieg* (Düsseldorf: Lintz, 1927), pp. 82, 87, 89, 243. *VZ*, October 8, 10, 1914.

88　*VZ*, November 7, 21, December 30, 1914. Berten, p. 137.

89　Institut für Marxismus-Leninismus beim ZK der SED, ed., *Dokumente und Materialien zur Geschichte der deutschen Arbeiterbewegung*, Reihe 2, Vol. I (Berlin: Dietz, 1958), pp. 26–7.

90　Berten, pp. 143–4.

91 *VZ*, October 31, 1914.
92 *VZ*, August 27, 1914.
93 *VZ*, September 24, 29, October 3, 6, 7, 1914.
94 Miller, p. 72.

11. War

1 Gerald Feldman, *Army, Industry and Labor in Germany, 1914–1918* (Princeton, N.J.: Princeton University Press, 1966), pp. 45–116, passim.
2 Ibid. Jürgen Kocka, *Klassengesellschaft im Kriege, 1914–18* (Göttingen: Vandenhoeck und Ruprecht, 1973), pp. 21–33.
3 Oehler, pp. 242–3. Weidenhaupt, p. 156.
4 *MdH*, No. 1–2, January–February 1916, p. 5.
5 Kocka, pp. 17–21, 25–7. *MdH*, No. 8–9, August–September 1915, pp. 319–20.
6 Oehler, p. 243. *SM*, 1915, p. 3; 1917, p. 131. For a discussion of the effects of rationalization, see Carmen Sirianni, "Workers' Control in the Era of the First World War: a Comparative Analysis of the European Experience," *Theory and Society* 9 (January 1980):29–88.
7 Oehler, pp. 330–1. *SM*, 1915, p. 6; 1917, p. 7.
8 Feldman, p. 136.
9 Miller, pp. 75–113. Schorske, pp. 291–320.
10 Hans-Joachim Bieber, "Die deutsche Gewerkschaften, 1914–20" (Ph.D. diss., University of Hamburg, 1975), p. 233.
11 Feldman, p. 30.
12 Ibid., pp. 73–96.
13 Fischer, *World Power or Decline*, p. 84.
14 *VZ*, January 20, 1915.
15 *VZ*, March 4, 1915.
16 *VZ*, March 26, 1915.
17 Jürgen Reulecke, "Der erste Weltkrieg und die Arbeiterbewegung im rheinisch-westfälischen Industriegebiet," in Reulecke, ed., pp. 213–14.
18 StADd, Reg. Dd. 15985, May 1915.
19 Ibid. *VZ*, April 27, 1915.
20 StADd, Reg. Dd. 15985, May 1915.
21 Berten, pp. 145–8. *VZ*, April 30, 1915. Institut für Marxismus-Leninismus beim ZK der SED, ed., *Dokumente und Materialien*, Vol. I, pp. 135–6, 157–9.
22 Institut für Marxismus-Leninismus beim ZK der SED, ed., *Dokumente und Materialien*, Vol. I, pp. 170–85. Miller, p. 107.
23 *VZ*, July 9, 1915.
24 Fritz Opel, *Der deutsche Metallarbeiter Verband während des ersten Weltkrieges und der Revolution* (Hannover: Norddeutscher Verlagsanstalt Goedel, 1957), pp. 47–9.
25 Schorske, p. 303–5. *VZ*, December 31, 1915.
26 *VZ*, December 22, 1915.
27 Miller, p. 132.
28 *VZ*, March 25, 1916.
29 Reulecke, in Reulecke, ed., pp. 224–5.
30 *VZ*, May 15, 1916.
31 *VZ*, May 2, 1916.
32 Oehler, pp. 349–57.

33 Arthur Rosenberg, *Entstehung der Weimarer Republik* (Frankfurt: Europäische Verlagsanstalt, 1961) pp. 101–14. Feldman, pp. 150–68.

34 Feldman, pp. 197–249.

35 *VZ*, January 2, 1917.

36 Feldman, p. 318.

37 Feldman, pp. 255–7, 272–3. Kuczynski, 4:393. Kocka, pp. 43–4. Oehler, pp. 94, 97, 103–4, 356–7, 377, 388–95. Weidenhaupt, p. 157.

38 Arno Mayer, *Wilson vs. Lenin, Political Origins of the New Diplomacy, 1917–1918* (New York: Meridian, 1964), pp. 22–36, 61–140. Halévy, pp. 214–43. For a discussion of German war aims, see Fischer, *Germany's Aims*.

39 Kocka, pp. 33–49. Reinhard Rürup, Gerald Feldman, and Eberhard Kolb. "Die Massenbewegungen der Arbeiterschaft in Deutschland am Ende des ersten Weltkrieges (1917–1920)," *Politische Vierteljahresschrift* 13, No. 1 (August 1972):86–9.

40 Feldman, p. 445.

41 Hans W. Gatzke, *Germany's Drive to the West* (Baltimore: Johns Hopkins University Press, 1950), p. 294.

42 *VZ*, February 3, 5, 1917. Miller, pp. 143–7.

43 Institut für Marxismus-Leninismus beim ZK der SED, ed., *Dokumente und Materialien*, Vol. I, pp. 582–3.

44 *VZ*, March 31, April 23, 1917.

45 SADd, III 4604, April 1917. *VZ*, May 2, 1917.

46 David W. Morgan, *The Socialist Left and the German Revolution* (Ithaca, N.Y.: Cornell University Press, 1975), p. 68. Reulecke in Reulecke, ed., p. 227. Jürgen Tampke, "The Ruhr and Revolution" (Ph.D. diss., n.d. Australian National University), p. 115.

47 Schorske, pp. 314–18. Wheeler, *USPD*, p. iii. Eberhard Kolb, *Die Arbeiterräte in der deutschen Innenpolitik, 1918–1919* (Düsseldorf: Droste, 1962), p. 38.

48 Opel, p. 68. *VZ*, September 7, 1917.

49 SADd, III 4604, April 1917. Institut für Marxismus-Leninismus beim ZK der SED, ed., *Dokumente und Materialien*, Vol. I, pp. 562–4.

50 Kuczynski, 4:271.

51 Oehler, pp. 96–7.

52 StADd, Präsidialbüro 29, April 30, 1917.

53 SADd, III 4604, April 5, 1917.

54 Rürup et al., p. 88. SADd, III 4604, April 1917.

55 SADd, III 4604, April 1917, September 12, 1917. *VZ*, July 14, 1917. Kuczynski, 4:278–9. Oehler, p. 363.

56 Ehrhardt, p. 109. StADd, Präsidialbüro 29, November 3, 1917.

57 Oehler, pp. 267–8, 297. *VZ*, September 7, 1917. StADd, Präsidialbüro 29, November 3, 1917.

58 Reulecke, in Reulecke, ed., pp. 232–3. SADd, III 4604, March 1918. StADd, Präsidialbüro 29, June 4, 1917. *VZ*, January 11, 1918.

59 *SM*, 1915, p. 6; 1918, p. 7. SADd, III 4604, March 1918. Kocka, p. 18.

60 SADd, III 4604, March and September 1918. *VZ*, April 12, 18, 1918.

61 *VZ*, January 8, April 27, August 7, 24, September 7, 14, 1918. Feldman, pp. 484–6.

62 *VZ*, April 2, 1918.

63 Feldman, p. 523.

64 SADd, III 4604, March and September 1918.

65 *VZ*, April 25, 26, May 3, 5, 6, 17, 24, 27, October 25, 31, November 2, 1918.

66 Hartfrid Krause, *USPD* (Frankfurt: Europäische Verlagsanstalt, 1975), pp. 108–9. Miller, p. 253.

67 Krause, pp. 108–9. StADd, Präsidialbüro 29, April 30, 1918.

68 SADd, III 4604, November 17, 1917. StADd, Präsidialbüro 29, May 6, 1918.
69 SADd, III 4604, September 23, 1918.
70 SADd, III 4604, October 18, 1918.
71 Kolb, pp. 56–9.
72 Miller, p. 396.

12. Revolution

1 Kolb, pp. 42–5, 81–3. See also Reinhard Rürup, ed., *Arbeiter- und Soldatenräte im rheinisch-westfälischen Industriegebiet* (Wuppertal: Peter Hammer, 1975); and Francis L. Carsten, *Revolution in Central Europe* (Berkeley, Calif.: University of California Press, 1972).
2 *VZ*, November 1–7, 1918, passim. Oehler, p. 532.
3 SADd, XXI 336, November 14, 1918.
4 Feldman, pp. 521–7.
5 SADd, XXI 336, November 8, 14, 1918.
6 SADd, XXI 336, November 14, 1918. *VZ*, November 9, 1918.
7 *WdH*, No. 46, November 16, 1918. SADd, XXI 73, November 14, 1918. *VZ*, November 11, 1918.
8 Kolb, pp. 56–60. Robert Wheeler, "'Ex oriente lux?' The Soviet Example and the German Revolution, 1917–1923," in Charles L. Bertrand, ed., *Revolutionary Situations in Europe, 1917–22: Germany, Italy, Austria-Hungary,* (Montreal: Centre Interuniversitaire d'Etudes Européennes, 1977), p. 40.
9 Reulecke, in Reulecke, ed., p. 238. Rürup et al., p. 96. Kolb, pp. 87, 91, 158, 168–9.
10 Eberhard Kolb, "Rätewirklichkeit und Räteideologie in der deutschen Revolution von 1918/19," in *Vom Kaiserreich zur Weimarer Republik,* (Cologne: Kiepenheuer und Witsch, 1972), pp. 174–5.
11 Rürup et al., p. 86.
12 Rürup, ed., pp. 15–16, 21–3.
13 *VZ*, November 11, 14, 1918.
14 SADd, XXI 336, November 1918, passim. Oehler, pp. 638–9.
15 *VZ*, November 11, 20, 21, 1918. Oehler, pp. 644, 648.
16 Rürup, ed., p. 23. Peter von Oertzen, "Die grossen Streiks der Ruhrbergarbeiterschaft im Frühjahr 1919," in Kolb, ed., p. 187.
17 *WdH*, No. 46, November 16, 1918, pp. 656–8; No. 14–15, April 25, 1919, p. 136. *SM*, January 1919, pp. 11, 112.
18 *VZ*, November 13, 19, 29, 1918. *WdH*, No. 46, November 16, 1918; No. 50, December 14, 1918.
19 Rürup, ed., p. 23. Kolb, *Arbeiterräte*, p. 99.
20 *VZ*, November 16, 1918.
21 *VZ*, November 21, 25, 1918.
22 *VZ*, November 1918, passim.
23 Berten, p. 177. See notes 36 and 56.
24 Institut für Marxismus-Leninismus beim ZK der SED, ed., *Dokumente und Materialien,* Vol. II, p. 511. SADd, XXI 332, November 29, 1918.
25 *VZ*, November 28. 1918.

26 *VZ*, November 29, December 2, 1918.
27 *VZ*, December 12, 1917, and November–December 1918, passim.
28 Kolb, *Arbeiterräte*, p. 113. Oehler, p. 650. Rürup, ed., pp. 110–14, 172–3, 249. Comfort, pp. 46–52.
29 Berten, p. 179. SADd, XXI 332, n.d.
30 Rürup, ed., pp. 92–106, 166–77, 247–61.
31 Lucas, pp. 155–92. See also Tampke, passim.
32 *VZ*, December 9, 1918. Berten, p. 184.
33 Institut für Marxismus-Leninismus beim ZK der SED, ed., *Dokumente und Materialien*, Vol. II, p. 516. *VZ*, December 5, 12, 20, 1918.
34 *VZ*, December 1918, passim.
35 Rosenberg, *History*, pp. 35–67. For the most thorough discussion of Social Democratic military policy, see Ulrich Kluge, *Soldatenräte und Revolution* (Göttingen: Vandenhoeck und Ruprecht, 1975).
36 Berten, pp. 179, 184–5. *VZ*, December 28, 1918. For the Congress, see Kolb, *Arbeiterräte*, pp. 197–204.
37 *VZ*, December 27, 1918.
38 Kolb, *Arbeiterräte*, p. 220. *VZ*, December 27, 1918. Institut für Marxismus-Leninismus beim ZK der SED, ed., *Vorwärts und nicht vergessen* (Berlin: Dietz, 1958), pp. 480–1.
39 Kolb, *Arbeiterräte*, pp. 158–61, 244–82.
40 Peter von Oertzen, *Betriebsräte in der Novemberrevolution* (Düsseldorf: Droste, 1963), pp. 89–153. Brian Peterson, "Workers' Councils in Germany, 1918–19," *New German Critique* 4 (Winter 1975):113–24.
41 Institut für Marxismus-Leninismus beim ZK der ZED, ed., *Dokumente und Materialien*, Vol. III, pp. 440–1.
42 SADd, XXI 333, January 9, 1919.
43 Oehler, p. 653. *Beiträge zu den statistischen Monatsberichten der Stadt Düsseldorf*, December 1919, n.p. SADd, XXI 333, January 9, 1919; III 7886, April 12, 1919.
44 *Beiträge*, December 1919, n.p. Institut für Marxismus-Leninismus beim ZK der SED, ed., *Vorwärts und nicht vergessen*, pp. 484–5. Kolb, *Arbeiterräte*, p. 307.
45 J. S. Drabkin, *Die November Revolution 1918 in Deutschland* (Berlin: VEB, 1968), p. 527.
46 *WdH*, No. 16, March 3, 1919, p. 152. Oertzen, *Betriebsräte*, p. 124.
47 Dick Geary, "Radicalism and the Worker: Metalworkers and Revolution, 1914–23," in Evans, ed., pp. 271–2.
48 Wheeler, *USPD*, p. 44. SADd, XXI 333, January 9, 1919.
49 SADd, XXI 333, January 9, 1919.
50 Lucas, p. 195.
51 *VZ*, January 10, 11, 1919. SADd, XXI 333, January 9, 1919; III 7886, March 6, 1919.
52 SADd, XXI 333, January 9, 17, February 4, 1919. Institut für Marxismus-Leninismus beim ZK der SED, *Dokumente und Materialien*, Vol. III, p. 441.
53 Morgan, p. 448. *SdR, Erstes Ergänzungsheft*, 1919, pp. 51–2.
54 SADd, XXI 333, n.d. *VZ*, February 6, 7, 1919.
55 *VZ*, February 7, 1919.
56 *VZ*, February 8, 1919.
57 *SM*, January 1919, p. 11; June 1919, p. 112. SADd, XXI 333, January 14, February 4, 1919.

58 SADd, XXI 333, January 30, 1919.
59 SADd, XXI 334, February 4, 1919.
60 Oehler, p. 656.
61 SADd, XXI 334, February 12, 1919.
62 Oertzen, *Betriebsräte*, pp. 114–19.
63 *VZ*, January and February 1919, passim.
64 Lucas, p. 226.
65 Ibid., pp. 181–2, 280–1. Oertzen, *Betriebsräte*, pp. 278–9.
66 Oertzen, *Betriebsräte*, pp. 190–1, 276–7.
67 See Hinton for a discussion of the relationship between different structures of work and protest in the British metal industry. There is no comparable study for Germany.
68 Stephen Hickey, "The Shaping of the German Labour Movement: Miners in the Ruhr," in Evans, ed., pp. 220–35.
69 Oertzen, *Betriebsräte*, pp. 69–108.
70 *WdH*, No. 9–10, March 15, 1919, pp. 86–7. SADd, III 7886, February 24, 1919; XXI 334, February 21, 1919. Gerald Feldman, "Socio-Economic Structures in the Industrial Sector and Revolutionary Potentialities, 1917–22," in Bertrand, ed., p. 167.
71 SADd, XXI 333, February 20, 1919; XXI 334, February 1919, passim. *VZ*, February 26, 1919.
72 SADd, XXI 334, February 24, 1919.
73 *VZ*, February 28, 1919. Institut für Marxismus-Leninismus beim ZK der SED, ed., *Vorwärts und nicht vergessen*, p. 485.
74 SADd, XXI 335, March 1, 1919. *VZ*, March 3–7, 1919.
75 *VZ*, March 7, 1919.
76 SADd, XXI 335, March 10, 1919.
77 *VZ*, March 8, 1919.
78 *VZ*, March 10, 1919. SADd, XXI 335, March 10, 1919.
79 SADd, XXI 335, March 10, 1919.
80 *VZ*, March 18, 1919.
81 *VZ*, March 5, 31, 1919, SADd, III 7886, March 29, 1919.
82 *WdH*, No. 14–15, April 26, 1919, pp. 136–40.
83 Rürup et al., p. 90.
84 Oertzen, *Betriebsräte*, p. 117.
85 *VZ*, April 5, 16, 18, 1919. SADd, III 7668, n.d.
86 *VZ*, April 18, 1919.
87 This was true in many other areas as well. Rürup et al., p. 100.
88 *Beiträge*, December 1919, n.p. SADd, III 7668, April–June passim; III 5518, June 4, July 18, 1919. Wheeler, *USPD*, pp. 96–7.
89 *WdH*, No. 15–16, April 30, 1919.
90 Opel, pp. 104–6. Wheeler, *USPD* pp. 148–9. Morgan, p. 449.
91 Wheeler, *USPD*, pp. 239–55. Berten, p. 193. Krause, p. 324.

Bibliography

I. Archival material

Staatsarchiv Koblenz, Abteilung 403: Akten des rheinischen Oberpräsidiums

403 6832–56	Ausführung des Gesetzesgegen die Bestrebungen der Sozial Demokratie.
403 6862	Arbeiter Radfahrerbund "Solidarität" in Düsseldorf, 1913–14.
403 6864–71	Nachweisungen der Sozialdemokraten und Anarchisten, der sozialdemokratischen Vereine, der Führer, usw.
403 8323–9	Lage der Industrie, Arbeiterentlassungen, Arbeitereinstellungen, usw.
403 9047–9	Zeitungsberichte der Regierung zu Düsseldorf, 1888–97, 1905.

Staatsarchiv Düsseldorf

Akten der Regierung zu Düsseldorf, Präsidialbüro

25–29	Zeitungsberichte, 1898–1900, 1901–4, 1906–10, 1911–14, 1914–18.

Akten der Regierung zu Düsseldorf

8843–5	Berichte über den Stand der Sozial Demokratie.
8867–8	Agitation der Sozialdemokratie, Verbreitung von Schriften, Maifeier, 1891–5.
9028	Spezial- und Sammelberichte zu generellen Angelegenheiten über die sozialdemokratische Bewegung und anarchistische Bewegung, 1893–1900.
9039–41	Terminalberichte über die sozialdemokratische Bewegung, 1895–1907.
9043–59	Sammelberichte zu den Terminalberichten, 1895–1907.
9067	Agitation der Sozial Demokratie gegen das preussische Landtagswahlrecht, 1905–6.
15921	Die konfessionellen Arbeitervereine und die christlichen Gewerkschaften, 1901–15.
15923	Die nationalen Werkvereine, 1910–13.
15985	Spezial- und Sammelberichte zu generellen Angelegenheiten über die sozialdemokratische Bewegung und anarchistische Bewegung, 1901–15.
30411–12	Ueberwachung der Arbeiterbewegung, 1903–15.
42781	Sammelberichte zu den Terminalberichten, 1910.
42786	Sozialdemokratische Maifeier, 1902–13.
42787–8	Agitation der Sozial Demokratie gegen das preussische Landtagswahlrecht, 1906–10.
42809	Terminalberichte über die Sozialdemokratie, 1912–14.
42810–13	Sammelberichte zu den Terminalberichten, 1912–14.
42814	Die sozialdemokratische und anarchistische Bewegung, 1906–13.

Stadtarchiv Düsseldorf

III 4589–604	Zeitungsberichte, 1886–1918.
III 4649	Statistik über Ein- und Auswanderung, 1871–1905.
III 5372–2a	Wohlfahrtseinrichtungen in den gewerblichen Anlagen, 1878–1934.

III 5373–7	Beschäftigung jugendlicher Arbeiter in Fabriken, 1876–1926.
III 5381–6	Arbeiterentlassungen und Aussperrungen, 1886–1911.
III 5389–92	Arbeitsordnungen, 1892, 1901–13.
III 5393	Die Ueberarbeit von Arbeitern in den gewerblichen Betrieben, 1872–1928.
III 5518	Die öffentliche Sicherheit. Generalia, 1891–1923.
III 5700–8	Oeffentliche Versammlungen, 1886–1912.
III 5738–84	Die Presse, Spezialia, 1889–1909.
III 5757–64	Verteilung und Verkauf von Druckschriften auf öffentlichen Strassen und Beschlagnahme der Druckschriften, 1905–11.
III 5791–2	Polizei über die Presse: *Die Wacht, Organ der christlichen Arbeiter und Handwerker*, 1897–1908; *Die Rheinische-Westfälische Wacht*, 1897–1908.
III 5803	Polizei über die Presse: *Gewerkvereinsbote*, 1901–8.
III 5816	Polizei über die Presse: *Die Düsseldorfer Arbeiterzeitung*, 1889–1891.
III 5825	*Agitations-Material*, (Herausgeber, Dr. H. Laufenberg), 1906–8.
III 5931	Der deutsche Arbeiterverein in Oberbilk, 1887–1902.
III 5932	Arbeiter-Sängerbund Rheinlands, 1898–1901.
III 5933	Arbeiterverein der Marienhütte zu Oberbilk, 1887–98.
III 5934	Arbeiter-Vertreter Verein, 1898–1901.
III 5939	Verein christlicher Arbeiter und Handwerker: Sektion Düsseldorf-Nord, 1896–7.
III 5981	Verband der Bau- Erd- und gewerblichen Hülfarbeiter Deutschlands, Zahlstelle Düsseldorf, 1898–1903.
III 6000	Bildungsverein für Frauen und Mädchen.
III 6080–1	Verein für christliche Arbeiter und Handwerker, 1886–98.
III 6159–64	Evangelische Arbeitervereine, 1899–1909.
III 6165	Gewerkverein der Fabrik und Handarbeiter, 1892–1907.
III 6166	Vereinigung der Fabrik und gewerblichen Hilfsarbeiter Deutschlands, 1906.
III 6184	Die Former Deutschlands, Allgemeiner Metallarbeiter Verein, 1888–90.
III 6185	Centralverein der deutschen Former, 1892–1904.
III 6188	Frauen-Agitations Commission.
III 6219	Freie Vereinigung der Gewerkvereine, Hirsch-Duncker, 1897–1906.
III 6396–7	Katholische Arbeiter Verein, 1896–1904.
III 6556	Leseklub "Heinrich Heine."
III 6557	Der Leseverein Lassalle.
III 6559	Die Lese- und Diskutiergesellschaft "Liberte."
III 6704	Vereinigung der Metallarbeiter Deutschlands, 1884–93.
III 6712–15	Deutscher Metallarbeiter Verband, 1891–1905.
III 6915–33	Die sozialdemokratische Vereine, 1878–1910.
III 6224–6	Gewerkschafts-Cartell, 1892–1904.
III 6921	Der christlich-soziale Verein, 1881–92.
III 7027	Verband aller in der Textil Industrie beschäftigten Arbeiter und Arbeiterinnen Deutschlands, 1893–1901.
III 7032	Theater Verein "Morgenröthe."
III 7143	*Die Wacht*, 1896.
III 7168	Wohnungs- und Konsum Verein der Arbeiter, 1897.
III 7774–9	Anarchisten. Spezialia, 1889–1914.
III 7886	Streiks, Unruhen und Ausschreitungen, 1919–24.
III 9354–5	Berufs- und Gewerbezählung, 1895, 1907.

III 9372a	Arbeitslosenstatistik, 1902–9.
III 10103–14	Wahlen für den Reichstag, 1884–1920.
III 10125–33	Wahlen für den Abgeordnetenhaus, 1888–1913.
III 10143–52	Stadtverordnetenwahl, 1885–1916.
XXI 72–3	Protokolle der Zentrumspartei der Wahlkreis Düsseldorf, 1908–10, 1911–18.
XXI 74	Protokolle der Geschäftsleitung der Wahlkreis Düsseldorf (Zentrum), 1910–11.
XXI 75	Protokolle über Versammlungen der Vertrauensmänner in den Vororten (Zentrum), 1909.
XXI 185–7	Windhorstbund (Jungzentrum) 1903–13.
XXI 232	Sammlung zur Geschichte des Düsseldorfer Zentrums.
XXI 332–6	Arbeiter- und Soldatenrat, 1918–19.

II. Newspapers

Social Democratic Party
Düsseldorfer Arbeiterzeitung
Düsseldorfer Volkszeitung
Niederrheinische Volkstribune
Catholic Center Party
Düsseldorfer Tageblatt
Düsseldorfer Volksblatt
National Liberal Party
Düsseldorfer Zeitung

III. Protocols, reports, and journals

Bericht des Gewerkschaftskartells, Düsseldorf, 1902–6, 1911–12.
Christlicher Metallarbeiter Verband Deutschlands, Ortsverwaltung Düsseldorf, Jahresbericht vom Jahre 1912.
Die Internationale, I, April 1915.
Jahresbericht des Bezirksverbandes katholischer Arbeitervereine von Düsseldorf Stadt und Land für das Jahr 1912.
Jahresbericht des christlichen Gewerkschaftskartell Düsseldorf, 1911–12.
Jahresbericht der Handelskammer zu Düsseldorf, 1888–1903.
Jahresbericht der Handwerkskammer zu Düsseldorf, 1902–3, 1906–7.
Jahresbericht des statistischen Amts Düsseldorf, 1908–14.
Mitteilungen zur Statistik der Stadt Düsseldorf.
  No. 1, *Die städtische Arbeitslosenbeschäftigung im Winter 1901–2 in Düsseldorf,* n.d.
  No. 2, *Die Grundstücks- und Wohnungszählung vom 1. Dezember 1905,* 1907.
  No. 3, *Industrie und Handelsgewerbe in Düsseldorf nach der Betriebszählung vom 12. Juni 1907,* 1908.
  No. 4, *Die Nichteinheimischen in Düsseldorf nach der Volkszählung vom 1. Dezember 1905,* 1912.
  No. 8, *Die Grundbesitz- und Wohnungsverhältnisse in Düsseldorf und ihre Entwicklung seit 1903,* 1912.
Monatsschrift der Handelskammer zu Düsseldorf, 1904–18.
Protokoll über die Verhandlung des Parteitages der sozialdemokratischen Partei Deutschlands, 1890–1913.

Bibliography 357

Sozialdemokratische Parteitage für die Rheinprovinz und den Niederrhein, 1889–1909.

Statistik des deutschen Reiches, n.s., Vol. 108, 207.

Statistik über den Stand der katholischen Arbeitervereine des Bezirks Düsseldorf für das Jahr 1903–5, 1907, 1911.

Tätigkeitsbericht des Vorstandes und Ausschusses des Rheinisch-Westfälischen Ausbreitungs-Verbandes der deutschen Gewerkvereine, 1902–3, 1906.

Wochenschrift der Handelskammer zu Düsseldorf, 1918–20.

IV. Works on Düsseldorf

Albrecht, Helmut. "Die Entwicklung der Düsseldorfer Arbeiterwohnung." Med. diss., University of Düsseldorf, 1939.

Bär, Max. *Die Behördenverfassung der Rheinprovinz seit 1815*. Bonn: Publikationen der Gesellschaft für Rheinische Geschichtskunde, Vol. 35, 1919.

Beckers, Hubertus. "Entwicklungsgeschichte der Industrieunternehmungen in Düsseldorf, 1815–1914." Ph.D. diss., University of Cologne, 1958.

Brandt, Otto. "Düsseldorfs Wirtschaftliche Entwicklung," in Hans Arthur Lux, ed., *Düsseldorf*. Düsseldorf: Deutsche Kunst und Verlagsanstalt, 1921–2.

Studien zur Wirtschafts- und Verwaltungsgeschichte der Stadt Düsseldorf im 19. Jahrhundert. Düsseldorf: n.p., 1902.

Bringmann, Karl. *Die konfessionell-politische Tagespresse des Niederrheins im 19. Jahrhundert*. Düsseldorf: n.p., 1938.

Eberstadt, Rudolf. *Rheinische Wohnungsverhältnisse und ihre Bedeutung für die Wohnungs-wesen in Deutschland*. Jena: G. Fischer, 1903.

Froelich, Fr. *Die Stellung der deutschen Maschinenindustrie im deutschen Wirtschaftsleben und auf dem Weltmarkte*. Berlin: J. Springer, 1914.

Fürsorge für den Bau von Kleinwohnungen in Düsseldorf. Denkschrift der Handelskammer zu Düsseldorf. Düsseldorf: August Bagel, 1911.

Gerlach, Paul. "Die Düsseldorfer Arbeiterbewegung." In Hans Arthur Lux, ed., *Düsseldorf*, pp. 69–72. Düsseldorf: Deutsche Kunst und Verlagsanstalt, 1921–2.

Görgen, Hans Peter. *Düsseldorf und der Nationalsozialismus*. Düsseldorf: Schwann, 1969.

Hansen, Josef. *Preussen und Rheinland von 1815–1915*. Bonn: A. Marcus und E. Webers, 1918.

Hatzfeld, Lutz. *Die Handelsgesellschaft Albert Poensgen, Mauel-Düsseldorf*. Cologne: Rheinische-Westfälisches Wirtschaftsarchiv, 1964.

Heinson, Ernst, "Düsseldorf als Sitz wichtiger industrieller Verbände," in Hans Arthur Lux, ed., *Düsseldorf*, pp. 54–8. Düsseldorf: Deutsche Kunst und Verlagsanstalt, 1921–2.

125 Jahre Industrie- und Handelskammer zu Düsseldorf, 1831–1956. Düsseldorf: n.p., 1956.

Kauhausen, Paul. *Chronik der Stadt Düsseldorf*. Berlin: C. H. Weise, 1938.

Kelleter, Heinrich. *Die Geschichte der Familie Poensgen*. Düsseldorf: August Bagel, 1908.

Kieber, Wilhelm. "Stadtentwicklung und Wohnungsfrage in Düsseldorf." Ph.D. diss., University of Münster, 1922.

Köllmann, Wolfgang. "Die Bevölkerung Rheinland-Westfalen in der Hochindustrialisier-ungsperiode." *Vierteljahresschrift für Sozial- und Wirtschaftsgeschichte* 58 (1971):359–70.

"Industrialisierung, Binnenwanderung und 'soziale Frage'." *Vieteljahresschrift für Sozial- und Wirtschaftsgeschichte* 46 (1959):45–70.

Kuske, Bruno. *Geschichte der rheinischen Städte*. Essen: G. D. Baedeker, 1922.

Liewer, Hans. "Die wirtschaftliche Entwicklung von Benrath-Reiholz." Ph.D. diss., University of Coburg, 1926.

Lux, Hans Arthur, ed. *Düsseldorf*. Düsseldorf: Deutsche Kunst und Verlagsanstalt, 1921–2.

Metzmacher, Helmut. "Der Novemberumsturz 1918 in der Rheinprovinz." *Annalen des Historischen Vereins für den Niederrhein* 168/9 (1967):135–265.

Meydenbauer, Hans. *Die Stadt Düsseldorf und ihre Verwaltung im Ausstellungsjahr 1902.* Düsseldorf: August Bagel.

Most, Otto. *Düsseldorf als Handels- Industrie-, Kunst- und Gartenstadt.* Düsseldorf: August Bagel, 1914.

Die Gemeindebetriebe der Stadt Düsseldorf. Leipzig: Duncker und Humblot, 1909.

Ortsverein Düsseldorf im Verbande der Deutschen Buchdrucker, ed. *75 Jahre Organisation der Düsseldorfer Buchdrucker, 1849–1924.* Düsseldorf: August Bagel, n.d.

Ottsen, Otto. *Der Regierungsbezirk Düsseldorf.* Moers: August Steiger, 1925.

Renard, Georg. *Struktur- und Konjunkturtendenzen im Düsseldorfer Wirtschaftsraum.* Essen: Essener Verlagsanstalt, 1939.

Schmitz, Heinrich Karl. *Anfänge und Entwicklung der Arbeiterbewegung im Raum Düsseldorf.* Hannover: Verlag für Literatur und Zeitgeschehen, 1968.

Schubert, Friedrich, *Düsseldorfer Zeitungswesen in Vergangenheit und Gegenwart.* Düsseldorf: Mathias Strucken, 1932.

Seeling, Hans. *Geschichte der Gerresheimer Glashütte, Ursprung und Entwicklung, 1864–1908.* Düsseldorf: Ed. Lintz, 1964.

Steller, Paul. *Führende Männer des rheinisch-westfälischen Wirtschaftsleben.* Berlin: Reimar Hobbing, 1930.

Stöcker, Hans. *250 Jahre Düsseldorfer Presse.* Düsseldorf: Rheinisch-Bergische Druckerei und Verlagsgesellschaft, 1962.

Stump, Wolfgang. *Geschichte und Organisation der Zentrumspartei in Düsseldorf, 1917–1933.* Düsseldorf: Droste, 1971.

Stüwer, Alex. *Die Entwicklung der Eisenindustrie in Düsseldorf.* Düsseldorf: Deutsch Kunst und Verlagsanstalt, 1925.

Weidenhaupt, Hugo. *Kleine Geschichte der Stadt Düsseldorf.* Düsseldorf: Verlag L. Schwann, 1962.

Wilden, Joseph. *Düsseldorf: die Lichtstadt im Industrierevier.* Düsseldorf: L. Schwann, 1952.

Gründer und Gestalter der Rhein-Ruhr Industrie. Düsseldorf: August Bagel, 1951.

Düsseldorf, Fürstenhof, Kunststadt, Wirtschaftsraum. Düsseldorf, n.p., 1938.

Grundlagen und Triebkräfte der Wirtschaft in Düsseldorf. Düsseldorf: Deutsche Kunst und Verlagsanstalt, 1923.

100 Jahre Düsseldorfer Wirtschaftsleben. Düsseldorf: Kommissionsverlag A. Bagel, n.d.

Winkels, Hans. *Die Entwicklung des Handwerks in Düsseldorf seit dem Jahre 1816.* Ph. D. Diss., University of Cologne, 1933.

V. General works

Abendroth, Wolfgang. *Sozialgeschichte der europäischen Arbeiterbewegung.* Frankfurt: Suhrkamp, 1965.

Adam, Paul. *Lebenserinnerungen eines alten Kunstbuchbinders.* Stuttgart: Max Hettler, 1951.

Adelmann, Gerhard, "Führende Unternehmer im Rheinland und in Westfalen, 1850–1879." *Rheinische Vierteljahresblätter* 35 (1971): 335–52.

Anders, Karl. *Stein für Stein.* Hannover: Verlag für Literatur und Zeitgeschehen, 1969.

Anderson, Evelyn. *Hammer or Anvil: The Story of the German Working Class Movement.* London: Victor Gollanz, 1945.

Aubin, Hermann; and Zorn, Wolfgang, eds. *Handbuch der deutschen Wirtschafts- und Sozialgeschichte,* Vol. II. Stuttgart: Ernst Klett, 1976.

Bachem, Karl. *Vorgeschichte, Geschichte und Politik der deutschen Zentrumspartei*, Vol. 3. Cologne: Bachem, 1927.

Barkin, Kenneth P. *The Controversy over German Industrialization, 1890–1902*. Chicago: University of Chicago Press, 1970.

Bartel, Walter. *Die Linken in der deutschen Sozialdemokratie im Kampf gegen Militarismus und Krieg*. Berlin: Dietz, 1958.

Basler, Frolinda. *Aufbruch zur Freiheit, 1863–1963*. Hannover: Verlag für Literatur und Zeitgeschehen, 1963.

Bauer, Clemens. "Wandlungen der sozialpolitischen Ideenwelt im deutschen Katholizismus des 19. Jahrhunderts." In Sektion für Sozial- und Wirtschaftswissenschaft der Görres-Gesellshaft, ed., *Die Soziale Frage und der Katholizismus*. Paderborn: Ferdinand Schöning, 1931.

Bebel, August. *Die Frau und der Sozialismus*. Berlin: Dietz, 1929.

Beck, Hermann. *Lohn- und Arbeitsverhältnisse in der deutschen Maschinenindustrie am Ausgang des 19. Jahrhundert*. Berlin: Leonhard Simion, 1902.

Berger, Michael. "Arbeiterbewegung und Demokratisierung. Die wirtschaftliche, politische und gesellschaftliche Gleichberechtigung der Arbeiter im Verständnis der katholischen Arbeiterbewegung im Wilhelmischen Deutschland zwischen 1890 und 1914." Ph.D. diss., University of Frieburg, 1971.

Berghahn, V. R. *Germany and the Approach of War in 1914*. New York: St. Martins Press, 1973.

Berlepsch, Hans. *Sozialpolitische Erfahrungen und Erinnerungen*. Mönchen-Gladbach: Volksvereinsverlag, 1925.

Bernays, Marie. "Berufswahl und Berufsschicksal des modernen Industriearbeiters." *Archiv für Sozialwissenschaft und Sozialpolitik* 35 (1912):123–76 and 36 (1913):884–915.

Bernstein, Eduard. *Die Berliner Arbeiterbewegung*. Berlin: Dietz, 1924.

Berten, Peter. *Lebenslauf eines einfachen Menschen*. Düsseldorf: Selbstverlag, 1958.

Bertram, Jürgen. *Die Wahlen zum deutschen Reichstag vom Jahre 1912*. Düsseldorf: Droste, 1964.

Bertrand, Charles L., ed. *Revolutionary Situations in Europe, 1917–1922: Germany, Italy, Austria-Hungary*.Montreal: Centre Interuniversitaire d'Etudes Européennes, 1977.

Bieber, Hans-Joachim. "Die deutschen Gewerkschaften, 1914–20. "Ph.D. diss., University of Hamburg, 1975.

Bieligk, Fritz; Eckstein, Ernst; Jenssen, Otto; Laumann, Kurt; and Wagner, Helmut. *Die Organisation im Klassenkampf*. Berlin: Verlag der Marxistischen Verlagsgesellschaft, 1931.

Blackbourn, David G. "The Problem of Democratisation: German Catholics and the Role of the Center Party." In Richard J. Evans, ed., *Society and Politics in Wilhelmine Germany*. London: Croom Helm, 1978.

"The *Mittelstand* in German Society and Politics, 1871–1914." *Social History* 4 (January 1977):490–33.

"Class and Politics in Wilhelmine Germany: the Social Democrats in Württemburg." *Central European History* 9, No. 3 (September 1976):220–49.

Blank, R. "Die soziale Zusammensetzung der sozialdemokratischen Wählerschaft Deutschlands." *Archiv für Sozialwissenschaft und Sozialpolitik*, n.s. 4 (1905):507–50.

Bock, Hans Manfred. *Geschichte der "Linken Radikalismus" in Deutschland*. Frankfurt: Suhrkamp, 1976.

Boettcher, Ulrich. *Anfänge und Entwicklung der Arbeiterbewegung in Bremen von der Revolution 1848 bis zur Aufhebung des Sozialistengesetzes 1890*. Bremen: Carl Schünemann, 1953.

Böhme, Helmut. *Deutschlands Weg zur Grossmacht.* Cologne: Kiepenheuer und Witsch, 1966.

Prolegomena zu einer Sozial- und Wirtschaftsgeschichte Deutschlands im 19. und 20. Jahrhundert. Frankfurt: Suhrkamp, 1968.

Bologna, Sergio. "Class Composition and the History of the Party at the Origin of the Workers' Council Movement," *The Labour Process and Class Struggle.* CES Pamphlet 1 (1976), pp. 68–91.

Born, Karl Erich, *Staat und Sozialpolitik seit Bismarcks Sturz.* Wiesbaden: Franz Steiner Verlag, 1957.

Braun, Adolf. *Die Gewerkschaften vor dem Kriege.* Berlin: Dietz, 1925.

"Bildungsprobleme in der Arbeiterbewegung," *Der Kampf* 8 (1915):240–50.

Gewerkschaften und Sozialdemokratie. Berlin: Verlagsanstalt des Deutschen Holzarbeiterverbandes, 1915.

"Realismus und Utopismus in den Gewerkschaften," *Der Kampf* 8 (1915):45–7.

Braverman, Harry. *Labor and Monopoly Capital.* New York: Monthly Review Press, 1974.

Brepohl, Wilhelm. *Industrievolk im Wandel von der agraren zur industriellen Daseinsform, dargestellt am Ruhrgebiet.* Tübingen: Mohr, 1957.

Bringmann, August. *Geschichte der deutschen Zimmerer-Bewegung.* Stuttgart: Dietz, Vol. 1, 1903; Vol. 2, 1905.

Broch, Ernst-Detlef. *Die Katholische Arbeitervereine in der Stadt Köln, 1890–1901.* Wentorf/ Hamburg: Einhorn Presse, 1977.

Brockhaus, Eckhard. *Zusammensetzung und Neustrukturierung der Arbeiterklasse vor dem ersten Weltkrieg.* Munich: Trikont, 1975.

Bromme, Moritz William Theodor. *Lebensgeschichte eines modernen Fabrikarbeiters.* Ed. Paul Göhre. Jena: Diederichs, 1905.

Bruck, W. F. *Social and Economic History of Germany from William II to Hitler.* London: Oxford University Press, 1938.

Bry, Gerhard. *Wages in Germany, 1871–1945.* Princeton, N. J.: Princeton University Press, 1960.

Buchheim, Karl. *Ultramontanismus und Demokratie: der Weg der deutschen Katholiken im 19. Jahrhundert.* Munich: Kösel, 1963.

Budde, Heinz. *Die Arbeitnehmerschaft in der Industriegesellschaft.* Essen: Hubert Wingen, 1963.

Büddenburg, Theodor. "Das soziologische Problem der Sozialdemokratie." *Archiv für Sozialwissenschaft und Sozialpolitik* 49 (1944):108–32.

Carsten, Francis L. *Revolution in Central Europe.* Berkeley, Calif.: University of California Press, 1972.

Cassau, Theodor. *Die Gewerkschaftsbewegung. Ihre Soziologie und ihr Kampf.* Halberstadt: H. Meyer, 1925.

Christliche Arbeiterpflichten. Berlin: Buchhandlung Vorwärts, 1903.

Clapham, J. H. *Economic Development of France and Germany.* Cambridge: Cambridge University Press, 1966.

Comfort, Richard. *Revolutionary Hamburg.* Stanford, Calif.: Stanford University Press, 1966.

Conze, Werner. "Sozialgeschichte 1850–1918." In Hermann Aubin and Wolfgang Zorn, eds., *Handbuch der deutschen Wirtschafts- und Sozialgeschichte*, 2:602–84. Stuttgart: Ernst Klett, 1976.

Craig, Gordon A. *The Politics of the Prussian Army, 1640–1945.* Oxford: Oxford University Press, 1955.

Croon, Helmuth. "Die wirtschaftlichen Führungsschichten des Ruhrgebietes in der Zeit von 1890–1933." *Blätter für deutschen Landesgeschichte* 108 (1972):143–59.

Danneberg, Robert. "Die Ergebnisse sozialdemokratischer Bildungsarbeit." *Der Kampf* 8 (1915): 272–89.

DeMan, Henry. *The Psychology of Socialism*. London: Allen and Unwin, 1928.

Dowe, Dieter. "The Workers' Choral Movement Before the First World War." *Journal of Contemporary History* 13, No. 2 (April 1978):269–96.

Dyos, H. J., ed. *The Study of Urban History*. New York: St. Martin's Press, 1968.

Drabkin, J. S. *Die November Revolution 1918 in Deutschland*. Berlin: VEB, 1968.

Eckert, Georg. *100 Jahre Braunschweiger Sozialdemokratie, I. Teil: Von den Anfängen bis zum Jahre 1890*. Hannover: Dietz, 1965.

Die Braunschweiger Arbeiterbewegung unter dem Sozialistengesetz. I. Teil, 1878–1884. Braunschweig: Waisenhaus, 1961.

Aus den Lebensberichten deutscher Fabrikarbeiter. Braunschweig: Alfred Limbach, 1953.

Eckert, Hugo. *Liberal- oder Sozialdemokratie, Frühgeschichte der Nürnberger Arbeiterbewegung*. Stuttgart: Ernst Klett, 1969.

Ehrhardt, Heinrich. *Hammerschläge*. Leipzig: Koehler, 1922.

Eley, Geoff. "Defining Social Imperialism: Use and Abuse of an Idea." *Social History* 3 (October 1976):265–89.

Erdmann, August. *Die christlichen Gewerkschaften, insbesondere ihr Verhältnis zu Zentrum und Kirche*. Stuttgart: Dietz, 1914.

Die christliche Arbeiterbewegung in Deutschland. Stuttgart: Dietz, 1909.

Evans, Richard J., ed. *Society and Politics in Wilhelmine Germany*. London: Croom Helm, 1978.

Faulhaber, Alfons. "Die christliche Gewerkschaftsbewegung." Ph.D. diss., University of Nürnberg, 1913.

Feldman, Gerald. *Army, Industry and Labor in Germany, 1914–1918*. Princeton, N. J.: Princeton University Press, 1966.

Feldman, Gerald; Kolb, Eberhard; and Rürup, Reinhard. "Die Massenbewegungen der Arbeiterschaft in Deutschland am Ende des ersten Weltkrieges (1917–1920)." *Politische Vierteljahresschrift* 13, No. 1 (August 1972):84–105.

Fischer, Franz Louis. *Arbeiterschicksale*. Berlin: Buchverlag der *Hilfe*, 1906.

Fischer, Fritz. *World Power or Decline*. New York: W. W. Norton, 1974.

Germany's Aims in the First World War. New York: W. W. Norton, 1967.

Fischer, Wolfram. *Wirtschaft und Gesellschaft im Zeitalter der Industrialisierung*. Göttingen: Vandenhoeck und Ruprecht, 1972.

"Arbeitermemorien als Quellen für Geschichte und Volkskunde der industriellen Gesellschaft." *Soziale Welt* 9 (1958):228–98.

Foster, John. "Nineteenth Century Towns: a Class Dimension." In H. J. Dyos, ed., *The Study of Urban History*. New York: St. Martin's Press, 1968.

Frey, Georg. *Die Streikbewegung in Deutschland 1900 bis 1910*. Bamberg: St. Otto Verlag, 1927.

Frey, Ludwig. *Die Stellung der christlichen Gewerkschaften Deutschlands zu den politischen Parteien*. Berlin: Christlicher Gewerkschaftsverlag, 1931.

Fricke, Dieter. *Die deutsche Arbeiterbewegung 1869–1914*. Berlin: Dietz, 1976.

Zur Organisation und Tätigkeit der deutschen Arbeiterbewegung, 1890–1914. Leipzig: Verlag Enzyklopädie, 1962.

Fricke, Dieter, ed. *Die bürgerlichen Parteien in Deutschland, 1830–1945*. Berlin: das europäische Buch, 1970.

Fuchs, Peter. "Die Geschichte der Kölner Sozialdemokratie." Programmheft für das 2. Deutschlandtreffen der SPD am 26. Mai. 1962 in Köln, pp. 20–37.

Gärtner, Georg. *Die Nürnberger Arbeiterbewegung, 1868–1908.* Nürnberg: Fränkische Verlagsanstalt, n.d.

Gatzke, Hans. W. *Germany's Drive to the West.* Baltimore: Johns Hopkins University Press. 1950.

Gay, Peter. *The Dilemma of Democratic Socialism.* New York: Collier Books. 1962.

Geary, Dick. "Radicalism and the Worker: Metalworkers and Revolution, 1914–23." In Richard J. Evans, ed., *Society and Politics in Wilhelmine Germany.* London: Croom Helm, 1978.

"The German Labor Movement, 1848–1919." *European Studies Review* 6, No. 3 (1967):297–330.

Gellately, Robert. *The Politics of Economic Despair: Shopkeepers and German Politics, 1890–1914.* London: Sage, 1974.

Gerschenkron, Alexander. *Bread and Democracy in Germany.* Berkeley, Calif.: University of California Press, 1943.

Gewehr, Wilhelm. *Kann ein Christ Sozial Demokrat sein?* Elberfeld: Molkenbuhr, 1903.

Geyer, Curt. *Der Radikalismus in der deutschen Arbeiterbewegung.* Jena: Thüringer, 1923.

Göhre, Paul. *Drei Monate Fabrikarbeiter.* Leipzig: Grunow, 1891.

Goldenberg, Boris. "Beiträge zur Soziologie der deutschen Vorkriegssozialdemokratie." Ph.D. diss., University of Heidelberg, 1932.

Gramsci, Antonio. *Prison Notebooks.* New York: International Press, 1971.

Gray, Robert Q. *The Labour Aristocracy in Victorian Edinburgh.* Oxford: Clarendon Press, 1976.

"Styles of Life, the 'Labour Aristocracy' and Class Relations in Late Nineteenth Century Edinburgh." *International Review of Social History* 18, No. 3 (1973):428–52.

Groh, Dieter. "The Relationship Between the Intensification of Work and Industrial Conflict in Germany, 1896–1914." *Politics and Society* 8, No. 3–4 (1978):349–97.

Negative Integration und revolutionäre Attentismus. Frankfurt: Ullstein, 1973.

Grote, Heiner. *Sozialdemokratie und Religion.* Tübingen: J. C. Mohr, 1968.

Habersbrunner, Franz X. "Lohn-, Arbeits- und Organisationsverhältnisse im deutschen Baugewerbe."Ph.D. diss., University of Regensberg, 1903.

Halévy, Elie. *The Era of Tyrannies.* Garden City, N.Y.: Anchor Books, 1965.

Handbuch für sozialdemokratische Wähler. 1893/8. Berlin: Vorwärts, 1898. *1907/11.* Berlin: Vorwärts, 1911.

Haupt, Georges. "Why the History of the Working-Class Movement?" *New German Critique* No. 14 (Spring 1978):7–27.

Socialism and the Great War: The Collapse of the Second International. Oxford: Oxford University Press, 1972.

Heberle, Rudolf; and Meyer, Fritz. *Die Grossstädte im Strom der Binnenwanderung.* Leipzig: Verlag von F. Hirzel, 1937.

Heiddiger, Hermann. *Die deutsche Sozialdemokratie und der nationale Staat, 1870–1920.* Berlin: Munsterschmidt, 1956.

Henning, Hansjoachim. *Der westdeutsche Bürgertum in der Epoche der Hochindustrialisierung, 1860–1914.* Wiesbaden: Franz Steiner, 1972.

Herberts, Hermann. *Zur Geschichte der SPD in Wuppertal.* Wuppertal: Molkenbuhr, 1963.

Herkner, Heinrich. *Die Arbeiterfrage, Vol. 1, Arbeiterfrage und Sozialreform.* Berlin: Walter de Gruyter, 1922.

Hibbs, Douglas. A. *Long-Run Trends in Strike Activity in Comparative Perspective.* Cambridge, Mass.: MIT, 1976.

Hickey, Stephen. "The Shaping of the German Labour Movement: Miners in the Ruhr." In Richard J. Evans, ed., *Society and Politics in Wilhelmine Germany*. London: Croom Helm, 1978.

Hinton, James. *The First Shop Stewards Movement*. London: Allen and Unwin, 1973.

Hobsbawm, Eric. J. "Inventing Traditions in the Nineteenth Century." In *Past and Present Society Annual Conference*. Oxford: Past and Present Society, 1977.

"Class Consciousness in History." In Istvan Meszaros, ed., *Aspects of Class Consciousness and History*. New York: Herder and Herder, 1972.

Labouring Men. Garden City, N.Y.: Anchor, 1967.

Hochstadt, Steve. "Rural Migrants and Urban Population in Nineteenth Century Germany." Paper delivered at the American Historical Association Convention, Dallas, 1977.

Holek, Wenzel. *Lebensgang eines deutsch-tschechen Handarbeiters*. Jena: Diederichs, 1930.

Vom Handarbeiter zum Jugenderzieher. Jena: Diederichs, 1921.

Homburg, Heidrun. "Anfänge des Taylorsystems in Deutschland vor dem ersten Weltkrieg." *Geschichte und Gesellschaft* 4, No. 2 (1978):170–227.

Hommer, Otto, *Die Entwicklung und Tätigkeit des DMV*. Berlin: Carl Heymanns, 1912.

Institut für Marxismus-Leninismus beim ZK der SED, ed., *Dokumente und Materialien zur Geschichte der deutschen Arbeiterbewegung*, Reihe 2, Vols. I–III, *1914–1919*. Berlin: Dietz, Vol. I, l958; Vol. II, 1957; Vol. III 1958.

Institut für Marxismus-Leninismus beim ZK der SED, ed. *Vorwärts und nicht vergessen*. Berlin: Dietz, 1958.

Jaeger, Hans. *Unternehmer in der deutschen Politik, 1890–1918*. Bonn: Ludwig Röhrscheid, 1962.

Jantke, Carl. *Der vierte Stand*. Freiberg: Herder, 1955.

Joll, James. *The Second International*. London: Routledge and Kegan Paul, 1975.

Jones, Gareth Stedman. "Working-Class Culture and Working-Class Politics in London, 1870–1900." *Journal of Social History* 7 (1973–4):460–508.

Joos, Joseph. *Antworten an einem sozialdemokratischen Agitator*. Mönchen-Gladbach: Volksverein, 1911.

Kaelble, Hartmut. *Industrielle Interessenpolitik in der Wilhelmischen Gesellschaft*. Berlin: Walter de Gruyter, 1967.

Kantorowicz, Ludwig. *Die sozialdemokratische Presse Deutschlands*. Tübingen: Mohr, 1922.

Kautsky, Karl. *The Economic Doctrines of Karl Marx*. London: A. and C. Black, 1925.

Kehr, Eckert. *Primat der Innenpolitik*. Berlin: Walter de Gruyter, 1965.

Schlachtflottenbau und Parteipolitik, 1894–1901. Vaduz: Kraus Reprint, 1965.

Kemp, Tom. *Industrialization in Nineteenth-Century Europe*. London: Longman, 1960.

Kesseler, Gerhard. *Die deutschen Arbeitgeberverbände*. Leipzig: Duncker and Humblot, 1907.

Klein, Fritz. *Deutschland von 1897/8 bis 1917*. Berlin: VEB Deutscher Verlag der Wissenschaft, 1961.

Klocker, Alois. *Konfession und sozialdemokratische Wählerschaft*. Ph.D. diss., Mönchen-Gladbach, 1913.

Klöcker, Michael. *Die Sozialdemokratie im Regierungsbezirk Aachen vor dem 1. Weltkrieg*. Wentorf/Hamburg: Einhorn, 1977.

Kluge, Ulrich. *Soldatenräte und Revolution*. Göttingen: Vandenhoeck und Ruprecht, 1975.

Knopp, Gisbert. *Die preussische Verwaltung des Regierungsbezirks Düsseldorf in den Jahren 1897–1919*. Cologne: Grote, 1974.

Koch, Adelbert. "Arbeitermemorien als sozialwissenschaftliche Erkenntnisquelle." *Archiv für Sozialwissenschaft und Sozialpolitik* 61 (1929):128–67.

Kocka, Jürgen. *Klassengesellschaft im Kriege, 1914–18*. Göttingen: Vandenhoeck und Ruprecht, 1973.

Kolb, Eberhard. *Die Arbeiterräte in der deutschen Innenpolitik, 1918–1919.* Düsseldorf: Droste, 1962.

Kolb, Eberhard, ed. *Vom Kaiserreich zur Weimarer Republik.* Cologne: Kiepenheuer und Witsch, 1972.

Köllmann, Wolfgang. *Bevölkerung in der industriellen Revolution.* Vandenhoeck und Ruprecht, 1974.

"The Process of Urbanization in Germany at the Height of the Industrialization Period." *Journal of Contemporary History* 4 (July 1969):59–76.

"Politische und soziale Entwicklung der deutschen Arbeiterschaft, 1850–1914." *Vierteljahresschrift für Sozial- und Wirtschaftsgeschichte* 50 (January 1964):480–504.

Sozialgeschichte der Stadt Barmen im 19. Jahrhundert. Tübingen: J. G. B. Mohr, 1960.

Korn, Karl. *Die Arbeiterjugendbewegung,* Parts I and II. Berlin: Arbeiterjugendverlag, 1922–3.

Koszyk, Kurt. *Anfänge und frühe Entwicklung der sozialdemokratische Presse im Ruhrgebiet, 1875–1903.* Dortmund: Fr. Wilhelm Ruhfus, 1953.

Krause, Hartfrid. *USPD.* Frankfurt: Europäische Verlagsanstalt, 1975.

Krieger, Leonard; and Stern, Fritz, eds. *The Responsibility of Power.* Garden City, N.Y.: Anchor Books, 1969.

Kuczynski, Jürgen. *Die Geschichte der Lage der Arbeiter unter dem Kapitalismus.* Part I, Vol. 4. *Darstellung der Lage der Arbeiter in Deutschland von 1900 bis 1917/18.* Berlin: Akademie, 1967.

Geschichte der Lage der Arbeiter unter dem Kapitalismus. Vol. 18. *Studien zur Geschichte der Lage der Arbeiterin in Deutschland von 1700 bis zur Gegenwart.* Berlin: Akademie, 1963.

"Oekonomische Basis und Zusammensetzung der Arbeiteraristokratie im Wandel eines Jahrhunderts." *Zeitschrift für Geschichtswissenschaft* 2 (1954):666–80.

A Short History of Labor Conditions Under Industrial Capitalism, Vol. 3, Part 1, *Germany, 1800 to the Present.* London: Frederick Muller, 1945.

Landes, David. S. *The Unbound Prometheus.* Cambridge: Cambridge University Press, 1969.

Lange, Helene; and Bäumer, Gertrud, eds. *Handbuch der Frauenbewegung.* Berlin: W. Moeser, 1901.

Langewiesche, Dieter. "Wanderungsbewegungen in der Hochindustrialisierungsperiode: regionale, interstädtische und innerstädtische Mobilität in Deutschland, 1850–1914." *Vierteljahresschrift für Sozial- und Wirtschaftsgeschichte* 64, No. 1 (1977):1–40.

Laschitza, Annelies. *Deutsche Linke im Kampf für eine demokratische Republik.* Berlin: Dietz, 1969.

Laubier, Patrick de. "Esquisse d'une theorie du syndicalisme." *Sociologie du Travail* 10 (1968):362–92.

Laufenberg, Heinrich. "Gorreslexikon." *Neue Zeit* 28 (October 15, 1909):76–85; (October 22, 1909):110–19; (October 29, 1909):137–49.

"Dogma und Klassenkampf," *Neue Zeit* 27 (January 15, 1909):564–74.

"Klerikale Zweiseelentheorie." *Neue Zeit* 26 (May 22, 1908):263–71.

Lug und Trug oder christliche Reaktion und christliches Geschäft. Düsseldorf: A. Gerisch, 1906.

Kann ein Katholik Sozialdemokrat sein? Düsseldorf: Düsseldorfer *Volkszeitung,* 1905.

Die Legende vom Arbeiter-Pabst. Düsseldorf: A. Gerisch, 1905.

Leckenbusch, Roswitha. *Entstehung und Wandlungen der Zielsetzungen, der Struktur und der Wirkungen von Arbeitgeberverbänden.* Berlin: Duncker and Humblot, 1966.

Lepsius, M. Rainer. "Parteiensystem und Sozialstruktur: zum Problem der Demokratisierung der deutschen Gesellschaft." In G. A. Ritter, ed., *Die deutschen Parteien vor 1918*, pp. 56–80. Cologne: Kiepenheuer und Witsch, 1973.

Levenstein, Adolf. *Die Arbeiterfrage*. Munich: Reinhardt, 1912.

Lichtheim, George. *Imperialism*. New York: Praeger, 1971.

Lidtke, Vernon. "Songs of the German Labor Movement, 1864–1914." Unpublished paper. [A German version has appeared in *Geschichte und Gesellschaft* 5, No. 1 (1979):54–82.]

——— "Social Democratic Cultural Organizations in Imperial Germany." Paper delivered at the American Historical Association Convention, Chicago, December 1974.

——— "Songs and Politics: an Exploratory Essay on *Arbeiterlieder* in the Weimar Republic." *Archiv für Sozialgeschichte* 14 (1974):253–73.

——— "August Bebel and German Social Democracy's Relation to the Christian Churches." *Journal of the History of Ideas* 27, No. 2 (April–June 1966):204–45.

——— *The Outlawed Party: Social Democracy in Germany, 1878–1890*. Princeton, N.J.: Princeton University Press, 1966.

Lipset, Seymour Martin; Trow, Martin A.; and Coleman, James S. *Union Democracy*. Garden City, N.Y.: Anchor Books, 1956.

Loreck, Jochen. *Wie man früher Sozialdemokrat wurde*. Bonn-Bad Godesberg: Verlag neue Gesellschaft, 1977.

Lucas, Erhard. *Zwei Formen von Radikalismus in der deutschen Arbeiterbewegung*. Frankfurt: Roter Stern, 1976.

——— *Die Sozialdemokratie in Bremen während des ersten Weltkrieges*. Bremen: Carl Schunmann, 1967.

Ludwig, Franz. *Die Reichstag-Wahlen von 1907 und die Sozialdemokratie*. Berlin: Schestsche, 1907.

Lug und Trug der Sozialdemokratie im Kampfe gegen das Zentrum. Mönchen-Gladbach: Verlag der *Westdeutsche Arbeiterzeitung*, n.d.

Lützenkirchen, Ralf. *Der sozialdemokratische Verein für den Wahlkreis Dortmund-Hörde*. Dortmund: Verlag des Historischen Vereins Dortmund, 1970.

Maehl, William H. *German Militarism and Socialism*. Neb. Wesleyan Press, 1968.

Mann, Michael. *Consciousness and Action Among the Western Working Class*. London: Macmillan, 1973.

Martiny, Martin. "die politische Bedeutung der gewerkschaftlichen Arbeiter-Sekretariat vor dem ersten Weltkriege." In Heinz Oskar Vetter, ed.,*Vom Sozialistengesetz zur Mitbestimmung*. Cologne: Bund Verlag, 1975.

Maslowski, Peter. *Was ist die deutsche Zentrumspartei? Klerikalismus und Proletariat*. Berlin: Vereinigung Internationaler Verlagsanstalten, 1925.

Massing, Paul. *Rehearsal for Destruction*. New York: Harper & Bros., 1949.

Mattheier, Klaus J. "Werkvereine und wirtschaftsfriedlich-nationale (gelbe) Arbeiterbewegung im Ruhrgebiet." In Jürgen Reulecke, ed., *Arbeiterbewegung an Rhein und Ruhr*. Wuppertal: Peter Hammer, 1974.

Matthias, Erich. "Kautsky und Kautskyanismus." *Marxismusstudien* 2 (1957):151–97.

May, Eugen. "Mein Lebenslauf, 1889–1920." In Eugene Rosenstock, ed., *Werkstattaussiedlung*, pp. 16–72. Berlin: Julius Springer, 1922.

Mayer, Arno. "Domestic Causes of the First World War." In Leonard Krieger and Fritz Stern, eds., *The Responsibility of Power*. Garden City, N.Y.: Anchor Books, 1969.

——— *Wilson vs. Lenin, Political Origins of the New Diplomacy, 1917–1918*. New York: Meridian, 1964.

Mehring, Franz. *Geschichte der deutschen Sozialdemokratie*. Part 2. Stuttgart: Dietz, 1898.

Mendelssohn-Bartholdy, Albrecht. *The War and German Society*. New Haven: Yale University Press, 1937.

Mergner, Gottfried. *Arbeiterbewegung und Intelligenz*. Starnberg: Werner Raith, 1973.

Meszaros, Istvan, ed. *Aspects of History and Class Consciousness*. New York: Herder and Herder, 1972.

Michels, Robert. *Political Parties*. New York: Free Press, 1962.

"Die deutsche sozialdemokratische Parteimitgliedschaft und soziale Zusammenset-zung." *Archiv für Sozialwissenschaft und Sozialpolitik*, n.s. 5 (1906):471–556.

Miller, Suzanne. *Burgfrieden und Klassenkampf*. Düsseldorf: Droste, 1974.

Mitchell, Harvey; and Stearns, Peter. *Workers and Protest*. Itasca, Ill.: Peacock, 1971.

Möllers, Paul. "Die Essener Arbeiterbewegung in ihren Anfängen." *Rheinische Viertel jahresblätter* 25 (1960):42–65.

Molt, Peter. *Der Reichstag vor der improvisierten Revolution*. Cologne: Westdeutscher Verlag, 1963.

Moore, Barrington. *Injustice: the Social Bases of Obedience and Revolt*. New York: M. E. Sharpe, 1978.

Moorhouse, H. F. "The Marxist Theory of Labour Aristocracy." *Social History* 3, No. 1 (January 1978):61–82.

Morgan, David. W. *The Socialist Left and the German Revolution*, Ithaca, N.Y.: Cornell University Press, 1975.

Moring, Karl-Ernst. *Die sozialdemokratische Partei in Bremen, 1890–1914*. Hannover: Verlag für Literatur und Zeitgeschehen, 1968.

Moss, Bernard H. *The Origins of the French Labor Movement, 1830–1914*. Berkeley: University of California Press, 1976.

Most, Otto. *Die deutsche Stadt und ihre Verwaltung*, Vols. I and II. Berlin: G. J. Goschen'sche Verlagshandlung, 1912–13.

Müller, Richard. *Vom Kaiserreich zu Republik*. Vienna: Malik, 1924.

Nettl, Peter. *Rosa Luxemburg*. London: Oxford University Press, 1969.

"The German Social Democratic Party, 1890–1914 as a Political Model." *Past and Present* 30 (April 1965):65–95.

Nipperdey, Thomas. "Interessenverbände und Parteien in Deutschland vor dem ersten Weltkrieg." In Hans-Ulrich Wehler, ed., *Moderne deutsche Sozialgeschichte*, Cologne: Kiepenheuer und Witsch, 1966.

Die Organisation der deutschen Parteien vor 1918. Düsseldorf: Droste, 1961.

Oehler, Adalbert. *Düsseldorf im Weltkrieg*. Düsseldorf: Lintz, 1927.

Oertzen, Peter von. "Die grossen Streiks der Ruhrbergarbeiterschaft im Frühjahr 1919." In Eberhard Kolb, ed., *Vom Kaiserreich zur Weimarer Republik*. Cologne: Kiepenheuer und Witsch, 1972.

Betriebsräte in der Novemberrevolution. Düsseldorf: Droste, 1963.

Opel, Fritz. *Der deutsche Metallarbeiter Verband während des ersten Weltkrieges und der Revolution*. Hannover: Norddeutscher Verlagsanstalt Goedel, 1957.

Osterroth, Franz. *Biographisches Lexikon des Sozialismus*. Hannover: Dietz, 1960.

Parkin, Frank. *Class Inequality and Political Order*. New York: Praeger, 1971.

"Working-Class Conservatives: A Theory of Political Deviance," *British Journal of Sociology* 18, No. 3 (September 1967):278–90.

Pelger, Hans. "Zur sozialdemokratischen Bewegung in der Rheinprovinz vor dem Sozial-istengesetz." *Archiv für Sozialgeschichte* 5 (1965):377–406.

Peterson, Brian. "Workers' Councils in Germany, 1918–1919." *New German Critique* 4 (Winter 1975):113–24.

Peukert, Josef. *Erinnerungen eines Proletariers aus der revolutionaren Arbeiterbewegung*. Berlin: Verlag des sozialistischen Bundes, 1913.

Pinner, Felix. *Deutsche Wirtschaftsführer*. Charlottenburg: Verlag der Weltbühne, 1924.

Pogge von Strandmann, Hartmut; and Geiss, Imanuel. *Die Erforderlichkeit des Unmöglichen. Deutschland am Vorabend des ersten Weltkrieges*. Frankfurt: Europäischer Verlagsanstalt, 1965.

Popp, Adelhaide. *Jugendgeschichte einer Arbeiterin*. Munich: Ernst Reinhardt, 1909.

Puhle, Hans-Jürgen. "Parlament, Parteien und Interessenverbände." In Michael Stürmer, ed., *Das kaiserliche Deutschland: Politik und Gesellschaft, 1870–1918*. Kronberg: Athenäum, 1977.

Quataert, Jean. "The Social Basis of Socialist Feminism." Paper delivered at the Berkshire Women's History Conference, South Hadley, Mass., August 1978.

Ragenfeld, Norma N. von. "The Attitude and Behavior of the Prussian Civil Service Toward the Working Class in the Rhineland, 1889–1905." Ph.D. diss., University of Connecticut, 1976.

Reichard, Richard. "The German Working Class and the Russian Revolution of 1905," *Journal of Central European Affairs* 13 (July 1953):136–53.

Reichelt, Heinrich. "Die Arbeitsverhältnisse in einem Berlin Grossbetrieb des Maschinen-industrie." Ph.D diss., University of Berlin, 1900.

Reulecke, Jürgen, ed. *Arbeiterbewegung an Rhein und Ruhr*. Wuppertal: Peter Hammer, 1974.

Rheinisch-Westfälische Wirtschaftsbiographien. Münster: Aschendorffsche Verlag, Vol. 3, 1974; Vol. 4, 1974; Vol. 7, 1960; Vol. 8, 1962.

Rimlinger, Gaston. *Welfare Policy and Industrialization in Europe, America and Russia*. New York: John Wiley & Sons, 1971.

Ritter, Emil. *Die katholisch-soziale Bewegung Deutschlands im 19. Jahrhundert und der Volksverein*. Cologne: J. P. Bachem, 1954.

Ritter, Gerhard A. "Workers' Culture in Imperial Germany." *Journal of Contemporary History* 13, No. 2 (April 1978):165–90.

Arbeiterbewegung, Parteien und Parlamentarismus. Göttingen: Vandenhoeck und Ruprecht, 1976.

Die Arbeiterbewegung im Wilhelmischen Reich. Berlin: Colloquium Verlag, 1959.

Ritter, Gerhard A., ed. *Die deutschen Parteien vor 1918*. Cologne: Kiepenheuer und Witsch, 1973.

Rosenberg, Arthur. *A History of the German Republic*. New York: Russell and Russell, 1965.

Entstehung der Weimarer Republik. Frankfurt: Europäische Verlagsanstalt, 1961.

Democracy and Socialism, New York: Alfred A. Knopf, 1939.

Rosenberg, Hans. "Political and Social Consequences of the Great Depression of 1873–96 in Central Europe." *Economic History Review* 13 (1943):58–73.

Rosenstock, Eugene, ed. *Werkstattaussiedlung*. Berlin: Julius Springer, 1922.

Ross, Ronald J. *Beleaguered Tower: the Dilemma of Political Catholicism in Wilhelmine Germany*. Notre Dame, Ind.: University of Notre Dame Press, 1976.

Roth, Guenther. *The Social Democrats in Imperial Germany*. Totowa, N.J.: The Bedminster Press, 1963.

Roth, Karl Heinz. *Die "andere" Arbeiterbewegung*. Munich: Trikont, 1976.

Rürup, Reinhard, ed. *Arbeiter- und Soldatenräte im rheinisch-westfälischen Industriegebiet*. Wuppertal: Peter Hammer, 1975.

Rürup, Reinhard; Kolb, Eberhard; and Feldman, Gerald. "Die Massenbewegungen der Arbeiterschaft in Deutschland am Ende des ersten Weltkrieges (1917–1920)." *Politische Vierteljahresschrift* 13, No. 1 (August 1972):84–105.

Ryder, A. J. *The German Revolution of 1918*. Cambridge: Cambridge University Press, 1967.

Sabel, Charles Frederic. *Industrial Conflict and the Sociology of the Labor Market*. Cambridge: Cambridge University Press (in press).

Salvadori, Massimo L. *Kautsky e la revoluzione socialista 1880/1938.* Milan: Feltrinelli, 1978.

Saul, Klaus. *Staat, Industrie und Arbeiterbewegung im Kaiserreich.* Düsseldorf: Bertelsmann, 1974.

Scharrer, Manfred. *Arbeiterbewegung im Obrigkeitsstaat.* Berlin: Rotbuch, 1978.

Schauff, Johannes. *Die deutschen Katholiken und die Zentrumspartei.* Cologne: Bachem, 1928.

Schippel, Max. *Sozialdemokratische Reichstag-Handbuch.* Berlin: Vorwärts, 1902.

Schirmer, Karl. *50 Jahre Arbeiter.* Duisburg: Bücher der Arbeit, 1924.

Schmidt, Rudi. "Die Geschichtsmythologen der 'anderen' Arbeiterbewegung." *Internationale Wissenschaftliche Korrespondenz zur Geschichte der deutschen Arbeiterbewegung* 11, No. 2 (June 1975):178–99.

Schmierer, Wolfgang. *Von der Arbeiterbildung zur Arbeiterpolitik, Die Anfänge der Arbeiterbewegung in Württemberg, 1862/3–1878.* Hannover: Verlag für Literatur und Zeitgeschehen, 1970.

Schofer, Lawrence. *The Formation of a Modern Labor Force in Upper Silesia, 1865–1914.* Berkeley, Calif.: University of California Press, 1975.

Schöller, Peter. *Die deutschen Städte.* Wiesbaden: Franz Steiner Verlag, 1967.

Schorske, Carl. *German Social Democracy, 1905–17.* New York: John Wiley & Sons, 1955.

Schröder, Wilhelm *Geschichte der sozialdemokratischen Parteiorganisation in Deutschland.* Dresden: Raden, 1912.

Schröder, Wilhelm Heinz. *Arbeitergeschichte und Arbeiterbewegung.* Frankfurt: Campus, 1978.

Schwer, Wilhelm; and Müller, Franz. *Der deutsche Katholizismus im Zeitalter des Kapitalismus.* Augsburg: Literarisches Institut Haas und Grabheir, 1932.

Scott, Joan Wallach. *The Glassworkers of Carmaux.* Cambridge, Mass.: Harvard University Press, 1974.

Sektion für Sozial- und Wirtschaftswissenschaft der Görres Gesellschaft, ed. *Die soziale Frage und der Katholizismus.* Paderborn: Ferdinand Schöningh, 1931.

Selter, Fr. *Ueber die Einführung von Tarifverträgen in den Grossbetrieben der Maschinenbau und verwandter Industrien.* Berlin: A. Seydel, 1911.

75 Jahre Mannesmann, 1890–1965. Berlin: Tempelhof, 1965.

Sheehan, James. *Imperial Germany.* New York: New Viewpoints, 1977.

"Liberalism and the City in Nineteenth Century Germany." *Past and Present* 51 (May 1971):116–37.

Shorter, Edward; and Tilly, Charles. *Strikes in France, 1830–1968.* Cambridge: Cambridge University Press, 1974.

Sinowjew, G. *Der Krieg und die Krise des Sozialismus.* Vienna: Verlag für Literatur und Politik, 1924.

Sirianni, Carmen. "Workers' Control in the Era of the First World War: a Comparative Analysis of the European Experience." *Theory and Society* 9 (January 1980):29–88.

Die Sozialdemokratie in München. Berlin: Verlag von Wilhelm Baensch, 1902.

Die Sozialpolitik der deutschen Zentrumspartei 1907. Gesammelte sozialpolitische Flugblätter des Volksverein für das katholische Deutschland nach dem Bestande des jahres 1907. Mönchen-Gladbach: Volksverein Verlag, 1910.

Spael, Wilhelm. *Das katholische Deutschland im 20. Jahrhundert, 1890–1945.* Würzberg: Echter Verlag, 1964.

Stearns, Peter N. *Lives of Labor.* New York: Holmes and Meier, 1975.

"The European Labor Movement and the Working Classes, 1890–1914." In Harvey Mitchell and Peter Stearns, *Workers and Protest.* Itasca, Ill.: Peacock, 1971.

"Adaptation to Industrialization: German Workers as a Test Case." *Central European History* 3 (December 1970):303–31.

Stegmann, Dirk. *Die Erben Bismarcks*. Cologne: Kiepenheuer und Witsch, 1970.

Steinberg, Hans-Josef. *Sozialismus und deutsche Sozialdemokratie*. Hannover: Verlag für Literatur und Zeitgeschehen, 1967.

Stephan aus Strang, Cora. "Das Verhältnis von Strategik und Theorie in den Debatten der deutschen Sozialdemokratie von der Anfängen bis zum Sozialistengesetz." Ph.D. diss., University of Frankfurt, 1976.

Stern, Fritz. *The Failure of Illiberalism*. Chicago: University of Chicago Press, 1976.

Stürmer, Michael, ed. *Das kaiserliche Deutschland: Politik und Gesellschaft, 1870–1918*. Kronberg: Anthenäum, 1977.

Tampke, Jürgen. "The Ruhr and Revolution." Ph.D. diss., Australian National University, n.d.

Tänzler, Fritz. *Die deutschen Arbeitgeberverbände, 1904–29*. Berlin: Elsner, 1929.

Thernstrom, Stephen; and Sennett, Richard, eds. *Nineteenth Century Cities*. New Haven, Conn.: Yale University Press, 1969.

Thompson, E. P. *The Making of the English Working Class*. New York: Vintage Books, 1966.

Thönnessen, Werner. *Frauenemanzipation*. Frankfurt: Europäische Verlagsanstalt, 1969.

Timmermann, Walter. "Entlohnungsmethoden in der Hannoverischen Eisenindustrie." Ph.D. diss., University of Berlin, 1906.

Tischer, Alfred. *Der Kampf im deutschen Baugewerbe, 1910*. Leipzig: Duncker und Homblot, 1912.

Tormin, Walter. *Zwischen Rätediktatur und sozialer Demokratie*. Düsseldorf: Droste, 1956.

Tureck, Ludwig. *Ein Prolet erzählt*. Berlin, 1930.

Ullrich, Volker. *Die Hamburger Arbeiterbewegung vom Vorabend des Ersten Weltkrieges bis zur Revolution 1918/19. Bd. 1–2*. Hamburg: Hartmut Lüdke, 1974.

Varain, Heinz Josef. *Interessenverbände in Deutschland*. Cologne: Kiepenheuer und Witsch, 1973.

Freie Gewerkschaften, Sozialdemokratie und Staat: Die Politik der Generalkommission unter der Führung Carl Legiens, 1890–1920. Düsseldorf: Droste, 1956.

Veblen, Thorstein. *Imperial Germany and the Industrial Revolution*. Ann Arbor, Mich.: University of Michigan Press, 1966.

Vetter, Heinz Oscar, ed. *Vom Sozialistengesetz zur Mitbestimmung*. Cologne: Bund Verlag, 1975.

Vorstand des Deutschen Metallarbeiter Verbandes, ed. *Die Schwereisenindustrie im deutschen Zollgebiet. Ihre Entwicklung und ihre Arbeiter*. Stuttgart: Schlicke, 1912.

Wachenheim, Hedwig. *Die deutschen Arbeiterbewegung, 1844 bis 1914*. Cologne: Westdeutscher Verlag, 1967.

Weber, Adna Gerrin. *The Growth of Cities in the Nineteenth Century*. Ithaca, N.Y.: Cornell University Press, 1967.

Wehler, Hans-Ulrich. *Das deutsche Kaiserreich, 1871–1918*. Göttingen: Vandenhoeck und Ruprecht, 1973.

Krisenherde des Kaiserreichs, 1871–1918. Göttingen: Vandenhoeck und Ruprecht, 1969.

Sozialdemokratie und Nationalstaat. Würzburg: Vandenhoeck und Ruprecht, 1962.

Wehler, Hans-Ulrich, ed., *Moderne deutsche Sozialgeschichte*. Cologne: Kieperheuer und Witsch, 1966.

Weiner, Karl-Gustav. *Organisation und Politik der Gewerkschaften und Arbeitgeberverbände in der deutschen Bauwirtschaft*. Berlin: Duncker und Humblot, 1968.

Werner, Karl-Gustav. "Gründung des deutschen Arbeitgeberbundes für das Baugewerbe 1899 und seine Entwicklung bis 1910." In Heinz Josef Varain, ed., *Interessenverbände in Deutschland*. Cologne: Kiepenheuer und Witsch, 1973.

Organisation und Politik der Gewerkschaften und Arbeitgeberverbände in der deutschen Bauwirtschaft. Berlin: Duncker und Humblot, 1968.

Wettstein-Adelt, Minna. *3½ Monate Fabrikarbeiterin.* Berlin: J. Leiser, 1893.

Wheeler, Robert F. "Organized Sport and Organized Labor: the Workers' Sports Movement." *Journal of Contemporary History* 13, No. 2 (April 1978):191–210.

" 'Ex oriente lux?' The Soviet Example and the German Revolution, 1917–1923." In Charles L. Bertrand, ed., *Revolutionary Situations in Europe, 1917–1922: Germany, Italy, Austria-Hungary.*. Montreal: Centre Interuniversitáire d'Etudies Européennes, 1977.

USPD und Internationale. Frankfurt: Ullstein, 1975.

"German Labor and the Comintern: Problem of Generations." *Journal of Social History* 7 (Spring 1974):306–18.

Winkler, Heinrich August, ed. *Organisierter Kapitalismus.* Göttingen: Vandenhoeck und Ruprecht, 1974.

Wrigley, E. A. *Industrial Growth and Population Change.* Cambridge: Cambridge University Press, 1961.

Zeender, John K. *The German Center Party, 1890–1906.* Philadelphia: American Philosophical Society, 1976.

Zeitlin, Jonathan H. "Rationalization and Resistance: Skilled Workers and the Transformation of the Division of Labor in the British Engineering Industry, 1830–1930." B. A. thesis, Harvard University, 1977.

Zeitz, Alfred. *Zur Geschichte der Arbeiterbewegung der Stadt Brandenburg vor dem ersten Weltkrieg.* Potsdam: Veröffentlichungen des Bezirksheimatsmuseums Potsdam. 1965.

Zunkel, Friedrich. *Industrie und Staatssozialismus.* Düsseldorf: Droste, 1974.

"Industriebürgertum in Westdeutschland." In Hans-Ulrich Wehler, ed., *Moderne deutsche Sozialgeschichte*, pp. 309–41. Cologne: Kiepenheuer und Witsch, 1966.

Index